Teaching, Training and Learning

A Practical Guide

Ian Reece and Stephen Walker

Business Education Publishers Limited 2000

© Ian Reece and Stephen Walker 2000

ISBN 1 901888 17 7

First published in 1992
 Reprinted 1993
Second Edition 1994
 Reprinted 1995
 Reprinted 1996
Third Edition 1997
 Reprinted 1998
 Reprinted 1999
 Reprinted 2000
Fourth Edition 2000
 Reprinted 2000
 Reprinted 2001
 Reprinted 2001
 Reprinted 2001

Cover Design by Tim Murphy Creative Solutions

Published in Great Britain by Business Education Publishers Limited,
The Solar Building, Doxford International,
Sunderland, Tyne and Wear, SR3 3XW

Telephone: 0191 5252410   Fax: 0191 5201815

British Library Cataloguing-in-Publications Data
A catalogue record for this book is available from the British Library

The publisher has made every effort to obtain permission to reproduce material in this book
from the appropriate source. If there are any errors or omissions please contact the publisher
who will make suitable acknowledgement in the reprint.

Printed in Great Britain by Athenaeum Press, Gateshead

Preface

The status of Further Education in the UK appears to be improving. The DfEE, through FENTO, (Further Education National Training Organisation), has produced a set of occupational standards for all FE Lecturers. It would appear that all college lecturers will have to undergo some form of teacher training and that there may be a body established which will govern the standards of the profession. This is good news for all concerned with Post-Compulsory education.

At the time of writing, the FENTO standards are at the consultation stage; these appear to be reasonable and relevant. We have reproduced these draft standards in the appendix and have shown how this book relates to the standards. There are some "gaps" but these are generally where the standards can be obtained by working in FE (eg induct learners into the organisation).

We are grateful for readers who have taken the time to contact us with suggestions for improvements and we have used many of these. In particular, we have added some new materials on the curriculum.

We have used many sources to write this book and have made every effort to cite original materials. If we have failed to give due credit, we sincerely apologise and will do so in the next reprint. Please contact us if you have ideas or suggestions for the next edition. We will be pleased to hear from you.

Ian Reece.
Stephen Walker is at New College Durham.

Acknowledgements

We would like to thank members of the Further Education Teacher Training team at New College Durham for their contribution to debates and discussions over many years and, in particular Phyll Bryning and Alan Lilley. We would also like to pay tribute to our teacher students from whom we have learned a great deal, especially during practical teaching visits. Of these, special thanks must go to Carl Gill, Janice Flint, Janet Ford, Andrew Lindley and Carolyn Piggford, whose original ideas have greatly enhanced this book.

The authors would particularly like to express their thanks to Sid Knight of the FETT team at New College Durham for his continued support and suggestions for changes in the second edition.

We are particularly grateful for the comments and suggestions for the third edition made by two of our colleagues Carole Rosethorn and John Hunt.

Gwyn Rose, Gail Thompson, Richard Harvey and Denise Heslop have been particularly helpful with ideas for this fourth edition.

Our thanks go to all at Business Education Publishers, particularly Sonya Miller and Moira Page whose help was invaluable in producing this publication, and Paul Callaghan, whose positive attitude and professionalism have been a constant source of motivation in writing this book. Andrea Murphy has managed the production of this fourth edition with well timed and pertinent e-mails. Proof reading is a demanding task so our thanks go to Susan Walker.

Finally thanks to Margery, Susan, Timothy, Martin and Ruth for their tolerance and understanding as this book was being written.

Durham
March 2000
IHR
SW

Table of Contents

Chapter 1   An Introduction to Teaching

Competences Related to this Chapter   3

FENTO Standards Related to this Chapter   4

1.   The Role of the Teacher   5

2.   Plan and Organise Learning   22

3.   The Management of Learning   40

4.   Assessment of Learning and Evaluation of Teaching   49

5.   Giving a Presentation   58

Further Reading and References   63

Chapter 2   Student Learning

Competences Related to this Chapter   67

FENTO Standards Related to this Chapter   68

1.   Introduction   69

2.   The Three Domains   69

3.   Learning Taxonomies   70

4.   Why use Models?   75

5.   Learning and the Cognitive Domain   76

6.   Learning and the Psychomotor Domain   91

7.   Learning and the Affective Domain   96

8.   Motivation   100

9.   The Main Theories   105

Further Reading and References   127

Chapter 3   Teaching Strategies and Learning Styles

Competences Related to this Chapter   133

FENTO Standards Related to this Chapter   134

Teaching Strategies   135

1. Introduction   135

2. Application of Teaching Strategies   135

3. Teaching Strategies   144

4. Evaluation of Teaching Strategies   181

Further Reading and References   189

Chapter 4   Learning Aids

Competences Related to this Chapter   193

FENTO Standards Related to this Chapter   194

1. What are Learning Aids and Resources?   195

2. Preparation of Learning Aids   197

3. Boards   203

4. Charts   205

5. Handouts   209

6. The Overhead Projector (OHP)   215

7. Other Techniques   221

8. Copyright   225

9. Selection of Visual Aids   225

10. Evaluation of Aids   230

Further Reading and References   234

Chapter 5   Planning and Design for Teaching and Learning

Competences Relating to this Chapter   237

FENTO Standards Related to this Chapter   238

1. Curriculum Development   239

2. The Process of Specifying Learning Outcomes   243

3. Course and Subject Aims   243

4. Learning Outcomes   250

5. Product Objectives: A Concept   253

6. Process Objectives   275

7. Competences   286

8. Scheme of Work (sequence of topics)   306

9. Topic Analysis   317

10. Scheme of Work (Planning Document)   324

11. Lesson Planning   329

12. Negotiation   338

13. Classroom Management   342

Further Reading and References   349

Chapter 6   Communication and the Teacher

Competences Related to this Chapter   353

FENTO Standards Related to this Chapter   354

1. Model of Communication   355

2. Reading Age and Readability   357

3. Listening Skills   363

4. Questioning   365

5. Transactional Analysis   371

6. Body Language   377

7. Equal Opportunities   379

8. Classroom Control   383

9. Spider Diagrams   384

10. Study Skills   388

11. Key Skills   395

12. References, Citation, Bibliographies and the Harvard System   400

Further Reading and References   403

Chapter 7   Assessment of Student Learning

Competences Related to this Chapter   407

FENTO Standards Related to this Chapter   408

1. Introduction   409

2. Formative Assessment   410

3. Norm and Criterion Referenced Assessment   417

4. Accuracy of Test Instruments   418

5. Increasing the Validity and Reliability   421

6. The Accreditation of Prior Achievement   438

7. Assessment of Student Practical Work   443

8. Assessment of Assignments and Projects   451

9. Student Profile Formats   458

10. Motivate Students Through Feedback   470

11. Assessment in Overall Lesson Design   471

12. Revising Assessment Procedures   471

Further Reading and References   475

Chapter 8   Evaluation of Self Teaching

Competences Related to this Chapter   479

FENTO Standards Related to this Chapter   480

1. Introduction   481

2. Autonomy and Accountability   481

3. Central Teaching and other Professional Tasks   482

4. Course Evaluation   494

Further Reading and References   511

Chapter 9   Evidence of Competence in Teaching

Competences Related to this Chapter   515

FENTO Standards Related to this Chapter   516

1. Introduction   517

2. Competences Related to Teaching and Learning   517

3. Learning Competences   519

4. Generation of Evidence   520

5. Competence Learning   531

Further Reading and References   535

Appendix

The FENTO Standards   539

Glossary of Terms

541

Bibliography

545

Index

553

Teaching, Training and Learning

A Practical Guide

Ian Reece and Stephen Walker

Chapter 1

An Introduction to Teaching

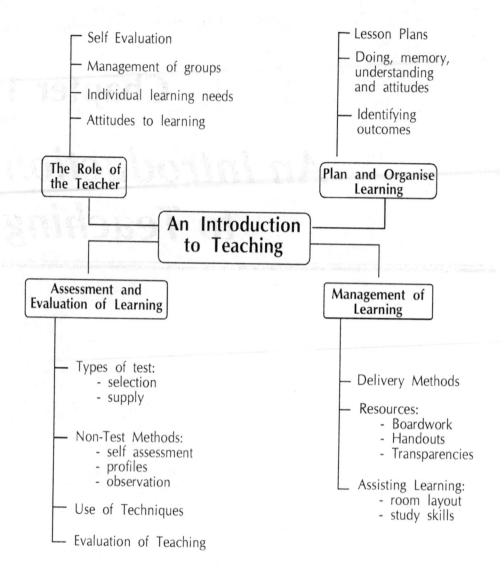

Overview of Chapter 1

This chapter is a free standing basic teacher training course for teaching adults. It equates to the requirements of the Stage One of the City and Guilds 730 courses. It discusses the role of the teacher together with the basic techniques of planning, management and assessment of learning. Thus, it covers the *basic* competences required by the teacher to teach adult students.

Competences Related to this Chapter

The teacher competences and associated performance criteria related to this chapter are:

Overall Competence - *Establish an Effective Approach to Teaching and Learning*

Competence	Performance Criteria
1. Adopt a Teaching Role	(a) Comment upon individual learning needs within a group. (b) Create positive attitudes to learning. (c) Discuss methods of group management. (d) Initiate self evaluation of teaching.
2. Plan and Organise Learning	(a) Identify learning outcomes. (b) Relate topics to outcomes. (c) Produce plans for learning sessions. (d) Identify ways in which learning is recognised. (e) Use learning resources. (f) Relate content structure and sequence to student needs.
3. Manage Learning	(a) Use methods of delivery that are appropriate to the group. (b) Organise the environment in a way that assists learning. (c) Use appropriate language. (d) Use appropriate resources. (e) Use appropriate methods to assess learning. (f) Encourage feedback from learners.
4. Assess Learning and Evaluate Teaching	(a) Assess prior learning of the group. (b) Analyse strengths and weaknesses of the learners. (c) Identify and confirm strengths and weaknesses of learners. (d) Give constructive feedback on progress to learners. (e) Carry out evaluation of teaching and learning.

FENTO Standards

FENTO Standards Related to this Chapter

A.	**Assessing Learners' Needs**
a1	Identify and plan for the needs of potential Learners
a2	Make an initial assessment of the learners' needs
B.	**Planning and Preparing Teaching and Learning Programmes for Groups and Individuals**
b1	Identify the required outcomes of the learning programme
b2	Identify appropriate teaching and learning techniques
C.	**Developing and Using a Range of Teaching and Learning Techniques**
c2	Facilitate learning in groups
D.	**Managing the Learning Process**
d2	Plan and structure learning activities
d5	Select and develop resources to support learning
F.	**Assessing the Outcomes of Learning and Learner'sAchievement**
f1	Use appropriate assessment methods to measure learning and achievement

Based on the FENTO Draft standards by kind permission

1. The Role of the Teacher

1.1 Creating Positive Attitudes to Learning

Traditionally the role of the teacher has been as a purveyor of information: the teacher was the fount of all knowledge. This suggests a picture of students sitting in rows in front of the teacher who is talking and passing information to students with the aid of a blackboard, while the students either listen passively or, if the teacher is lucky, take their own notes.

This, of course, is not true any more. The modern teacher is a facilitator: a person who assists students to learn for themselves. Instead of having students sitting in rows, they are likely to be in groups, all doing something different; some doing practical tasks, some writing, some not even in the room but in another part of the building using specialist equipment or looking up something in the library. All of the students might well be at different stages in their learning and in consequence, the learning is individualised to suit individual requirements and abilities.

This change from the traditional model is the result of a number of factors. First, it is recognised that adults, unlike small children, have a wealth of experience and are able to plan their learning quite efficiently. Second, not all individuals learn in the same manner, so that if a teacher talks to students some might benefit, but others might not. Third, everyone learns at their own pace and not, of necessity, at the pace set by the teacher. Hence, the individualising of learning has definite advantages.

Research into the ways that people learn has not provided teachers with any specific answers. If it had, all teachers would be using the same techniques. However, researchers have identified that learning is generally more effective if it is based on experiences: either direct experiences or experiences that have been read about. Of the two types of experiences, the former is more likely to be effective than the latter. Thus concepts that are able to be practised or seen are more likely to be learned. To apply this in a practical situation in post-16 education and training, learning is more likely to be effective when it is related to, and conducted in, the knowledge of a student's (work) experience.

We need, at this stage, to consider how we as teachers might best provide the experiences so as to make the learning as easy and quick as possible. We might consider two possible approaches to the design of a teaching programme.

(i) A programme where the content is carefully derived from an analysis of the student's personal, social and/or vocational needs, and which is implemented by you in such a controlled and organised manner that the student is almost certain to learn, and is aware when the learning has taken place. By this method motivation is generated by immediate success and the avoidance of failure.

Unfortunately this rarely takes place because it has a fundamental drawback. Apart from the requirement for the students to place themselves in the hands of the teacher and thus tend to develop a relationship of dependency, it confirms to them that learning is a process which is organised by someone who knows better. It does not help students to learn on their own.

(ii) The other approach starts from the experience of the student, experience that has taken place as part of life or which has been organised as part of the programme. It then depends upon the student identifying and accepting a need to learn. Such an approach has been described as 'problem solving', 'student-centred learning', 'participative learning', and so on.

The problem with this approach is to ensure that important areas of learning are not omitted and that the 'right' balance is struck between these areas, and that each area is learned as effectively as possible.

Teaching methods which allow this second approach to be implemented include:

- project work derived from students' current experiences;
- discussions which allow students to recognise and consolidate what the experience has taught them, and also lead them to identify what else they need to learn and practise;
- the learning of specific problem-solving techniques which can be applied to a range of situations;
- activities designed to provide opportunities for specific learning outcomes.

Such a list of teaching approaches identifies a second problem associated with the approach; that of (over) concentrating upon the activities - the practical work which tends to be more enjoyable, and neglecting to recognise the possible learning that can accrue from such activities.

As long ago as 1981, FEU documented a suggested model of lesson design to help overcome the problems associated with the second and more readily applied of the approaches. This *Experience, Reflection, Learning* Model, they suggested, embodied the principles that:

(i) the process should be focused on the student's current experience,

(ii) it recognises the adult nature of the learner by according responsibility for what is learned, and how, and

(iii) the learning can take place in a variety of contexts.

The suggestion was that the learning process should be considered in three phases; first, the student's *experience* needs to be followed by, secondly, some organised *reflection*. This reflection ensures that the student learns from the experience and also helps, thirdly, to identify any need for some *specific learning* before further experience is acquired. This model is expressed diagrammatically in Figure 1.1.

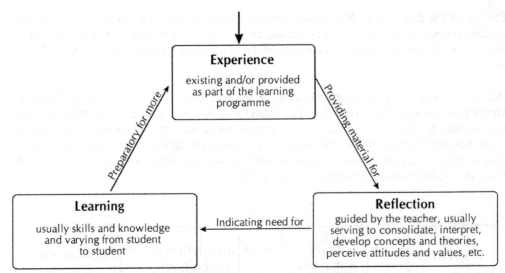

Figure 1.1   Experience, Reflection, Learning Model to Optimise Learning

The diagram shows that (i) the model is cyclic in nature and (ii) it has a definite starting point. Such a cyclic nature probably reflects an individual's learning process which takes place naturally. What is not so natural, but very important, is that reflection takes place to ensure the learning from the experience that has taken place. Many teachers recognise the importance of the provision of experiences in their classrooms and workshops, but then forget to provide an activity which is designed not only to consolidate the learning, but also to ensure that all of the learning opportunities take place.

Although the three activities are shown as separate entities in the diagram, they should not be seen as separate lessons; they may well be part of the same lesson. Indeed, if they are separated by too long a time span, some of the aspects may be forgotten. The **experience** may be any student-centred activity such as simulation, role play, workshop task, watching a TV programme, and so on. However, as suggested above, the experience may not be part of the programme but may be something that has previously taken place at work and away from the learning environment: they may be past experiences.

When the experience is part of the learning process, the **reflection** can very effectively be undertaken in groups. The teacher's role is very much an enabling one. When this is the case it will be the intention to elicit ideas, perceptions and views from the students and also to enable them to learn from each other. For this to take place effectively, the basic teacher requirement is that of good listening. Some stimulus materials might facilitate this process, such as a well designed questionnaire, or a problem solving strategy.

The **specific learning** part of the cycle will often take the form of specific skills to be practised or learned and particular information to be acquired. It is likely that individual students will vary greatly in what they need to learn and how they might best learn it. For example a text might be available for students to read through when they need help in the learning of specific information. This might be associated with a particular piece of written work which will allow the practise of the application of the information.

The use of the *Experience, Reflection, Learning* Model allows us to devise a teaching and learning scheme or it can be used to analyse an existing scheme. The format could well be used for the design of a lesson where each of the three components form part of the lesson itself.

Our task as teachers is to make this process work in some way and the Basic Teaching Model gives us some help with this. The Model suggests that we start with what we want our students to learn (the objective or 'terminal behaviour' of the students), go through 'entry behaviour' (what the students already know about the topic), 'instructional techniques' (this involves experiences and reflections) until finally assessing what has been learned. Thus, the model involves the aspects in Figure 1.2.

Figure 1.2   Aspects of the Basic Teaching Model

The model sub-divides the teaching process into four components and, in so doing, provides us with an uncomplicated yet fairly adequate concept of the teaching process, allowing us to plan and implement an effective learning sequence.

Objectives involve the determination of what our students should be able to do when they have completed a segment of instruction. Objectives vary in scope and character and we will discuss them in some detail in Chapter 5. They can consist of very general statements of aims or much more specific objective statements or competences. Determining our objectives is first in the sequence because knowing where we are taking the students, means there is more likelihood of us getting them there.

Entry behaviour describes the student's level of understanding of the topic before instruction begins. It refers to what the students have previously learned about the objective, their intellectual abilities and development, their motivational state and their learning abilities.

Instructional techniques describes the teaching process, which results in those changes in student behaviour that we call 'learning'.

Finally **assessment** consists of tests and observations that we use to determine how well the student has achieved the objectives. If this assessment tells us that all of the students, or even some of them, have fallen short of their objectives, then one or more of the previous components of the model may need adjustment. The feedback loops shown in Figure 1.3 provide the complete diagram.

Figure 1.3   Complete Basic Teaching Model

Both the Experience, Reflection, Learning Model and the Basic Teaching model give you the basis on which you can establish a positive attitude towards learning by your students. In order to be motivated to learn, students have to be interested in their work. One of the best ways to motivate your students, is to provide a variety of student activity: variety coming from the direct experiences and the subsequent reflection. The Basic Teaching Model tells you that you need to know where you are going (the objectives), to focus the learning on the needs of the students, to ensure that the level is neither too low or too high (entry behaviour) and, finally, after you have provided a variety of learning activity, to assess how much has been learned.

Your role as a teacher is to provide a positive learning environment and it will help you to do this if you take all of these aspects into consideration. Without a positive environment, your students will not reach their full potential. They will find their learning boring, will not devote the required time to it and, even during periods of learning, will find their minds wandering.

1.2 Individual Learning Needs - Adult Expectations

All students are individuals and no two students learn in the same way. One student may prefer to read information and to learn individually. Another student may have problems with reading and only learn through direct experiences by actually doing things. A third may learn through a mixture of experience and being made to think about that experience and learn best as a member of a group where competition is an important element in the learning process. Thus, although you may have a number of students in a class, they are all individuals and need to be treated as individuals.

The question for you is 'How do you treat a class of students as individuals?' Adult students (and, in this context, post-16 year olds are classed as adults) all have their own individual expectations and it is important that you meet these. Your students have all, either successfully or unsuccessfully, completed at least eleven years of primary and secondary education and some will have also completed a number of years of tertiary education. During this time they have built up a series of expectations which have been based on their previous experiences. Your task is to discover their preferences, to concentrate upon those that have been successful and play down those that have been unsuccessful. There are four main general expectations that are common in adult learners and we describe each of these below.

First, adults *expect to be taught*. Adults become involved in post-16 education and training for a variety of reasons but in the main they come of their own volition. This, often for the first time in their life, is education because they choose it. Previously at school, their attendance had been mandatory. Because the students choose to give up their own (or their employer's) time, they have expectations that they *will* learn as a result of their attendance and their hard work. In consequence they expect you to teach them.

This, of course, does not mean that you have to talk or lecture to them the whole time. Kolb, 1984, shows us the importance of variety in instructional techniques. It does, however, mean that you need to find out the techniques that are most appropriate to individuals and to teach each individual according to their needs and preferences.

Second, adult students *expect to have to work hard*. Adults have already come to the realisation that education does not come easily and that success only comes from hard work on an individual basis. They know that not only will they have to concentrate in the learning environment, but that they will also have to devote some time to private study. Your task is to make sure that they do work hard both in the learning environment and outside it at home.

The third main adult expectation is that the *work is related to the vocation*. All too often, especially in secondary education, students are not too sure why they have to learn the subjects they are asked to study and may be too immature to recognise that learning for its own sake is a useful exercise, and will be useful in later life. In post-16 education, it is important to make these links clear and to make sure that all of our students know why they are being encouraged to work hard. Generally, classes of students are grouped into specific vocations like secretaries, caterers, or electricians. Even so, a secretary who is employed by one firm has slightly different needs to one who is employed by a different firm. In consequence, you not only have to relate the work to that required by secretaries in general but to an individual secretary employed by a specific firm. This means that you must set exercises that can be adapted to individual requirements, making sure that some of the exercises are work based.

The fourth and final adult expectation is that your learners *expect to be treated as adults*. In childrens' education it is necessary to establish a degree of discipline and much of the role of the teacher is related to this. Adults do not need this and, although we may become exasperated on occasions, we must not show it. We must accept the students' comments and questions with all of the seriousness with which they are presented. We must not be rude to our students as they are liable to remember this rather than the subject matter. Adults tend to be much more intense about their learning and this is what makes teaching adults so satisfying. In consequence, we must not treat them in an offhand manner. In short, we must treat our students as adults with all that this entails.

Each of these four expectations, although stated in general terms, need to be interpreted as an individual need. Your students may vary in age from sixteen to over sixty. They are of different sexes, of different marital states, have different backgrounds, different requirements and all have been through different experiences. If you are to treat them as individuals, the more you can find out about them (both in class and outside of it) the greater the likelihood of your being able to treat them as individuals, relate their learning to their needs and, in consequence, improve their learning potential. Kindness, empathy and sincerity will always reap dividends with the adult learner.

The following assumptions, values and beliefs relate to how adults learn and the conditions under which they learn. The statements emerge largely from the growing literature on **Andragogy** but they have been extended by tutors experienced in working with adults. The following is based on work by Farrington (1996). In general, it is assumed that adults learn best when they:

Are involved in negotiation: Negotiation and evaluation should be continuous, beginning before the course begins. There should be a mechanism for mutual planning. Overall, the adult accepts a share of the responsibility for planning, implementing and evaluating the course.

Derive their own goals: Adults need to derive their own goals from their own practice, experience and future needs.

Diagnose their own needs for learning: Adults should be helped to diagnose their own learning needs, beginning with the decision to attend the course in the first place (pre-course counselling) and ending with plans for further study when the course is completed.

Accept that learning is an internal process: that is, learning is something that occurs 'inside' the adult and not something that the teacher 'does' to them.

Become autonomous: The adult learner is enabled to move from a state of dependency (on the teacher as 'appointed leader') to one of inter-dependency and autonomy. This involves learning how to learn from one's own experience and from that of others.

Have responsibility for learning: Adults should have (and be prepared to take) equal responsibility for their own learning and that of others.

Share ideas and feelings: Adults in a group should be encouraged to share their ideas and feelings with others in the group from a very early stage. This will be harder for some than for others and it will be a major initial responsibility for the tutor to help build the sense of trust and membership that will enable sharing to take place fully and fairly.

Experience openness, trust, respect, commitment etc: There should be an emphasis on the development of equality, mutual trust and respect, mutual helpfulness, openness, care, commitment, freedom of expression and acceptance of differences.

Are in a climate conductive to learning: The establishment of a suitable 'climate' should follow upon the successful building of a group feeling and the attainment of earlier values.

Are willing to alter their way of thinking: This might be another way of saying 'willing to learn'. For some adults their presence on a course indicates that they are passing through a major transition in their life requiring a new way of thinking (redundancy, training for a new job, a change of marital status, enforced leisure, etc.). Others will resist changing long established habits, assumptions and beliefs.

Are able to accept uncertainty: This follows immediately upon the point above and carries equal risk. For many adults, their earlier education (and their own need for security) makes it difficult for them to accept that some questions don't have answers!

Learn and think with others: Teaching adults is a process which involves learning and thinking with others who are also learning and thinking. It is a reciprocal process with a need to be both learner and teacher. Only in this way is it possible to facilitate the learning of others.

Make use of their experience: That is, a course and a tutor should try to take account of each adult's reservoir of experience. The adult may well have a highly structured understanding of the world which has been created over a lifetime and this can enhance or inhibit learning.

Fully utilise their willingness to learn: Adults will tend to have a readiness to learn which will come from their need to undertake developmental tasks associated with existing or proposed social roles, e.g. as workers, professional, parents, members of sports groups, etc.

Are present-centred: The interests of the adult tend to be more present-centred. They look for more immediate gratification of needs and are less willing to postpone that gratification.

Learn from problems rather than subjects: There should be an emphasis on the tackling of problems and issues which are grounded in the present practice of course members rather than on the teaching and learning of 'subjects'.

Are activity-based: Adults should be helped to move from passivity to activity in their approach to their own learning. They learn best when they are actively involved in the learning process.

Focus on principles: there may well be a need to move from an initial focus on particulars (specific details and concrete examples) to the development of principles (general rules, concepts and, ultimately, theory) for each individual.

Reflect upon experience: Adults should be encouraged to reflect upon their own experience and praxis and use this as a source of learning. This may require an initial 'unfreezing' and learning how to learn from experience.

Acknowledge the importance of process: A group of adults should acknowledge the importance of the process of learning. They should be willing to reflect upon and help change their own and other people's learning processes.

Have a sense of progression: Adults need to have a sense of progression towards the goals which they agree are worth achieving.

Value Transitions: Adults should welcome the contribution that life's transitions make towards their learning. In this sense, even 'failure' can be interpreted as an opportunity to learn and change.

Are integrated in their thinking: There is value in integrated thinking and learning. Fragmentation and the separation of ideas and practice should be avoided.

Can create knowledge: Adults should come to understand that knowledge is something that can be created as well as used. Not all knowledge comes from 'authoritative sources'.

Can change: Adults have the potential to undergo further qualitative changes in their thinking throughout their entire life-span. In so doing they move towards increasing control over their own thinking.

Think critically: Education for adults is about critical thinking, questioning, problem-posing, synthesis and discovery in a cycle so that from each end emerges a new beginning.

Knowles (1978) is generally regarded as being a key figure in the development of the andragogical model. Tennant (1988) in his discussion of Adult Learning, questions five assumptions made by Knowles. Tennant agrees that children do move from being dependent to being independent, (assumption one) but would then argue that they may not be independent in all aspects of their lives. With regard to assumption two, Tennant argues that because adults have had more life experience, this does not a particularly relevant characteristic for good learning. Tennant also dismisses the relevance of assumption three, namely, in adults, that readiness to learn is a function of the need to perform social roles.

The fourth assumption involves adults preferring to learn via problem solving and applying their new learning immediately. Tennant suggests that adults may be more willing than children to postpone the application of new-found knowledge. The fifth assumption is that internal motivators are more salient with maturity is contested by Tennant as having no base in the literature. Having said all that, Tennant continues to recognise the contribution of Knowles and the destructive nature of adult learners.

1.3 The Management of Groups

Much of the art of the management of groups of students lies in preparation. You must always be prepared and be ready for any eventuality. This means that you must be ready to change your prepared teaching plan and strategy both for the group and for individuals.

Generally, all sessions, whether they are classroom, laboratory or workshop based, should have an introduction, a development and a conclusion and as such, all of these lesson phases present you with opportunities for both group and individual activities.

Follow the basic teaching model that we discussed earlier and relate this to the three phases of a lesson. In the introduction (which includes an assessment of the immediate needs of individuals - their entry behaviour) the group activities can include question and answer or a discussion of the objectives of the session to find out what your students already know about the topic. The development phase may involve you in some formal input of the material to be covered but, following the Experience, Reflection, Learning Model, students should then reflect and conceptualise the material. This can be achieved by completing some sort of group exercises (discussion groups, role play, group problem solving, gaming) to assist the learning process. The final conclusion phase is to find out how much the students know and this might be achieved through, for example a group assignment. The activities related to each of the lesson phases are summarised in Figure 1.4.

Lesson Plan	Basic Teaching Model Aspect	Group Activity	Individual Activity
Introduction	Objectives	Question and answer or discussion	Notes on session ojectives
	Entry Behaviour		Entry behaviour test
Development	Instructional Techniques	Group work to apply learning	Notes on lecture
			Completing examples to apply learning
Conclusion	Assessment	Group assignment	Test

Figure 1.4   Activities Related to Lesson Phases

With this type of group activity, the question is asked "How do we manage the groups?" In effect, the role of the teacher in group work is very different to that when students are working individually or when you are controlling the learning through lecture or other forms of formal teaching methods. With group work the students control both the pace and the direction of the learning; they need to pool their knowledge and learning styles so that they learn from each other. Your role is to provide information *only* when it is asked, to point your students in the right direction (for example, where they might find the information that they require) but *not* to supply the answers. If groups are straying from the point or from the right direction, you can ask questions to bring their minds back but do not tell them the direction. Your role is that of guide and counsellor and not as the purveyor of information. This is summarised in Figure 1.5 giving the possible teacher and student roles for the different learning situations.

Learning Situation	Teacher Role	Student Role
Lecture-type situation	Control of time and pace of learning. Giving information and help.	Listening and taking notes.
Individual work	Assisting learners to know and apply their learning.	Asking questions. Working at own pace.
Group work	Guiding groups of students but not telling them.	Learning from each other by pooling knowledge. Learning and displaying group skills (leading and following). Working at pace of the group.

Figure 1.5   Teacher and Student Roles in Learning Situations

1.4 Good Teachers

There is no single good way to teach. Good teachers come in different guises and have different techniques. Much research has been undertaken (and continues to be undertaken) regarding effective teaching. We shall look at what American educators found in the Sixties and Seventies, and see how similar it is to current views of Further Education and Higher Education in this country.

Perrott (1982) considered issues with respect to effective teaching and listed observable factors. She noted that Ryan (1960) identified three main factors which he polarised as follows. Good teachers are:

- Warm and understanding rather than cold and aloof.
- Organised and business-like rather than unplanned and slipshod.
- Stimulating and imaginative rather than dull and routine.

Also reported by Perott, is the work of Rosenshine and Furst (1973). This research identified similar characteristics associated with observed good teaching. These factors are:

- teacher is enthusiastic;
- teacher is business-like and task orientated;
- teacher is clear when presenting instructional material;
- teacher provides opportunities for learning.

Moving onwards to the further education sector brings us to an interesting survey of Tertiary Colleges. HMI (1987) stated that:

> "Good practice was characterised by a high level of participation by the students, thorough preparation by the lecturers and a clear and shared sense of direction, spelled out in syllabus and lesson plans. In the best practice teachers had high expectations of their students and provided them with an appropriate variety of challenging learning activities. The best teachers had prepared written specifications of strategies to ensure that effective learning took place".

Cox and Ingleby (1997) report the outcomes of good teaching sessions which have been observed by Higher Education Assessors. They say that the best sessions included features such as:

- Clear aims and objectives, good planning and clear structure to the session.
- Classes characterised by enthusiastic and well-informed teaching, and consistently high quality of student contributions.
- Student contributions to discussions encouraged by tutors who provided a challenging but supportive environment.
- Much of the teaching being imaginative, innovative and participative and well-grounded in principles of adult learning.
- Some excellent lecturing supported by a range of audio visual aids.

- High levels of student interaction and participation in classes.

Maier P et al (1998) noted the popular qualities of lecturers by student interview (which may not necessarily equate with good teaching and effective learning). The top qualities were in order:

- Subject Expert.
- Good preparation.
- Related to life.
- Student questions and opinions encouraged.
- Enthusiastic.
- Approachable and opinions encouraged.
- Humour.

When we have a new group of students working towards the C & G 730, Cert Ed or PGCE, we often use the following activity:

> "Think of the best teacher you ever had, at school, at university or during your own training - think of a real person - and then list the qualities that made them so good". After this we ask individuals to contribute their thoughts and we write these on the board as a basis for discussion. The following are the thoughts of one of the groups and you can see the close relationship of these to what the literature says.

The ideal teacher is described as having the following characteristics:

- is expert in own subject
- is expert in the teaching role, well organised, well prepared
- is confident, open to suggestions, other viewpoints, is flexible and approachable
- is interested in individual students, and spends time with them
- is consistent in the treatment of everyone
- is consistent in behaviour - always fair, always even tempered
- is friendly, with a sense of humour
- shares with students the teaching aims and objectives
- knows the students as individuals - their strengths and their weaknesses
- communicates well in a variety of modes, including non-verbal
- leads well, with appropriate pace
- is flexible and willing to change the approach
- gives feedback within an appropriate timescale

In addition to this paragon, the ideal learning process is described as one where students like:

- to be stimulated and motivated

- to be involved

- to have clear goals

- to feel a sense of openness and trust

- to enjoy the lesson and feel part of it

- to have a role model

- to see the overall picture and the underlying model

- the topic to be relevant or be made relevant

All of the above research can be used gauge the qualities that are required by a 'good' teacher. They indicate:

(i)   The qualities that are necessary (e.g. enthusiastic, warm, approachable); and

(ii)   The teaching attributes that are required (e.g. have clear aims and objectives, be a subject expert, and be open to other views).

1.5 Self Evaluation of Teaching

Evaluation needs to be systematic if you are to get a realistic picture of what you are good at and what aspects need more thought and practise. The only true evaluation is self-evaluation. Only when we learn to assess our own performance and make judgments on our own can we really change ourselves.

Checklists, rating scales and questionnaires all help us to evaluate what we do with our students. Probably one of the most helpful methods is to keep a diary of what has gone on in our learning sessions. The type of headings that you might consider in such a diary are given in Figure 1.6 with associated questions. These questions can be used as a checklist, or alternatively you can rate yourself on, say, a four point scale (one for poor and four for excellent) for each of the aspects, or you might make comments alongside each of the aspects.

Alternatively, you might like to design a pro-forma that can be used to make a diary for each of a series of lessons. You can use the proforma to write a sentence or two about each of the aspects of your teaching. The summation of the completed pro-formas can then form a diary for the series of lessons. Such a pro-forma is shown in Figure 1.7 with some suggested headings.

Aspect	Question
Preparation	Have you: * analysed the topic/subject area? * indicated expected student learning? * identified the needs of your students? * selected appropriate teaching strategies? * written systematic lesson plans?
Presentation	* implemented selected teaching strategies? * responded flexibly to classroom situations? * used learning resources effectively? * conformed to safety requirements?
Classroom Relationships	*secured student participation in your lesson? *provided leadership to your students? *promoted a classroom climate which facilitated learning?
Communications	* used appropriate language registers? * developed students' communication skills? * effectively employed skills of non-verbal communication?
Assessment	* used an assessment method to consider if the objectives have been achieved?
Subject Matter	* demonstrated mastery of your subject matter?

Figure 1.6   Headings and Questions for a Self-Evaluation Diary

Preparation:	How successful was the preparation?
Entry Behaviour:	Was the entry behaviour as expected?
Aims/Objectives:	Were the aims/objectives achieved?
Teaching Strategies:	What teaching methods were most successful?
Aids:	Were the aids successfully designed and used?
Classroom Relationships:	Why was the class climate either successful or unsuccessful?
Assessment:	What assessment techniques were most successful and why?
Subject Matter	What was most successful in achieving the required learning?

Figure 1.7   Pro-forma for Self-Evaluation of a Lesson

The questions in the above example not only ask *what* but they also ask *why* and that second part is important in your self evaluation. Whatever system you devise for yourself, it should be quick and easy to complete; if it is long and complex you will tend not to do it. However, the type of form above, when completed for, say, eight to ten consecutive classes, will form a comprehensive 'diary' of your activities, indicating what went well and what went not so well, for that group of students.

Possible Evidence

> *Possible Evidence to Show you have*
> *Achieved the Competence*
> *'Adopt a Teaching Role'*

The type of evidence that you might collect to show that you have achieved the competence involves:

(a) Take one of your classes and find out what the students expect from attending the course. You might ask questions like:

   (i)   Why did you join the course?

   (ii) What do you expect to do on the course?

   (iii) What will you do at the end of the course?

(b) For one of your classes, show how you have applied either The Experience, Reflection, Learning Model of learning, or the Basic Teaching Model, or a combination of each of these.

(c) Take, say, three individual students (a good student, an average student and one who is not so good) and, by talking to them, find out what are their expectations in terms of:

   (i)   What they expect from you?;

   (ii) What work they expect to do in the teaching environment and at home?;

   (iii) How the work on the course is related to what they do at work?

   (iv) How the course is different/the same as their work at school?

Using these expectations, indicate how you will treat these learners as individuals.

(d) Design a series of 'diary' headings for one of your classes or for individuals and complete these for successive sessions for a period of time. On completion, state what you have found out in general terms, what you have learned and what you might do differently and why, if you were starting the teaching again.

> *If you want to check your understanding of your Role as a Teacher, try the following progress check*

Progress Check 1.1

1. Complete the diagram of the Basic Teaching Model by naming each of the four components of the teaching process.

A	B	C	D

2. Identify the three phases that are used in the majority of lessons. Suggest at least two activities that could be used for each of these phases.

3. The following activities are identified by a teacher teaching 'Safety' in the Workshop.

   A.   Visiting a factory where machines are in operation.

   B.   Discussing own experiences in the College workshop.

   C.   Taking notes in a lecture about the importance of machine guards.

   D.   Operating a machine safely in the College workshop.

Complete the table below to identify a suitable sequence for the learning of 'safety'. You may use some of the activities above or you may chose others of your own.

Classification	Activity
Experience	
Reflection	
Specific Learning	

Progress Check

2. Plan and Organise Learning

2.1 Identify Learning Outcomes

It is important for you to know where you want your students to finish and what you want them to learn. In this way you know when they have got there. In educational language, this involves you identifying the learning outcomes. These *learning outcomes* can be stated as aims and objectives. They are dealt with in greater detail in Chapter 5 but, at this stage, it is only necessary to state that they are what the students will be able to do by the end of their learning.

Aims are *goals* that are set, either by you as teacher or by the curriculum designers in the curriculum documents (syllabus), to state what the learning will achieve. They are 'ultimate' goals to indicate what the students will be able to do at the end of the course, or subject; they give direction for both the teaching and the learning. Aims can be written at different levels. Course aims are fairly general and are designed to describe the overall purpose of the course. At a subject level they are more specific and are even more specific at lesson level. Examples at the different levels are:

Course Aim:	To provide an introduction to the vocation of catering;
Subject Aim:	To develop the skills required in kitchen work;
Lesson Aim:	To give a working knowledge of the standard methods of cooking by roasting.

These statements are of most use when they are stated in terms of student behaviour; what the learners will be able to do at the end of the course, subject or lesson. Learning outcomes at lesson level are often stated in terms of objectives as opposed to aims. However, at this stage, it is sufficient to identify these as student terminal behaviour. Chapter 5 gives details of writing objectives and competences.

2.2 Doing, Memorising, Understanding and Attitudes

The way in which we learn depends to a certain extent on the type of learning that is involved. There are three main types (or domains) of learning and each type has different 'rules' associated with it for the teaching. The three domains are:

Psychomotor:	relates to the measurement of the student's manual skill performances and, therefore, the performance required will involve the manipulation of objects, tools, supplies or equipment. Performances which are primarily psychomotor include: *typing a letter; constructing a wall; driving a car; drawing a picture.*
Cognitive:	includes those learning behaviours which require 'thought processes' for specific information such as 'define the terms',

'select a suitable material' and 'summarise the topic'. All of these involve thought processes (i.e. thinking).

Affective: the behaviour required in this domain involves the demonstration of feelings, emotions or attitudes towards other people, ideas or things. For example the student might be asked to:

- demonstrate an increased awareness of environmental pollution;

- show concern for safety in the workshop;

- display an appropriate attitude towards a frightened patient.

The learning required of the student related to each of the domains is quite different and, indeed, the learning in the cognitive domain at the level of knowledge is different from that required for understanding (as these are two different levels within that domain).

Teaching Students to Learn to DO Something (Psychomotor Domain)

Learning to do something (learning a psychomotor skill) usually involves three distinct aspects:

(i)   *Purpose*   In order to learn a skill the student needs some understanding of what it is that is to be achieved - that is the aim or objective.

(ii)   *Procedures*   Skills need some procedures or rules that are necessary in order to complete them efficiently.

(iii)   *Practice*   All skills need practice so that they are completed correctly, quickly and, like riding a bicycle, automatically. This part is very important so that the movements are *right* from the start, unlearning of wrong movements can be difficult to rectify.

Thus, as the word 'psychomotor' suggests, learning in this domain involves a 'psycho' aspect - a cognitive aspect which must be remembered or understood, and a 'motor' aspect - the movement and co-ordination between brain and limbs (usually, but not always, the hands).

Psychomotor skills are usually learned either from a demonstration or from written instructions or, preferably, from a mixture of the two.

When demonstrating a skill to students you should:

(i)   give emphasis to the required body movements; which hand and foot is being used, when sight, sound, smell and touch are required;

(ii)   encourage students to *ask questions* until they understand what is being done;

    (iii) emphasise the key points so that the sequence is learned and any difficult aspects can be concentrated upon. These points could be highlighted on a chalkboard or in a handout or noted by the students themselves.

    (iv) ensure that all safety aspects are covered.

Demonstrations should be short because, in the main, students will be inactive, watching what is being done. Anything that you do that can give students an activity will help them to concentrate upon the important points, for instance getting them to complete a handout, noting the key points, sketching some aspects, or even assisting. If the demonstration is too long consider dividing it into two parts.

Demonstrations are designed to assist with the cognitive aspects of learning. Give the students some practice as soon as possible; too long a gap between the demonstration and the subsequent practice will mean that they may have forgotten many of the points.

Teaching Students to Memorise (Cognitive Domain)

Some students have good memories while others are not so good (and the same might be said of teachers!). Memory relates to the factual information which is the basis of all subjects. It is not concerned with understanding but only with the *recall* of the factual information.

You can help your students to memorise information by:

    (i)   verbal or visual association; that is grouping things together verbally (like knife, fork and spoon) or keeping the location of things always the same (like the layout of the kitchen and the drawers so that equipment can always be visualised in the same place and, hence, remembered).

    (ii) repetition; we remember our telephone number by dialling it time and time again. We can do the same with facts. By writing them out a number of times, repeating them aloud as in poetry, listening to a tape several times or reading a number of times.

    (iii) testing; this is a form of repetition which asks learners to recall and repeat the information either verbally or in writing.

    (iv) special aids like rhyme rules (30 days has September, etc.) or mnemonics (ROYGBIV) which can either be designed by you for your learners or by the learners themselves.

A number of conditions help good recall. These include: (a) trying to avoid errors; (b) testing frequently to increase learning; (c) the more the students concentrate, the more they will be able to recall; (d) the greater the importance of the learning, the more effective it will be, and (e) the more students can relate the material to other things that have been learned previously, the greater the likelihood of recall.

Teaching Students to Understand (Cognitive Domain)

Learning to *understand* something involves giving answers to the questions of "Why?" and "How?". Students need to give explanations or summaries to show that they understand something.

To summarise these points, learning to *do* something involves learning a procedure and then practising it; avoiding errors if possible.

Memorising involves using various methods to enable students to recall facts; practice, in the form of repetition or testing is helpful and, as with learning to do something, errors must be prevented if possible. Learning to *understand* something is different in a number of crucial aspects. Repetition is *not* helpful whereas errors can be. Another difference lies in the fact that memorising and doing, once accomplished, are always practised or repeated in the same way. By contrast, understanding is an active mental process involving thoughts which link or group ideas together in a *new* way in our minds.

An aid to understanding two similar concepts is to "compare and contrast" them. So we can list the features they have in common i.e. compare, and then list features which are distinct to each, i.e. contrast.

For example, Guidance and Counselling are often used interchangeably or together but they are different. Figure 1.8 shows how you can start to compare and contrast the two activities.

Same	Different	
	Guidance	**Counselling**
Helping students to make informed choices	• May be in small groups	• Usually one-to-one
Helping students with problems	• Usually not confidential	• May be confidential
May need to seek information for a student	• Usually concerned with future	• Usually concerned with now
May need to refer to another for help	• Planned event in student life	• Often response to unexpected event
Appointment basis		

Figure 1.8   Compare and Contrast as an Aid to Understanding

Helping students to understand involves making sure that they ask questions so that the topic makes sense to them. They must be made to work at making comparisons and trying to solve problems. Thus, there are three techniques that you might use to help students understand; questioning, making comparisons and solving problems.

Getting students to ask questions can be achieved by them asking you as teacher or by them asking other students. Thus, a discussion on the topic can assist understanding. Questions such as 'Why' usually identify the reasons for what goes on and are likely to be helpful. 'Who?', 'What?', 'Where?' and 'When?' only gain information and are not helpful for understanding.

After finding out by questioning as much as they can about the new facts or ideas, you can ask students 'How is the information the same or different from ideas that you have already'? Questioning is being used here for the specific purpose of comparing what is known with what has been recently learned.

Working out a problem expands students' understanding by making them adapt and transfer the body of knowledge that they have to a variety of different circumstances. Figure 1.9 summarises helpful and unhelpful activities for doing, memory and understanding types of learning.

Type of Learning	Helpful Activities	Unhelpful Activities
Doing	Identifying key points from a demonstration followed by practice.	Errors must be prevented
Memorising	Practice in the form of repetition and testing.	Errors must be prevented
Understanding	Errors can be helpful. Learners should ask questions, make comparisons and solve problems.	Repetition is unhelpful

Figure 1.9   Helpful and Unhelpful Activities for Different Learning

Teaching Students to Learn Attitudes (Affective Domain)

The learning of attitudes is equally, if not more, important than the learning of cognitive and psychomotor elements. It could be argued that, unless your students have the 'correct' attitude (whatever that might be), then other learning is superfluous.

Attitudes like 'showing concern for safety', 'working effectively as a group member' and 'checking work after completion' are all important aspects for your students. But, how do you teach them? You can tell students again and again about an incorrect attitude but, unless they really see the necessity for it and internalise it as part of their character, then they are not likely to display it.

The most effective technique for the teaching of attitudes is to set up a discussion (that is a discussion itself, or case study, role play and so on, all of which involve students discussing with each other) where students can learn from each other. Adult students are more likely to listen to their peers about the importance of attitudes than they are to you.

2.3 Production of Plans for Learning Sessions

It is evident from the previous section that:

(a) the type of plan for a learning session depends upon the learning that is required for that session. The requirements are different for a psychomotor skill session compared with a knowledge session;

(b) it is important to classify the requirements of a session into the domain that it predominantly falls and, if it involves cognitive learning, the level in that domain.

We have already said from the Basic Teaching Model (Section 1.1) that the formulation of objectives (or aims) for a session provides the starting point. Within these objectives (or aims) lie the clues to the required domain through the verbs that are used. These are summarised in Figure 1.10.

Domain	Possible Verbs (student behaviours)
Psychomotor	Show skill in, assemble, build, cook, design, fillet, mend, paper, sing, weigh
Cognitive (Knowledge)	Know, define, label, list, name, outline, state
Cognitive (Understanding)	Understand, interpret, translate, explain, give new examples, summarise
Affective	Appreciate, ask, choose, answer, comply, study, check

Figure 1.10 Student Behaviours Related to Domains of Learning

Thus, the wording of the required student behaviour can indicate the domain into which the learning predominantly falls. Of course, as we have already said, the requirement of a psychomotor skill also relies upon cognitive knowledge and attitudes and vice-versa. What we have discussed in the previous section now has to be put into practice with the design and production of a plan for a learning session (lesson plan).

Lesson Planning

A lesson plan has two functions:

1. a strategy or plan for 'teaching'.

2. a series of cues to be used during the lesson.

It is not to be confused with *lesson notes* which are details of the actual subject matter content of the session. The lesson plan is intended to help you to proceed logically without being bound to your notes, but, even with detailed planning, every eventuality cannot be catered for, so the lesson plan is essentially tentative and flexible. A lesson plan should not limit you in your approach and it should contain sufficient flexibility to cater for circumstances as they arise in the session.

You can usefully divide your lesson plans into two:

(a) Initial information; and

(b) Body of the plan.

The initial information should contain:

1. The title of the lesson.

2. Details of the class (name, size, etc.).

3. The time of the lesson.

4. The expected entry behaviour of the class (expressed in terms of what the students should know or be able to do).

5. The aims/objectives of the lesson (expressed in the same sort of terms as the entry behaviour)

An example of initial information is shown in Figure 1.11.

Title:	Calculating Area
Class:	First Year Business Studies - 18 Students
Time:	9.00 - 10.00
Entry Behaviour:	Multiplication of numbers, shapes of plane figures
Objectives:	1. Explain how to calculate the area of plane shapes 2. Solve problems relating to area

Figure 1.11 Sample Initial Information in a Lesson Plan

Once the essential preliminaries have been completed you need to plan the strategy. Planning should relate to the principles stated at the start of this chapter (that is following the Experience-Reflection-Learning and Basic Teaching Models). You will need to plan an introduction, a development and a conclusion within the time available, give students an experience, make them reflect on the experience and provide variety for them so that they are motivated throughout the session.

Planning a Cognitive Lesson

The expansion of the three phases of a lesson (introduction, development and conclusion) depends upon the type of learning and the subject matter.

Planning a cognitive lesson depends on whether the aim or objective relates to knowledge (memorising) or understanding. For a lesson based on knowledge there needs to be an emphasis on verbal or visual association, repetition and testing, whereas, for a lesson based on understanding, questioning, comparing with what is already known, and problem solving is appropriate.

You may find the following steps helpful when you are planning a lesson where **information** is to be remembered:

1. Tell the student *what* is expected to be learned and *why* it is important that it is learned.

2. Provide a meaningful context to the information to be learned. Logically organise the information.

3. Relate new information with previous experience or learning.

4. Provide for adequate practice and reinforcement of correct responses.

5. Assess students' performances.

If, on the other hand, the objectives of the lesson require that the students understand the subject matter and are required to solve problems to show their understanding, you will find the following steps useful.

1. Tell the students the lesson objectives

2. Assess the students' entry behaviour for the concepts and principles they will need in order to solve the problem.

3. Have students recall the necessary concepts and principles.

4. Provide verbal direction to the students' thinking (an algorithm or paradigm) short of giving them the solution to the problem.

5. Verify students' learning by requiring them to give a full demonstration of the problem solution.

The headings that can usefully be employed for the expansion of the three phases are:

1.	*Time*	It is helpful to give an indication of the time that is likely to be needed for each of the phases and each of the sub-topics within a phase.
2.	*Content*	This should be restricted to brief cues or key words and they should be made to stand out clearly.
3.	*Teacher Activity*	This should specify the strategies which are intended to be used during the lesson. If a question or questioning technique is to be used then key questions should be stated.
4.	*Student Activity*	The parts played by students should be clearly stated so that variety can be planned. Students should have a change of activity at least every 15 minutes.
5.	*Aids*	All audio-visual materials should be specified.

An example of the body of the plan using the introductory information from Figure 1.11, might be as shown in Figure 1.12.

Time	Content	Teacher Activity	Student Activity	Aids
9.00	**Introduction** Assess entry behaviour	Questions about multiplication	Answering	
9.05	Objectives	Tell students objectives and the importance of them	Listening	OHP
9.10	**Development** Area of Square	Exposition	Listening	Handout A1
		Individual Tutorials	Examples	
9.20	Area of triangle	Individual Tutorials followed by chalkboard	Groups to predict the formula	Handout A2
		Individual Tutorials	Examples	
9.35	Area of parallelogram	Individual Tutorials	Individuals to predict formula	Handout A3
9.45	**Conclusion** Review of formulae	Questions with C/B overview	Answers	
	Test		Individual work	
10.00	**End**			

Figure 1.12 Sample Body of a Plan for a Cognitive Lesson

Planning a Psychomotor Skills Lesson

We have all learned psychomotor skills. These include walking, tying our shoe laces and riding a bicycle. These, however, were learned automatically. They might have taken quite a long time to learn and might have been learned by trial and error. You are required to teach psychomotor skills so that they are learned in the most effective way and this generally means them being learned quickly and with a minimum of error.

Five steps can be identified in the teaching and learning of a skill. These are:

1. Analyse the skill.

2. Assess the entry behaviour of the student.

3. Arrange for training in the component parts.

4. Describe and demonstrate the skill.

5. Arrange for the three basic learning conditions of contiguity, practice and feedback.

Each of these steps will be examined in detail.

1. Analyse the Skill

The first step involves a detailed analysis of the skill so that it is broken down into its constituent parts, the sequence of operation is identified, and the key abilities are noted. For example, if you assume that you are teaching 'sharpening a Pencil with a Knife' the skills analysis will involve for a right handed person:

To cut wood:

1.   Hold pencil in left hand about 2.5 cm from the end.

2.   Hold knife in right hand and rest blade with blunt edge uppermost at an angle of about 30 degrees to the centre line of the pencil.

3.   Cut off wood with slow, sure cuts removing pressure at the end of the stroke.

4.   Rotate pencil in left hand to take equal cuts around the pencil.

5.   Cut until about 5 mm of lead is exposed from the wood, equally around the circumference.

To put point on lead:

6.   Position knife so that it makes an angle of approximately 90 degrees with the centre line of the pencil.

7.   Sharpen lead with swift sure strokes rotating pencil in left hand.

From this analysis the key abilities can be identified as:

(a)   Ability to keep the angle of the knife around the pencil constant.

(b)   Ability to judge angle of knife for correct depth of wood.

(c)   Ability to remove pressure towards the end of the stroke of the knife.

(d)   Ability to sharpen exposed lead to a point without breaking the lead.

2. Assess the Entry Behaviour

The skills analysis results in a chain of activities in the form of a sequence of component skills. You must make sure that the students have learned all of the pre-requisite skills. For example, in the sharpening of a pencil you must make sure that the student can cut with a knife, hold the knife at 30 and 90 degrees and so on.

3. Arrange for Training of Component Skills

This provides opportunity for the student to:

(a)   learn any missing links in the chain and to develop the required abilities; and

(b)   learn the skill components (or some of them) so well that they can focus attention on new aspects of the more complex task that is being learned.

4. Describe and Demonstrate the Skill to the Student

Describing and demonstrating is a very important and skilled part of your job. It is necessary to show students the chain involved in the skill and the links in the chain. This part of the learning of the skill is, for the students, the cognitive part; they must learn to verbalise the skill so that they *know* what is required and, secondly, the demonstration provides a clear visual picture of what is required in completing the skill, what the task will look like after each stage. The demonstration method is described in Chapter 3 and will not be discussed here. Sufficient to say that it is an important part of your job.

5. Arrange for the Three Basic Learning Conditions

The first condition for efficient and effective learning is *contiguity*, that is the almost simultaneous occurrence of the links in the chain so that each part of the chain is linked. Once the links are contiguously formed, they occur almost simultaneously. Thus, you must teach students the correct sequence, co-ordination and timing. To achieve this you can teach students (a) the whole method involving all of the links being learned at one time, or (b) the part method involving sub-dividing the skill into sections and learning a section at a time. For a complex skill, the part method has the advantage that the simple skills can be mastered before the more complex ones. It does, however, have the disadvantage that the sections have then to be joined.

The other conditions are *practice* and *feedback*. Practice should be given directly after the demonstration so that students do not have the chance to forget what is required. Feedback is the information to the students about their performance. Feedback can be intrinsic (which comes from within the student by, for example, noting the finish produced or by the kinaesthetic or sensory feel of doing the job right) or extrinsic (which is provided by someone else like you as the teacher). The best type of feedback is intrinsic because you will not always be available to provide information to the student. In consequence, any form of extrinsic information should always lead to the provision of intrinsic feedback. For this reason feedback should be immediate or given as soon as possible after the event.

Using the pencil example, intrinsic feedback could be given through telling students the criteria of acceptable performance and them ensuring that the lead does not break during the sharpening process. Extrinsic feedback could be given by you commenting upon the angles of the knife during the practice periods and through assessment of both process and product.

The Skills Lesson Plan

As with a the cognitive lesson, the main components of a skills lesson involve introduction, development (demonstration, explanation, practice and assessment) and conclusion.

Introduction

It is vital to arouse interest in the first few minutes of a skill lesson. For a new topic, a short clear statement of what the students are going to be doing (the aim/objective) and why it is important for them to be doing this. The importance can often be the link with what they are doing at work. In a continuation lesson testing the work already completed will focus attention on the subject and provide the necessary link with the previous lesson.

Development

A demonstration of the skill to be learned can follow the introduction. This should be followed by an explanation of the key points which can usefully be reinforced with questions and answers. As soon as possible each student should be given the opportunity to practice the skill so that the sub-tasks are integrated. The necessary extrinsic feedback can be given on a one-to-one basis during the practice period to complement the intrinsic feedback that should be encouraged.

When students have practised the skill sufficiently to become competent, they can be tested. This assessment may need to be followed by a further period of practice if sufficient competence has not been achieved.

Conclusion

You should plan the ending of the lesson with just as much care as the introduction and development. Sufficient time must be allowed for the cleaning of the practical area, returning tools and equipment and washing (if this is required). You should plan a short period in which you summarise what has been learned and prepare students for the next session. A useful summary is to place all of the student work on the bench and to formally, but anonymously, assess each piece of work. In this way the students see what their peers have achieved as well as having the main points emphasised.

The example plan given in Figure 1.13 on the next page shows the design of a lesson to teach the sharpening of a pencil with a knife.

Title:	Pencil Sharpening
Class:	First Year - 18 Students
Time:	2.00 - 3.00
Entry Behaviour:	Use of knives - Know 30 and 90 degrees
Objectives:	1. Show skill in sharpening a wood pencil with a knife so that 5 mm of lead is exposed concentrically

Time	Content	Teacher Activity	Student Activity	Aids
2.00	**Introduction** Assess entry behaviour	How do you use a knife?	Answering	
2.05	Objectives	Tell students objectives and importance of sharp point in drawing	Listening	OHP
2.15	**Development** Removal of wood	Demonstration	Watching	
		Tutorials	Practice	Pencils & Knives
2.30	Sharpen to a point	Demonstration	Watching	
		Tutorials	Practice	
		Assessment	2nd Practice	Template
2.45	**Conclusion**	Display on front desk of all pencils for critique Identification of criteria	Listening Identification and notes	
2.55			Clearing away and returning equipment	
3.00	**End**			

Figure 1.13 Sample Psychomotor Skills Lesson Plan

Introductions and Conclusions

When we are planning our lessons we have a tendency to concentrate upon the main body of the lesson and then consider the start and the end. However, the start of a lesson and the end, are very important and should be part of our normal planning process.

Introduction

The **introductory** phase is intended to motivate the students to want to know more; it shold motivate the students by providing links with what has gone on before, by informing them of what is to take place in the lesson and suggest why the topic is important and how the information might subsequently be used. Figure 1.14 shows some of the possible purposes (the inner circle) and processes (outer circle) that might be used in this introductory phase of the lesson.

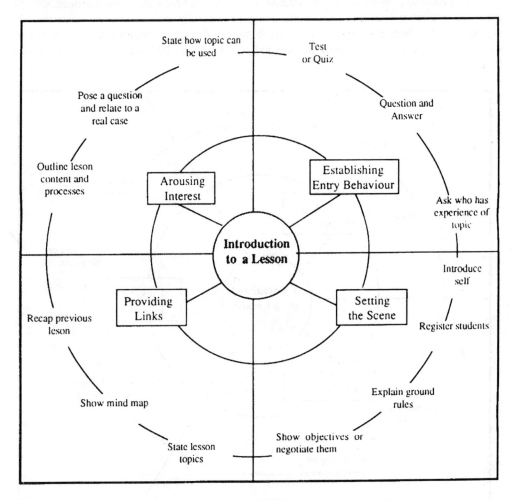

Figure 1.14 Possible Purposes and Processes of Introductions

This indicates that there are four possible purposes, and for each purpose, there are a number of possible processes that can be used. It is not, however, suggested that only one of these are used or that all of them are used for each introduction. The intention is to indicate the options that are available so that you can choose those options that are most appropriate for your students and for a particular topic.

So, how do we choose what is appropriate for a particular lesson. The over-riding criterion must be that which is to motivate the students. If the lesson is in the middle of a sequence of topics you might establish the entyr behaviour of the students through question and answer of the previous lesson's content, set the scene by informing the students of the objectives of the session, and arouse interest by stating how the topic might be used in the future

Conclusion

The **conclusion** to a lesson shold be planned with as much precision as the introduction. All too often a teacher who does not watch the time carefully will suddenly realise that the allotted time has been completed and, in consequence, there is either no conlusion or a very short one. The conclusion should be planned to take about 10% of the total time of the lesson.

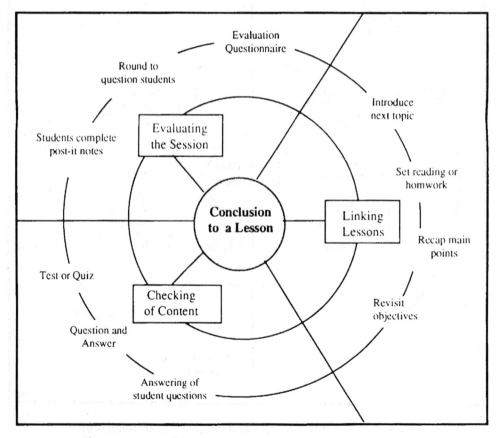

Figure 1.15 Possible Purposes and Processes of Conclusions

In any lesson much information passes between you, the eacher and your students. The intention of a conclusion is to remind students of the main aspects covered during the lesson and to start the transfer of the information from the short-term to the long-term memory. If this is repeated in the introduction to the next session this will further assist the process.

Figure 1.15 provides an overview of the possible purposes (the inner circle) and processes (the outer circle) that may be used. The three purposes that are suggested include (i) checking the student understanding of the content, (ii) linking the content and structure to other learning and (iii) evaluating the session. Each of these purposes have their own suggested processes associated with them. Thus, the checking of the understanding of the content might includea test or quiz of the main points that have been covered, it may involve question and answer based on the objectives of the session or it may involve you answering any questions that students may have for you. Some of these are teacher-centred and some student-centred. The former can check the understanding of all the students whilst the latter can only check some of the students. The decision of which might be more appropriate, will probably rest on how much time you have available as any student-centred activity is likely to take longer than teacher-centred ones.

A useful ploy in any session is to have your objectives displayed for students on either an OHP transparency or on the whiteboard or flipchart. In this way they can be displayed in the introduction phase as an advance organiser and motivator; they can be ticked off in the development phase as they are covered; ans they can be used as the basis of questions during the conclusion phase to remind students of the main points that have been covered and to check on their understanding of them. Any visual aid that can be used on three occasions during a session must be worth the time and effort that you put into its preparation!

Possible Evidence

**Possible Evidence to Show you Have
Achieved the Competence
'Plan and Organise Learning'**

The type of evidence that you might collect to show that you have achieved the competence involves:

(a) Stating the aims/objectives of either a course, subject or lesson in which you are involved and stating how they will be achieved and why.

(b) Classifying each of the aims/objectives into the domain which they predominantly fall and, for those in the cognitive domain, stating whether they are at the knowledge or understanding level.

(c) Choosing an aim/objective in each of the domains and stating, with reasons, how you would achieve the necessary learning.

(d) For a session that you are to teach in the near future, writing a lesson plan and giving a rationale for activities that you have included in each of the phases of (a) introduction; (b) development; and (c) conclusion.

(e) For the planned lesson asking your tutor, or a colleague, or your line manager to sit in on the session and to provide for you a critical analysis of your performance using the headings and questions in section 1.4 of this chapter as the basis.

> *If you want to check your understanding of your
> role in Planning and Organising Learning,
> try the following progress check*

Progress Check 1.2

1.   What are the three phases of a lesson plan?

2.   Describe a lesson plan in your own words.

3.   The two sections of a lesson plans are:

   (a)   introductory information; and

   (b)   a breakdown of the topic.

   Indicate what might be included in each of these sections.

4.   What is the difference between 'memory' and
     'understanding'?

5.   What are the helpful activities that can be given to students
     for:

   (a)   learning to 'do';

   (b)   learning to 'memorise'; and

   (c)   learning to 'understand'?

Progress Check

3. The Management of Learning

3.1 Methods of Delivery

A teaching strategy is defined as "a combination of student activities supported by the use of appropriate resources to provide a particular learning experience (process) and/or to bring about the desired learning (product)". Notice, in the definition, the emphasis is placed firmly on the needs of the student and not on the teacher. A teaching strategy is what you do for the benefit of student learning. There is a vast range of teaching strategies, some of which are detailed in Chapter 3. Here it is sufficient that you familiarise yourself with that range and know what each of them entails. Some of the more popular strategies are outlined below.

Lecture
One way communication by the teacher with no feedback from students. May last from 5 minutes to more than two hours.

Question and Answer
Teacher-centred interaction with the students.

Group Discussion
A network of interaction between students with the teacher setting the discussion but subsequently playing only a minor role.

Practicals
Real or simulated situations with students learning from experience.

Tutorial
Interaction between the teacher and one or a small group of students providing opportunity for guidance and support.

Individual Learning
Situations where students work alone with books, equipment and other resources.

Demonstration
Teacher shows the basic steps and sequence of a skill, or the main attributes of a concept with students watching.

Seminar
Students either individually or in small groups are set a task to research and from which they report their findings to the whole group and lead a subsequent discussion.

Case Study
The examination of a real or simulated situation so that learning can take place through the discussion of each of its facets.

Role Play
Students are invited to enact, in the training situation, the role they will be called upon to play in their job of work.

Project
The particular task is laid down by the teacher but the lines to be followed to achieve the objectives are left for the student to decide. Projects have an end product and tend to be integrated activities.

Assignment	Similar to a project but usually of shorter duration and not as open-ended.
Problem Solving	Teacher sets a problem which students solve either individually or in groups.

It has already been suggested that the use of one strategy may be more appropriate in a given situation than another. Research into the advantages and limitations of the various methods, however, is not always clear cut. It is possible to make some crude choices, based on the way that you analyse your objectives. Figure 1.14 makes suggestions for the general choices of matching strategies to objectives.

When your objective is to teach a motor skill	When your objective is to impart knowledge and understanding	When your objective is to change attitudes
Assignment Demonstration Individual Practice Tutorial Project	Case Study Project Seminar Individual Learning Problem Solving Lecture Question and Answer Assignment	Case Study Discussion Role Play

Figure 1.14 Matching Strategies to Objectives

Making the choice, of course, does not mean that a lecture (for instance) cannot change attitudes, or that role play will not impart knowledge.

3.2 Resources to Supplement Strategies

You will remember from the previous section that the definition of a teaching strategy was given as a combination of student activities supported by appropriate resources. The main resources with which you should have familiarity and be able to use fairly effectively are:

Chalk and whiteboard or flipchart	can be used as a planned visual aid but also to give a résumé of student work like responses to questions.
Handout	information given to students on paper which can either be given complete to supplement a lecture or incomplete to provide a student activity. Worksheets fall into this latter category.
OHP transparency	pictures or words projected onto a screen which are used to provide students with the information needed to reach the lesson objectives. Used like a chalkboard but with the advantage that the transparencies can be prepared prior to the lesson to save time in writing.

Chapter 4 goes into some detail about the design and use of resources. You must remember that resources are an extremely useful aspect of your teaching repertoire. They can:

(a) provide concrete experience (Experience-Reflection-Learning Model);

(b) motivate and arouse learner interest;

(c) increase retention (we remember more of what we see than we do of what we hear);

(d) provide variety in learning,

(e) provide experience not otherwise easily obtained;

(f) make better use of class contact time;

(g) improve your communicative skills.

With all of these advantages, you must ensure that you are skilful in the design and use of resources.

Boardwork

Figure 1.15 suggests some guidelines that you can use for your boardwork including chalk, white or flipchart.

Boardwork	
Preparation:	Keypoints and diagrams should be planned on lesson plan.
Lettering:	Minimum size should be 5cm upper case and 3cm lower case. Lower case is easier to read than upper case. Emphasis can be given by: * UPPER CASE *colour *underlining *s p a c i n g Avoid symbols, abbreviations, vertical or angled words
Diagrams:	Avoid clutter. Use colour but not too much to be confusing. Label directly, avoid a key. Use templates for accuracy and recurring need.
Location:	Ensure it is visible to all learners and is suitably lit.
Testing:	Check visibility from rear of room. Avoid Obscuring students' vision.

Figure 1.15 Guidelines for Boardwork

Handouts

Handouts are useful in the presentation of information and as worksheets. They may be loosely categorised as:

Information handouts

These aim to provide learners with the information needed to achieve the lesson objectives. They may be further divided into:

(a) Notes that relate directly to the content of the lesson, for example an overview of the main points of a lecture, a summary or outline of an experiment, a full transcript of a seminar.

(b) Supporting handouts which may be used to introduce a session, give formal statements such as definitions or formulae, present data to support arguments, e.g. graphs or maps.

Worksheets (Incomplete handouts)

The student is expected to write on the handout either during the lesson or afterwards. Workcards are similar to worksheets but the crucial difference is that they are reusable because the students do the associated work on a separate page.

You should consider various things when using handouts. The following questions need answering before you decide to design and duplicate the handout.

(a) Why use a handout? Is it to save time and make the learning easier for the students?

(b) At what stage in the lesson do you intend using the handout? Remember that, if they are Information Handouts, it is better to give them at the start of your lecture/exposition as the students can read them at the same time as listening to you.

(c) Are the students clear as to how they can use the handout? Do they use it as background to be read later? Do they make their own notes on it? There is nothing worse than spending time, effort and money on their design and duplication and finding that they are subsequently left on the desks or, even worse, in the wastebasket at the end of the lesson!

(d) What type of handout do you intend to use? In general, an incomplete handout is preferable to the information type. The former can be personalised and you can ensure that they are read and used.

(e) Do you intend to assess the students' use of the handout? This is a useful way to ensure that the material that they contain is learned. One way which this can be achieved is to plan the questions that you are to ask in order to draw out the information from the class, which students then write in the appropriate spaces provided.

Preparing Handouts

Choose the best format to clearly and simply illustrate the idea you are seeking to teach. Remember your aim is to provide motivation and to ensure achievement. The handout should be clear, logical, straightforward, concise, error free and legible.

You must write at a vocabulary level which will be understood by the student. Simple, short sentences rather than complex, compound ones are more likely to be understood. Illustrations are invaluable; a picture can be worth much more than words and a table is more likely to be looked at than a paragraph.

You should avoid large blocks of type. 'White space' makes a handout easier to read. If possible colour should be used where it is necessary to differentiate between different aspects. For differentiation purposes, different phases, topics or subjects can be duplicated on different coloured paper.

OHP Transparencies

The Overhead Projector, has several advantages including: (a) it can be used in daylight conditions; (b) you face the class and can therefore more easily control the group; (c) it can be used in conjunction with other aids; (e) material can be prepared before a lesson or can be developed as the lesson proceeds; (f) material can be stored and used again.

You should site the OHP 'off centre', and then turned so that the projected image is directed diagonally towards the screen which should be placed in the darkest corner at the front of the room.

You may find it necessary to adjust the screen to avoid a 'keystoning' effect where the image at the bottom of the screen is wider than at the top with the result that it is distorted. To prevent this, tilt the top edge of the screen towards the projector.

Operating the OHP

You should follow the following principles when using the OHP: (a) face the students at all times; (b) stand or sit to one side of the projector and not behind it. All writing on the transparencies should be done while standing at the side; (c) place the prepared transparencies on the projector with the light off. Switch off between each transparency; (d) if it is necessary to *point* at the transparency this should be done by pointing at the projector; (e) do not move the projector while it is hot as this may reduce the bulb life.

Preparing Transparencies

(i) Materials

The transparency material is made from acetate sheet and different thicknesses are available. The thicker material is easier to use and handle than the very thin.

Two types of ink pen are available: spirit based and water based. If a permanent transparency is to be produced, then use a spirit based ink pen. If you have to erase the ink from a spirit-based pen, special erasing spirits are available, but Gin or Whiskey is just as good!

Adhesive lettering such as *'Letraset'* can be applied directly to the acetate film.

Care should be taken when using photocopies from books, magazines or other published material. Apart from the laws relating to copyright, the printing can be too small for classroom purposes. If you do resort to this, ensure that you enlarge the print prior to copying onto acetate film.

(ii) Considerations of use

Many teachers prepare their own transparencies. If you do this, careful thought must be given to how you will use the aid and how you will integrate it with other learning activities. For instance: (a) what do you expect the students to do while the transparency is being projected?; (b) are they to make notes or copy in full the displayed material and should an associated handout be prepared?; (c) what questions are to be asked to draw out information from the students?

(iii) Key Design Principles

Often, transparencies have far too much material on them. The overall principle relates to simplicity: So you should: (a) keep the transparency simple. Preferably, a transparency should deal with only one main point; (b) use large lettering (a minimum of 6 mm in height) and, as with boardwork, lower case is easier to read than upper case; (c) do not overuse colour; (d) water based pens can easily be so use spirit based permanent ones when you intend to store the transparency for future use;

3.3 Assisting Student Learning

It is evident that a very important task for you is to make learning as easy and as enjoyable as possible for your students. We have already laid down some principles like: all students learn differently, at their own pace and in their own way; students' experiences should be interspersed with periods of reflection; different strategies are applicable for different domains of objectives; a variety of teaching strategies are most likely to be useful to a class of students to maintain motivation; well designed and correctly used visual aids assist the learning process.

All of these, and more, are means which you can use to assist your students in their learning. You must think about the environment of your classrooms and workshops and make them as amenable to the learning process as possible.

Room Layout

The traditional image of post-16 teaching is fast disappearing and you should assist it to disappear. This old image is one which involves a lecturer, chalk and talk, teacher centred methods that are syllabus bound and examination oriented, dictated notes, pitching the teaching at the average ability level, rows of desks and despotic teacher control.

You should see yourself as a facilitator with much of your work being done out of the classroom in preparation for individualised learning: you should value resource-based learning where student participation and activity is high, curriculum negotiation is common and the teaching of transferable skills takes place at all stages.

In order to accommodate this change, your classroom has to become more of a resource centre and less of a lecture room. You need to have books, magazines and articles readily available for your students. The walls need to be covered with charts, drawings, photocopied articles and the like, about the subject. They also require constant changing so that they keep up with the changes in the curriculum area being followed. The desks need to have a flexible format so that they can easily be moved from the more formal situations, to groups of them being put together for discussions and then apart for individual work.

Study Skills

Why should you try to introduce new approaches? There are a number of possible reasons which were given by Anne Robinson (FEU, 1987) and adapted here:

- The exam results might be better.

- You should not rely on always teaching traditional courses and should be developing some of the skills that the newer FE courses require.

- Even if it does not improve the end product (exam results), development of more interactive teaching may improve the quality of experience of the course and the process of learning.

- You should value some degree of student independence in learning for its own sake which should make students more adaptable and able to learn for themselves.

If students are to be asked to learn for themselves then you should assist them in this process and teach them the study skills that are necessary for this to take place. In its many forms, teaching study skills basically means teaching people to learn effectively from whatever 'delivery mode' is being used either presently, or in a more general sense, as a life skill. The common study skills are described in detail in Chapter 6 but, in general terms those often required by adults are:

- planning a project or an assignment
- reading (SQ3R - Survey, Question, Read, Recall, Review)
- taking notes
- (a) from a lecture
- (b) from a book
- essay writing
- planning study time

You need to consider including the teaching of these skills, particularly in the beginning part of your courses, in order to assist your students in their learning. They are going to have enough difficulty with the subject matter without having the added problem of not knowing how to study effectively.

**Possible Evidence to Show you have
Achieved the Competence
'Manage Learning'**

The type of evidence that you might collect to show that you have achieved the competence involves:

(a) for a lesson plan that you have designed, stating why the teaching strategies that you have chosen are appropriate for that session;

(b) for a session that you have taught, describing how you have organised the environment in a way that assists learning. In this you should include, not only the room and the groupings that you might have used, but the resources that you have chosen together with the reasons for their choice;

(c) giving a description of the techniques that you have used with both individuals and groups of students to assist them with learning. This can include organising the environment as well as the teaching of study skills.

Possible Evidence

Progress Check

*If you want to check your understanding
of your role in Managing Learning,
try the following progress check*

Progress Check 1.3

1. For each of the teaching strategies below, write a short description to indicate what is involved in each.

    (a) Demonstration

    (b) Lecture

    (c) Discussion

    (d) Project

    (e) Question and answer

    (f) Tutorial

2. State at least five advantages of using visual aids.

3. For one of your classes, identify a study skill that is lacking in some of the students and decide how you would introduce it to them and improve their proficiency with it.

4. Assessment of Learning and Evaluation of Teaching

You must make many decisions in your teaching job. Some of these are:

- which students are successful;
- what teaching strategies to use;
- where to start instruction depending on the ability of the students;
- what additional instruction is to be given to less successful students;
- when students have achieved the objectives.

The basis upon which you make these decisions is generally related to information that you collect. This information is often based on tests that you give to your students. A test is:

> a systematic procedure for measuring a sample of a student's behaviour in order to evaluate that behaviour.

Thus a distinction is drawn between assessment and evaluation. Assessment is the provision of information (generally through testing) whereas evaluation involves the making of judgements based on the information that has been collected.

So, assessment is the process of *obtaining information* about how much the student knows and evaluation involves using that information to form *judgements* which, in turn, are to be used in *decision making*.

The three concepts that are outlined are:

Information: facts about students, materials, resources, processes, and so on that you need to collect.

Judgements: interpreting the facts or information to help determine present conditions or predict future performance.

Decisions: deciding upon a course of action from among several alternatives.

The Basic Teaching Model earlier in this chapter in Figure 1.3 indicates that assessment is required at two major stages of the process. You will need to assess the entry behaviour of your students and you will need to make an assessment to see how well they have achieved the objectives after the learning has taken place. Thus, assessment of the student is necessary for the following types of instructional decisions. The list is not exhaustive and you could think of many more decisions that follow assessment tests. It does, however, illustrate the various points.

- identifying where to start instruction
- planning remedial action for students
- identifying student learning difficulties
- finding student readiness for learning new topics

- improving teaching methods or aids
- planning activity-wide groupings of students
- grading students.

4.1 Types of Assessment Test

Achievement testing usually involves the use of certain instruments. These include:

- a written test;
- an oral test, or;
- a practical test.

There are, however, many objectives in education for which tests are not appropriate. For these objectives, non-test methods need to be employed. Some of the techniques used for this purpose are:

- self-report techniques;
- observational techniques;
- profiles.

As all courses require a variety of objectives for their successful completion, it is necessary that you use a variety of test and non-test instruments to decide if all your objectives are being met by your students.

It is not our intention in this chapter to make you expert in the design of the various types of test, only to make you familiar with the different types together with where they might be most appropriately used. In this way you can include them in your lesson plans in order to take the decisions described above. Greater detail will be found in Chapter 7.

A written test is made up of a variety of questions. One way of classifying these is from the point of view of how the students are expected to respond. They can either:

- select the right response from a set of given responses (called selection-type questions) or
- supply the answer to a given question (called supply-type questions).

Selection Type Questions

Items of the selection type include alternative choice, multiple choice and matching block types. The time needed to answer this type of question is only a matter of seconds.

Alternative Choice Type

Items of this type, also known as true-false items, contain statements for which there are only two possible responses. The type of responses can be: true or false; yes or no; agree or disagree.

Multiple-Choice Questions

Multiple-choice questions consist of two parts: a stem and a number of options. The stem consists of the question or statement which must be answered by choosing one of the options. The *options* are plausible answers or concluding statements from which one option must be selected.

Matching Block Questions

The matching block type consists of a series of premises in one column, and the response options are listed in another column. The student is asked to select the response options that match each of the stems.

Example

Here are two columns. Match the decimals in the left-hand list with the appropriate prefix in the right-hand list by completing the table.

Decimal	Prefix
(i) 0.000 001	a. centi
(ii) 0.000 000 001	b. milli
(iii) 0.001	c. pico
(iv) 0.01	d. micro
	e. nano
	f. deca

Table

Decimal			
0.000 001	0.000 000 001	0.001	0.01
Letter of Appropriate Prefix			

Supply Type Questions

Questions of this type include short answer, structured response essay, extended response essay and practical questions. The time needed to answer this type of question is much longer than for the selection type.

Short Answer Questions

There are two types of short answer questions:

   (a)   Where a question is posed and the student supplies the answer by using a word or phrase.

         e.g. In what year did the first person land on the moon?

(b) Where an incomplete sentence is given and students must complete it by inserting the appropriate word or phrase.

e.g. In the year .... the first person landed on the moon.

Structured Essay Questions

This is an essay-type question taking 15-25 minutes to answer, but the response is structured for the student. This type can include calculation questions.

Example

Using the following headings, state briefly how to grow a lettuce crop in the open:

(a) soil preparation

(b) sowing

(c) thinning

(d) harvesting

Essay Type

In this type no restrictions or limits are placed on the student responses. Again, they are usually allocated 15-25 minutes to answer.

Example

Give a brief account of growing an outdoor lettuce crop.

Practical Test

The term practical 'test' refers to a test in which students perform a practical exercise according to instructions prepared in advance and assessed according to a marking scheme.

The practical test involves the completion of psychomotor skills. This type of test might also be called an assignment or project when it involves the completion of written work to accompany the psychomotor skills.

Example

The following example shows how such a test can be operated and consists of specific instructions for the students and a marking scheme which will also be given to them.

Task

Apply undercoat and gloss paint to wall surfaces by brush.

Preparation

You will require a wall area (plaster, plaster board or building board) of between 7 and 8 sq. metres with a height of at least 1.5 metres and a cutting edge of at least 4 metres. The surface should be prepared, made good and ready to receive undercoat.

The test is to be organised over two days to allow sufficient drying time. Colours must be selected with care to ensure that no opacity weaknesses reduce your chance of meeting the standards.

Instructions

1. Protect the surrounding area.
2. De-nib surfaces.
3. Apply one coat of undercoat by brush.
4. Wet or dry flatten to a smooth even surface.
5. Apply one coat of alkali type gloss finish by brush.
6. Check and clean tools and equipment and return to store after each process.
7. Clean surroundings after each process.
8. Check assessment schedule for standards to be achieved.

Assessment

Standard of Finish	Tolerances	Yes	No	Comments
Are bits and nibs visible but not excessive?				
Are brush marks laid off correctly and not pronounced?				
Is work free from grinning				
Does work have full even gloss?				
Free from runs and tears?	1 run 5mm max			
Free from curtains?	1 allowed 50mm max.			
Free from misses?	Invisible from 1m			
Etc.				

4.2 Non-Test Methods

The objectives that are applicable to these methods include:

- Communicating effectively with a range of people and in a variety of situations.
- Showing a capacity for organisation and leadership.
- Working safely with a range of equipment and materials to an agreed standard.
- Identifying own strengths and weaknesses.
- Recognising the need for a personal career plan.

These objectives are all affective domain objectives which deal with attitudes and personal competences.

Self Assessment Techniques

You can argue, especially in the case of adults, that the only true assessment of the type of objective or competence identified above, is self assessment. No one else really can know how well a person is able to 'communicate with a range of people' or 'recognise the need for a personal career plan'. The only true assessment is that made by the individual. Hence, self-assessment is becoming widely recognised as an important assessment technique especially when used with adults.

When you adopt this technique, you will need to identify the objectives or, even better, competences that are to be achieved together with explicit criteria for assessment for each of the competences, so that students have a clear idea upon which to base their self-assessment.

Profiles

A profile is a way of reporting student achievements; it is not an assessment technique in itself. Profiles can be used during the course of study to provide a basis for action by both students and teachers and, at the end of the course, to provide a basis for action by employers and teachers. They also provide a system of reporting progress on areas (that is the affective domain areas) that are difficult to assess when using the traditional techniques of assessment. Thus, profiles attempt to pass on information to students, employers and other teachers about student progress and achievements in all areas of study.

You will see that several types of profile are discussed in Chapter 7. One type, the 'Free Response' type is given as an example in Figure 1.16. Others have much greater structure than this and are more firmly linked to lists of objectives or competences.

The intention is that this will be completed by you as the teacher but that you will discuss it with your students and, more importantly, get the student to sign it. This is of particular importance where goals are to be set for the student in the space for areas where improvements need to be made. It has already been stated that profiling is a process; it takes place in an on-going (formative) framework. There are four basic principles that you should follow when profiling. It:

1.   requires one-to-one teacher-student reviews on a regular basis;

2.   involves negotiation with individual students;

3.   is a strategy which allows students to:

   • reflect on their success and failure;

   • take responsibility for their own learning, development and assessment;

4.   should record positive statements of achievement with respect to:

   • abilities and skills demonstrated;

   • personal qualities exhibited;

   • tasks and activities experienced.

Please comment on the following: **Communication Skills:**
Practical and Numerical Skills:
Attitude to Training:
Planning and Problem Solving:
Manual Dexterity:
Computer Literacy:
Aptitude and Areas for Improvement: (give here areas in which the student shows a particular aptitude and areas in which improvements need to be made)

Signed:	Teacher:	Student:	Date:

Figure 1.16 Sample Free Response-Type Profile Sheet

Observation Techniques

It has come to be realised over the past few years that the traditional techniques of assessment (like examinations involving paper and pencil tests) are very unreliable and are not really achieving the intended result. They only assess the end product and, generally, completely neglect the process that is involved in achieving that product. In consequence, the instruments that have been used for some time in the assessment of practical work have become more widely accepted for other tasks and are based on *direct observation*.

This observation is necessary to increase the validity and reliability of the assessment procedures. The observation may take place over a relatively long period of time or may be related to the assessment of a specific task. It is evident that this technique can assess the process elements of a task as well as the finished product.

There are four common methods of direct observation but the first of these, global impressions, although included here for the sake of completeness, is unreliable and not really suggested for common use. The four methods are:

(i)   *Global impression*: which is essentially a 'look and see' technique. The method is very unreliable but is a useful first step when starting to develop an assessment procedure.

(ii) *Semi-structured*: consists of a number of open questions which have been determined in advance and are relevant to the different aspects of the task. The observer writes answers and/or comments during and after the observation.

(iii) *Rating schedules*: are where the rater gives a score on a scale of the impression of each component of the task on a scale from poor to good.

(iv) *Checklists*: are where the rater marks, usually with a tick or a cross, whether the student did or did not carry out the specific features of a task.

Examples of each of these methods are detailed in Chapter 7.

4.3 When to Use the Different Techniques

Each of the type of assessment techniques can be used in a variety of situations. One of your roles is to decide which type to use in a particular situation. Some suggestions for this are made in Figure 1.17.

Assessment Type	Possible Uses
Multiple Choice	Measurement of a variety of learning outcomes such as vocabulary, facts, explanations and applications. Providing diagnostic assessment of entry behaviour or to assess objectives quickly at the end of a session.
Alternate-Choice	These are not particularly helpful as they are very susceptible to guessing.
Matching Block	Testing of lower level knowledge (matching dates with events and symbols with units). When associations between things are to be identified.
Short Answer/Completion	When the learning outcome is to recall rather than to recognise information. Simple computational problems. When a selection type is too obvious.
Structured and Extended Essay	When the objectives specify writing or recall rather than recognition of information. When the sorting and presentation of an argument is required.
Practical	When the assessment of psychomotor skills is necessary.
Self Assessment	Especially useful for adults where affective and high level cognitive assessment required.
Profile	For recording on-going assessment during a course to give and negotiate specific feedback to students.
Observation	Particularly for psychomotor and affective domain objectives.

Figure 1.17 Situations where Different Assessment Techniques may be Used

4.4 Evaluation of Teaching

The Basic Teaching Model which was first given on page 8 of this chapter, and is reproduced again on the next page, gives you the basis for the evaluation of your teaching performance. Here if the feedback loop from the assessment tells you that the objectives have not been achieved by the students, you must consider: (a) if the objectives were correct, or (b) if the entry behaviour of the students was lacking, or (c) whether the teaching strategies that you adopted were inappropriate.

Feedback to inform evaluation

We have already suggested that you evaluate your own teaching. As part of this process you should also involve your students in your evaluation. Students, especially adults, can provide invaluable information about your performance that cannot be collected from any other source.

Information needs to be collected from students about the aspects of the Basic Teaching Model. Such information can be collected by questionnaire or through interviewing students (or a mixture of both). You need to design your own questionnaire or schedule but it is not the intention to go into questionnaire design in this chapter. However, an example questionnaire is presented in Figure 1.18.

It will be seen that this questionnaire has both open response aspects where students are invited to write their own comments, and closed response ones where students rate their choice on a 5-point scale.

In deciding the design of your questionnaire you should first consider what you want to find out. This can reflect the things that you think that you do well and things that you think could be improved. The answers that students give to the questions can either confirm or otherwise challenge these thoughts.

5. Giving a Presentation

What is your first reaction when you are asked to give a presentation? For most people, even those with lots of experience, there is some anxiety. Some anxiety, or nerves, is good because you tend to be more alert and do not take the situation for granted. However, if you become too nervous, you can use deep breathing and relaxation techniques. Careful preparation reduces anxiety. Collins (1998) says if you fail to prepare then be prepared to fail.

You need to ask a number of questions as you prepare. Why are you doing this presentation? What do you want your audience to learn? Who are your audience and what do they already know? How should the audience learn? Where will the session take place and when? Experienced presenters will double-check the answers to these questions. Be clear about the aims and objectives - be as precise as you can. Keep your presentation clear and simple. Using a mind map can help you to organise the key points in the most logical sequence. Remember, most presentations have an introduction, a development and a summary. Concentrate on your opening because a good introduction helps both you and your audience to relax. You need to show the audience why they need to learn, and establish the ground rules such as when to ask questions, use of handouts, etc. Design a good lesson plan and you may use cue cards rather than using a full script.

In relation to your course, indicate your views on the following issues by circling the appropriate numbers or ticking the appropriate methods:

1. Are the subject aims being fulfilled?

    Fully   5   4   3   2   1   Not at All

2. Do you think that the work done in class assists you with the learning process?

    Helpful   5   4   3   2   1   Unhelpful

3. Do you feel that there are adequate resources?

    Adequate   5   4   3   2   1   Totally Inadequate

4. Are the resources used effectively?

    Effective   5   4   3   2   1   Under-used

5. Which of the teaching methods have you experienced? Tick as appropriate those experienced and those which you would like to experience.

Experienced	Method	Wish to Experience
	Lecture Group Discussion Seminar Role Play Practical Demonstration Use of Handouts One-to-one talks Other (state)	

6. Have you found the content of the subject:

    Simple   5   4   3   2   1   Difficult

7. Do you feel that your progress has been monitored:

    Adequately   5   4   3   2   1   Not at all

8. Do you feel that your progress is:

    Satisfactory 5   4   3   2   1   Unsatisfactory

9. Any other comments:

Figure 1.18 Sample Questionnaire for Students on the Effectiveness of their Course

Take care with the design and preparation of your visual aids and resources because these will have an impact for good or ill. Size of writing and careful use of space will help with the design of overhead transparencies and handouts. Do allow everyone time to read the aids rather than you reading them all aloud by saying "Take a minute or two to read .....".

It is usually better to stand when you present as this helps with voice projection. Establish good eye contact with all areas of the room because this helps you to look confident. Another feature which helps you to appear confident is to move into the body of your audience, if you can, as it reduces the communication barriers. Have some pauses, especially when you are about to say something important. You can use "signposts" to assist with emphasis, such as, "Now we come to the unique feature of this process".

Opportunities for questions are essential to most presentations. With small groups, you may wish to take questions at anytime but with large groups, you usually ask for questions at the end of the presentation. You may avoid silences at this time by "planting" some friends in the audience with suitable questions. Repeating the question allows you some thinking time and ensures everyone hears the question as well as your answer.

Finally, do try to evaluate your presentation by using questionnaires or by talking to members of the audience at the end. There are many useful books which give advice on presentations with Collins (1998), Rawlins (1993) and Parry (1991) being simple and effective.

> *Possible Evidence to Show you have*
> *Achieved the Competence*
> *'Assess Learning and Evaluate Teaching'*

The type of evidence that you might collect to show that you have achieved the competence involves:

(a) For a lesson plan that you have designed, plan a test to assess:

  (i)   the entry behaviour of the students, and

  (ii) the achievement of the objectives.

  State why you have chosen a particular type of test question.

(b) Using the results of the tests in (a,ii) above, evaluate how the students, individually, and as a group, have achieved the objectives of the session.

(c) Design and distribute a questionnaire to students about the effectiveness of either a lesson or a subject. Analyse the results given by students and judge the effectiveness of the teaching. If you were to repeat the session(s), what changes would you make?

Possible Evidence

Progress Check

> *If you want to check your understanding of your role in Assessing Learning and Evaluating Teaching, try the following progress check*

Progress Check 1.4

1. State three different types of assessment technique and, for each type, state the possible uses.

2. Describe the main differences between assessment and evaluation.

3. Under what headings would you evaluate one of your lessons?

Further Reading and References

Further Reading relating to the topics in this chapter can be found in the following:

Armitage, A. et al, (1999)   *Teaching and Training in Post-Compulsory Education*. Open University Press.

Bligh, D. (1971)   *What's the Use of Lectures?,* Penguin. Gives a good comparison (from research) of different teaching and learning methods

Brookfield, SD. and Preskill, S. (1999)   *Discussion as a Way of Teaching*. Open University Press.

Buzan, T. (1989)   *Use Your Head*, BBC, 2nd Edition. A book written from a series of BBC TV programmes which gives suggestions for thinking and studying (e.g. mind maps)

City & Guilds (1979)   *Constructing Practical Tests*, City & Guilds. A short practical guide to the construction of practical tests which is useful for teachers of practical subjects

Collins, J. (1998)   *Perfect Presentations*. Marshall Publishing.

Cox, B. and Ingleby, A. (1997)   *Practical Points for Quality Assessment*. Kogan Page.

Curzon, L. B. (1985)   *Teaching in Further Education*, Holt Education.

De Cecco, J. P. (1968)   *The Psychology of Learning and Instruction*, Prentice Hall. A very useful tome dealing with the theory of instruction of cognitive, affective and psychomotor learning. Not easy first reading but is a useful volume for 'dipping' into

Farrington, I. (1996)   Journal of Further and Higher Education 20. (1) Spring.

FEU (1981)   Experience, Reflection, Learning, FEU.

Fry, H. Ketteridge. S, & Marshall, S. (1999)   *Teaching and Learning in Higher Education*. Kogan Page.

Gronlund, N. L. (1970)   *Stating Behavioural Objectives for Classroom Instruction*, Macmillan. A product of the '60s approach to instruction but very helpful in the design of aims and objectives.

HMI (1987)   *Tertiary Colleges*. DES

Huddleston, P. & Unwin, L. (1997)   *Teaching and Learning in Further Education*. Routledge.

Knowles, M. (1978)   *The Adult Learners. A Neglected Species*. Gulf Publishing.

Kolb, D. A. (1984)

Experiential Learning - Experience as a Source of Learning and Development, Prentice Hall.

Law, D. (1984)

Uses and Abuses of Profiling, Harper. A practical guide to both the design and use of profile documents.

Lovell, R. B. (1980)

Adult Learning, Croom Helm. The mechanisms and processes of adult learning, covering individual characteristics to the social context in which learning takes place are included in this easy to read book.

Maier, P. and Barnet, L. (1998)

Using technology in Teaching and Learning. Kogan Page.

Minton, D. (1991)

Teaching Skills in Further and Adult Education, Macmillan. All aspects of study skills, lesson preparation and communication skills to visual aids, assessment and testing are covered. There is also a section giving an overview of the major theories of learning.

Newble, D. (1987)

A Handbook for Medical Teachers, 2nd Edition, MTP Press.

Nierenderg, G. (1982)

The Complete Negotiator, Souvenir Press, (London). Guidelines to the negotiating process.

Parry, H. (1991)

Successful Business Presentations. Croner.

Perrott, E. (1982)

Effective Teaching: A Practical Guide to Improving Your Teaching, Longman. A very practical book giving guides to lesson planning, questioning and communication in the classroom.

Rawlins, K. (1993)

Presentation and Communication Skills. Macmillan Magazines.

Reece, I. and Walker, S. (1995)

A Practical Guide to the Overhead Projector and Other Visual Aids. Business Education Publishers.

Robinson, A. (1987)

Study Skills, FEU.

Rosenshine, B. and Furst, A. F. (1973)

The use of direct observation to study teaching in Travers. Second Handbook of Research on Teaching. Rand Mc Nally.

Rowntree, D. (1977)

Assessing Students: How Shall We Know Them?, Harper and Row. A practical guide to student assessment.

Ryan, D. (1960)

Characteristics of Teachers. American Council on Education.

Tennant, M. (1988)

Psychology and Adult Learning, Routledge.

Walkin, L. (1990)

Teaching and Learning in Further Education, Stanley Thornes Ltd. A practical book covering all of the topics in this introductory chapter.

Chapter 2
Student Learning

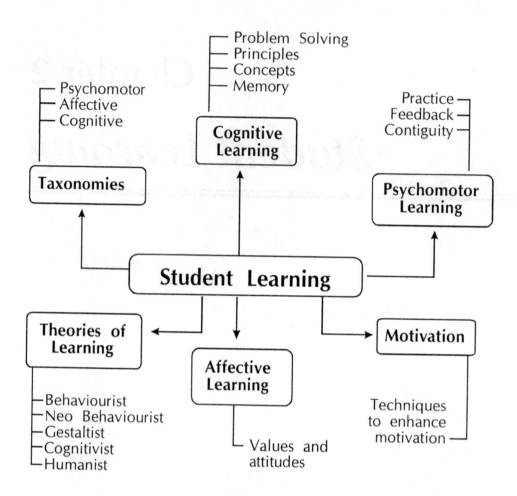

Overview of Chapter 2

Competences Related to this Chapter

The teacher competences and associated performance criteria related to this chapter are:

Overall Competence - *Use positive aspects of theory in the design of lessons*

Competence	Performance Criteria
1. Identify the characteristics of the three taxonomies.	(a) The levels in the taxonomy of at least two of the domains are used.
2. Demonstrate effective design of learning sessions through the identification of variables which effect learning.	(a) Uses psychological factors when teaching concepts, principles and problem solving. (b) The factors which enhance student memory are used effectively. (c) In the teaching of motor skills, uses contiguity, feedback and practice effectively. (d) Plan to have an influence on student attitudes.
3. Use the components of a range of theories of learning.	(b) Evaluate the effectiveness of the models for your own teaching.
4. Identify variables which influence student motivation.	(a) Consider student motivational techniques.

FENTO Standards

FENTO Standards Related to this Chapter

A. a1 a2	**Assessing Learners' Needs** Identify and plan for the needs of potential Learners Make an initial assessment of the learners' needs
B. b1 b2	**Planning and Preparing Teaching and Learning Programmes for Groups and Individuals** Identify the required outcomes of the learning programme Identify appropriate teaching and learning techniques
C. c2	**Developing and Using a Range of Teaching and Learning Techniques** Facilitate learning in groups
D. d2 d5	**Managing the Learning Process** Plan and structure learning activities Select and develop resources to support learning
F. f1	**Assessing the Outcomes of Learning and Learner'sAchievement** Use appropriate assessment methods to measure learning and achievement
G. g1	**Reflecting upon and Evaluating One's Own Performance and Planning Future Practice** Evaluate one's own practice

Based on the FENTO Draft standards by kind permission

1. Introduction

Learning is about change: the change brought about by developing a new skill, understanding a scientific law, changing an attitude. The change is not merely incidental or natural in the way that our appearance changes as we get older. Learning is a relatively permanent change, usually brought about intentionally. When we attend a course, search through a book, or read a discussion paper, we set out to learn!

Other learning can take place without planning, for example by experience. If you wallpaper a room and then paint the ceiling you could learn that you should paint the ceiling first. Some of our learning can be more dangerous; for example we might discover that a knife is very sharp by cutting ourselves. Generally with all learning there is an element within us of wishing to remember and understand why something happens and to do it better next time.

This chapter is about the theoretical underpinning that is provided for us by educational psychology. It is important that we are able to relate what we do in the classroom to some theory. If we do not do this, then the way that we teach is likely to be ad hoc. Unfortunately, for every aspect of research that tells us to do something a particular way, there is another piece that suggests, not necessarily the opposite, but a different way.

Educational theory has, as its base, psychology and the study of behaviour. As teachers, it is argued, we need to know how people behave under certain circumstances so that we can optimise their learning through the provision of conditions that make it as easy a process as possible. For instance, how do we help our students to memorise the material in our subject, how do we help them understand the concepts and principles, does their attitude to both learning and the subject have a bearing on how they learn, and so on?

2. The Three Domains

Writers tend to separate learning into three main groups or domains. These are the psychomotor, cognitive and affective domains. Each will be considered in turn.

Those skills which are concerned with physical dexterity, for example changing a wheel and giving an injection, fall into the *psychomotor* domain. Both of the tasks do need knowledge but, predominantly, they are physical skills which need practice.

Knowledge and knowing the 'how' and the 'why', the thinking skills, fall into the *cognitive* domain. Examples include 'stating the names of the major bones in the body', 'explaining why we have tides'. Both of these require thought processes to be accomplished.

The third domain, and one we often neglect, is the *affective* domain. This is concerned with attitudes. Examples in this domain include 'the need to eat a healthy, balanced diet', 'the need for equality of opportunity for all', and 'politeness'. These deal with feelings and emotions and are different from the examples in the other domains.

Already, in Chapter 1, we have introduced these three domains but here we need to look at them in more detail in order to consider the conditions that are likely to make learning easier.

Learning in these three domains often needs different teaching and learning approaches. They are often considered in isolation but in practice learning may occur simultaneously in all three.

3. Learning Taxonomies

As teachers we tend to concentrate upon teaching our subject matter and the best or most logical order in which to teach the topics. As we see in this chapter, we teach a variety of topics at different levels and the educational literature leads us to believe we need to teach each issue in the most appropriate way. This prompts us to consider the importance of domains and levels, or degrees of difficulty, within each domain. This classification of levels is known as a 'taxonomy'. Each of the three domains needs to be considered in turn.

The levels in the cognitive domain were identified by Bloom (1960) and the levels in the affective domain by Krathwohl et al, (1964). Modified versions of these are shown in Figure 2.1 and Figure 2.2 respectively. When learning is taking place at one of the higher levels, it is important that the student has the requisite lower levels of learning upon which to base the subsequent learning. This, again, shows the importance of entry behaviour.

Levels in the cognitive domain range from the lowest level of knowledge (remembering or recall) to the more complicated thinking processes required for evaluation. As you will see from Figure 2.1, to accomplish objectives at any level, objectives at the lower level need to be achieved first. For example, in order to achieve the application level the student must first possess knowledge and comprehension.

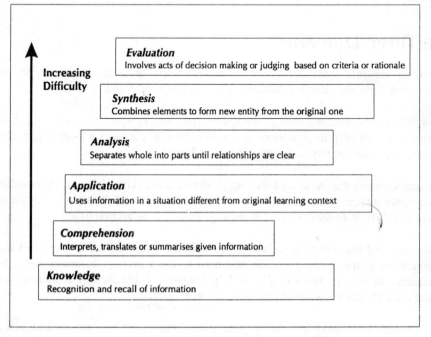

Figure 2.1   Major Categories in the Cognitive Domain

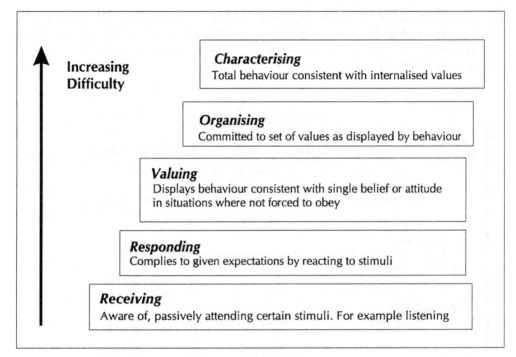

Figure 2.2   Major Categories in the Affective Domain

The affective domain also includes levels, but instead of the development from the simple to the complex found in the cognitive domain, each succeeding level involves more internalising of the feeling or attitude. That is, the behaviour becomes a part of our total way of responding. In the lower levels of the domain the student is simply provided with the necessary information to know what an appropriate response is: the student is only required to *passively* attend to and be aware of the information. The highest level is only achieved when the student has *internalised* the information. At this level the feelings or attitudes have become a way of life. Thus, if this is related to, say, safety in the workshop, at the lower level the student is told about the safety rules and, in order to achieve the objective, listens attentively to them. At the highest level these rules will be automatically applied without thinking about them no matter what the situation or place as they have become internalised, automatic, and a way of life.

Dave (1975) has produced a taxonomy for the psychomotor domain and this is shown in Figure 2.3. This taxonomy is similar to that in the cognitive domain in that it progresses from the simple to the complex, in this case, skill development. A psychomotor skill consists of tasks that are integrated into a co-ordinated whole. It is developed in stages from the imitation of a model to the point at which performance becomes automatic or habitual. As can be seen from Figure 2.3 each successive level within the domain requires more complicated forms of psychomotor skills and/or a combination of several skills into a co-ordinated sequence.

The usefulness of each of these taxonomies lies in their operation in the classroom as they are applied to learning. There are three aspects of importance: (i) identifying and writing entry behaviour; (ii) writing and identifying levels of objectives; and (iii) assessing the learning of the objectives.

Figure 2.3 Major Categories in the Psychomotor Domain

In terms of entry behaviour its assessment relates to a level lower than that required by the objectives. The writing of objectives need to be at an appropriate level within the domain and the choice of methods are more applicable for some levels than they are for others. Also, the classification of objectives into levels allows you to sequence your teaching from the simple to the complex. Finally, the assessment needs to be at the level at which the objectives have been stated. Thus, the construction of test questions needs to be at the appropriate level of the objectives.

Possible Evidence to Show You Have
Achieved the Competence
'Identify the characteristics of the three taxonomies'

The type of evidence that you might collect to show that you have achieved the competence involves:

1. Classification of the aims of your subject into:

    (a) the domain into which each predominantly falls;

    (b) identification of the highest level within that domain that is intended by each.

2. Writing a series of objectives at different levels in each of the domains.

Possible Evidence

Progress Check

> *If you want to check your understanding of the three taxonomies, try the following progress check.*

Progress Check 2.1

1. Define the:

    *   six levels in the cognitive domain;

    *   five levels in the affective domain; and

    *   five levels in the psychomotor domain.

2. State the three main aspects of importance of the use of the taxonomies in the classroom as they are applied to learning.

4. Why use Models?

There is a good deal written about, 'how to teach', and 'how students learn', which often comes from the experience of many people over many years. These books often contain theories and models which the writers feel 'work' and are useful. You need to be careful to consider the context of the model how old were the students, what was their previous experience, what resources were available, how long did it take? You can try some of these models. If they help your teaching, then that is something that you can use in future. However, some models do not work well at the first attempt. You can reflect upon this and try to find out why in order to give the model another chance.

4.1 Pedagogical vs. Andragogical Models

A pedagogical approach may be described as a teacher dominated learning situation. Often the teacher does all or most of the talking, dictates the pace of learning (or rather the pace of teaching!) and the students are rather passive.

An andragogical approach places more emphasis on what the learner is doing. Andragogy is all about how adults learn. Knowles (1970) stated that adults prefer to learn in a different way from that of children. Much of educational theory is based upon assumptions. Knowles identified assumptions such as, adults prefer to be self directing rather than being totally dependent on a teacher and adults have a fund of experience which helps them to learn. Mezirow (1981) considered andragogy to be an organised and sustained effort to assist adults to learn in a way which enhances their capability to function as self directed learners. Aspects which assist the andragogical process include:

(i)   helping students to understand how to use learning resources;

(ii) helping students to assume responsibility for their own learning, (some validating bodies such as BTEC expect this);

(iii) helping the students make decisions about how they learn best;

(iv) helping the students to think about the learning process and reflect upon what they have learned;

(v)   making the learning as active and participative as possible.

At first glance this appears to make the teacher redundant! This is far from true. What it does mean is that the teacher role is different and many feel much more enjoyable.

5. Learning and the Cognitive Domain

The cognitive domain, like the other domains, as we have seen has various levels of learning. The easiest is remembering facts, relationships, laws etc,. More difficult is understanding; why relationships occur, and predicting, requires concept attainment and ability to link concepts to form principles. A further step is the ability to use all these skills in order to solve problems. Perhaps the most logical approach is to consider how memory works and then move up the taxonomic hierarchy to problem solving.

5.1 Memory

As teachers we sometimes present our students with facts and knowledge and leave it to them to select and find a means of remembering these key issues. We should plan the learning to enhance memorability and a study of how we think memory works is helpful.

The model shown in Figure 2.4 is a simplified vision of how we think the memory system functions. Although it is simple it appears to be helpful.

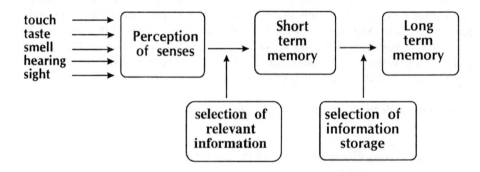

Figure 2.4   Simple Model of Memory

The ability to retain and recall information is called memory. Experience and experiments suggest there are three stages to the memorising process: sensory stage; short-term memory; and long-term memory. Each may be considered in turn.

The first stage is perception. The senses gather a vast amount of information and it appears that much of this is ignored. However some signals are given particular attention and active use of these signals is known as perception. Gathering of the same signals by different people leads to differences in perception because of their different experiences and abilities.

In your teaching you can help the perception process by using a variety of signals, appealing to the senses, perhaps by the use of audio visual aids. You may have to supply information, i.e. set the scene, before the appearance of the stimuli.

The short-term memory appears to retain the immediate interpretation of events. Information goes into the short term memory quickly and is available for rapid recall. The short term memory is a very busy area which perhaps accounts for the fact that its capacity is limited.

The long term memory appears to have a huge capacity. If you can get information into the long term memory - and the purpose of the first two stages is to filter material that is appropriate to long term storage - then it may be stored almost indefinitely.

Our task then is to help students to remember. Here are some common ways to do this:

1. *Verbal Association*	Group or pair things together e.g. bat and ball; knife, fork and spoon.	
	Make unlikely associations e.g. chalk and cheese, oil and water.	
	Make up a story linking things together.	
2. *Visual Association*	Group things together and visualise them in their relative positions.	
	Write a list and visualise that list.	
3. *Repetition*	Write out a number of times, repeat aloud a number of times.	
	Listen to a tape several times.	
	Read over and over again.	
4. *Self test*	Used with repetition.	
5. *Part test*	If there is a great deal to be learned then break the material into manageable lots and remember these smaller parts.	
6. *Rhyme rule*	30 days has September, etc.	
7. *First letter*	Colours of the Rainbow - Red, Orange, Yellow, Green, Blue, Indigo, Violet. *R*ichard *O*f *Y*ork *G*ave *B*attle *I*n *V*ain	
8. *Spelling Association*	Stationery - E for envelopes.	

The following conditions appear to help recall:

•	*Errors*	Try to avoid making errors.
•	*Recency*	You tend to remember things which have happened recently.
•	*Frequency*	The more you make recall active, via testing, the more likely you are to remember.
•	*Intensity*	The better the concentration the better the recall.

- *Importance*   You remember the most important things to you (at the time).

- *Feelings*   Your state of mind affects the quality of learning. If you are upset about a domestic issue then your ability to enhance recall will be reduced.

- *Association*   The more you can associate and relate new material to existing knowledge, the better the recall.

5.2 The Learning of Concepts

When learning a new topic or subject, the key to understanding lies in our ability to grasp the basic concept(s). This makes teaching concepts a key skill. We probably teach many concepts without analysing how we teach them.

Before we can teach concepts we need to understand what a concept is. It is considered to be 'a class of stimuli which have common characteristics'. These can be objects, events or persons. For example a *book* is an object - there are many different varieties of books but we can differentiate between what is a book and what is a newspaper, or magazine. A *party* is an example of the 'event concept' while *teachers* , *bakers* and *doctors* are examples of 'people concepts'. Note that 'War and Peace', 'Ruth's 18th Birthday Party', and 'Mr Chips' are not concepts, they are particular examples of each concept.

Concepts have attributes and an attribute is a distinctive feature of a concept. For example a red triangle has two attributes; colour and shape. The more complex the concept then, generally speaking, the greater the number of attributes. Some attributes are more important than others and these are known as dominant attributes.

Perhaps you are wondering why we have concepts and need to teach them. Concepts reduce the complexity of learning because we can categorise objects according to their concept rather than having to remember each individual set of stimuli. Concepts also reduce the need for constant learning. We can classify new sets of stimuli ourselves rather than having to be told what they are. Concepts help in communicating with each other and hence with the learning.

There are two main types of concept: concrete and abstract. Concrete concepts are often those we can see, for example, a car, a house, a book. Abstract concepts are a little more difficult and are often defined in many ways, for example democracy, poverty. Clearly concepts are important in learning and it is useful to consider how we can help our students attain them. De Cecco and Crawford (1974) provide a step by step approach to their teaching and this is shown in Figure 2.5.

Step 1	Describe the performance expected of the students after they have learned the concept. *This is what we often call the objective, the competence or the learning outcome.*
Step 2	Reduce the number of attributes to be learned in complex concepts and make the important attributes dominant. *This is part of your planning process.*
Step 3	Provide the students with useful verbal mediators. *Here we help the students by giving the names of attributes and features to ensure that they know these before we attempt to teach the concept itself.*
Step 4	Provide positive and negative examples of the concept. *This is seen as a very important step. It helps the students to discriminate among the attributes: those which form part of the concept and those which do not.*
Step 5	Present examples in close succession or simultaneously. *This process helps with contiguity and reduces unwanted learning.*
Step 6	Provide a new positive example and ask the students to identify it. *Here you are checking that students have learned the necessary attributes.*
Step 7	Provide occasions for student responses and the reinforcement of these responses. *This really takes place with steps 4, 5 and 6 and gives feedback (and praise) to the students.*
Step 8	Ask students to define the concept in their own words. *This should be done individually, and in writing, with each student using their own words to define the concept. They should not use the 'textbook' definition but should translate this into their own words.*
Step 9	Assess the learning of the concept. *This final step may not be considered as part of the formal teaching and learning of the concept attainment process but is obviously important and helpful feedback.*

Figure 2.5   De Cecco's Model of Concept Teaching

If we take an application of the De Cecco model of teaching the concept of a **bridge** we can see the way in which the learning might be structured.

Step 1	"The student shall be able to identify bridges given a range of structures", is the objective that we tell the students at the start of the learning.
Step 2	Show a picture of a simple bridge and discuss the main features (attributes) such as span, support, communication.
Step 3	Use names for the attributes e.g. span, support, structure, communication.

Step 4   Present pictures of several structures, some of which are bridges, some of which are similar e.g. pylon, crane or road.

Step 5   Display pictures on wall or in quick succession using a slide projector, OHP, or charts.

Step 6   Show a new example of a bridge and ask students whether it is a bridge or not and ask them to give reasons for their choice.

Step 7   With steps, 4, 5 and 6.

Step 8   Ask students to write their own definition of a bridge.

Step 9   Test, perhaps in the local area.

De Cecco's model can be used in the teaching and learning of both concrete and abstract concepts. A concept has been defined as 'an idea existing in the mind' but it is associated with experience. Every concept, even the most abstract, has something to which it refers (a referent). The concept "one" is learned through experience with one book, one ice cream, one toy. In other words it is learned through experience with things. De Cecco's steps gives us a sequence to help students with the provision of experiences. The provision of positive and negative examples provide experiences for students and this is probably better if it can be provided with real objectives (or pictures of them) to make the experiences as realistic as possible. Even abstract concepts like *viscosity* or *sibling* require referents, or examples, in their learning. If, then, the effectiveness of the learning is based on experience, it is important to provide as many and as varied a set of experiences as possible. With abstract concepts we have to make individual pictures in each of the students' minds. Much of post-16 education and training relates to processes (like the concept of work), qualities (like the concept of viscosity) or relationships (like the concept of sibling or electric current). Consequently, and in order to provide the necessary experiences for our students, we need to provide the necessary simulations. These might be actual experiences or vicarious ones that we ourselves might have had experience with.

The following list of 'rules' might be incorporated for the teaching of concepts:

- can the idea be expressed symbolically, or displayed in the form of a diagram?
- if students make specific points get them to generalise and move away from the specific so as to help others understand what they are getting at;
- be ready to try a variety of teaching procedures because repetition of ideas using the same words often does not work;
- get students to think and talk **actively** about ideas and what they mean;
- encourage students to look for both similarities and differences between the new and existing ideas.

The following example of the application of De Cecco's model to teaching a concept is based on an idea in Towers et al (1987). Imagine we need to ensure our students need to know the new concept of a Reklaw.

Step 1   "The students will be able to identify Reklaws when given a range of shapes".

Step 2   Figure 2.5a shows a range of shapes, some of which are Reklaws and some are not. The patterns and colours are not important to the teaching and learning so, before presenting to the students, we reduce the diagram to the key attributes as shown in Figure 2.5b.

Step 3   We ask the students to study the shapes in Figure 2.5b and ask them to describe what they see.

Steps 4 & 5   The students are told that Figure 2.5b contains four shapes which are Reklaws and three shapes which are not Reklaws. The students are asked to identify the four Reklaws.

Step 6   The students are shown Figure 2.5c and asked to confirm that they agree that this is a Reklaw.

Step 7   This step allows the students to check their understanding by answering questions similar to Figure 2.5d.

Step 8   The students are asked to define a Reklaw in their own words.

Step 9   Further assessment can take place now and at later dates.

Figure 2.5a   A Variety of Shapes

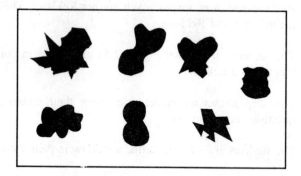

Figure 2.5b   Shapes Simplified to Remove Patterns and Colours

Figure 2.5c   An Example of a Reklaw

Figure 2.5d   Assessing or Identifying a Reklaw

Other writers have similar models. Stones (1983) stresses the importance of planning how to teach concepts. His model is based upon 12 stages which are in three phases as shown in Figure 2.6.

A	**Pre-Active**
1.	Make a task analysis of the teaching objectives to identify the key concepts involved, the subordinate concepts, specific examples, methods of presentation, students' activities and modes of evaluation.
2.	Ascertain students' prior knowledge. If this is not possible plan for diagnosis at the interactive stage.
B	**Interactive**
3.	Give a preliminary idea of the nature of the new learning.
4.	Explain terms to be used in labelling the new concepts and their attributes and call to mind existing concepts relevant to the new learning.
5.	Provide initially a series of simplified exemplars with few attributes to facilitate identification of the criterial attributes.
6.	Increase the salience of the criterial attributes to enable students to discriminate between criterial and non-criterial attributes.
7.	Provide a series of exemplars sequenced to provide a complete range of criterial attributes as economically as possible.
8.	Provide non-exemplars in counter position to exemplars to enhance discrimination between criterial and non-criterial attributes.
9.	Provide new exemplars and non-exemplars and ask the students to identify the exemplars. Provide feedback for each discrimination.
10.	Encourage the students to use their own language in explaining the nature of the concepts.
11.	Provide suitable cueing throughout to ensure that students gradually become independent in their ability to identify novel exemplars of the concepts.
C	**Evaluative**
	(This process is naturally much the same procedure as would be applied in diagnosing prior level of ability.)
12.	Present novel exemplars of the concepts for the students to identify and/or discriminate from non-exemplars.

Figure 2.6   Stones' Model of Concept Teaching

Rowntree (1982) has a similar model but considers that there is no need to apply each step every time you teach a concept. He thinks this is too time consuming and that the model should be reserved for the more difficult concepts. This model is shown in Figure 2.7.

Isolate the concepts	- from the facts, principles, examples, etc of our subject matter.
Define each concept	- dictionary-type definitions to begin with, perhaps.
Examine model examples	- to sharpen the definition by deciding which features of the examples are essential to the concept and which are incidental.
Examine counter examples	- to further establish the essential character of the concept by identifying features that would negate it.
Examine border line examples	- to clarify our understanding of the crucial features of the concepts by considering cases where it 'almost' applies or applies only 'in a way'.
Consider invented examples	- testing the concept by inventing imaginary cases that might really stretch the features we have identified for the concept.
Compare personal contexts	- in recognition that the concept will have different connotations for different individuals (which may or may not hinder communication).
Examine related concepts	- studying one concept leads us into seeing how it fits into the surrounding network of concepts.
Elucidate the principles	- concepts are related to other concepts in principles (rules, theorems, axioms, generalizations, statements) which constitute the message(s) of the subject matter, and the key principles need to be identified and classified (e.g. as empirical,, evaluative,, or semantic statements).

Figure 2.7   Rowntree Model of Concept Teaching

Joyce and Weil (1990) have a three phase model (Figure 2.8) which has ten stages. Although each model has differences, they contain many similarities. It may be useful to think about a concept which you will be teaching in the near future and use one of the models to structure your teaching.

PHASE ONE Presentation of Data and Identification of Concept	PHASE TWO Testing Attainment of the Concept
Teachers present labelled examples. Students compare attributes in positive and negative examples. Students generate and test hypotheses. Students state a definition according to the essential attributes.	Students identify additional unlabelled examples as yes/no. Teacher confirms hypotheses, names concept, and restates definitions according to essential attributes. Students generate examples.

PHASE THREE Analysis of thinking strategies
Students describe thoughts. Students discuss role of hypotheses and attributes. Students discuss type and number of hypotheses.

Figure 2.8   Joyce and Weil Syntax of the Concept Attainment Model

5.3 The Learning of Principles

In the literature, concept and principle teaching are closely related because a principle is a statement of the relationship between two or more concepts. Principles are sometimes called rules, laws, theorems, or generalisations.

Some examples of principles are:

(i)   four plus ten equals fourteen;

(ii)   all men are created equal;

(iii) an object with six sides is three dimensional.

The following are statements but are *not* principles:

(i)   evergreen trees;

(ii)   the Conservative party won the last election;

(iii) John made the strongest structure.

The first set of statements qualify as principles because they state relationships among concepts. The first, for example, states the relationship among five concepts: four; plus; ten; equals; and fourteen. The second relates four concepts: all; men; created; and equal. The second set of statements are not principles: evergreen trees is a concept, in the second statement the Conservative party is the only concept and so no relationship is stated.

It is sometime useful to think of principles as 'if-then' statements. For example, *if* you add four to ten, *then* you obtain fourteen; *if* an object has six sides, *then* it is three dimensional.

The advantage of phrasing a principle as an if-then statement is that the statement then indicates the proper ordering of the component concepts. Only the proper ordering of the concepts results in satisfactory learning of the principle.

De Cecco (op cit) has a model (Figure 2.9) which is similar to the concept attainment model.

1.	Describe the performance expected of the students after they have learned the principle.
2.	Decide and indicate which concepts or principles the students must recall in learning the new principle.
3.	Assist the students to recall component concepts.
4.	Help the students to combine the concepts in the proper order.
5.	Require the students to demonstrate the principle fully.
6.	Require the students to give a full statement of the principle.
7.	Verify the students' learning of the principle.
8.	Provide for practise of the principle and reinforcement of the students' responses.

Figure 2.9   De Cecco's Steps in the Teaching of a Principle

When teaching principles in the near future you may wish to use this model as a framework for your teaching.

5.4 The Learning of Problem Solving

Moving further up the taxonomy of the Cognitive domain brings us to Problem Solving. Problem Solving may be regarded as a high level activity since it usually involves using two or more principles. This separates it from lower order puzzle solving.

A similar model to those used in the teaching of concepts and principles may be used for problem solving. The steps are:

Step 1	State the learning intentions.
Step 2	Ensure students know the relevant concepts and principles and ask the students to recall them.
Step 3	Give indications or guidelines to the solution without providing the solution.
Step 4	Assess the learning outcomes.

Practice with problem solving, in a structured manner, often helps students.

The following, reported in Gage and Berliner (1983) of Mager's work, are considered important principles in the solving of problems:

- habitual ways of doing things do not solve difficult problems;
- problems would not be difficult if they could be solved through habitual ways of solving problems;
- a person should not stay in a rut but should keep an open mind for new meanings;
- if someone fails to solve a problem, they should put it out of their mind and seek a new problem;
- solutions to problems appear suddenly and cannot be forced.

Experiments have been completed which suggest that problem solving can be enhanced through careful structuring of the teaching. The suggested sequence is:

(i)　ensure students understand the problem completely and then get them to state it in general terms;

(ii)　find the major solution strategies;

(iii)　list alternatives within the solution strategies;

(iv)　evaluate the alternatives and choose the best.

Figure 2.10 is an example of the use of this sequence as suggested by Gage and Berliner (op cit).

State the problem in general terms	Find major solution strategies	List alternatives within the solution strategies	Evaluate and choose the best
Increase the attention of students in class.	Vary the methods of presentation of the subject matter.	Shout at them.	Will work if used occasionally; could frighten some students.
		Move about; create novelty and surprise; stop talking, etc.,	Must gather evidence of attitude change.
	Vary materials to be learned.	Switch texts.	Must gain approval of course team. Expensive. More exercises in new text will help.
		Add films/videos. Use programmed learning.	As above.
	Change rewards being offered.	Give consumable rewards for best test performances.	Expensive to provide sweets. May foster competition.
		Release class early; Punish when inattentive.	

Figure 2.10   Application of Problem Solving Model

This is only one of the models of problem solving that is suggested by educational psychologists and it is usually applied to technological problems. However, not all problems are of a technological nature, and different techniques are suggested for (a) science and (b) business studies. These other models are described in Chapter 6 where they are considered as a study skill which, when taught, will assist students in their study habits.

> *Possible Evidence to Show You Have Achieved the Competence 'Demonstrate effective design of Cognitive lessons through the identification of variables which effect learning'*

The type of evidence that you might collect to show that you have achieved the competence involves:

1. From a lesson plan that you have designed, identify the conditions that you have applied to assist the students to memorise the relevant information.

2. For one or more of the following, using a lesson plan, identify the steps that you have used to assist the learning of:

    *   a concept

    *   a principle

    *   a problem solving situation.

Possible Evidence

Progress Check *(vertical text in left margin)*

If you want to check your understanding of your ability to demonstrate effective design of learning sessions through the identification of variables which effect learning in the cognitive domain, try the following progress check

Progress Check 2.2

1.   State at least four of the common ways to assist students to memorise information.

2.   State at least four conditions that are necessary to aid the memory process.

3.   Define a concept.

4.   What sequence of steps might be used in the teaching of a concept?

5.   Define a principle.

6.   What sequence of steps might be used in the teaching of a principle?

7.   What sequence of steps might be used to assist the learning of a technique of problem solving?

6. Learning and the Psychomotor Domain

We have all seen skilled tradesmen performing their trade, skilled demonstrations on the television such as 'throwing' pottery, hanging a door, and so on. We often pause and watch with much admiration. It can be motivating and we want to emulate their performance. We usually fail to achieve their high standards even when it looks so easy. Even when we match their standards, with say home decorating, the skilled person is so much quicker. This brings us to the realisation that there are two types of performance;

- Unskilled performance which tends to lack consistency and smoothness
- Skilled performance which is consistent, smooth, co-ordinated, in fact 'second nature'.

Although we tend to concentrate upon the physical part when we teach psychomotor skills, there usually is, of course, a cognitive element and an affective aspect.

A person skilled in a range of the professional tasks of, say, a nurse, a graphic designer, a carpenter, or hairdresser usually exhibits the following characteristics:

- adaptable/flexible;
- clear sense of purpose;
- quick;
- accurate;
- professional/stylish;
- consistently good results;
- good condition;
- smooth and rhythmic;
- cool and calm.

All of the above need training, thought, effort and practice. Fitts (1967) suggests that there are three phases to achieving a skilled performance. These are

(i) the cognitive phase

(ii) the fixative phase

(iii) the autonomous phase.

It can be argued that, in post-16 education, only the very basic skills are learned to the third of these phases. Many of the skills that we teach are only learned to the second, fixative, phase where they are correctly completed but still require thought and, in consequence, do not have the speed associated with them that are exhibited by the craftsman who can complete them without thought (that is, automatically, with all of the attributes suggested above).

The *cognitive phase* involves considering and talking about the background information. It consists of 'knowing' how to complete the skill, the nature of the steps involved, and how they might be combined.

This would include:

- procedures;
- essential knowledge;
- precautions;
- standards;
- things to look for;
- things to avoid.

This should be quite a short phase and is usually completed through a teacher demonstration. Thus, the main teaching skill in this phase involves assisting the students to memorise the information, and the conditions for this are the same as those described earlier for the cognitive domain.

The *fixative phase* involves acquiring the correct patterns of behaviour and the elimination of errors through initial practice. Thus we need to:

- give the students an opportunity to inquire about the skill;
- practise the skill;
- give feedback on performance.

The *autonomous phase* is the final stage. Speed and accuracy are enhanced as the skill becomes more automatic. Speed, rhythm and concentration should increase at this stage. It may be difficult to notice when the student changes from one phase to another since the process is gradual.

Clearly, a key feature of skill acquisition is practice. Practise can be massed or distributed. Massed practise involves large blocks of time where the students practise without breaks. Distributed practise involves short practise periods, say ten minutes with breaks between each period. It is considered that distributed practise is the most effective of the two because, in massed practise, fatigue soon sets in when initially practising. There needs to be high concentration in the initial stages of practise and students find such a high level difficult to sustain. Thus, short bursts of practise are more effective.

Feedback is an important part of learning a skill. Intrinsic feedback comes from the task itself, i.e. through the senses, and is immediate. Extrinsic feedback comes from outside the task. Feedback of this nature often comes from ourselves, the teachers. Feedback on knowledge and skills is needed until mastery is achieved. Feedback at the mastery stage is still needed so that the learners can feel confident that they have achieved the standard.

A good deal of the literature used in the UK related to educational psychology is indigenous or from the USA. An interesting writer is the Russian, Galperin. (Galperin in Simon (1957)) He experimented with two main approaches.

The first, and traditional approach, was to explain how to perform the task, and allow the student to perform the task under teacher supervision.

The second method was the teacher carrying out the task: the student watches and helps by directing and prompting. The second method was found to produce better results, perhaps because the students concentrate upon the task elements and organisation of their own learning.

De Cecco discusses some useful conditions which enhance the learning of skills. He suggests that contiguity, the almost simultaneous occurrence of the stimulus and the response, is important. We may call this timing or co-ordination. This means that the proper order of sub skills is important.

Feedback, De Cecco suggests, is also of prime importance for the successful learning of a skill during student practice. Students should complete the skill correctly from the start of their practice as unlearning of incorrect movements is difficult. Hence, teacher feedback can assist in stopping these incorrect movements.

Part training is where the students receive instruction on the first subtask, then the second sub task whilst still practicing the first subtask and so on. This may be compared with the whole training method where the students receive instruction and practice on the entire sequence. There is evidence to show that the whole training is more effective.

Gilbert (1973) perhaps confuses the situation by reporting that Mathetics produces superior results. Mathetics is reverse contiguity i.e. first teach the student the final task, then the penultimate task whilst practising the final task and so on.

As you can see the effectiveness of teaching psychomotor skills would benefit from more research. What are the implications for teaching? De Cecco would advocate an approach similar to the following:

Step 1 *Analyse the skill*
At the planning stage, you need to consider body position, movements, sequence of movements, turning, etc.

Step 2 *Assess the entry behaviour*
This is where you determine what the students can do already. It is important to look for bad practice and eliminate it at this stage.

Step 3 *Describe and Demonstrate the skill*

Step 4 *Provide opportunity for the three basic learning conditions viz, contiguity, practice and feedback*

Perhaps your best approach is to select and try a range of methods, consider the outcomes and develop an approach which you find suits you and your learners. What may happen is that one approach suits a particular skill or task, where a second approach is more appropriate to a different skill.

Possible Evidence

> *Possible Evidence to Show You Have*
> *Achieved the Competence 'Demonstrate*
> *effective design of Psychomotor lessons*
> *through the identification of variables*
> *which effect learning*

The type of evidence that you might collect to show that you have achieved the competence involves:

1. From a lesson plan that you have designed, identify the conditions that you have applied to assist the students to complete the skill effectively.

2. For one or more of the following, using a lesson plan, identify the steps that you have used to assist the learning of:

   • memorising the skill; and

   • practising the skill.

> *If you want to check your understanding of*
> *your ability to demonstrate effective design*
> *of learning sessions through the*
> *identification of variables which effect*
> *learning in the psychomotor domain,*
> *try the following progress check*

Progress Check 2.3

1. State the components of a 'second nature' skilled performance.

2. What are the three stages, according to Fitts, of a skilled performance?

3. What is meant by distributed practise and why is it considered preferable when learning a psychomotor skill?

4. Identify the suggested four steps in the teaching of a psychomotor skill.

Progress Check

7. Learning and the Affective Domain

The affective domain is perhaps the most difficult domain in which to teach and there tends to be relatively less literature concerning attitudes. We could set out to change attitudes and in fact we are often required to change attitudes with regard to health and safety, or alternatively we may change attitudes unconsciously. The latter category is where attitudes are caught not taught! For example if we are perpetually late starting our classes then we often find students late in attending; if our boardwork is untidy then students' notes often reflect this. In these cases, the students are using us as a role model and we need to be aware of this. Attitudes are learned and may have roots in the emotions but they may also have a major element of knowledge.

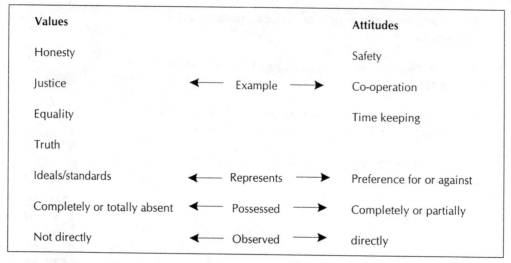

Figure 2.11 Comparison between Values and Attitudes

We all tend to have a value framework i.e. a set of standards or ideals and these are linked to attitudes. Figure 2.11 compares values and attitudes. Attitudes have three components each of which may vary in intensity. These are:

Knowledge   What the student knows

Emotion   What the student likes or dislikes about the subject

Action   What the student does to express feelings of like or dislike

Davies (1981) believes that you cannot change attitudes before the appropriate change of behaviour but it is better to change behaviour before there is an attitudinal change. A great many intelligent people smoke or eat an unhealthy diet, and know they do so but are unable to change. However, if the behaviour is changed first then attitudinal change is more likely to take place. So, how can we plan to change students' attitudes? The following guidelines appear to be helpful:

1. State intended learning outcomes (e.g. objective);

2. Small group discussions;

3. Student centred rather than teacher centred;

4. High levels of participation by each individual. Peers can have a major influence on attitudes (Think of fashion!);

5. Role play and simultaneous discussion.

Attitudinal change often takes a long time. You can force change by using rewards or punishments and gain what appears to be rapid results but it is usually only a short term change. However, if you encourage participation, then this slower process tends to be long term and to all intents and purposes - permanent.

Possible Evidence

> *Possible Evidence to Show You Have*
> *Achieved the Competence 'Demonstrate*
> *effective design of Affective lessons through*
> *the identification of variables which effect*
> *learning'*

The type of evidence that you might collect to show that you have achieved the competence involves:

1. From a lesson plan that you have designed, identify the conditions that you have applied to assist the students to learn an attitude.

2. Comment upon the conditions that have been helpful in changing attitudes.

3. Explain why you think some students are reluctant to change their attitudes.

> *If you want to check your understanding*
> *of your ability to demonstrate effective design*
> *of learning sessions through the*
> *identification of variables which effect*
> *learning in the affective domain, try the*
> *following progress check*

Progress Check 2.4

1. What are the main differences between 'values' and 'attitudes'?

2. What are the three components of an attitude?

3. Why is discussion generally thought to be helpful in the learning of attitudes?

8. Motivation

8.1 Concepts related to Motivation

Motivation is a key factor in successful learning. A less able student who is highly motivated can achieve greater success than the more intelligent student who is not well motivated. Students may come to us highly motivated and all we have to do is maintain this motivation. However most student groups tend to have some highly motivated students, across the range to one or two who appear to have no motivation. Our task, then, is to maximise motivation. To do this we need to consider the concepts related to motivation.

Interest - Students with an interest in a subject tend to pay more attention to it and study it to a level greater than we demand. Their attention and workrate is high with a correspondingly higher quality of learning. Our task is to develop and maximise this interest.

Need - There are several possible needs but the most common student needs are:

- need for achievement e.g. success in reaching a goal;

- need for affiliation e.g. friendly relationship with other persons including you, the teacher;

- need for dominance, and this is attained by obtaining leadership, power or control over others e.g. getting the best results in the class.

Attitude - Emotions, and feelings are important. So if students get pleasure out of calculations then they will enjoy working with activities involving calculation, or if they get satisfaction from working with their hands, they will learn psychomotor skills well.

Aspirations - Students may have a particular aim in mind. If they pass your course then they can enter another course which will then qualify them to practise a chosen profession. Motivation can be classified into intrinsic motivation and extrinsic motivation. Intrinsic motivation may be defined as motivation without apparent reward i.e. studying for its own sake. Many writers say this is the best form of motivation. Extrinsic motivation depends upon external stimuli, which we, as teachers, may have to provide.

8.2 Maslow's Hierarchy of Basic Needs as Applied to the Classroom

Abraham Maslow's (1962) hierarchy of Basic Human Needs is well known and is based on ensuring that lower needs are met before moving upwards in a step-by-step progression from basic physical needs to self-actualisation. Figure 2.12 is an attempt to place the five needs identified by Maslow (physical, safety and shelter, love and belonging, self esteem and self-actualisation) into a 'classroom' setting with examples of what we as teachers might do to promote an individual's achievement of that need.

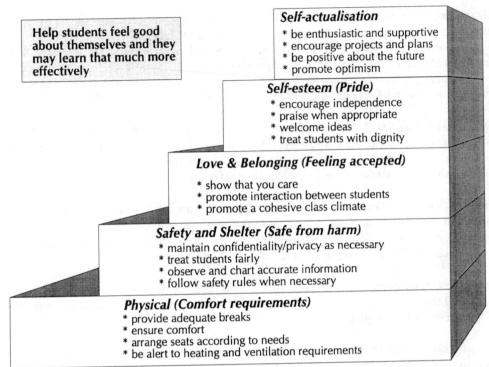

Adapted from "Study Guide for Health, Social Care and Support Workers". Beverly Robertson

Figure 2.12   Maslow's Hierarchy of Basic Needs as Applied to the Classroom

8.3 Teaching Techniques to Provide Extrinsic Motivation

The following guidelines for the provision of extrinsic motivation are the result of the experience of many teachers. Most of the techniques appear to be effective with most groups most of the time. They are relatively easy to use.

Verbal Praise - Feedback to the students such as 'good answer' or 'that's an interesting observation' give the students social approval and such praise appears to be a powerful motivational technique. Some students, mostly extroverts, appear to respond to blame rather than praise. Your comments to your learners are important.

Test results/marks - Results of periodic tests and feedback on assignments are important to your students so that they can see that they are making progress. Poor results should be used to diagnose and remedy learning difficulties, not just left and ignored.

Arousal - Humans, even your students, are naturally curious and like suspense and to explore. We need to use this natural curiosity to enhance motivation. Most subjects have features which perplex and baffle students with their apparent contradictions. 'Why should that happen when I expected this to happen?'. This is a powerful stimulant provided the puzzlement does not last too long and leads to frustration.

Unexpected - As teachers, we tend to have our favourite ways of teaching which allows the students to predict the style of learning. This may allow the learner to relax and feel comfortable but it is motivating to have an unexpected event so that the interest of the students is aroused. For example, if the problem-solving has been theoretical - introduce a very practical problem. Change the arrangement of the furniture in the room. Instead of setting the test yourself ask the students to design the test.

Use material familiar to the students - When students are learning, they often have problems with new material, and research shows that using examples that are familiar to the students eases the learning. This may involve you in learning a little yourself, like the current fashions so that these can be used in your teaching.

Unusual Contexts - Once you feel concepts or principles are learned you can ask your students to apply them in unusual situations. For example, the law of supply and demand applied to say 'classic cars'. Note that students learn better when attaining concepts with familiar examples but applying them in an unfamiliar situation.

Games and Simulations - Games and simulations motivate students to participate in the learning. Take care to ensure that the learning is reinforced and by the end of the topic the students know why they played the game.

Minimize adverse effects - There are a great many issues which reduce motivation and your job is to try to *minimize* these influences. You can add to this list no doubt:

- listening to a dull, boring, uninteresting teacher;
- test which are too hard or too easy;
- no feedback on progress;
- pace too fast/too slow;
- sitting for too long;
- poor lighting/heating/acoustics;
- being told they are unlikely to understand something;
- waiting for help from the teacher;
- being told that the topic is difficult.

> ### Possible Evidence to Show You Have Achieved the Competence 'Identify variables which influence student motivation'

The type of evidence that you might collect to show that you have achieved the competence involves:

Carry out some of the motivational techniques below and evaluate their effectiveness:

- verbal praise;
- good test marks;
- puzzlement;
- an unexpected event;
- unusual contexts;
- games.

Possible Evidence

Progress Check

> *If you want to check your understanding of your ability to identify variables which influence motivation, try the following progress check*

Progress Check 2.5

1. Explain three concepts related to motivation.

2. Identify five teaching techniques which you might use to enhance the motivation of your students.

3. Why is intrinsic preferable to extrinsic motivation?

9. The Main Theories

There is a great deal written about how we learn and there is a great range of theories. The purpose of the final part of this chapter is merely to introduce you to some theories so that you can read in those areas which appear to be most useful to you at the moment.

The five main areas are Behaviourism, Neo-behaviourism, Gestalt (Insight), Cognitive Development, and Humanists.

9.1 The Behaviourists

The origins of behaviourism are in the early 20th century. At that time it was thought that human activity or learning could be predicted and explained by studying the behaviour of animals. The essentials of the work involved animals responding to stimuli, that is stimulus-response (S - R). The learning model became more refined with the study of the effect of conditioning.

Pavlov, one of the early workers in the field, proposed the hypothesis of conditioned learning and used experiments with dogs to provide evidence to support the hypothesis. Basically, he linked a specific sound with the provision of food which, of course, caused salivation. After some time the mere sound caused the dogs to salivate.

Watson, another of the early workers in the field, thought that sensations, feelings and instinct were not a necessary part of the study of learning. The only area of interest is what the 'subject' is doing in response to the stimulus. He rejected the concept of memory. Instead, he said that responses were due to learning and we respond when we meet those stimuli again. Learning, he said, was a question of strengthening stimulus-response bonds. Conditioning, therefore, became important and habit forming was considered to be significant.

Both Pavlov and Watson have been criticised as they were considered to only think in mechanistic terms and extrapolated the results of their work with animals to predict human behaviour. Stimulus-Response, however, is quite a powerful action as we all know when we smell our favourite food cooking. The effect of conditioning is also important. We can all probably remember an unpleasant episode at school which put us off a subject for the rest of our lives.

Another early worker, Thorndike, showed in experiments that pleasurable experiences tended to reinforce stimulus-response bonds and 'discomfort' reduced these bonds. There are clear links to rote learning when Thorndike said that there was a need to maximise the strength of a bond. To do this, he suggested that the number of times and duration of the link should be maximised. Also associated with this work was the fact that an external reward was seen as being effective, whereas punishment was less important.

The behaviourist learning theory suggests that we learn by receiving a stimulus that provokes a response. So long as that response is reinforced in some way that response will be repeated. As a teacher we may direct this process by selecting an appropriate stimulus (say, teaching method) and by reinforcing the 'correct' responses while discouraging the 'wrong' responses. Behaviourists say that learning is brought about by association between the response and reinforcement.

Such a theory stresses the active role of the teacher with the student often seen as passive. Although the student is responsible for the responses, it is the teacher who controls the stimuli, who chooses the 'correct' response and who rewards it appropriately. Feedback from the teacher is largely seen as related to the reward and this part of the process is seen as separate from, and following after, the learning process.

Behaviourists do not see the theory as only applied to low level cognitive learning. They argue that stimulus-response applies at more advanced levels of learning as well. Nor is it confined to psychomotor skill learning: it is the basis of attitudinal learning as well; for example the appreciation of music. Stimulus and reinforcement, behaviourists argue, are elements of all different types of learning.

So, how can we apply behaviourist theory in the classroom? The following guidelines show potential of stimulus-response theory:

1. Use reinforcement to strengthen behaviour that you want to encourage. For example to encourage effective remembering:

    (a) when students are learning factual materials, give feedback frequently and quickly:

    (b) when students are learning to understand and apply factual information, use delayed feedback to encourage trial and error learning so assisting the understanding process;

    (c) use several kinds of reinforcers (e.g. praise, marks, prizes) so that each keeps its effectiveness.

2. Take advantage of the different schedules of reinforcement to encourage the learning process. For example:

    (a) when students first attempt a new kind of learning, supply frequent reinforcement, but, at a later stage, supply rewards less often

    (b) if you want to encourage spurts of activity, use a fixed-interval schedule of reinforcement.

3. Use programmed learning approaches by describing the terminal behaviour, organising what is to be learned, and finally provide feedback. For example:

    (a) in the introduction to your lessons, list and tell the students exactly what you want them to learn by the end of the lesson;

    (b) arrange the materials to be learned into a series of steps;

(c) provide feedback to each of the steps so that correct responses will be reinforced and students will be aware of correct responses.

4. When students lose motivation, use special forms of reinforcement to motivate them to persevere. For example:

    (a) negotiate a contract with a student for the work to be completed to earn a particular reward;

    (b) use short-term, frequent, immediate rewards.

You can see that this is very much 'controlled' education with the teacher controlling what goes on in the classroom. Control is based upon the specification of behavioural, product objectives. (See Chapter 5). We should be aware that there is some considerable criticism of the use of this approach and such criticisms are mainly based upon cases being made both 'for' and 'against' the specification and use of product objectives. MacDonald-Ross (1973) provides a very useful critical review of the use of behavioural objectives. The points for and against are summarised below.

Benefits Claimed	Case Against
1. The only well-worked-out method of rational planning in education.	1. No consistent view as to where objectives come from or how they are best derived.
2. Encourages teachers to think and plan in detailed, specific terms.	2. Defining objectives before the event can be limiting in a number of learning situations.
3. Encourages teachers to make their plans explicit.	3. In some disciplines criteria can only be applied after the event.
4. Provides a rational basis for assessment.	4. Objectives are inherently ambiguous and lead to ambiguity if told to students.
5. Provides guidelines for choice of teaching methods.	5. Trivial (knowledge) objectives are the easiest to operationalise.
6. Objectives communicate curriculum from designers to teachers to students.	6. Lists of behaviours do not adequately represent the structure of knowledge.
7. Objectives can be made the basis for individual programmes.	7. Can lead to teachers not thinking for themselves.

Figure 2.13   Review of Objectives model

9.2 The Neo-behaviourists

Tolman, Skinner and Gagné are, perhaps, the best known neo-behaviourists. They provided a more human perspective in that they considered the human mind to be selective in its actions and not simply responsive to stimuli.

Tolman's work showed that he felt that humans use their beliefs and feelings when responding to stimuli and that there is a need to consider the whole rather than isolated stimulus-response incidents. In other words, humans seek a purpose and people have a 'cognitive map'. This is a set of relationships appropriate to different stimuli. So the student has to fit new learning into a pattern, that is 'what leads to what'. Motivation comes into learning theory according to Tolman. The importance of a logical learning sequence is shown and the students need to *apply* their new learning in order to test its validity.

Skinner placed great importance on 'operant conditioning' where an operant is a series of actions which a learner completes. Through reinforcement of the learning, the learning quality becomes greater. Skinner's approach was highly structured. He stated that teachers need to identify what learning they wish to take place and then select 'reinforcers' which will help to maintain the desired behaviours. Such a reinforcer may only be a nod of the head in agreement. Skinner's work showed that it is important to reward the learner frequently in the early stages of learning, then at random or at a fixed interval subsequently. In the early stages of learning, each successive step in the learning process should be as small as possible so that rewards can be given as reinforcement.

Gagné recognised that the design of the teaching had to match the type of learning that was taking place. He listed eight learner characteristics which would influence the way in which the 'instruction' would take place. His eight types of learning are:

1. *Signal Learning*: learner associates exact response to stimuli.

2. *Stimulus-Response Learning*: learner associates exact responses to stimuli.

3. *Chaining*: learner acquires a number of S-R bondings as, for example, in changing a car wheel.

4. *Verbal Association*: verbal chains are acquired.

5. *Multiple Discriminations*: learner discriminates between apparently similar stimuli and makes the correct response.

6. *Concept Learning*: concepts are classes of stimuli and the learner can recognise these classes.

7. *Rule Learning*: chains of two or more concepts often called 'principles' or 'laws'.

8. *Problem Solving*: the discovering of relationships where rule learning is applied.

Gagné suggests that these eight types of learning are in a hierarchy with the lower types being needed as pre-requisites for the higher ones. He also suggests that it is valuable to have a sequence to instruction and such a sequence can usefully be based on the learning types. This, he suggests, might be:

- inform the students what they are expected to do, that is, tell them the objectives;

- question the students to determine their entry behaviour;

- use cues to form the chains of concepts or rules;

- question students so that they can demonstrate their learning;
- ask students to make a verbal statement of the rule.

This list can be compared with De Cecco's model for concept attainment.

As may be seen, the teacher designs the learning programme to ensure that students have the lower orders of learning before they progress to the higher levels. Planning for feedback is the key feature of the approach advocated by Gagné and is a characteristic of neo-behaviourism.

9.3 The Gestaltists

'Gestalt' comes from the German for pattern or structure. This indicates that the Gestaltists are interested in the overall perspective as opposed to the behaviourists who are concerned with a series of incremental actions. In other words, the whole is greater than the sum of the individual parts: it is the pattern which is important. Understanding, according to Gestaltists, is based upon *insight*. Insight has a particular meaning to those of the Gestalt school. It is when the student suddenly becomes aware of the relevance of the behaviour or learning. We have all experienced a sudden flash of inspiration - and this is a form of insight. The characteristics of insight are that the solution to a problem comes suddenly, the solution can be applied to similar problems in different contexts and the solution can be retained over a period of time.

Gestalt psychology has some basic laws which are of interest. They may well be evident from your own teaching.

1. *Figure-ground relationships:* Perceptions are organised into figures or features which stand out from their background. As you look at this page, the print is, as you think, the key part, but the spaces are just as important.

2. *Contiguity:* Proximity in time and space influences how we group things. The closer they are, the more likely they are to be grouped and linked together.

3. *Similarity:* Items which are similar tend to be grouped or classed together.

4. *Law of Praganz:*Figures will be perceived in their best possible pattern of form.

5. *Closure:* Figures, or items, which are incomplete, may be perceived as complete because we tend to complete the figure or 'fill in the gaps'.

6. *Transposition:* Patterns and figures may be distorted or changed to some degree but they can still be recognised.

As with all the schools of psychology, Gestaltists have their critics. The above laws have never been 'proved' and there appears to be a lack of factual or empirical evidence. Insight is also difficult to observe and measure (although this does not mean that it does not happen). Many subjects, or parts of subjects, do not need insight. For example, learning the times tables does not require a 'flash of inspiration'; rote learning is probably the most efficient way.

However, Gestalt theory has implications for us to use in our classrooms. The following techniques can be used to encourage the use of insight by our students.

1.   Group similar things together so that the 'pattern' can be more easily.

2.   Use diagrams where possible as this shows the whole at one glance.

3.   Allow times for students to apply information to their own situations so that they can make their own patterns and have insight in terms of their own previous experiences.

4.   Let students solve problems in their own way.

9.4 The Cognitivists

Behaviourists place their focus on the task and the Stimulus-Response model. The Cognitivists, on the other hand, place their focus on the students and how they gain and organise their knowledge (that is, cognize). Students do not merely receive information, but actively create a pattern of what it means to them. The implications of this are that, if you have a class of sixteen students, they probably have sixteen slightly different understandings. The students 'fit' their new learning onto their own existing mental structure.

Dewey defined learning as 'learning to think' and the process of learning is not just doing something, such as a task, but *reflecting* and learning from this.

The teacher is the key to Dewey's work because, he says, the teacher must plan for reflective thinking to take place. Education being firmly linked to social growth was one of Dewey's main claims.

Bruner was insistent that students must be taught *how* to analyse problems and *how* to think for themselves in order to become independent learners. The implications of this include the idea that teaching a lot of factual information is unproductive since the learner forgets most of it in a relatively short time and will use very little of it. However, teaching generalities is efficient as generalities can be applied in a number of situations over a period of time.

Bruner considers the learning process as the acquiring of new information, transforming that learning with regard to existing knowledge and then checking it against the new situation. So, knowledge is a process rather than a product. Models are constructed by the learner which explain the existing but can also predict what might be.

Bruner sees the teacher's role as one of facilitating the student's own discovery known as 'inquiry training'.

Ausubel sees the key to effective learning as the students relating their new learning to existing cognitive structures. He advocates the use of 'advance organisers' (that is, bridges between what the students know and what they need to know). Such an organiser is a short description of the new material *before* the lesson so that the students are prepared to accept the new materials.

These theories point to the active engagement of the mind in relation to the subject matter under consideration. They stress the **processes** involved in creating responses (as opposed to the responses themselves that are the aspect of behaviourism) and the organisation of perceptions that go on in the mind. The theory is similar to behaviourism, however, because in order to learn, understanding is necessary: the materials must be marshalled step by step and then mastered. The setting of goals is related to each part of the materials, and feedback is an essential element in the process of learning, **but** not separate from it.

Cognitive psychologists argue that we are not passive receptors of stimuli when we learn: the mind actively processes the information it receives and converts it into new forms and categories. So how do we apply cognitive theories in the classroom? The following suggestions may assist you.

1. Call attention to, and take advantage of, the structure of the subject. Stress relationships in what you present. Use advance organisers where appropriate and urge students to seek patterns of their own.

2. Take advantage of students wanting to find answers to problems that have personal significance to them, so relating the learning to their own personal situations.

3. Arrange the learning so that students discover things for themselves.

4. Structure discussions by posing specific questions.

5. Use discussions and give students themselves the responsibility for leading them.

Through the use of these techniques, which are all related to the importance of the structure of the subject, you are attempting to promote learning through insight of the cognitive structures of the subject: the concepts that are embodied within it. It is argued that students learn the best when they gain insight into, and understanding of, the underlying structure of the knowledge embodied within the subject. They need to be active in seeking new information and need to be active in participating in the teaching methods. They learn best when they discover concepts and principles for themselves.

9.5 The Humanists

Since about 1960, beginning with the publication of A S Neill's 'Summerhill', a new movement aimed at criticising and improving education in fundamental ways has gathered momentum. The movement has been particularly attractive with post-16 education whose students have been unhappy with their own schooling. It seemed to respond to their own resentment with the regimentation, pressure, competition, and so on. The movement has had several names: 'new romanticism', 'open schooling' and 'alternative education', but is now generally termed 'humanistic education'.

Summerhill, in southern England, is an 'open', private school where the education of the whole person is considered more important than subject matter. No pupil is forced to attend classes but go only when they want to. The school 'rules' are made through a school committee on which every pupil and staff member have one vote.

Neill recounts the story of how he tried to get football stopped in the corridor outside his office through the committee. Initially he was outvoted and it was not until he had brought it up on several occasions that he managed to get it accepted.

Neill argues that the apparent freedom allowed pupils to gain an education that the conventional kind of schooling was not capable of providing. Although the academic successes of the school were low, and HMI tried unsuccessfully to close the school on several occasions, Neill argued that if one of the ex-pupils of Summerhill gained an interview, they were more likely to get the job than someone from a conventional educational background.

The Humanist school of psychology, then, was developed as a reaction against behaviourism because its proponents saw behaviourism as reducing the concept of the human being. The person was seen as being worthy of dignity and teachers needed to develop qualities of worth and self esteem. This involved helping every person to make the most of themselves that they could.

Maslow, as described earlier, is best remembered for his work on motivation. His hierarchy of human needs is well known and is a feature of many management books. Essentially, Maslow states that needs must be satisfied before effective learning can take place. If a student is tired, cold and hungry, then the quality of learning will be reduced. The student who feels threatened in the learning situation is unlikely to learn effectively. Our task as teachers is to create an environment where students feel part of a group and feel that their contribution has worth.

Rogers' thinking is similar to Maslow's. He felt the need to place the student at the centre of the learning process through active self discovery rather than having to respond to stimuli. He stated that humans are essentially 'good' and that they have a desire to develop and grow. The job of the teacher, in his view, is to generate the conditions and environment for students to develop their own self concept.

The key to effective, long term learning is based upon experiential learning which has the following features: personal involvement, stimulation of feelings and thinking, self initiation and self evaluation. The behaviourists see the need to structure and control the learning whereas the humanists see it as essential to trust the learners to follow their own learning programme at their own pace and direction. Active learning by doing is seen as the key, but some form of reflection through evaluation is essential. More recently, Kolb has completed work in the humanist vein.

The humanist approach is quite different to what was (and, perhaps, is) the perceived way in which adults learn. Schools have always stated that they want to educate the whole person rather than train them for an occupation. Colleges tended to keep to subject matter and link their courses to specific occupational areas - in fact the recent legislation ensures that employers have considerable influence over colleges via their corporation.

The humanist learning theories are not so coherent as the behaviour or cognitivist theories. Like cognitivism, they stress the active nature of the learner. Indeed, the student's actions largely create the learning situation. They emphasise:

- the urges and drives of the personality;
- movements towards increased autonomy and competence;
- the compulsion towards development and growth of the individual;
- the active search for meaning;
- the goals that individuals set for themselves; and
- the social setting in which students operate.

The theories state that learning and setting goals for oneself are natural processes calling into play the persona; learning abilities that students already have and seek to enhance. Learning is largely by imitation and identification with others. Motivation for learning comes from within.

These views also stress the autonomy whereas other views stress learning in terms of 'control': that the learner is controlled by the stimuli, by the teacher or by the subject. The materials, humanists argue, on which students exercise their learning skills are less important than the goals that they have set themselves. This means that the role of the teacher is to increase the range of experiences so that the students choose how to achieve their own learning changes.

So, how do we, as teachers, apply the humanist perspective? Perhaps we could:

1. be aware of the extent to which we control the learning and, where possible, allow students to make choices and to manage their own learning;

2. establish a warm, positive class atmosphere so that every student believes that they can learn and that you want them to learn;

3. act as a facilitator to learning and encourage, help and assist the learning process;

4. consider participating as an individual in group settings;

5. do our best to help students to develop positive feelings about themselves;

6. use role-play and simulation exercise when they are appropriate;

7. use the taxonomy of educational objectives in the affective domain to identify specific goals of humanistic education;

8. provide learning activities that will lead to the development of the habits and attitudes that we want to foster.

9.6 Teaching and Learning Approaches

Inductive and deductive approaches

The differences and similarities of inductive and deductive approaches are, perhaps, best seen through simple examples.

Suppose we wished our students to gain an understanding of magnetic forces. We could give the students a magnet and a number of items made from a range of different materials. The students are then allowed to explore the use of the magnet and the various items made from the different materials. The students may then list items attracted to magnets and those not attracted. You may have to prompt this stage. The list may be as follows:

ATTRACTED BY MAGNET	NOT ATTRACTED BY MAGNET
Pen	plastic pen
chair leg	paper
watch	cup
paper clip	wood
hair clip	clothes
spoon	
zip	

You can then ask the students to make a statement which summarizes their observations. It may be that they say metals are attracted by the magnet. A more sophisticated test would indicate only some metals are attracted by the magnet. The students can then be given more objects and asked to predict which items would be attracted.

An alternative approach could be to give out magnets, telling the students that magnets attract (some) metals but not objects made from other materials. Question and answer could then be used to ask the students to predict, then test, whether the magnets will attract various materials.

The two methods have some commonality. Essentially the content and equipment are the same. Both methods depend upon the generalization that magnets attract (some) metals.

However there are significant differences. In the first case the students make observations about specific examples and then make and test a general statement. This process of moving from specific examples to generalized statement - or law is called an *inductive* approach and would be advocated by humanists. In the second case the generalization was stated and then tested using specific examples. This process of working from a general statement and using specific examples is known as a *deductive* approach and would be advocated by behaviourists.

Example	Deductive	Inductive
Mixing Colours	• Teacher states "Yellow and Blue mixed make Green". Students mix colours and test.	• Teacher "How can we make green?" • Students experiment.
Interview Skills	• Lists process of do's and don'ts • Practice role play interview • Playback video and discuss in relation to do's and don'ts.	• Students interview each other. • Design guidelines • Apply guidelines in new practice interviews • Playback.
Needs of a Stroke Patient	Teacher states needs of Stroke Patient.	• Students visit Stroke Patients and their relatives. • Students meet in a group and generate the list of needs.

Both approaches have their benefits, and choice of approach may depend upon the topic under consideration. Also some students in your class will prefer an inductive approach whilst the other students may learn better with the deductive one. It could well be that the best approach is to use a mix of the two throughout the course.

A Constructivist's approach to Learning

As teachers we tend to make assumptions about the 'entry behaviour' of our students. We tend to think that the students know nothing about the topic or that they know a good deal. The truth is likely to be somewhere between the two extremes and will differ from student to student. As we saw with concept attainment, it is important that the students do not have misconceptions before they even start to learn the concept.

The constructivists' view is that we identify the students' current ideas which they may well have to modify or abandon before they can construct new meaning.

The key assumptions of this constructivist perspective [as described by Driver and Bell (1985)] include:

1. What the student currently believes, whether it is correct or incorrect, is important.

2. Despite having the same learning experience, each individual will construct on individual meaning which only they hold.

3. Understanding or constructing a meaning is an active and continuous process.

4. Learning may well involve some conceptual changes.

5. When students construct a new meaning, they may not believe it but may give it provisional acceptance or even rejection.

6. Learning is not a passive process, but active, and depends upon the students taking responsibility to learn.

A simplified model of the Constructivist approach is shown in Figure 2.14 below.

Figure 2.14   Model of the Constuctivist Approach

The process starts with an outline of what is going to be learned. This allows the student to prepare the way for new ideas. The teacher should then try to ascertain the entry behaviour of the students (i.e. what they think now) by, say, question and answer. This may reveal quite a high level of learning or some strange ideas which will inhibit the correct learning which it is hoped will take place. Correction of these misconceptions may then be addressed.

The restructuring phase follows and although this restructuring process is the responsibility of the student, the teacher needs to lead and facilitate this approach. The teacher may achieve this by designing appropriate practical activities and/or discussions or explorations. The students can try their ideas in new, different situations. The review stage is when the students reflect upon their ideas and how they have changed since the start of the learning.

9.7 Andragogy

In section 4.1 above we discussed the differences between pedagogical and andragogical models and defined andragogy as 'how adults (as distinct from children) learn'. The following provides an overview of the important facets of adult learning.

Malcolm Knowles (1983) identified six assumptions made about adult learning. These are related to:

(i) the need to know. Adults need to know **why** they need to learn something before starting to learn it;

(ii) self-concept. The self-concept moves from teacher dependence to self-direction in the learning process. Adults have a self-concept of being responsible for their own lives. Once they have arrived at this self-concept a need is developed to be seen by others, and treated by others, as being capable of self-direction;

(iii) experience. Adults have a reservoir of experience upon which to draw for their learning;

(iv) readiness to learn. Adults are motivated to learn those things they need to know and be able to do in order to cope effectively with their real-life situations. For example ten year-olds are not ready to learn about infant nutrition and marital relations, but when they get older they will be more ready to learn;

(v) orientation to learning. Adults are motivated to learn when it will help them to perform tasks or deal with problems that they meet at work or in real-life situations;

(vi) motivation. While adults are responsive to some external motivators (like promotion) the best motivators are internal pressures (like increased job satisfaction and self-esteem).

Andragogy, says Mezirow (1981), as a professional perspective of adult educators, must be defined as an organised and sustained effort to assist adults to learn in a way that enhances their capability to function as self-directed learners. We, as teachers of adults, need to help the learning that will continue after our students have left us. Mezirow provides us with a 'Charter' which gives us suggestions as to how we may achieve this. His suggestions are outlined in Figure 2.15.

Figure 2.15   Charter for Andragogy (Mezirow - 1981)

It will be seen that Mezirow's Charter operationalises the assumption made by Knowles about how adults learn. As such, it provides you with a set of principles upon which to base your lesson planning. For instance, your should always tell students the objectives of the session(s); you should negotiate with students about the objectives that they are to achieve and how they, as individuals might achieve them; you should get them to make their own decisions and encourage their own self-valuation. Therefore, in order to achieve the Charter, you should treat students as individuals who will **not** be dependent upon you as the teacher, but help them to be self-dependent. In short, it is suggested that a move from behaviouristic principles towards the more humanistic is appropriate for adult learning.

9.8 Overview of Models - The Learning Continuum

The three main models of learning, humanism, cognitivism and humanism, provide us with a choice: which is most appropriate for your students and for your subject area? Should we stick to one model, or should we use different models for different occasions? If we should use different models, upon what principles do we make the choice?

Behaviourism is based on stimulus-response theory and is about teacher control. The teacher uses external reinforcement to motivate the students and uses prompting techniques. Variety of approach comes from strategies like role play and simulations but, in the main, the sessions are teacher-centred. The advantages of the approach are that the objectives are clear, it is highly specific and it is measurable. The **humanistic** approach is founded on the theory that learning is individual. The work of the teacher is to extract lessons from the students' own insight and experience and get them to reflect upon things. The theory is based on the Socratic approach where you do not need to tell students anything, just ask them the right questions so that they will find out for themselves. The teaching strategies involve discussion, with the teacher asking questions, action planning. self-assessment and guided reflection. The advantages claimed for this approach include building on individual experiences, treating people as adults and developing critical thinking and creativity. **Cognitivism** is an academic approach based on the principle that learning accrues through exposure to logically presented information. Such logic comes from the subject itself. The teaching strategies associated with the theory include videos, class presentations, readings, case studies and debates. The advantages claimed include treating people as adults (again), faster learning, and the building upon a base of information, concepts and principles to provide a rationale for action.

So how do we choose? Knowles (1983) suggests relating one's teaching approach to a mixture of topic and student analysis. The topic is related to both the type (cognitive, affective or psychomotor) and level of learning that is required. Simpler tasks, he says, are probably best learned by behaviouristic techniques, while higher level learning needs more cognitive input and humanistic insight. The student analysis depends upon the ability of the student's thought processes. Less able learners are often satisfied with behaviouristic approaches while the more able require greater cognitive information and a chance to discuss and share what they already know. It might also be argued that the stage in a course is a factor in deciding which approach to use. To begin with a behaviouristic approach can provide all with the basic levels of information before proceeding to the cognitivist approaches to provide high level information and a rationale for its existence. Finally, a humanistic approach can stimulate initiative, creativity and independent thinking which allows students to individualise the learning and apply it to their own situations.

Figure 2.16 (adapted from Kramlinger and Huberty - 1990) provides a guide to the selection of different learning strategies for each of the theories. The diagram indicates that the behaviourist methods are the most structured and teacher-centred and the humanist the least structured and more student-centred.

It is also possible to link the three models with student learning styles. Honey and Mumford (1986) describe four learning styles as theorist, activist, pragmatist and reflectivist. They also provide a questionnaire so that individuals can find their own preferred style. it is argued by Kramlinger and Huberty (op cit) that:

- the theoretical learner learns best with cognitivist methods such as reading;

- the pragmatist learns best with a mixture of behaviourist and humanist approaches such as tasks and case studies;

- the reflective learner learns best with humanist approaches such as group discussion; while

- the activist responds to a mixture of behaviourist and humanist approaches.

Theory / Type of Learning		Methods		
		Behaviourist	Cognitivist	Humanist
Knowledge	Transmit	Memory Association	Lecture Class presentation Case Study/Reading	Discussion Games
Knowledge	Assess	Question/Answer	Test	Discussion
Psychomotor Skills	Initial	Demonstration	Demonstration	Discuss action
Psychomotor Skills	Practice	Worksheets	Case Study	Project Simulation
Psychomotor Skills	Application	On-the-job	Coaching/Feedback	Action Plan/Contract
Attitudes	Transmit and Assess	Assessment Reinforcement	Vicarious experience Debate	Self assessment Discussion of beliefs

Figure 2.16   Guide to Selection of Learning Strategies

Kramlinger and Huberty (op cit) conclude that humanistic techniques answer the **why** questions; cognitivist approaches answer the **what** questions; and methods that are predominantly behaviourist but with some humanist techniques answer the **how** questions.

Figure 2.17 provides an overview of the three main models together with their prominent aspects. The implication for us is to decide which approach best suits our students and to organise accordingly. That is not to suggest that we use only one approach: at different times and with different subjects, we may use a combination. Indeed, often the curriculum materials lead us to a combination. For example Ed Excel, formerly BTEC use a mixture of process and product approaches where both the subject matter and key (core) skills require product and process learning.

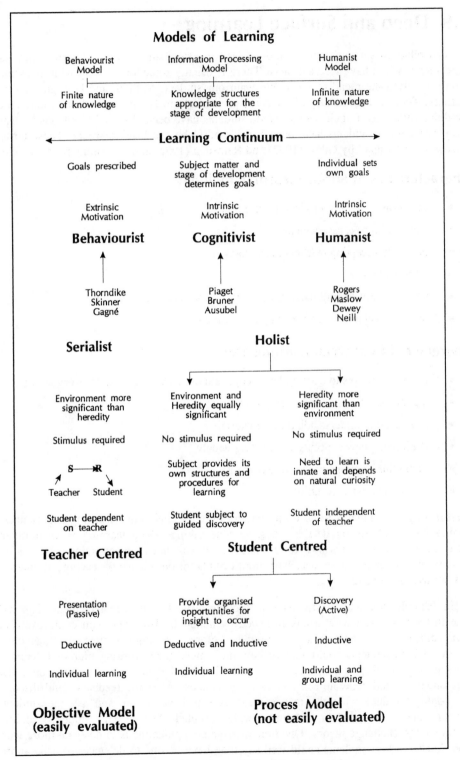

Models of Learning

Behaviourist Model	Information Processing Model	Humanist Model
Finite nature of knowledge	Knowledge structures appropriate for the stage of development	Infinite nature of knowledge

← ——— **Learning Continuum** ——— →

Goals prescribed	Subject matter and stage of development determines goals	Individual sets own goals
Extrinsic Motivation	Intrinsic Motivation	Intrinsic Motivation

Behaviourist	**Cognitivist**	**Humanist**
Thorndike Skinner Gagné	Piaget Bruner Ausubel	Rogers Maslow Dewey Neill

Serialist   **Holist**

Environment more significant than heredity	Environment and Heredity equally significant	Heredity more significant than environment
Stimulus required	No stimulus required	No stimulus required
S ——➤ R Teacher Student	Subject provides its own structures and procedures for learning	Need to learn is innate and depends on natural curiosity
Student dependent on teacher	Student subject to guided discovery	Student independent of teacher

Teacher Centred   **Student Centred**

Presentation (Passive)	Provide organised opportunities for insight to occur	Discovery (Active)
Deductive	Deductive and Inductive	Inductive
Individual learning	Individual learning	Individual and group learning

Objective Model   **Process Model**
(easily evaluated)   **(not easily evaluated)**

Figure 2.17 Overview of Models of Learning

9.9 Deep and Surface Learning

We can relate to students who have done well in examinations simply because they have a good memory and have recalled facts. There is usually something wrong with assessment if it only involves the recall of facts. We want our students to think and be highly motivated learners. There is a good deal of concern, particularly in Higher Education, where students are doing little to earn their degree. Good students have been observed to be "deep" learners whereas mediocre students have been considered to be "surface" learners. These terms are discussed "inter alia" by Gibbs (1992) and Ramsden (1992) and are summarised as follows.

Characteristics of Surface learning include:

- intention to recall/reproduce lecture notes
- sole aim to pass assessments
- passively accepting teachers ideas/notes
- no reflection
- no concept of overall patterns or themes – focus on elements only
- treating assignments and reading as a burden

Characteristics of Deep learning are:

- relating concepts to existing knowledge and understanding, and to everyday life
- organising and structuring new information
- an interest in understanding new materials
- challenging new concepts and reading widely
- examining the logic of the development
- determining what is significant

We can help our students to be deep learners by designing active learning experiences and placing less emphasis on detailed, passive note taking. Deep learning is encouraged by engaging in applying learning to problem-based situations, encouraging discussion and structuring reflection. These ideas have implications for our choice of teaching strategies and how we assess learning.

As an example, you may be involved in teaching aspects of time management. This can be done in the traditional way; a talk followed by handouts. However, you could ask each of your students to record a day's activities before you discuss time management. As individuals, the students could analyse how they spend their working time and decide how they can improve their time management skills. During the class, small groups could discuss their outcomes and generate some rules or guidelines. After the feedback, and discussion, you could introduce what the management experts have to say and ask the students to compare and contrast their outcomes with accepted theory. The students should be encouraged to challenge theory. One time management guideline is to delegate more work to subordinates – your students could well say they have no-one to delegate to! This approach helps the students to relate to everyday life, and to debate and discuss the key points: A much more active approach!

9.10 Models of Teaching

Introduction

A great deal is written about how students learn but not so much is written about how we should teach. Teaching, inevitably, responds to and reflects how students learn. Never-the-less it is useful to spend some time examining how we teach by reflecting upon some teaching models.

Teaching strategies are relatively straightforward but teaching models are less accessible and largely ignored.

Perhaps, we should have an understanding of the term 'model'. De Cecco (1968) suggests that models are similar to theories but have yet to be fully tested and have not achieved the necessary rigour.

Joyce and Weil (1992) were probably the first to write extensively about models of teaching and their work has been the base for interesting work by others such as Eggen and Kauchak (1998) and Joyce et al (1997). Joyce and Weil grouped a number of models into four families as follows:

The Social Interaction group emphasises the way in which people relate to others and their role in society. Great weight is placed upon the development of the person and how they learn academic subjects. Role play and Jurisprudential models are in this family.

The Information Processing Family is concerned with the way in which we handle stimuli, organise, generate concepts and solve problems. Models in this family include: Inductive thinking, concept attainment, advanced organiser, inquiry training and synetics.

The Personal Family sees the individual as the source of ideas. The development of individuals and their emotions are crucial as they consider personality and self-image. The work of Carl Rogers and A S Neill would fall within this family and an example of a model would be non directive teaching.

The Behavioural Family is the fourth and final and is concerned with the careful sequencing of learning activities to shape behaviour. The work of Skinner and Bloom would fall into this family.

David Ausubel (1968) developed a model called the **advanced organiser**. This is a **deductive** approach in which the broader ideas are presented first, i.e. the organiser statement is presented first (the advanced organiser) which acts as a cognitive road map in order to guide the learning. The new ideas or concepts are connected to existing cognitive structures or knowledge and emphasis is placed on making relationships between existing ideas and new ideas.

The Suchman Inquiry Method as its name suggests, attempts to develop thinking skills through inquiry. Both inductive and deductive approaches are used. The process is interesting and usually follows the pattern:

- Teacher states the problem which requires the students to explain a phenomenon.

- Students hypothesis about a solution or exploration.

- Students' gather data in the form of questions to which the teacher can answer either "Yes" or "No".

This last stage makes the students think quite deeply.

The **Jurisprudential** model, developed by Oliver and Shaver (1966) uses controversial topics as a basis for discussion. It is ideal for addressing problems with legal, ethical and social questions. It requires students to consider value, factual, and definitial problems. There are six phases to the Jurisprudential approach: the first three are concerned with analysis and the second three with argument. The phases are as follows:

- Orientation, where the students are introduced to the issue.

- Identifying the issues, where the students determine the facts, and values.

- Position, where the students take (or are given) one side of the case to argue.

- Exploring, where the teacher challenges the views of the students.

- Refining, where the students reconsider their position in the light of the dialogue.

- Testing, where the teacher helps the students to examine their final position.

Gordon's **Synetics** model (1961) attempts to develop creativity. (Synetics is the study of creative processes). Gordon believes that we are all creative but often need help to develop that creativity. He suggests a three stage process as follows:

- Personal analogy – individual students are encouraged to identify with an item in a problematic situation e.g., be a pair of pliers and imagine cutting through wire. How do you feel?

- Direct analogy – individuals practice inventing relationships between two items not usually considered together. For example, consider how alike the pliers and a dish cloth are.

- Compressed conflict – individual students think of opposite words (antonyms) which could be characteristic of the pliers, e.g., joining – cutting

The process encourages students to break free of traditional approaches and can lead them to redesign the pliers with changes to shape, colour, size, materials etc.

Not included in the Joyce and Weil approach is Galperins approach to teaching psychomotor skills (see Stone, 1979). Emphasis is placed on demonstration – but demonstration in a different way. Firstly, when teaching a new skill, the teacher explains the finished performance, the component skills and how they are linked. The teacher repeats the demonstration but this time under the direction of the students. The teacher gives no commentary. The reason for this approach is that the students are freed from the physical tasks so can concentrate on the cognitive aspects i.e., tasks of "doing". Then the roles are reversed into the traditional manner i.e., students manipulating while the teacher directs and supervises.

> ## Possible Evidence to Show You Have Achieved the Competence
> ## 'Use the Components of a Range of Theories of Learning'

The type of evidence that you might collect to show that you have achieved the competence involves:

1. Showing how you use a particular model of learning and state the reasons why you consider it appropriate.

2. Evaluating the effectiveness of a particular model through some determination of how it is better than other models.

Possible Evidence

Progress Check

> *If you want to check your ability to use a range of learning theories try the following progress check*

Progress Check 2.6

1. Define each of the following through giving their main characteristics:

   - behaviourism;

   - gestaltism;

   - cognitivism;

   - humanism;

   - constructivism.

2. Choose a topic that you have taught recently using a deductive approach and state how you would teach it inductively.

3. Classify the following theorists into behaviourists, cognitivists and humanists:

   - Rogers - Maslow

   - Piaget - Skinner

   - Thorndike - Ausubel

   - Bruner Gagné

   - Neill - Dewey

Further Reading and References

Further Reading and References relating to the topics in this chapter can be found in the following:

Argyris, C. and Schon, D.   *Theory in Practice: Increasing Professional Effectiveness.* Jossey-Bass

Ausubel, D. P. (1968)   *Educational Psychology: a cognitive view.* Holt, Rinehast and Winston.

Bloom B. S. (1960)   *Taxonomy of Educational Objectives, Handbook 1: Cognitive Domain,* David McKay.

Boud, D. et al. (Eds) (1985)   *Reflection: Turning Experience into Learning*, Kogan Page.

Boud, D. and Griffin, V. (Eds) (1987)   *Appreciating Adults Learning: From the Learner's Perspective*, Kogan Page.

Brandes, D. and Ginnis, P. (1986)   *A Guide to Student-Centred Learning*, Basil Blackwell.

Brookfield, S. D.   *Developing Critical Thinkers: Challenging Adults to Explore Alternative Ways of Thinking*, Jossey-Bass, 1987

Burbales, N. (1993)   *Dialogue in Teaching: Theory and Practice,* Teachers College Press.

Claxton, G. (1990)   *Teaching to Learn - a Direction for Education.* Cassell: London.

De Cecco, J. P. (1968)   *"The Psychology of Learning and instruction: Education Psychology".* Prentice Hall.

De Cecco, J. P. and Crawford, W. R. (1974)   *The Psychology of Learning and Instruction*, Prentice Hall.

Dave, R. H. (1975)   in Armstrong, R. J. et al. *Developing and Writing Behavioural Objectives*, Educational Innovators Press.

Davies, I. K. (1981)   *Instructional Technique*, McGraw Hill.

Driver, R. and Bell, B (1986).   Students' Thinking and the Learning of Science, *School Science Review*, March pp 443-456.

Entwistle, N. (1990)   *Student Learning and Classroom Environment.* in 'Refocusing Educational Psychology, Eds Jones, N and Fredrickson, D. P. Falmer London.

Eggen, P. D. and Kauckak, D. (1988)   *Strategies for Teachers.* Prentice Hall: New Jersey.

Eggen, P. D. and
Kauckak, D. P. (1998)
Strategies for Teachers 2nd Edition. Prentice Hall.

Fitts, P. M. and
Posner, M. I. (1967)
Human Performance , Brooks Cole.

Gage, N. L. and Berliner,
D. C.(1983)
Educational Psychology, Houghton Mifflin.

Gagné, R. M. (1973)
The Conditions of Learning, Holt Rienhart and Winston (NY).

Galperin, D. (1957)
in Simon, B, *Psychology in the Soviet Union*, Routledge and Kegan Paul.

Gibbs, G. (1984)
Learning by Doing, FEU.

Gibbs, G. (1992)
Improving the Quality of Student Learning, Technical and Educational Services.

Gilbert, T. F. (1973)
Mathetics: The Technology of Education, *Journal of Mathetics*, 1st July.

Gordon, W. J. J. (1961)
Synetics. Harper & Row.

Howard, R. W. (1987)
Concepts and Schemata, Cassell.

Joyce, B. and
Weil, M. (1986)
How to Learn a Teaching Repertoire, in Models of Teaching, Prentice Hall.

Joyce, B. and
Weil, M. (1992)
Models of Teaching 4th Edition. Allyn and Bacon.

Joyce, B. Calhoun, E. and
Hopkins, D. (1997)
Models of Learning – tools for teaching. Open University Press.

Krathwohl, D. R. et al.
(1964)
Taxonomy of Educational Objectives, Handbook 2: Affective Domain, David McKay.

Kramlinger, T. and
Huberty, T. (1990)
Behaviourism Versus Humanism *Training and Development Journal*, Dee.

Knowles, M. (1970)
Andragogy: an emerging technology for Adult Learning, in Tight, M, *Adult Learning and Education*, Croom Helm, 1983

Knowles, M. (1984)
The Adult Learner: A Neglected Species, Gulf Publishing.

Lovell, R. B. (1984)
Adult Learning, Croom & Helm.

MacDonald-Ross, M
(1973).
Behavioural Objectives - A Critical Review. Instructional Science 2.

Meziorow, J. (1981)   A Critical Theory of Adult Learning in Tight (op cit).

Mezirow, J. et al. (1990)   *Fostering Critical Reflection in Adulthood*, Jossey-Bass.

Minton, D. (1991)   *Teaching Skills in Further and Adult Education*, MacMillan.

Oliver, D. and Shaver, J. P. (1966)   *Teaching Public Issues in the High School*. American Educational Publishers.

Ramsden, P. (1992)   *Learning to Teach in Higher Education*. Routledge.

Rowntree, D. (1982)   *Educational Technology in Curriculum Development*, Harper.

Roders, J. (1984)   *Adult Learning*, Penguin Press.

Schon, D. A. (1983)   *The Reflective Practitioner: How Professionals Think in Action*, Basic Books.

Schon, D. A. (1987)   *Educating the Reflective Practitioner: Toward a New Design for Teaching and Learning in the Professions*, Jossey-Bass.

Stones, E. (1982)   *Educational Psychology - A Pedagogical Approach*, Methuen: London.

Stones, E. (1983)   *Psychology of Education: A Pedagogical Approach*, Methuen.

Tight, M. (1983)   *Adult Learning & Education*, Open University Press.

Towers, M. et al (1987)   *Learner Psychology in Training*, Parthenon Publishing.

Chapter 3

Teaching Strategies and Learning Styles

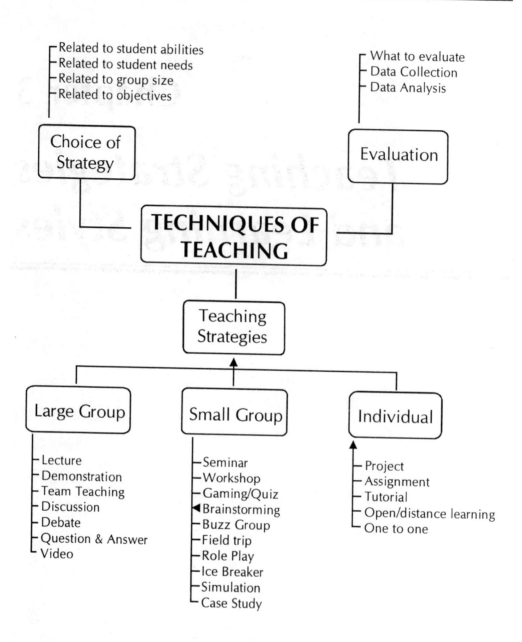

Related to student abilities
Related to student needs
Related to group size
Related to objectives

Choice of Strategy

What to evaluate
Data Collection
Data Analysis

Evaluation

TECHNIQUES OF TEACHING

Teaching Strategies

Large Group

Lecture
Demonstration
Team Teaching
Discussion
Debate
Question & Answer
Video

Small Group

Seminar
Workshop
Gaming/Quiz
Brainstorming
Buzz Group
Field trip
Role Play
Ice Breaker
Simulation
Case Study

Individual

Project
Assignment
Tutorial
Open/distance learning
One to one

Overview of Chapter 3

Competences Related to this Chapter

The teacher competences and associated performance criteria related to this chapter are:

Overall Competence - *Use a range of teaching strategies appropriately.*

Competence	Performance Criteria
1. Deliver a programme of learning sessions.	(a) Deliver teaching sessions to meet specified and/or negotiated group needs. (b) Ensure strategies are relevant to specific objectives and characteristics of students. (c) Encourage a positive attitude to learning.
2. Manage learning activities.	(a) Adapt the learning environment to optimise learning. (b) Encourage a positive attitude to learning. (c) Use a variety of teaching strategies. (d) Manage both your own and your students' time. (e) Manage and lead group learning.

FENTO Standards

FENTO Standards Related to this Chapter

B.	**Planning and Preparing Teaching and Learning Programmes for Groups and Individuals**
b2	Identify appropriate teaching and learning techniques
b3	Enhance access and provision in learning programmes
C.	**Developing and Using a Range of Teaching and Learning Techniques**
c1	Promote and encourage individual learning
c2	Facilitate learning in groups
c3	Facilitate learning through experience
D.	**Managing the Learning Process**
d1	Establish and maintain an effective learning environment
d2	Plan and structure learning activities
d3	Communicate effectively with learners
d4	Review the learning process with learners
d5	Select and develop resources to support learning
d6	Establish and maintain effective working relationships
d7	Contribute to the organisations' quality assurance system
E.	**Providing Learners with Support**
e2	Provide effective learning support
e4	Provide personal support to learners
G.	**Reflecting upon and Evaluating One's Own Performance and Planning Future Practice**
g1	Evaluate one's own practice
g2	Plan for future practice
H.	**Meeting Professional Requirements**
h1	Work within a professional value base

Based on the FENTO Draft standards by kind permission

Teaching Strategies

1. Introduction

During your first few months in teaching, you tend to adopt an approach with which you are comfortable and which enables you to feel in control of things. Often you model your teaching upon those who taught you. This may mean you give out information by talking and working on the chalkboard. Perhaps there are some question and answer sessions and even a test. This is the usual way to gain confidence in teaching a group of students.

Once you feel confident in the teaching role, you are then able to experiment with how students learn and with ways in which to improve the effectiveness of their learning. You should start to consider the range of teaching strategies available, explore them and build up your experience, expertise and confidence over a wide range of approaches.

2. Application of Teaching Strategies

There are many teaching strategies described in the literature and we will examine the most common or popular in this chapter. You will find considerable overlap between them and so we have grouped the strategies into those which are suitable for large groups, small groups and for individuals. Of course, you can use most of these strategies in all three situations. As usual in education, there are few answers which are totally right or totally wrong. Some strategies appear to be more effective with certain students in certain situations. Figure 3.1 shows the possible applications of various teaching strategies and relates each of them to the three domains, indicating the objectives that may be achieved by each strategy. A lecture will be likely only to achieve low level cognitive objectives, a demonstration will be likely to achieve low level cognitive objectives and low level psychomotor objectives, and so on. Such a general relationship can only be a guide and in this chapter we will describe a range of strategies. Students appreciate variation and would tire of the same few strategies. Your task is to become adept at using as many strategies as you can and to choose the most appropriate ones for each group you teach.

2.1 Choice of Teaching Strategy

Your choice of teaching strategy is often related to your own individual style. However, there are some overall 'rules' that you might like to consider. These relate to two aspects. The first is the type of objective that you want your students to achieve. The second is the number of students you have to teach. Although we describe each separately, you should consider them together in making your final choice of which teaching strategy to use.

Teaching Strategy	Domain					
	Cognitive		Affective		Psychomotor	
	Low	High	Low	High	Low	High
Lecture	√√√					
Demonstration	√√				√√	
Team Teaching		√√			√	
Discussion		√√		√√		
Debate		√√		√√		
Question & Answer		√√√				
Video		√√	√√		√√	
Seminar		√√	√√			
Laboratory/Workshop		√√	√		√√√	
Gaming/Quiz		√√	√√			
Brainstorming		√√				
Buzz Group		√√				
Field Trip		√		√	√	
Role Play		√		√√		
Ice Breaker			√√			
Simulation		√		√	√√	
Case Study		√√				
Project/Assignment		√√	√√		√√	
Tutorial		√√	√√			
Open/Distance Learning		√√				
One to One		√√		√√		√

Figure 3.1 Application of Teaching Strategies in the Three Domains

2.2 Choice of Teaching Strategy related to Objectives to be Achieved

The basic teaching model that we described in Chapter 1 showed us that objectives are at the heart of teaching and that all other aspects flow from them. Thus, when you come to choose your teaching strategy it is logical that you make the domain and level of objective you are seeking to achieve the basis for the choice. In Chapter 1, we also linked objectives to teaching strategies. For example, we suggest that the most appropriate way to learn a motor skill is through demonstration and individual practice; to gain knowledge and understanding, a lecture and question and answer are appropriate; and to develop students' attitudes towards issues then you might use discussion to best achieve the objective. In Figure 3.1 we take this a stage further. The figure splits the domains into the different levels that we examined in Chapter 2 and then suggests that different strategies are more appropriate for the lower level objectives in a domain than for the higher levels. Thus a lecture might achieve low level objectives (such as knowledge and comprehension), while to achieve the higher levels (for instance, synthesis and evaluation) then you might find a debate or seminar more appropriate.

2.3 Choice of Teaching Strategies based on Group Size

Let us look at another means of categorising teaching strategies; a simple category, group size. At one extreme a 'group' may consist of only one student. In such circumstances you could use methods such as projects or assignments, tutoring and individually prescribed instruction such as open learning.

Next we have small groups of between 5 and 20 students. With such a group you may find that a discussion method is suitable. The conventional classroom size for post-16 education and training is a group of between 10 and 20 students. With such groups the approach often adopted is what is traditionally called 'classroom teaching' which consists of a mixture of methods. Because this form of teaching is most frequently used you might consider it a strategy in its own right. The nature of such classroom teaching will vary considerably from one teacher to another. It will often have a short lecture, followed by question and answer, some small group discussion and some individual work.

The final group size is a group greater than 20 students. Such large groups can lead to difficulties in dealing with individuals and so you may have to resort to strategies such as lecture and demonstration.

We have already said that little definite advice has emerged from research about teaching strategies. However, Gage and Berliner (1983) describe research completed by Olsen. 18,500 classrooms were observed by trained observers. They looked for 'indicators of quality' in student behaviour that fostered (a) individualisation, (b) interpersonal regard, (c) group activity and (d) creativity in classes of different sizes. A higher test score indicated a greater occurrence of the types of desirable activity.

Olsen found, as shown in Figure 3.2, that higher 'quality' scores were associated with the styles of classroom activity that entailed smaller groups (laboratory work and discussion), and, as shown in Figure 3.3, that mean 'quality' scores decreased regularly as class size increased. However, he concluded that class size should not be considered in isolation when choosing teaching strategy.

Figure 3.2 'Quality' - Teaching Strategy   Figure 3.3 'Quality' - Class Size

2.4 Choice of Teaching Strategy related to Needs and Characteristics of Students

We can think of choice of teaching strategy in terms of classroom management. How you choose your teaching strategy has a direct influence on how you manage your classroom. It has been said repeatedly in this book that students learn in different ways: an approach that is appropriate to one student may well be inappropriate for another. Some people learn better in a group through the interaction with both the teacher and other students. Others find interaction difficult and use the group sessions for gathering of information and only learn when they are on their own. Some learn by reading and listening, others learn through the application of the knowledge gained.

When we accept this premise we realise the importance of providing a variety of learning activities for our students. We might start off by *telling* them, next provide a group activity and finally provide an individual application activity. In this way, the coverage of the content is through a number of different strategies in the hope that one of them will appeal to all of the students and ensure that students learn in a manner appropriate to themselves.

The level of participation of the students in the learning process is an important factor. Figure 3.4 gives a general guide to participation levels, which will vary depending upon the way in which the strategies are implemented.

Strategy	Level of Participation
Lecture	Low
Demonstration	Low/High
Team Teaching	Low
Discussion	High
Debate	High
Question & Answer	Medium
Video	Medium
Seminar	Medium
Laboratory/Workshop	Medium
Gaming/Quiz	Medium
Brainstorming	High
Buzz Group	High
Field Trip	Medium
Role Play	High
Ice Breaker	High
Simulation	High
Case Study	Medium
Project	High
Assignment	High
Tutorial	High
Open/Distance Learning	High
One to One	High

Figure 3.4 Teaching Strategy and Level of Participation

We found at an early stage in our teaching careers that students learn in different ways. The differences may be slight, but also may be significant. You may have experienced a lesson and thought, "That was really good. I learned a lot from that". However, some of your friends may have said, "That was useless. What a waste of time". This may indicate your **learning styles** are different. Honey and Mumford (1986) published the Manual of Learning Styles which identified four main learning styles. Briefly, they said:

Activists enjoy the present, like the immediate experience and respond to short term issues.

Reflectors prefer to think about things and explore all aspects before coming to a conclusion.

Theorists like principles, theories, models and systems. Logic rules!

Pragmatists look for new ideas and are keen to experiment.

You can use Honey and Mumford's book, which contains a student questionnaire, to ascertain the preferred learning styles of your own students.

This leads us to think about what teaching strategies our students prefer. Many students often say they prefer "lectures" because they are passive and few demands are made of them. However, our own research which is on-going, gives a different view. The "top ten" teaching strategies are shown in Figure 3.5

1.	Group work
2.	Games
3.	Simulation
4.	Self directed (including open learning)
5.	Assignments
6.	Discussions
7.	Buzz groups
8.	Lectures
9.	Case study
10.	Field trips

Figure 3.5   Teaching Strategies: Student Preferences

One method that you might use when considering your choice of teaching strategy to meet students' needs is to negotiate with them. You might ask, from a range of options, the type of strategy they prefer and use this along with other aspects before you make your final choice.

2.5   Choice of Strategies related to Ability of Students

Your classroom management needs to be related to the ability of your student group and your choice of teaching strategy. It is no good lecturing to students and expecting them to take their own notes if they are either not able to do this or not used to it.

The ability of students relates to their temperament and special aptitudes. When choosing a teaching strategy you need to consider the attention span of the students and the ability they have to cope with the adopted approach. More mature students will be able to cope with the use of a similar method for a more protracted period while the less mature will need to benefit from more changes in approach. It may be that the less mature, or less able, will have an attention span of not more than ten minutes. If this is the case, changes in approach will have to be considered for each time span.

2.6   Choice of Teaching Strategies related to Motivation of Students

There is no doubt that the choice of teaching strategy can have an effect upon the motivation and interest of the student. The manner in which the teacher approaches the teaching strategy will have an effect upon motivation: an enthusiastic approach is more likely to motivate than a dull approach. In consequence, to encourage a positive attitude to learning, you should not yourself appear to be disinterested either in the content or the approach.

Some students enjoy working with others. If this is the case, group teaching approaches might give you better results than individual approaches. This could be particularly important in the achieving of affective domain objectives where the use of discussion groups, role play or seminars might be effective.

Figure 3.6 gives an overview of some of the aspects that you might consider in making your choice of teaching strategy. Added to this, of course, is your own personal preference and your ability to cope with specific methods.

Aspect Related to Choice	Points to Note
Objective to be achieved	Both the domain and the level in the domain need to be considered.
The size of the group	Different methods are more appropriate to different sizes of class.
The needs and characteristics of students	Student needs and the characteristics of students need to be considered. This might involve negotiation.
The ability of the student	Ability and 'intelligence' need to be considered.
The motivation of the student.	Appropriate strategies can motivate an individual to learn.

Figure 3.6   Aspects to be Considered when Choosing Strategies

Possible Evidence

---

*Possible evidence to show that you have
achieved the competence
'Deliver a Programme of Learning Sessions'*

---

1. For a series of lessons (say, three contiguous) state the teaching strategies that you have used or are to use. Justify your choice in terms of:

    *   intended learning outcomes;

    *   group size;

    *   the needs of the students;

    *   the ability of the students;

    *   the motivation of the students.

> *If you want to check your understanding of delivering a programme of learning sessions, try the following progress check*

Progress Check 3.1

1. List the teaching strategies you currently use and, for each of them, state:

    (a) whether they are teacher or student-centred;

    (b) the dominant domain with which you use them;

    (c) whether they are used with large, small or individual groups.

    Are your statements in line with the suggestions in the readings above?

2. Identify any domain(s) which is (are) not addressed. Are the strategies appropriate to the intended learning outcomes and objectives?

3. State two teaching strategies which are appropriate for each of the following;

    - cognitive domain objectives;

    - affective domain objectives;

    - psychomotor domain objectives;

    - large groups of students;

    - small groups of students;

    - individual work.

3. Teaching Strategies

In order to make the choice of teaching strategy it is important that you are familiar with each and know where they might best be used. The following pages give you a description of each of the strategies, where they might be used, guidelines relating to preparation and presentation and, finally, the merits of each. For ease of reference the methods are divided into the three group sizes to which they are most applicable: large groups, small groups and individual. The sub-division is shown in Figure 3.7.

Group Size	Appropriate Strategy
3.1 **Large Group** **(N = > 20)**	3.1.1 Lecture 3.1.2 Demonstration 3.1.3 Team Teaching 3.1.4 Discussion 3.1.5 Debate 3.1.6 Question and Answer 3.1.7 Video
3.2 **Small Group** **(N = 5 – 20)**	3.2.1 Seminar 3.2.2 Laboratory/Workshop 3.2.3 Gaming/Quiz 3.2.4 Brainstorming 3.2.5 Buzz Groups 3.2.6 Field Trip 3.2.7 Role Play 3.2.8 Ice Breaker 3.2.9 Simulation 3.2.10 Case Study
3.3 **Individual** **(N = < < 5)**	3.3.1 Project/Assignment 3.3.2 Tutorial 3.3.3 Open/Distance Learning

Figure 3.7   Teaching Strategies Related to Group Size

3.1 Strategies Appropriate to Large Groups

The strategies that are appropriate to large groups are lecture, demonstration, discussion/debate, question and answer and video.

In 1992 PCFC published an interesting resource pack called "Teaching more Students". Some of the problems it identified were students just being overwhelmed by the size of the campus, the number of people, everywhere being full, not knowing anyone and the problems of getting to know people. Lack of opportunity to discuss issues and to gain feedback were also highlighted.

Brown (1987) found that students wanted "good notes". Symptoms of barriers to this included lecturers saying too much, too quickly, no summaries, lack of stress of major points, no mention of reservations, no time to copy diagrams, poor organisation and so on.

There are two main avenues of approach to the problems of large groups. We can:

- Develop lecturing skills
- Make the students more active

We advise that it is beneficial to explore both of these avenues.

Lectures need to be planned carefully and delivered to a high standard. Let your students have an overview of the whole series of lectures at the outset, and keep reminding them where they are. Students like to see a structured approach as it helps them to organise themselves. You also need to share, with the students, the structure of each lecture.

You need to be heard. There is a limit to your voice projection, you may need a radio microphone. (Speak more slowly to give emphasis, use pauses and give cues.)

Your visual aids need to be seen by everyone. Larger writing, less content and better use of colour is helpful.

Always start on **time**, never over-run and, if possible, have short breaks in the lecture. **Moving** about indicates you are confident, relaxed and in control. Don't forget to smile.

Look at the students and try to detect when they are interested, bored or tired.

Students like examples. They bring the topic to life. However, it is beneficial to give negative examples because this helps with concept attainment and understanding.

Verbal signposts can help the students to make notes as they listen.

"Today I will .....", "First we shall look at ....." help the students to prepare for new materials.

"Now let's turn our attention to .....", "So that's how ....." help the students to see the material in "sub sets".

"Now this is crucial .....", "The key aspect is ....." help the students to identify main points.

"Similarly, ..." helps the students to make links to other aspects.

Students often try to make verbatim notes. This is boring, dreary and passive work. Why not help the students by showing or telling them the main points. Habeshaw et al (1992) give some helpful hints and tips such as pausing for a few minutes to allow students to exchange notes with someone else to see if they can improve their own notes. It also gives you a few minutes to re-group and re-organise!

All lecturers have views about handouts. Our view is that handouts should be given at the start of the lecture or event the week before. Trying to give them out during the lecture is too disruptive. They should be bound or stapled otherwise there could be total confusion. You want your students to **use** the handouts so give skeletal, framework, structured or gapped handouts. In other words, the handouts are incomplete and the students need to listen, **actively**, for the crucial points. This means that the handouts are useless unless they attend, and attend to, the lecture. Diagrams, key proofs or formulae can be given, saving valuable time. Students could then, say, complete a graph diagram, label a given diagram, list assumptions. Obviously, you need to indicate these activities at the appropriate times. You should ensure that all handouts are produced to a good standard, perhaps with coloured paper and your own "house style".

Jenkins (1992), Habeshaw et al (1992), Brown and Atkins (1988) all suggest that the one hour lecture is too long without a break of some kind. You can introduce a number of mini-breaks of two/three minutes in your lectures but remember that you might have to "train" your students who are unused to this technique. Establish ground rules such as switching the OHP on and off when you are ready to restart.

You might also say some of the following:

- Review your notes for two minutes.
- Swap notes with someone near you and compare.
- Write down a question you want to ask in the next seminar.
- Try to solve this problem.
- Try to answer these five multiple choice questions.
- Write down some aspect you want to know more about.
- Discuss for two minutes.....
- Complete the following sentence.
- Who agrees with x?

You could ask the students to work in pairs, to snowball, pyramid, rainbow or syndicate. Walk around as the students talk and gain some feedback on the quality of the discussions. The groups could then make a contribution.

You could undertake formal evaluation using questionnaires. Indeed, this may be a departmental procedure. However, you can get more useful feedback, on a more frequent basis, by issuing "postcards" and asking students to make constructive suggestions or to state any unresolved questions. This will reduce the feeling of (academic) impotency and help you to become a more effective lecture.

3.1.1 Lecture

What it is   - a lecture involves the teacher talking to the students about the subject. There is little, if any, chance of any two-way communication. An interesting description of a lecture is: "You tell them what you are going to tell them, you tell them, and you tell them what you have told them." In other words, the lecture has an introduction to the content, the detail is then presented, and finally there is a summary of the lecture. The word lecture comes from the Latin word "LETCARE" meaning to read aloud.

When is it used	- either in the classroom or workshop to pass information to the class in a cost-effective manner (i.e. to a group of students in a short time by one person). Thus, it is used to pass knowledge only: if understanding is required a subsequent different strategy will be used.
Example:	- explaining a concept to a group of learners.

Guidelines:

(a) Preparation:	- extract key points from the topic;
	- prepare visual aids (OHP transparencies, handouts, chalkboard) to supplement the verbal material;
	- consider how to introduce and conclude.
(b) Presentation:	- avoid monotone voice and be loud enough for the room;
	- emphasise (by repetition, visual aids etc.) key points;
	- assist learners in their note taking;
	- avoid words that learners will not understand and be sure to define technical words;
	- include an introduction and a summary.
Advantages:	- a teacher can reach a large number of students;
	- conveys a large amount of material in short time;
	- teacher has complete control (unless listeners rebel!).
Disadvantages:	- little opportunity to question teacher (often one way communication);
	- little or even no feed back regarding the effectiveness of the learning;
	- need for a large, comfortable perhaps purpose built room;
	- need to be a communication expert
	- large group could be off putting to teacher;
	- students are often passive;
	- little use of teaching skills
Summary:	- lecturing skills are an essential part of your teaching repertoire. The lecture is often completed without the preparation needed to ensure success. It must have a beginning, middle and end. (Introduction, development and conclusion) and must be supported by other strategies in order to both consolidate and assess the learning which has taken place

The period of concentration of students is not very long. Some authors tell us that ten minutes is the maximum amount of time that an individual can concentrate. To assist this, the development of a lecture should be carefully structured. For instance, if your topic is 'fishing' you might structure it as shown in Figure 3.8. Such an organisational breakdown into sub-topics allows breaks to be made so that the topic is divided into manageable 'chunks' of information which will cope with different concentration spans. The sub-topics need to be sequenced in such a way that students can follow the flow of information.

Making a case for active learning is especially relevant for lecturing. The case for having an incomplete handout, encouraging students to make their own notes, or asking questions even when the group is large, is easily made.

Figure 3.8   Topic Organisation for a Lecture

Other techniques that can be associated with the lecture so that you maintain attention include (a) showing enthusiasm for the topic; (b) ensuring vocal inflection, gesturing and maintaining eye contact; and (c) adding a touch of humour (but not too much).

3.1.2 Demonstration'

What it is — the technique is usually associated with demonstrating a practical skill. It often introduces the skill; its point and importance. The skill is demonstrated after which the students practice the skill.

When is it used — in the practical situation to introduce a new skill to a group of students to rectify faults with individuals.

Example: — giving an injection; changing a car wheel; wallpapering.

Guidelines:

   (a) Preparation: — identify key points;

               — relate theoretical underpinning to key points;

               — rehearse to ensure all equipment is working and that you can use it;

               — ensure all students can see even small equipment and processes;

- time your demonstration. If it is more than, say 10 minutes, consider sub-dividing into a series of demonstrations;

- consider how to make the students active (e.g. helping, completing a handout, answering questions, predicting the next step, noting results);

- consider how to emphasise safe working practices.

(b) Presentation:
- clear introduction;

- name of tools/equipment;

- check entry behaviour;

- do not show how not to complete the skill;

- stress key points and show links between them;

- monitor safety aspects;

- check learner understanding.

Advantages:
- when performed well, the demonstration can be highly motivating - better than a verbal description;

- theory and practice can be linked;

- pace of demonstration can be varied;

- students usually enjoy actively doing things;

- expert demonstrations may be available via the video;

- key points can be stressed and repeated;

- three dimensional, even sounds and smells;

- students see the sequence and build-up;

  may allow students to ask questions.

Disadvantages:
- a poor demonstration can be frustrating for the students;

- can be too fast or too slow for the learners;

- no permanent record;

- may be difficult to see;

- may be too long leading to loss of concentration;

- students may learn bad habits/techniques;

- can be expensive in terms of material costs;

- teacher needs to rehearse;

- students can be passive.

Summary:
- the first stage in learners acquiring a skill. It must be well prepared, key points identified, learners involved and must be followed by individual learner practice and feedback.

A skilled demonstration is characterised by its speed and dexterity.. Some skills are difficult for you to slow down because when you do, you loose the 'flow' (the links in the chain of stimulus-response relationships). A golf swing, slicing an onion, and plastering a wall are all difficult to slow down.

In order to overcome this problem of speed a useful sequence to follow is:

(i)   complete the demonstration at normal speed without commentary;

(ii)   repeat the demonstration with commentary stressing the key points, asking students questions (what comes next? can you hold this? will you fill that?);

(iii)   ask a student to repeat the demonstration with all of the students watching;

(iv)   ask another student to repeat the demonstration with a third one giving a commentary.

You do not need to complete all of these stages of course but they are possibilities. Remember that you are helping the students to **verbalise** (to remember in their own minds) the stages or steps involved in the skill. And, as you will remember, repetition is helpful in helping students to remember.

Points (iii) and (iv) above are useful because, when you are not directly involved in demonstrating the skill, you can concentrate more upon the teaching aspects: you can more easily identify the key points and tell students to expect them, to watch out for them, or ask them what they are, without having to stop the student who is completing the demonstration.

Also getting students to demonstrate is useful for highlighting the problems that exist in the completion of the skill. You should *not,* in your demonstration, show students the wrong way o doing things. They may remember only the wrong way and think that it is the correct one. However, when a student is completing the demonstration with the others watching, it is likely to be done incorrectly, and you can immediately point out any mistakes.

The above strategy has linked the method to the initial stages of skill learning but it can also be used for the teaching of concepts. If you are able to visually demonstrate the concept, then all of the above benefits of the strategy can be maintained. For example if you are teaching Pythagoras Theorem (in a right angled triangle the square on the hypotenuse is equal to the sum of the squares on the other two sides. We are sure that you all remember that!) then this can be demonstrated by using a model as shown in Figure 3.9.

A model can be made (either out of card or coloured acetate to go onto the overhead projector) of the triangle abc and of the squares on side 'a' and 'b'. The squares on these two sides can then be replaced onto side 'c' showing that the square on the hypotenuse (side 'c') is equal in area to the square on the other two sides. Students are more likely to remember this visual demonstration of the concept than they are a formula written on the chalkboard.

Figure 3.9   Demonstration of a Concept: Pythagoras Theorem

One of the problems of demonstrations is that students are often passive participants of the process: they sit and watch the demonstration but take no active part. As with any passive learning, the memory process is problematic and much of what is seen and heard might quite easily be forgotten. This can be overcome to some extent through the provision of an incomplete handout which students can complete as they watch the demonstration. Figure 3.10 shows the relative merits of handouts when used with demonstrations. As you can see, the limitations of one approach may be balanced by the advantages of the other.

Demonstration	Handout
Advantages Can be highly motivating; Students can see development/progress; Students can be supervised and errors prevented; Students can ask questions; Three dimensional; Students use same tools/equipment as the teacher.	**Advantages** Permanent record; Words and diagrams; Can be trial tested and hence error free; Can be designed by an expert; Accessible to teacher and student; Inexpensive; Work at own pace; Step by step.
Limitations No permanent record; Pace suits teacher and not individual students; All students may not be able to see easily; Students may not understand; Students must practise; Some skills (e.g. chopping an onion) cannot be slowed down; Students can be passive for too long; Costly in terms of teacher time, materials, room. etc.,	**Limitations** Needs to be clear and unambiguous; Cannot see real product/tools; No supervision; No-one to ask; Vocabulary may not be suitable; Must be error-free; Two dimensional.

Figure 3.10 Comparison between Demonstrations and Handouts.

3.1.3 Team Teaching

What is it	- two or more teachers co-operating in the planning, presentation, assessment and evaluation of a course, but mainly in the presentation.
When is it used	- where there are large groups of students and the teachers can take responsibility for parts of the course or where special expertise is needed.
Examples:	- communications in science;
	- nurse teacher training.
Guidelines:	- the course team need to prepare very carefully to avoid duplication of topics and to ensure contiguity. Tutorial or seminar support may be needed.
Advantages:	- reduces preparation time for each teacher;
	- teachers work to their strengths;
	- teamwork produces a better course;
	- curriculum development enhanced.
Disadvantages:	- communication breakdown;

- talking to large numbers of students can be daunting;

- large teaching room(s) needed;

- can be seen by the students as disjointed;

- variation in teaching quality.

Summary: - a well co-ordinated team teaching approach can lead to a high quality course.

3.1.4 Discussion

What it is   - the students are actively involved in talking to each other about an issue of mutual concern. Your job is to manage the situation so that learning takes place.

When is it used   - discussion is often used to help solve problems, or to explore issues and take decisions. It is a useful way of exploring attitudes and to help change unhelpful or antisocial attitudes.

Examples   - Treatment of Young Offenders; preventative medicine.

Guidelines: - discussion must be carefully planned. A clear intention or objective is needed and ground rules need to be established. Timing is a crucial issue as is the need to reduce your own involvement whilst trying to ensure all can participate. The topic should be easily understood by all students. Ensure that the room layout is conducive to a discussion.

(a) Preparation: - must be relevant to an objective;

- do learners need to research the topic?

- consider size of group and room layout so that all participate (i.e. small groups and intimate areas);

- consider if a semi-structured handout will assist coverage of topic.

(b) Presentation: - tell students how long they have for discussion;

- tell the students how the results are to be fed back;

- your role is (a) to provide information and not answers; (b) to monitor the discussion: and (c) to try to ensure that all participate;

- assist learners to summarise the main points as a conclusion, and finally you must summarise the main issues.

Advantages: - can be used following a video or lecture in order to reinforce the learning;

- very useful for changing attitudes;

- involves the students - and quiet members of the group can emerge as leaders;

- can be very creative;

- needs a summary;

- can encourage students to become more articulate;

- students can criticise each other's views and not the person;

- broadens views;

- does not feel like hard work;

- provides interesting feedback on students knowledge of the topic and their social skills;

- encourages "deep" learning.

Disadvantages:
- students and teachers need to develop discussion skills;

- can be risky;

- may take a relatively long time;

- you must not dominate;

- have something else prepared in case discussion is ineffective;

- may be difficult to keep to the point;

- may be noisy;

- can degenerate into an informal chat.

Summary:
- high learner participation but you need to develop the necessary management skills;

- remember to arrange the furniture in the room so that the communication in the discussion is enhanced.

The seating plan is very important for discussion. Figure 3.11 shows an ideal situation where desks have been removed and students are seated so they can both see and hear each other. The 'network' has been decentralised so that there is no focal point - the students are seated in a circle.

If there is a focal point (for example, someone sitting in the middle) some students are likely to look to this person for a lead and will not participate as an 'equal partner'. If it is not possible to remove the desks, then they should be arranged in a square or circle so that all of the students can see and hear each other and, again, there should be no focal point. However, desks can provide a barrier behind which the more introvert students might hide.

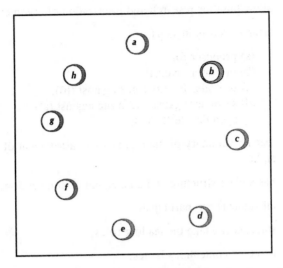

Figure 3.11 Decentralised Student Seating for a Discussion

Often the results of the discussion will need to be fed back to either the whole group or to you as teacher. This needs to be made clear at the start and it is useful to let students decide who is to do this. However, it is useful that they make this decision at the start of the discussion period so that the chosen individual can make the necessary notes and preparation (or ensure that another student does it for them).

3.1.5 Debate

What is it
- a debate is very similar to a discussion but tends to have more rules regarding procedure.

When is it used
- where there is no right answer and where both sides of the argument would benefit from exploration. To enhance formal communication skills in the presentation of an argument.

Examples:
- the use of nuclear power to generate electricity; bring back corporal punishment; the National Lottery.

Guidelines:

  (a) Preparation:
- nominate/elect a chair from the students to ensure rules are followed in an impartial manner;

- select a topic which will stimulate debate and allow argument for and against;

- select a main speaker for the motion and one against the motion and give them time to prepare;

- brief the chair.

  (b) Presentation:
- divide group into those in favour of the motion, those against and those uncommitted;

- allow time for research and preparation of arguments;
- arrange debate in steps:

    (a) proposer for;
    (b) proposer against;
    (c) seconder for (to argue against (b));
    (d) seconder against (to argue against (a));
    (e) open debate;(f) Vote.

- teacher summary of main points and assessment of communication skills.

Advantages:

- has a clear structure and an element of competition;
- all students can participate;
- students can take the leading roles;
- good for contentious issues;
- students can enhance their presentation skills;
- increases teamwork;
- both sides of the argument are exposed;
- students can enjoy the process.

Disadvantages:

- students may find the rules and procedures difficult to understand;
- a minority of the students may do most of the work;
- students must prepare thoroughly which may take some time.

Summary:

- student centred, structured technique for learning communication skills and extracting key points of a topic.

3.1.6 Question and Answer

What it is

- Posing a series of questions to students in order to promote thinking and understanding.

When is it used

- it is an informal assessment technique which is used with groups of up to 30 students. It is a way of ascertaining the existing level of learning or entry behaviour in the introduction to a lesson and/or, assessing the learning that has taken place at the end of a lesson (or during it).

Example:

- building concept attainment (e.g. a tourist).

Guidelines:

- questions need to be carefully considered so that the learners supply their knowledge and do not simply answer yes or no;
- ask simple questions first and then move to more complex ones;
- spread the questions so that all learners respond;
- ask the questions, allow thinking time and then ask students to

respond. This may involve setting rules to avoid chorus answers;

- praise a correct response, praise the correct part of a partially correct response and explore the reason for an incorrect response. Always accept the students' answers to ensure future participation.

Advantages:

- students are involved and feel they are contributing to learning;

- misconceptions may be identified at an early stage;

- can build from simple to complex;

- key questions can be pre-planned;

- feed back on quality of learning is gained;

- maintains concentration;

- can stimulate students;

- gives feedback on quality of teaching.

Disadvantages:

- you need to be able to respond quickly to the students answers;

- careful planning may be needed;

- may use too many closed questions;

- a minority of students may participate.

Summary:

- you need to develop this useful skill. Question and answer may last a few minutes or be developed into a longer session. The feed back showing misconceptions is very valuable. Encourage all answers and build upon wrong or partially correct answers.

When discussing lesson planning in Chapter 1 it was suggested that 'key questions' should not only be planned but be stated as part of the teacher activity in the body of the plan. This means that you need to plan the questions related to the level of the objectives. Figure 3.12 gives an indication of questions at the different levels. Each level in the Cognitive Domain has been included but only up to 'valuing' in the Affective Domain. You might want to combine the higher three levels in the cognitive domain into 'invention'. The reason that the higher levels in the affective domain have not been covered is that post-16 education and training tends not to go higher in this domain.

You will see that, not only do the levels of question get harder to answer the higher they go up the domain, but the length of the responses is also likely to increase. Those questions that warrant a one word answer are termed 'closed' questions: those that require a sentence or more to answer are 'open' questions.

Domain	Level	Example Question
Cognitive	Knowledge	What city is the capital of England?
	Comprehension	Explain, in your own words, the meaning of pollution.
	Application	Now that you have studied energy, if you leave a refrigerator door open and switched on in a sealed room, will the temperature rise or fall?
	Analysis	Why do you think that Labour party supporters, after World War II, said that the Conservatives were a party of warmongers?
	Synthesis	Now that you have studied static electricity, how could you stop getting a 'shock' when you slide over the plastic seat covers of a car?
	Evaluation	Describe the fallacies in reasoning in the statement "All ducks are birds. All robins are birds. Thus, all ducks are robins".
Affective	Receiving	How interesting was your visit to the factory?
	Responding	How did you feel after reading "Catcher in the Rye"?
	Valuing	What actions if any, would you take with a friend who wrote a 'Letter to the Editor' of a local newspaper?

Figure 3.12   Questions at Different Levels in Different Domains

It is useful to have both types in a lesson but it is often the case that closed questions will elicit a 'chorus' response as many will know the answer and want to show that they know.

When you use the question and answer technique, you will want as many of the class to respond as possible and you will want them to answer both low and high level questions. The type of questions that you ask are not only classified into levels but also into whether you 'nominate' a student to answer or whether the question is 'un-nominated' (any student in the class can answer). Consider the response pattern to teacher questions shown in Figure 3.13 which gives an overview of a question and answer session with 9 students siting in a semi-circle. From this you can see that the teacher has asked equal numbers of nominated and un-nominated questions. This is generally useful in that, if you want all of the students to respond, you can nominate individuals to get them to think, involve them in the session, and so on. You will also see that the total of teacher initiated interactions is 36 and the total student initiated interactions (them making comments and asking questions) is 16. Thus a third of the interactions are student initiated which is a good proportion: it is generally useful to get students to talk to you as well as you talking to them. Often this is very difficult and you may find in your classes a very small proportion of the interactions are student initiated.

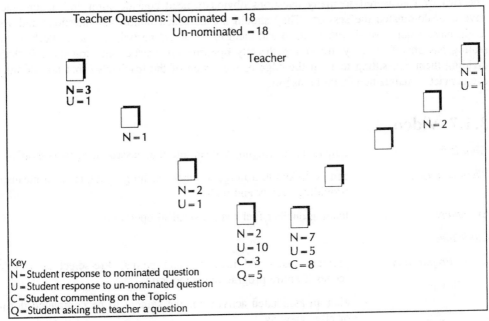

Figure 3.13 **Response Patterns to a Class Question and Answer Period**

However, when you look at the positions of the responses around the class, you will see that a total of 40 of the 52 interactions (77%) were from 2 members (22%) of the class: a very uneven distribution. Also, three members of the class (33%) did not interact at all or only interacted once. Thus 33% of the class were involved in only 2% of the interactions. The questions that need to be answered associated with this type of analysis include:

(a) did it matter that some students did not respond or make any contribution at all?

(b) if it does matter, what might be done to ensure that they participate?

(c) does it matter that 77% of the interactions came from 22% of the group?

(d) if it does matter, what might be done to make them respond less?

(e) does seating have any influence on the response pattern?

(f) what response pattern would be ideal?

The answer to question (a) depends upon the respective abilities of the students who did not respond. If they are bright students in your subject and they are not introvert, then perhaps it does not matter that they do not answer. They might not like question and answer and learn in spite of the use of this technique. If, on the other hand they are not concentrating and/or do not do very well in your subject, then a series of nominated questions to them will be an advantage. If they are introvert, then nominated questions will have to be handled carefully - you will need to make sure that they are easy questions that they should be able to answer and make sure that you give praise when they respond.

The two who answered so many questions obviously need consideration and action: they have over-dominated the session. They should not be asked nominated questions and you might have a quiet word with them to ask them to let others participate more. Perhaps the seating has an effect: they are sitting directly opposite the teacher and together. Perhaps dividing them and sitting them at the edge of the vision of the teacher so that not so much eye contact is maintained could be useful.

3.1.7 Video

What it is — a method of bringing realism into the classroom or workshop.

When is it used — can be linked to a range of other teaching strategies as a means of providing variety and realism.

Examples: — loading nuclear fuel rods; a surgical operation.

Guidelines:

  (a) Preparation: — preview video and identify main points. Pre-select appropriate scenes if entire programme is too long;

— plan an associated activity for the student to be completed during or after viewing;

— book necessary equipment (video, tape, room etc.).

— know how to operate the equipment;

  (b) Presentation: — introduce the video and the activity and alert students to the key points;

— after viewing assess the learning;

— stop for questions or replay any important points.

Advantages: — can bring a well known expert into the classroom;

— students can see dangerous or one-off situations;

— a permanent record;

— can provoke thought used as a trigger;

— relatively cheap and very convenient;

— can be taken home by (some) students;

— helps the students to visualise;

— freeze-frame and slow-motion available;

— movement, colour, sound;

— can choose to view small extracts;

— modern medium which is popular;

— video tapes may be hired or borrowed;

— an alternative to "teacher-talk".

Disadvantages	- may disrupt class;
	- class handed over to 'another';
	- may be perceived as merely entertainment;
	- can induce sleep;
	- can be seen as an easy option for the teacher;
	- technical problems;
	- availability of resources;
	- video from an "authoritative" source may be biased and bias the students.
Summary:	- video used with care can be a stimulating part of a lesson.

Used properly, the video can be an excellent addition to the classroom or workshop teaching of a large group of students. However, there is a danger when using a video to pass the responsibility for the teaching entirely over to the programme: to the voice on the TV and the picture on the screen. The 'good' use of a video, like so many other teaching strategies, must ensure that the students are *active*.

We have suggested that you preview the video and highlight the main points: the key features that it exhibits. Either before or after the showing of each main point, you can stop the recorder, emphasise the point, make a note of it on the chalkboard and ask students to note it before going on with the viewing.

You can also prepare an incomplete handout for the students which invites them to take notes under the main headings as they are viewing. If you consider that they have insufficient time to make the necessary notes you can again stop the recorder for the activity to take place. Another advantage of such a handout is that your students also have a permanent record of what they have watched.

3.2 Strategies Appropriate to Small Groups

Just as large group strategies are appropriate for certain educational purposes, there are times when you should use strategies that are appropriate to small groups. Students are likely to work in small groups in industry and commerce and, in consequence, we have a moral obligation to use such approaches in our controlled environments.

Industry and commerce are continually telling us of the importance of 'key' skills to be associated with our subject specialism skills and one of these relates to the ability to work 'as an effective group member'. This, generally, means the ability to work in small groups; to be an effective leader as well as an effective follower; to learn to cope with other people's idiosyncrasies; to be able to present a logical argument and analyse others' arguments; to co-operate with others and adopt a variety of roles when working co-operatively.

As educators have become dissatisfied with the conventional classroom, its basic assumptions, and its effectiveness, so the strategies associated with small group work have gained momentum. Such strategies include seminar, role play, case study, a simulation. These often employ different aspects of small group discussion where students are able to think things through for themselves without having the direct control of the teacher. Of course, this means that you automatically lose some of your control over what is being said and what is being done. You become more a manager of the situation as opposed to the purveyor of information. You need to set up the situation and take more of a 'back seat' and let the students proceed more at their own pace. This means a very different perspective for you and one that some teachers find, at least initially, very difficult to cope with. You become a more 'humanist' teacher with the concentration upon the need of the student as well as the need of the subject. Students learn from each other.

Because of the different approaches that you have to adopt with a smaller group, the range of objectives that you can achieve is greater. The higher level cognitive and affective domain objectives are more applicable to these methods. It has been argued that in some subjects the major concepts, principles, and methods are so well established that no competent person raises any doubt about them. At the introductory levels in such subjects like science, engineering and mathematics there is much agreement about what is important. In other subjects there is not such a consensus. In the social sciences - in history and economics, political science, psychology, literature, music and art, we do not agree nearly so readily about what is important, good, true, valid or significant. Consequently, in these low consensus subjects, discussion methods may be necessary. Similarly, the discussion method may also be better suited to the changing of attitudes and behaviour. During the discussion, students make public decisions committing themselves to a given course of action.

As with all forms of teaching, you need to be well prepared. Arranging the learning environment to suit small groupwork is important. Often just simply moving the chairs to form circles is sufficient.

You may want to identify the small groups in order to engineer some facet of the learning e.g. a good gender mix, or age mix. At other times, you may be content to give the students a free choice. Experience shows that a group size of four is ideal. This allows all to participate and reduces the chance of "passengers".

The students need to be clear about the activity and be clear about what they are learning. Giving written specification of the task, perhaps OHP, flipchart or hand-out, helps students to keep to the point. It is important to negotiate some ground rules. This may include time for task, mode of reporting outcomes, acceptable behaviour and so on.

A very important role for you when the students are busy is to monitor progress after ensuring that all of the groups are clear about the task. Give them a few minutes to discuss the task and to get started. Then join each group in turn. Sitting at the same level, rather than standing over them, encourages discussion to continue. Listen to the students. If they are progressing well, give some encouragement and positive feedback. If the students are having problems make a few suggestions and before the reporting-back stage, ensure all groups have something good to contribute even if it is really your own thoughts. Remind students about the time: when to start summarising: when to start writing and so on.

One of the problems with small group work is the time taken to feedback the outcomes. It is important to value the outcomes and to emphasise the key points. You have set time limits when you have lots of small groups. In this case OHPs can be photocopied for everyone or flipchart presentations can be typed, photocopied and distributed to all at a later date.

Do not destroy the feedback sheets when the students are in the room. Take the sheets away with you and, if they are not needed, put them in the waste bin in your own room! Some students resent seeing the results of their labour being destroyed and rightly so.

The final part of your role is to link the work done to the learning objectives. This demonstrates to the students that their work has been fruitful and you were not opting-out of "proper teaching".

Your role, when dealing with groups, is demanding. In order for the students to gain the maximum benefit from the group activity and interaction, you could consider the following:

- ensure students understand the objectives of the task and have a record of them
- answer questions regarding the purpose, procedures and limitations
- check progress and summarise progress made
- monitor timekeeping
- encourage contributions/diplomatically restrain the dominant
- reward contributions
- resolve internal conflicts
- keep the groups "on track"
- defuse emotional aspects
- delegate as many tasks to the groups themselves as possible so that, over a period of time, your role is minimised
- see that the group has all that it needs – e.g. pens, paper, flipchart, OHTs, clear (written) guidelines.

3.2.1 Seminar

What it is	- a student researches a topic, presents the findings to other students and leads the ensuing discussion.
When is it used	- widely used with mature students to explore specified topics.
Examples:	- how to deal with problem students; the causes of World War II.
Guidelines:	- a student should have time to consider relevant readings, view videos, listen to lectures etc. before the seminar. Some questions may be posed in advance. At the seminar, each student should be encouraged to share their views so that the range of issues can be explored;
	- students should be encouraged to use OHP, flipcharts, etc. You need to monitor the proceedings and avoid cross-talking, dominant individuals and unrelated discussion.

Advantages:	-	students involved in the preparation;
	-	students know what is to be discussed and that they will have the opportunity to participate;
	-	opportunity to ask questions of their peers and teachers;
	-	seminars are student led;
	-	ideal for very specialised topics;
	-	responsibility given to students;
	-	builds confidence;
	-	can link theory and practice.
Disadvantages:	-	students may be reluctant to participate at first;
	-	need to summarise the main issues at the end of the seminar;
	-	can be dull;
	-	students may not respect their peers;
	-	may be time consuming;
	-	student may be reluctant to criticise their peers;
	-	may be difficult to assess.
Summary:	-	a different way for learning and, if the group is small, then opportunities easiest for effective interaction.

The aims of the seminar method include the common skills of 'the ability to find information' and 'the ability to present an argument'. Often discussions take place in class without students having all of the facts and understanding the topic. The advantages of the seminar are that students are involved themselves in finding the information prior to giving a short input, and they then discuss its implications and sustain an argument through the answering of questions on it from their colleagues.

Thus, the phases in a seminar are:

(i)   finding information;

(ii) presenting the information to their colleagues;

(iii) answering questions from colleagues.

The assessment of the work, therefore, can give feedback on the subject matter; the ability to find information; the ability to present the information, and the ability to answer questions from their fellow students.

3.2.2 Workshop

What it is	- an opportunity to develop practical skills in a simulated situation and link the theory with practice.
When is it used	- in the development of skills.
Examples:	- using a CNC lathe; making a dovetail joint.

Guidelines:

(a) Preparation:
- ensure all equipment available and ready;
- consider how to introduce and conclude each session;
- prepare an assessment schedule related to key points;
- prepare worksheet to indicate task schedule and associated assessment points.

(b) Presentation:
- often starts with a demonstration;
- manage individuals working at their own pace (question, feed back, rectify faults);
- overtly link theory with the practical aspects;
- monitor safety aspects;
- allow time for a conclusion so that students can see/critically analyse others' work/progress.

Advantages:
- can take place before or after theoretical aspects;
- can be a good basis for problem solving;
- teacher can talk with the learners on a one-to-one basis;
- reinforces learning in a realistic and meaningful way;
- students work at own pace;
- students can work using a variety of skills;
- students can work in groups;
- a non-threatening environment.

Disadvantages:
- can be seen as tedious or boring;
- expensive in terms of time, equipment and rooms;
- implications for Health and Safety;
- teachers may lose control of learning.

Summary:
- a valuable, if not essential part of many courses. Usually enjoyable for the students as it often appears to be real and exciting.

3.2.3 Gaming/Quiz

What it is	- games are a learning situation with an element of competition and/or cooperation.
When is it used	- can stimulate and involve learners when they interact with other students and/or the game.
Examples:	- team building; effects of an oil spillage, healthy diet.
Guidelines:	
(a) Preparation:	- try out and test game prior to use with students;
	- ensure rules are clear and understood by students.
(b) Presentation:	- introduce the game in its learning context;
	- monitor programme and assist only when essential;
	- summarise and consolidate the learning outcomes.
Advantages:	- can be fun;
	- compete against a machine or situation rather than another student;
	- immediate feedback;
	- teacher has time to observe students.
Disadvantages:	- may have to make your own game;
	- game may not work;
	- immediate feed back;
	- may not be taken seriously;
	- may be difficult to control.
Summary:	- can be a different type of learning which the students generally enjoy.

The Quiz is a particular form of gaming. Teams or individuals may participate and an element of competition may be introduced. It can be an interesting way of obtaining feed back on the quality of learning and motivating students to revise and study their notes.

3.2.4 Brainstorming

What it is	- a problem solving technique used to generate a number of ideas (solutions) in a short time e.g. 5 to 15 minutes.
When is it used	- when a problem, real or manufactured, exists, the students are invited to generate possible solutions. Often used in management courses or with problem solving.
Example 1:	- warm-up - uses of a paper clip.

Example 2:	-	problem - how to prevent strikes.

Guidelines: - the 'problem' should be stated as "in how many ways can we .....". Restatements can be suggested by students to ensure that they understand the problem. The students may then be 'warmed up' using a trial brainstorm. The students are encouraged to shout out key words - these are all written down without criticism or censure. If the participants dry up, there can be an enforced two minutes silence. Then the brainstorm continues. The key words are then categorised and discussed. Possible solutions are then identified.

Advantages:
- unusual solutions may be identified;
- all can participate;
- needs few resources;
- seems to be part of the creative process;
- uses students experiences;
- encourages teamwork;
- no-one looks foolish.

Disadvantages:
- group needs to learn and obey rules;
- warm-up sessions may be needed;
- can be demanding and can only be used for short periods;
- some students can opt out.

Summary:
- a challenging and active learning situation.

3.2.5 Buzz Groups

What it is
- a relatively large group of students are divided into smaller groups of about 4 to 6, usually to discuss a problem/situation for a short time, say 5 minutes. The buzz of the several simultaneous discussions gives the strategy its name.

When is it used
- with large groups where you want the students to interact with each other.

Example:
- merits of an integrated transport system.

Guidelines:
- make sure the groups know what they have to discuss and how long they have. Nominate a leader or tell each group to appoint one. State the manner of feed back e.g. oral from the leader, OHT, flipchart etc.

Advantages:
- introduces student activity into what could be perceived as a teacher-centred situation;
- gives a change of activity and allows the students to express

themselves;

- can be used in a large, formal lecture theatre;

- gives feed back on the learning;

- gives teacher a break;

- can be used to recap;

- can be a safety valve;

- helps problem-solving;

- develops teamwork.

Disadvantages: - sometimes can be difficult to nominate groups;

- feed back could take some time (try a maximum of 60 second feed back from each group).

Summary: - small groups discussing giving a 'buzz' of conversation.

3.2.6 Field Trip

What it is   - usually the students are taken out of their normal learning situation to a 'real-life' situation.

When is it used   - where realism is essential, or very helpful, in reinforcing the learning.

Examples: - study of rock formation; a food processing plant.

Guidelines:

(a) Preparation: - plan links with the theory/learning intention;

- consider safety and make allowances for delays;

- prepare handouts and activities;

- plan for inclement weather;

- consider insurance and parent/employer permission;

- brief students before the visit;

- plan follow up activities;

- follow your organisations guidelines.

(b) Presentation: - ensure adequate supervision at all times;

- 'visit' students, use question and answer.

Advantages: - students can see the real situation;

- realistic and lifelike;

- motivating;

- clear links between learning and visit.

Disadvantages:	- time consuming for planning and visit;
	- may be costly;
	- legal/safety problems;
	- supervision of students on visit;
	- heavy responsibility.
Summary:	- can be a very valuable and rewarding experience but may turnout to be a nightmare.

3.2.7 Role Play

What it is	- students acting a part or a role in events before a situation, during the situation and after the situation.
When is it used	- helping the students to feel the influences and pressures in their role. It is suggested that role play is particularly effective with attitudinal issues.
Examples:	- conflict in the workplace e.g. receptionist and 'difficult' customer;
	- conflict within the team in the workplace;
	- situation where people are disadvantaged due to race, gender, etc.
Guidelines:	
(a) Preparation:	- have role cards for participants;
	- plan activities for those students not in role, i.e. observers for feed back; NB. players should not see each others' role-play cards;
	- set up physical environment to enhance realism.
(b) Presentation:	- introduce the role play and indicate its function in the learning, i.e. why you are doing it;
	- monitor the role play and only step in if things go badly wrong, i.e. a student is going to be embarrassed;
	- debrief the students so that they are no longer 'in role';
	- ensure that the role play is analysed and related to the intended learning outcome.
Advantages:	- a good way to address attitudinal issues;
	- high degree of student participation;
	- brings learning to life;
	- realistic;
	- emotions can be felt;
	- students can teach their peers about their feelings in their role rather than the teacher telling them;

	-	usually a safe environment.
Disadvantages:	-	can be threatening - especially for the shy participants;
	-	needs careful preparation;
	-	needs careful managing;
	-	essential to debrief the students;
	-	can take some time;
	-	may be difficult to manage;
	-	some students hate role play.

Summary: - once written and tested, the role plays can be used many times with different classes. High student involvement with the difficult area of attitudinal change.

3.2.8 Ice Breaker

What it is - a technique used to get the student to feel part of the group and part of the learning process.

When is it used - often used with the first meeting of a group or when a student or students join an established group.

Example 1: - ask the group to go into pairs; one person interviews the other and asks their name, their interests etc. (Nothing too personal). The roles are then reversed. The students then introduce each other to the whole group.

Example 2: - each student writes their first name on the board and tells as much as they know about it e.g. its origin, its meaning, how they feel about their name, famous people with the same name.

Example 3: - prepare a brief questionnaire which asks, what qualities do you bring to the group? What are you looking forward to? What are your concerns? Display the results and ask the students to look at the responses of the others in the group.
N.B. the questionnaires need to be anonymous.

Guidelines: - the balance between helping a group to get to know each other and causing embarrassment is a delicate one. Care needs to be exercised and judgment made so that the student is allowed to develop but is not threatened.

Advantages: - can help discussion and small group work to achieve maximum effectiveness very quickly;

- students feel part of a group;

- builds trust;

- no long silences;

	-	students pose more questions to the teacher earlier in the course;
	-	relieves tension;
	-	can be fun.
Disadvantages:	-	can take a long time;
	-	may not be perceived as being 'useful';
	-	some students may hate it;
	-	can be over-used.
Summary:	-	used with care and in a non-threatening way, icebreakers may help establish a group identity in an hour rather than weeks or months.

3.2.9 Simulation

What it is	-	the simulation of a real or a possible situation.
When is it used	-	in situations where it is not possible or desirable to undertake learning in the actual conditions.
Example 1:	-	computer simulation of the economy.
Example 2:	-	flight simulator.
Example 3:	-	managers trying to see own skills in prioritising and time management in a simulated situation.
Example 4:	-	job interview.
Example 5:	-	handling customer complaint.
Example 6:	-	running a reception desk.
Guidelines:	-	the simulation needs to be made as realistic as possible. Supervision of all students is essential at all times in order to avoid reinforcement of errors.
Advantages:	-	can be used where the real situation is dangerous, costly, 'difficult' or too time consuming;
	-	can be repeated until desired level of learning is achieved;
	-	can be stopped at any stage in order to inject concepts, principles etc.;
	-	students are active and take responsibility for their own learning;
	-	can be a good introduction to the real thing.
Disadvantages:	-	can be time consuming to set up;
	-	may be difficult to supervise all students all of the time.
Summary:	-	may be the only way to learn in some situations, with the students being able to stop and ask questions.

3.2.10 Case Study

What it is	-	it is an examination of a real or simulated problem which is structured so that learning can take place or be reinforced.
When is it used	-	often used on management and business study courses to analyse what went wrong in a given situation and to consider how failure could be avoided. It tends to be used in situations where rules or laws cannot be applied or where there is some ambiguity.
Examples:	-	why a particular company collapsed.
Guidelines:	-	what happened to the British Motor Cycle Industry.
	-	the situation needs to be as realistic and as accurate as possible. As much information as possible needs to be given and often superfluous information is given as in real life.
Advantages:	-	can be an individual or group activity;
	-	can be in class or at home;
	-	real, including current, situations can be studied.
Disadvantages:	-	the case study needs to have clear learning intentions;
	-	the aftermath of the study needs to reinforce learning;
	-	needs to be well structured;
	-	may seem unreal;
	-	a good deal of preparation may be needed.
Summary:	-	takes a good deal of preparation but can bring realism into the learning situation.

3.3 Strategies Appropriate to Individual Work

Just as some strategies are appropriate to large and small groups, there are times when you need to provide opportunities and activities for students to work on their own. What are these? When is a student best left alone with an assignment, a set of printed materials, a set of programmed instruction materials, or a broad mission to be carried out through independent effort and study?

The individualisation of instruction has gained momentum in recent years. Some educators have become dissatisfied with the conventional classroom, its basic assumptions and its effectiveness. The coming of the 'objectives' revolution provided the basis for this to happen and it has developed apace in recent years. Apart from helping achieve educational objectives in general, individual instruction can achieve the objectives of helping students to work and learn independently. It was realised that students must eventually learn on their own and education must assist this process. 'Learning to learn' is now a major objective in its own right with students continuing to learn throughout their lives. This *'humanist'* approach to education was promoted by Dewey (1933) with his 'Project Method', and A.S. Neill (1960) with his 'whole school approach' and has gathered momentum.

There are, of course, cautions in using individual work and there is a difference between 'independent' and 'self directed' study. Independent study is organised by the teacher with suggestions as to what might be completed and, perhaps, when. Self directed study, on the other hand, has its organisation base with the student and, in effect, is even more student centred. It is often the organisation that students find difficult. The 'Keller Plan' (F.S.Keller, 1974) found that students, when left to their own devices for too long a period, would be liable to flounder and the inclusion of teacher centred and group activities when associated with individual work made it much more effective in terms of the amount that was learned.

The 'Personalised System of Instruction' (PSI), which was the outcome of the work by Keller, has the following characteristics:

(i)	*Individually paced:*	- flexibility in timing can be achieved because students are working to meet specific criteria. The outcomes then are criterion and not norm referenced.
(ii)	*Mastery oriented:*	- unless students demonstrate mastery of a topic they cannot proceed. Testing can be at the request of the students when they feel that they are ready.
(iii)	*Tutoring:*	- help should be available to assist and answer questions which cannot be answered by the individual.
(iv)	*Study guides:*	- study guides, which contain objectives, offer suggestions for study, point out available resources, describe projects or experiments that could be attempted and provide sample assessment items, are given to the student.
(v)	*Supplemented with traditional methods:*	- lectures, demonstrations, and so on may be scheduled for stimulation or clarification; they may be used occasionally and attendance can be voluntary.

PSI has many variations but few meet with failure if the basic elements of the system stay intact.

You can use the elements of the Keller Plan in the three methods described below. More and more, effective classroom teachers are being asked to design their own 'study guides' for use with independent study and the elements of the Plan should be kept in mind during the design process.

3.3.1 Project/Assignment

What it is	- the students are usually given an individual topic for an in-depth analysis. They often have to work independently, do research and report either in writing or verbally to a group. The project could involve a group of students working together on different facets of the same problem.

| *When is it used* | - | often used in advanced courses for training in research techniques but now used in a wide variety of situations including practical work. |

Examples:	-	research the incidence of AIDS in the UK (individual);
	-	design and build a wind tunnel (individual);
	-	build a house (group project).

| *Guidelines:* | - | students may need help with the study skills involved, particularly when working on their own. The project and assignment has to be realistic in terms of time and cost. Clear learning intentions are needed. |

Advantages:	-	realistic situation for students;
	-	can promote independent learning;
	-	student feels in command;
	-	tutorial links may be on a one-to-one basis;
	-	can be highly motivating;
	-	enhances study skills and key skills;
	-	cross curricular;
	-	useful end-product
	-	some unpredictable aspects;
	-	can develop practical skills
	-	could involve groupwork;
	-	active learning;
	-	students find their own level.

Disadvantages:	-	supervision can take up a good deal of time;
	-	some students need a lot of managing;
	-	can be costly;
	-	resources, library, need to be available.

| *Summary:* | - | a recognised and realistic alternative to traditional examinations. |

3.3.2 Tutorial

| *What it is* | - | the teacher usually sets the student a task and the tutorial is a means of preparing the student for the task, assisting in the process and then discussing the quality of the learning outcomes. It is essentially a strategy to support and enhance the quality of learning. |

When is it used	- used in all spheres of learning but may not be called a 'tutorial'.
Examples:	- supporting work on an assignment;
	- checking progress on the course as a whole.
Guidelines:	- it is important to listen to students to see what they know and what the do not know. Positive outcomes should be planned. Tutorial could be on a one to one basis but when students have similar tasks a small group approach can generate valuable discussion and peer support. Students and teacher should prepare for tutorials.
Advantages:	- individual attention;
	- opportunity to see the quality of learning;
	- valuable support to progress;
	- opportunity to establish a rapport with students and improve communication;
	- confidential aspects can be discussed;
	- individual concerns addressed.
Disadvantages:	- costly because of one-to-one relationship;
	- student may feel pressurised;
	- finding a suitable room.
Summary:	- in widespread use and students should find tutorials to be of great value.

The following checklist may be a useful framework.

Checklist for Tutorial Supervision

| Observer: _____ | Person Observed: _____ | Date: _____ |
| Course: _____ | Subject: _____ | No of Students: _____ |

Make comments upon the following aspects

	Aspect	**Comment**
Methods of Supervising	Quick tutorial start to ensure that all know what to do.	
	Spend time with students who need help rather than those who demand it.	
	No students left waiting for assistance for too long.	
	Quick problem solving to identify and overcome student problems.	
	Mixture of teacher and student initiated visits.	
	Allow time for students to get on with the task(s) themselves.	
	Asking questions to help students solve their problems as opposed to doing things for them.	
	Praising students as appropriate.	
Timing and Number of Visits	Length of specific visits OK (not too long/short).	
	Optimum time between visits (not too long/short).	
	Number of visits and length related to ability.	
	Appropriate time spent with each student.	
Other	Others (please state)	

3.3.3 Open Learning/Distance Learning

What it is	- this is usually where the teacher and student meet infrequently (if at all). It may include videos, broadcast materials, audio tapes, written material, etc.
When is it used	- useful for students who cannot attend due to work commitments, or because of distance to travel.
Examples:	- Open University, Open College, Nursing up-dates.
Guidelines:	- the materials used must be tried and tested, unambiguous and interesting. Carefully consider the existing materials. If planning your own materials, build in as much activity and feedback as possible.
Advantages:	- helps students who cannot attend a given location at a given time;
	- student proceeds at own pace;
	- large number of students taught simultaneously;
	- convenient.
Disadvantages:	- may be seen as a cheap alternative 'to proper teaching';
	- can be expensive to design and produce;
	- teacher feed back could be infrequent;
	- can be difficult to maintain student motivation;
	- feeling of isolation and lack of peer group support
	- may be regarded as "second-best";
	- students may need access to a computer;
	- poorly designed materials.
Summary:	- the only option in some situations but tutorial support is often needed.

3.3.4 One-to-One (Coaching)

What is it	- the teacher and the student working together on a one-to-one basis which may be the full teaching strategy, say on a ward, or part of another teaching strategy, say demonstration followed by individual practice.
When is it used	- in all spheres of learning.
Examples:	- during lessons, IT, in a workshop as part of a practical.
Guidelines:	- it is tempting to be unplanned for one-to-one work. You need to consider the learning objectives, likely stumbling blocks, what to assess, when to give feedback, how to record progress, encourage reflection.

Advantages:	- individual attention;
	- opportunity to observe individual problems;
	- chance for student to question you about their concerns.
Disadvantages:	- time consuming;
	- expensive;
	- may be intimidating for shy students.

In a one-to-one situation the teaching is tailored to meet the individual students needs and abilities and to accommodate the difference between students.

There are unique differences in the way people learn and we must recognise this and not regard individuals as one group or body of students.

It is important to look for differences which affect learning. Sometimes these differences can be grouped into categories of a similar nature, e.g. experience, knowledge and skill but recognising the variety and range of individual differences is more important than categorising them. Being aware of them means that we can try to accommodate them in our teaching.

Individual Differences Between Students

- Using words: students differ in their abilities to use words with understanding and fluency. Verbal ability affects understanding of how to set about a task.

- Using numbers: number skills vary in accordance with ability to use numeric rules and with mental capacity.

- Remembering: varies in both ability to recall and reorganise material. Some students are better at remembering what they see, others at what they see and hear.

- Reasoning: often there are great variations in students capacities to solve problems and make decisions.

- Being creative: students have not only to solve problems, but the way in which they create original solutions by flexible thinking varies greatly.

- Achieving: students achieve at different rates.

- Studying: no-one studies in exactly the same way. Students all have styles of learning which they prefer and so use their own techniques to study.

- Using skills: apart from mental skills, students show great differences in mechanical abilities, in dexterity, in speed, precision and manipulative capacity, in co-ordination, in reaction times and in spatial ability, or the capacity to deal with relationships in different dimensions.

- Having interests: patterns of interest vary and are reflected in differing interests shown in training.

- Showing maturity: large variations are shown in the way in which students see themselves with objectivity, accept and show responsibility, believe their own worth, are active and curious, behave consistently with predictability and stability.

- Developing and holding attitudes: an important area especially in variations of students attitudes towards the value of the learning and behaviour in groups.

- Having motivation: probably the most important area of all, especially the degree to which students are self-motivated, rather than motivated by the teacher. Without adequate student motivation, little can be achieved.

- Showing perception: a lot of variation in individuals is shown in the area of differing student perception of the learning and the degree to which they attend to and select information.

- Seeing themselves: there is a wide range of personality variables, such as self-concept, need to achieve, a degree of self-discipline, measure of conformity and compliance; all affect learning. There are marked differences between younger and older students who are more anxious, fearful of failure, self conscious and cautious, more careful and resistant to changes. Older students are more demanding of effective learning and often more critical of the teacher.

- Having different backgrounds: variations in social background, parental attitudes, previous experience, create differences in values and beliefs and can radically affect learning.

- Persisting: the amount of time students are prepared to work is important in deciding their likely degree of achievement. Perseverance is only one part of personal psychology which affects the potential of students. There are others, all significant in themselves and including such aspects as the degree of introversion or extroversion, neuroticism or stability, need for affiliation, desire for certainty, dogmatism, etc.

- Having needs: establishing needs through Needs Analysis is perhaps one of the first actions to be taken when designing learning programmes. Students may have needs in common with others but will also entertain varying personal goals and this affects their motivation.

The possible variations of individual differences can be enormous and in any one situation they can vary across a wide range but it is likely that the teacher will become sensitive to the individual's learning style as the teacher-student relationship develops.

The following checklist may be helpful.

Checklist for Leading a Tutorial 1:1 Session

Observer: _____   Teacher Observed: _____   Date: _____

Course: _____   Subject: _____   No of Students: _____

Make comments upon the following aspects. Other aspects to be added as necessary.

		Aspect	Comment
Preparation		Setting goals for individuals	
		Planning work at correct level (not too easy/difficult)	
		Task sheets provided with attractive layout	
		Relevance of work to individual needs	
		Planned week-to-week progression	
Implementation	Introduction	Goals communicated to individual(s)	
		Student(s) motivated appropriately	
		Negotiation with student(s) regarding how to achieve goals	
	Development	Appropriate time spent with student(s)	
		Asking questions as opposed to answering them	
		Ensures that an acceptable result is achieved	
		Variety takes place for the student	
		Progress regularly reviewed	
	Conclusion	Feedback provided for student(s)	
		Records completed kept as appropriate	
		Appropriate goals set for next session	
Feedback		Appropriate praise provided for students(s)	
		Student(s) clear about performance achieved	
		Student(s) knows how to improve	
Others		Other (please state)	

4. Evaluation of Teaching Strategies

Improvement in your use of teaching strategies can come from better preparation but this is only a small part of the process. Your effectiveness in the use of the strategies can be achieved through (a) introspection involving you thinking about what you have done after the event, (b) asking a colleague to sit in with you and comment on your approaches, (c) using 'micro-teaching' where you teach a topic to a group of colleagues and they critically analyse what has taken place (this is often video recorded), or (d) asking students what they think of your approaches. Each of these will benefit from some sort of preparation; preparing a questionnaire for the observer(s) to complete; asking specific questions at the end of the lesson; or recording through either sound or video tape, what has taken place. This preparation will provide you with evidence or data upon which you can make judgments and decisions about what changes you might make. This, then, is the process of evaluation.

4.1 Deciding upon what to evaluate

It is all too easy for you to say that you want to improve your teaching and to look at too many things all at once. It is important that you decide the particular aspects that you want to improve and to concentrate upon those particular aspects at a specific time. You might want to improve a particular teaching strategy such as question and answer, or an introduction or conclusion to a session. You then need to prepare an instrument to ensure that you collect the information, or data, that you require in order that you can make the appropriate evaluative judgements.

The questions that you might want to find answers to include:

(i)   How can I improve my technique with ... (a specific teaching strategy)?

(ii) How can I improve the interaction of my students?

(iii) What is the effectiveness of my introductions/conclusions to my sessions?

(iv) How well do my students learn?

4.2 Data Collection

One of the easiest methods of collecting data is to audio-record, say, a question and answer part of your lesson, or an introduction to a lesson or a conclusion. The recording will give you specific data upon which to work. For instance, for a question and answer session you can find the following:

(a)   the total number of questions that were asked;

(b)   the number of questions that were open to all the class to answer and the number of questions that nominated a particular student to answer;

(c) whether you nominated a student to answer either before or after asking the question;

(d) the number of knowledge and the number of thinking questions;

and so on. The recording provides the evidence for finding out answers to the questions that you have planned. It might be useful to assist with the analysis of the data to make a transcript of either the whole or part of the recording.

Questionnaires to students can also form useful data upon which to make your judgments. The method of questionnaire design is discussed in Chapter 8, but Figure 3.14 gives an example of a questionnaire to be given to students to evaluate your explanations, Figure 3.15 your discussion, Figure 3.16 your demonstration, and Figure 3.17 your lecturing. The design of each of the questionnaires is slightly different and you should decide which you prefer and which will most likely give you the type of information that you require.

The Explanation guide (Figure 3.14) uses the principle that every explanation should have an introduction and conclusion and that the key aspects of the explanation should be stated and easily identified. It requires the students to answer yes or no (or not observed) and, in consequence is easy, and does not take much time, to complete.

The Explanation Guide

Please mark each aspect below with a 'Yes' or a 'No' or 'Not Observed'.

1. Introduction

    (a) The opening gained and held my attention.

    (b) The opening established rapport.

    (c) The opening told me what was to follow.

    (d) The opening said what was to be expected of me.

2. Key Points

    (a) The key points were clearly expressed.

    (b) The examples amplified the key points.

    (c) The examples added interest to the explanation.

    (d) The timing enabled me to understand the points.

3. The Summary

    (a) The summary brought together the key points

    (b) The conclusions were clearly stated.

Figure 3.14 Explanation Guide for Student Completion

The Teacher's Role in Leading a Discussion

Instructions to students:

Think back to the discussion we have just had and try to recall the role of the teacher in it. Examine each of the following statements and rate each one from 1 to 6 in terms of truthfulness. If you think that the statement is completely true then ring (1). If you think that it is completely untrue then ring (6). Ring numbers in between if you rate the statement as being somewhere between these opposites.

1.	The teacher explained the discussion task clearly.	1 2 3 4 5 6
2.	The teacher asked questions which encouraged group members to talk freely.	1 2 3 4 5 6
3.	The teacher did not interrupt constantly but listened.	1 2 3 4 5 6
4.	The teacher did not try to appear to be superior to the views expressed.	1 2 3 4 5 6
5.	The teacher encouraged the group to describe their own experiences when appropriate.	1 2 3 4 5 6
6.	The teacher attempted to involve each group member.	1 2 3 4 5 6
7.	The teacher did not show irritation with a particular viewpoint.	1 2 3 4 5 6
8.	The teacher did not force own views on the group.	1 2 3 4 5 6
9.	When desired,, the teacher gave information/shared experiences.	1 2 3 4 5 6
10.	The teacher allowed unpopular as well as popular views to be expressed.	1 2 3 4 5 6
11.	At the end, the teacher gave members of the group the opportunity to offer their own conclusions	1 2 3 4 5 6

Figure 3.15 Student Rating Schedule for Teacher's Role in Discussion

Rating Scale for Demonstration

Name: Group:

Topic: Date: :

Key: T = Transmission
        E = Emphasis
        V = Variation
        M = Meaningfulness

T1	Skilful performance by demonstrator.	Good	1 2 3 4 5	Poor	
T2	All equipment available.	All	1 2 3 4 5	Some	
T3	Equipment visible to all students.	All	1 2 3 4 5	Some	
T4	Clarity of commentary	Clear	1 2 3 4 5	Poor	
E1	Attention directed at specific points.	Clear	1 2 3 4 5	Confusing	
E2	Well paced step by step procedure	Good	1 2 3 4 5	Too	Fast Slow
E3	Use of Q & A for emphasis	Effective	1 2 3 4 5	Poor	
V1	Variation in student activity	Good	1 2 3 4 5	Too	much little
V2	Variation in teacher activity	Good	1 2 3 4 5	Too	little much
M1	Integration of demonstration with other subject matter.	Good	1 2 3 4 5	Disjointed	
M2	Involvement of students with other subject matter.	Good	1 2 3 4 5	Too	much little
M3	Best method of teaching the topic.	Suitable	1 2 3 4 5	Not suitable	
M4	Use of Q & A or other method to evaluate the learning	Effective	1 2 3 4 5	Poor	

Figure 3.16 Rating Scale for Demonstration

Feedback from Students
Lecture Rating Schedule

This questionnaire has been designed to inform me of your opinions concerning my presentation. They will be useful to me when giving future presentations. Please indicate your present thoughts by means of a mark on the 5 point scale below. For example, if you found the lecture quite interesting, you will show this as follows:

Interesting   1 ② 3   4   5   Boring

Use the reverse side of the sheet for additional written comments

The Lecturer

Clearly audible	1	2	3	4	5	Inaudible
Lively	1	2	3	4	5	Monotonous
Too fast	1	2	3	4	5	Too slow
Pleasant Manner	1	2	3	4	5	Unpleasant Manner
Well organised	1	2	3	4	5	Muddled
Interprets ideas clearly	1	2	3	4	5	Leaves me confused
Stressed important point	1	2	3	4	5	All points seem the same
Good use of examples	1	2	3	4	5	Examples were confusing
Is up to date with subject	1	2	3	4	5	Not aware of latest developments
Explanations clear	1	2	3	4	5	Incomprehensible explanations
Lectures confidently	1	2	3	4	5	Not confident

Subject Matter

Difficult	1	2	3	4	5	Easy
Too much material	1	2	3	4	5	Nothing much in it
Vocationally useful	1	2	3	4	5	Waste of time
Interesting	1	2	3	4	5	Boring
I will do further study	1	2	3	4	5	I will not pursue it

Use of Audio Visual Material

OHP Transparencies easy to read	1	2	3	4	5	Illegible
Sufficient time to read transparencies	1	2	3	4	5	Insufficient time to read

Activity

Too many different lecturer activities	1	2	3	4	5	Not enough
Too many different student activities	1	2	3	4	5	Not enough

Figure 3.17 Student Lecture Rating Schedule

The design of each of the questionnaires is based on the questions that are required to be answered. The data is provided by the students in answering the range of questions.

Data Analysis

The summation of the data can be achieved by taking a blank questionnaire and, on it, placing slash marks beside each question as to how the individuals have responded. Summation of the slash marks will give the overall response of the group.

The data from the questionnaires can be analysed by looking at the summation of all of the responses and finding those aspects that are very positive and those that are very negative. These, then, give the good aspects, those that should be kept, and the poor aspects, those that should be changed.

> *Possible evidence to show that you have achieved the competence 'Manage learning situations'*

1. (a) Choose one of your classes and relate the students and their needs to suitable learning activities and justify the choice of teaching strategy used.

   (b) Indicate your role in managing the learning situation.

   (c) Show how you have used a variety of teaching strategies.

2. State the techniques that you have used to ensure that your students have adopted a positive attitude to their learning.

3. Design a questionnaire for your students to answer to evaluate a specific aspect of your teaching. Give the questionnaire to a group of students to collect data, analyse the results by summating their responses and draw conclusions about what are:

   (a) the good aspects that you might accentuate in future;

   (b) the poorer aspects that you might consider changing.

Possible Evidence

Progress Check

*If you want to check your understanding of
managing learning activities,
try the following progress check*

Progress Check 3.2

1. Choose two strategies that are used with large groups and indicate, for each:

    (a) its advantages;

    (b) its limitations;

    (c) the main aspects of its preparation;

    (d) the main aspects of its presentation.

2. Choose two strategies that are used with small groups and indicate, for each:

    (a) its advantages;

    (b) its limitations;

    (c) the main aspects of its preparation;

    (d) the main aspects of its presentation.

3. Choose two strategies that are used with individual study and indicate, for each:

    (a) its advantages;

    (b) its limitations;

    (c) the main aspects of its preparation;

    (d) the main aspects of its presentation.

4. What are the possible methods of evaluating your effectiveness using the lecture method of teaching?

Further Reading and References

Further reading and references relating to the topics in this chapter can be found in the following:

Brown, G. (1975)   *Micro-teaching: A programme of teaching skills,* Methuen.

Brown, G. (1987)   *Lecturing Styles* in Engineering Design Education, Spring 1987

Brown, G. and   *Effective Teaching in Higher Education.* Methuen.
Atkins, M. (1988)

Dewey, J. (1933)   *How we think: A restatement of the relation of reflective thinking
                                     and the education process,* D. C. Heath, New York.

Eggen, P. D. and   *Strategies for Teachers*, Prentice Hall.
Kanchak, D. P. (1988)

Gage, N. L. and   *Educational Psychology*, Rand McNally.
Berliner, D. C. (1983)

Gibbs, G. Habeshaw, S.   *53 Interesting Things to do in your Lectures*, Technical and
and Habeshaw, T. (1988)   Educational Services.

Gibbs, G. and Habeshaw, T.   *253 Ideas for Teaching*, Technical and Educational Services.
(1988)

Gibbs, G. and   *Teaching Large Classes in Higher Education.* Kogan Page.
Jenkins, A. (1992)

Habeshaw, S. Habeshaw, T.   *53 Interesting Things to do in your Seminars and Tutorials*,
and Gibbs, G. (1984)   Technical and Educational Services.

Habeshaw, S. Gibbs, G. and   *53 Problems with Large Classes.* Technical and Educational Services
Habeshaw, T. (1992)   Ltd.

Heathcote, G. et al. (1981)   *Curriculum Styles and Strategies*, FEU.

Jenkins, A. (1992)   *Break up your Lectures.* Teaching and Learning Vol 8. Kogan Page

Joyce, B. and Weil, M.   *Models of Teaching*, Prentice Hall.
(1986)

Jacobsen, D. Eggen, P.   *Methods for Teaching: A skills approach*, Charles E. R. Merrill
et al. (1981)   Publishing Co.

Keller, F. S. and   *The Keller Plan Handbook: Essays on a personalised system of
Sherman, J. G. (1974)   instruction.*

Neill, A. S. (1960)   *Summerhill: a radical approach to child rearing*, Hart Publishing.

PCFC, (1992)   *Teaching More Students*. PCFC.

Perrott, E. (1982)   *Effective Teaching: A practical guide to improving your teaching*, Longman.

Race, P. (1992)   *53 Interesting ways to Write Open Learning Material*, Technical and Educational Services.

Reece, I. and   *A Practical Guide to the Overhead Projector and Other Visual Aids*.
Walker, S. (1995)   Business Education Publishers.

Rogers, J.(ed) (1978)   *Adults in Education*, BBC.

Walkin, L. (1990)   *Instructional Techniques and Practice*, Stanley Thornes.

Chapter 4

Learning Aids

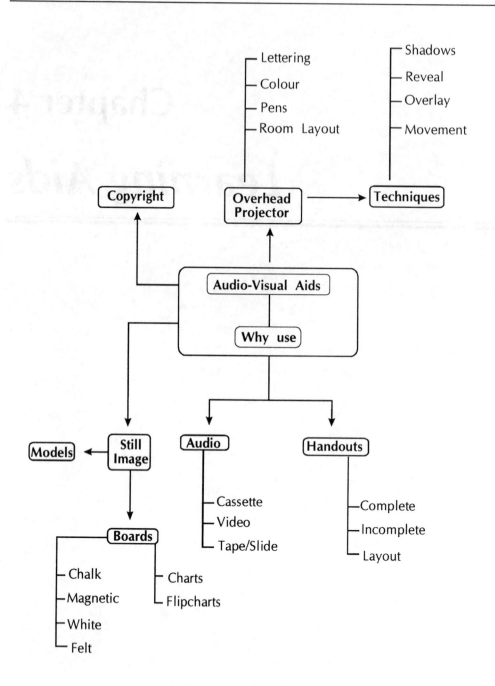

Overview of Chapter 4

Competences Related to this Chapter

The teacher competences and associated performance criteria related to this chapter are:

Major Competence - '*Produce, Use and Evaluate Learning Resources*'

Competence	Performance Criteria
1. Establish a basis for choosing learning aids.	(a) Classify learning aids. (b) Identify the principles of using learning aids. (c) Use or adapt the environment to optimise the use of learning aids.
2. Use board aids properly.	(a) Establish advantages and limitations of six types of board aids. (b) Design appropriate layouts for use on board aids.
3. Use handouts appropriately.	(a) Classify different types of handout. (b) Establish principles for handout design. (c) Produce and use effective handouts for student use.
4. Use the overhead projector (OHP) appropriately.	(a) Design clear and useful transparencies for the OHP. (b) Use the projector in a way to promote learning.
5. Select, adapt or construct learning resources for a specific programme.	(a) Identify factors which affect choice of visual aids. (b) Consider production and duplication costs, type of audience and content in choice of aids.
6. Evaluate the use of learning resources.	(a) Establish and meet criteria for evaluating the effectiveness of chosen resources. (b) Evaluate learning resources used in relation to established criteria and cost of production and use.

FENTO Standards

FENTO Standards Related to this Chapter

B.	**Planning and Preparing Teaching and Learning Programmes for Groups and Individuals**
b2	Identify appropriate teaching and learning techniques
b3	Enhance access to and provision in learning programmes
C.	**Developing and Using a Range of Teaching and Learning Techniques**
c1	Promote and encourage individual learning
c2	Facilitate learning in groups
c3	Facilitate learning through experience
D.	**Managing the Learning Process**
d2	Plan and structure learning activities
d3	Communicate effectively with learners
d5	Select and develop resources to support learning
E.	**Providing Learners with Support**
e2	Provide effective learning support
H.	**Meeting Professional Requirements**
h1	Work within a professional value base
h2	Conform to agreed codes of professional practice

Based on the FENTO Draft standards by kind permission

1. What are Learning Aids and Resources?

In Chapter 1, we defined a resource as "a support to teaching strategies which assists learning". We also discussed the use of the different types of board (chalk, white and flipchart), handouts and OHP transparencies. In this Chapter, using a spiral curriculum, we want to return to the topic of aids and resources, to expand upon what we described earlier to include a fuller range of resources and discuss the principles of choice of aids and to evaluate their use. You are also referred to Reece and Walker (1995).

Learning aids use all of the five senses. They use "hearing" through audio aids (like the cassette recorder), "sight" through visual aids like charts and posters and printed resources like handouts and books, "touch" through resources like specimens and models, and also, to a lesser extent, "taste" and "smell" in, for example, cookery. Also, more than one sense can be combined in a visual aid such as a film or a tape-slide presentation which combine both hearing and sight. Thus, anything that you use to augment your teaching or learning strategy, or anything that you get your students to use, can be termed a learning aid or a resource.

There is a great range of resources available to you as a teacher. Some are indicated in Figure 4.1. You should consider (a) those that you have used, (b) those that you have not used and (c) those that you would like to use.

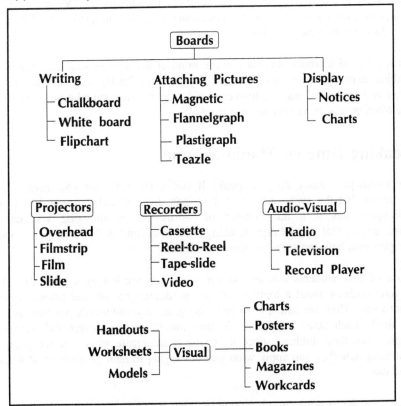

Figure 4.1   Range of Available Resources

1.1 Reasons for Using Learning Aids and Resources

Effective use of aids can really enhance your students' learning experience. Inspection reports, like those produced by FEFC, are a rich source of advice and such reports often link poor learning with the failure to use visual aids and similarly link effective learning to the professional use of well designed visual aids. This link tends to be implicit rather than explicit. There is little doubt that use of more than one sense, for example both sight and sound, enhances understanding and memory. As long as you do not overload your students' sensory input, then the more senses you use the better.

If you consider the traditional methods of teaching, the lecturer standing in front of the class talking, then the main sense the students are using is hearing. Psychologists tell us that only about 12 per cent of what we learn comes in this way. In comparison, they also tell us that 75 per cent of what we learn comes through what we see. Thus, six times more of what we learn is through sight than through listening. This, in itself, has implications for the range of teaching strategies that you use. Do you provide six times the opportunity for learning by sight as you do for learning through listening? Do you use visual pictures to accompany what you say? The television news is a good example of the use of pictures to associate with the spoken word. During the news there are invariably either picture stills associated with the news item, or, more often, video recordings of what is being talked about. Rarely do we only see the newscaster alone on the screen. Even when we do, there is often a still picture depicting the story in the background. Because of the media such as TV, radio, magazines and so on, students are used to the more sophisticated presentation and productions and you, as a teacher, have to compete with this.

It is said that all good learning aids start in the mind of the teacher with the idea of putting over the subject matter in the most convenient way to make the learning easy and interesting for both you and your students. Audio visual aids can be very stimulating to students and provide the often necessary variety to your teaching.

1.2 Speaking Time vs. Thinking Time

How many words per minute do you speak? If you speak very fast you might reach 200 words per minute but the average is much less than that - usually around 150 words per minute. Compare this with the number of words per minute that you can think. Psychologists tell us that the average thinking time is around 800 words per minute. So, there is a *differential* between *speaking time* and *thinking time*.

Consider one of your students listening to you when you are having a good day. You are talking to your students about a topic which has particular interest and relevance to them: they are motivated. They are listening to you talking at, say 160 words per minute but their minds can think much faster than that. So they are filling the differential between *your* speaking speed and *their* thinking speed by trying to anticipate what you are going to say next, by thinking how they can apply what you are saying in their projects or at work. That is on a good day.

Now consider one that is not so good. You are talking to them, for too long perhaps, about a topic which holds little interest to them and it is approaching lunch time, it is hot and they are hungry and thirsty. They start to listen to you but then say to themselves "What use is this to me? I will never use this topic." So they listen for a minute then their minds wander. "What shall I have for lunch? Shall I go to the canteen or just buy a sandwich at the snack bar?" They tune back in to you and realise that you are still on with the same boring topic. Their minds start to wander again. "What shall I do tonight. Shall I take my girl/boy friend to the cinema? What shall we do after we have been to the cinema?" This is a voyage upon which there is no return. The next thing that they hear is you saying "Thank you very much. I will see you next week" and the other students are putting their books together and leaving.

People *can* do two things at once. They can listen to you *and* they can do something else while they fill the differential between speaking and thinking speeds. The skill in teaching requires that you fill that differential for your students in a meaningful manner so that they are using the differential to further concentrate upon the topic. This is the place for visual aids. You can provide students with a handout which they can relate to whilst you are talking or, even better, provide them with an incomplete one which they can fill in whilst listening to you. You can get them to take their own notes, draw a diagram during a demonstration or some other activity which will allow some of the differential between the two speeds to be filled.

2. Preparation of Learning Aids

Well designed learning aids should:

1. *promote perception:* by adding senses there is greater likelihood that the learner will perceive what is intended;

2. *promote understanding:* with greater perception there is likely to be greater understanding;

3. *help reinforcement:* when you use learning aids to supplement your spoken words, as they are invariably, there is more likelihood of repetition and reinforcement. The reinforcement can be both during the teaching (for example with a chalkboard) and after it has taken place (for instance reading from a handout);

4.   *aid retention:*   as we said in Chapter 1, an important aspect of memory is repetition (remember learning your telephone number?). So, repetition leads to retention;

5.   *motivate and arouse interest:*   as your students use more than one of their senses when you use visual aids, you are more likely to arouse their interest;

6.   *provide variety in learning:*   the use of visual aids not only provides repetition, but repetition using a different medium. Hence the provision is more varied;

7.   *make effective use of time:*   as students are more motivated and show greater interest, then more effective use will be made of the time they spend learning.

Visual aids should be:

1.   simple;

2.   to the point;

3.   interesting.

An excellent visual aid is the map of the London Underground

- it is simple
- it makes good use of colour
- it is not accurate (in a geographical sense) but *representative*.

It does take time to make a good visual aid, but it will repay itself.

2.1 Room Requirements

Having made and designed appropriate visual aids, it is necessary to show them to their best advantage, through the appropriate positioning of tables, chairs, desks and equipment.

In order to motivate your students and allow them to concentrate upon their subject matter, you need to have a room that is :

- comfortable and quiet as possible;
- the right size for the number of students you have;
- adequately ventilated;
- acoustically good; and
- there should be no direct sunlight.

To apply these principles you should be able to move desks or tables about, have curtains or blinds at the windows, some covering on the floor, and chairs that are comfortable.

Your organisation of the room should depend on the number of students that you have. Figure 4.2 shows an optimum arrangement for up to 20 students, Figure 4.3 for between 20 and 30 and Figure 4.4 for more than 30

Figure 4.2 Rectangular Table for up to 20 Students

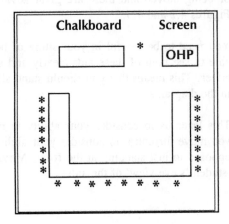

Figure 4.3 U-Shaped Arrangement for up to 30 Students

The arrangements shown in Figures 4.2 and 4.3 have the advantage that students have eye contact with each other. Consequently, with a relatively small class size, you can easily use question and answer and whole group discussion and the students will be able to see and hear what others are saying.

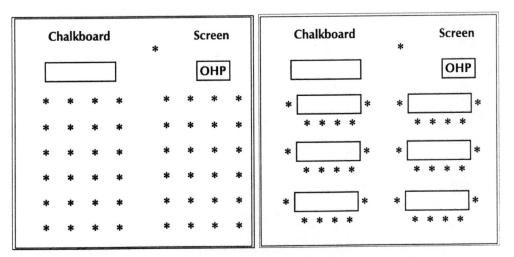

Figure 4.4   Theatre or School-Type Seating for larger Audiences

The arrangements shown in Figure 4.4 are, in effect, for lectures when the passage of information is from you, the teacher, to the students. The audience is too large for any meaningful interaction to take place and, in consequence, it does not matter that students are not able to see each other.

Each of the room layout diagrams have shown 'formal' arrangements. However, you will realise that many rooms are used as multi-functional accommodation, requiring a formal setting on one occasion and an informal one on another. Usually, desks or tables are capable of being moved and there are great advantages in the less formal arrangements shown in Figures 4.2 and 4.3.

You need to be careful in your siting of both a chalkboard and a screen. Students must be able to see both of these aids clearly and so your position must not obscure their vision of either. This means that you should stand slightly behind the overhead projector, as we show in the diagrams.

This leads us to consider your ability to move about the classroom. It is important, when you move furniture, to consider your ability to move freely about the whole of the room as opposed to just standing at the front. Moving to the back of the class allows you to have a 'student's eye view' of the aids.

> ## *Possible Evidence to Show You have Achieved the Competence 'Establish a Basis for Choosing Learning Aids'*

The type of evidence that you might collect to show that you have achieved the competence involves:

(a)   State the learning aids that you:

   (i)   already use; and

   (ii)   would like to use under the following headings:

   boards;
   projectors;
   recorders
   visual.

(b)   For a lesson plan that you have designed:

   (i)   decide which aids will assist learning;

   (ii)   state why you will use them.

State why you have chosen a particular type of test question.

Possible Evidence

Progress Check

> *If you want to check your understanding of your role in establishing a basis for choosing learning aids, try the following progress check*

Progress Check 4.1

1. State three different types of learning aid under the following headings:

   (a) Boards;

   (b) Projectors;

   (c) Recorders;

   (d) Visual.

2. Give at least SIX important aspects that well designed learning aids should achieve in the teaching and learning environment.

3. How many words per minute are, on average associated with:

   (a) speaking; and

   (b) thinking.

4. Give the advantages and limitations of three different types of room layout, stating, in each case, the size of group for which the layout is most appropriate.

3. Boards

Boards are probably the most popular and most used of all visual aids. The are quick and easy to use and are available in 99% of teaching accommodation. However, they are probably the most *misused* as well. It is all too easy to jot hurried notes on them; complete a quick sketch; or to place student responses to questions on them. To use them well, however, you need to plan carefully and be neat when using them.

There are several types of board in use: Chalkboard, Whiteboard, Feltboard, Magnetic board, and Flipchart.

Boards are in widespread use because of their advantages:

- always available
- easy to alter and amend work;
- versatile - suits any subject;
- colour is able to be used;
- simple;
- cheap;
- students can see the build-up of diagrams;
- easily cleaned;
- no special equipment required;

The disadvantages are few:

- many people have a tendency to 'talk to the board' as they write;
- you cannot see the students as you write;
- your writing needs to be larger than normal;
- if your presentation is unplanned it can be untidy;
- your notes on the board do not provide a permanent record.

You should remember that what you put on the board tends to go into your students notes in the same form. If your writing or drawing is untidy, if you have not drawn parallel lines when they should be parallel, if you have got half incomplete rubbing out, how can you expect your student's work to be neat and accurate.

At various times during the lesson, it is useful to go to the back of the room to make sure that your writing and drawings are visible to all of the class, that your writing does not drop towards the right hand side and that you have no spelling mistakes. It is only really from the rear of the class that you can get a true indication of the worth of your chalkboard work.

3.1 Chalkboard

Chalkboards tend be either rollerboards or fixed boards. Coloured chalk is very useful but make sure that the colours you use are visible. The main drawback of the chalkboard is that you, and your belongings, tend to be covered in dust - even with dustless chalk.

You can rotate the roller-board around top and bottom rollers. This has the advantage that it increases the amount of space that you have available through the up and down movement, as well as you being able to push up what you have just written to make it more visible to students. Also, you do not obscure what you have already written when you put more writing onto the board. A further advantage is that the height of the board can be adjusted to suit your own size. The advantage of the rollerboard type is that it can be made just the right height for you to be able to write on. This right height is your eye level. If you write at eye level, and walk along the board as you write, your lines should be straight and not drooping towards the end in an arc as you stretch.

However a corresponding fault of this type of board is that, when you rotate it, some of the writing that you have just completed goes over the back of the board and is obscured from the view of the students. You must be careful to avoid 'losing' important material in this way.

For difficult shapes you can use a template made from card or plywood. For some diagrams you can prepare the board using the 'pounce' method. First you draw the diagram (or a pattern of it) on paper and put small holes in the outline. Then before the lesson, you fix the paper pattern to the board and 'pat' the outline with the board duster so that when the pattern is removed it reveals an outline of dots that you can see but the students cannot. At the appropriate time during the lesson you can join up the dots to give the required, accurate outline.

Chalkboards are usually either black or green and probably the most effective colour of chalk on this background is *not* white as might be expected, but yellow. However, as we said in Chapter 1, the use of colour for highlighting and drawing distinctions between different aspects is very useful so long as you do not overdo it.

3.2 Whiteboard

Whiteboards are becoming more popular and are tending to replace chalkboards. They are used for exactly the same purpose and the principles of their use are the same. However, they are clean, bright and look modern. They have better visibility than the chalkboard especially when you use colour as they are more like a book with dark print on a white background. Additionally the white background gives the classroom a brighter atmosphere compared to the black of the chalkboard. Beware! you must use a drymarker - that is a non permanent pen. You can also use whiteboards as OHP screens but you must be careful of any glare that might be produced from the bright light. Many whiteboards have a steel backing which means they can be used as a magnetic board as well and we will discuss their use later. Writing on whiteboards tends to be more difficult than on chalkboards because there is less surface resistance. It is a little like using a ballpoint pen for the first time when you have been used to a fountain pen. You will find that the pens tend to 'flow' over the surface of the board. 'Poor' writers therefore tend to be even poorer when using a whiteboard. If you have not used one before, have a practise before you use it in front of a class of students.

3.3 Magnetic board

The great advantage of magnetic boards is that you can use them to depict movement. For instance, consider teaching a group of naval students how to dock three or more navy ships in harbour. What better way than making models of ships and sticking magnets to them, drawing the outline of the coast and harbour on a magnetic board, showing the movement of the ships in formation and the required docking procedures.

You should not just use the magnetic board when you want to show movement. You could cut out pictures from magazines or outlines could be cut from coloured card. Stick magnetic tape to the undersides, for display on the board. For example consider the concept formation of herbs in a horticulture class. You could cut out magazine pictures of basil, dill, parsley, rosemary, thyme, and marjoram and display them randomly with lettuce, tomato, cucumber and turnip. You can then ask your students to classify them into herbs and non-herbs.

3.4 Feltboard

This is the 'poorman's' magnetic board. It is less fashionable now due to the more widespread use of magnetic boards but was used a lot to depict movement. It operates on the same principle as your child's 'Fuzzyfelt' farm animals and consists of two pieces of felt, one of which is background and the other is the shape, which will stick together. The more modern version uses 'Velcro'.

4. Charts

Charts make an attractive display in a teaching base room. You can cover all of the walls with materials which are of interest and are informative to the students. You can make changes regularly depending upon the stage of the course you have reached. As the topic changes, the charts change. Charts form a useful, often colourful display.

Figure 4.5 shows a different type of chart; notices to be placed at strategic points to indicate the location of the class for the first meeting. You can make these colourful and with interesting shapes so that they catch the eye of the passer-by.

We have already said that charts should be regularly changed so that they maintain impact. They need therefore to be stored until they are required for the next class. Ideally they need to be kept flat and out of sunlight. Alternatively, roll them up and place them safely in a cupboard.

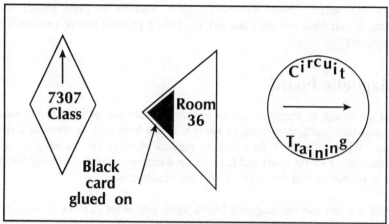

Figure 4.5   Notice for the First Class Meeting

4.1 Flipcharts

Flipcharts are essentially large pieces of paper placed on a stand and used instead of a white, or chalk, board. After the initial investment in the easel/stand, the flipchart:

- is low cost as you only need the paper and pens;
- is simple to use, and when one piece of paper is full, you just take another sheet;
- is easy to transport from one location to another;
- is unlikely to go wrong as there are no working parts or electricity required;
- can be used with charts, diagrams, and so on or whatever you wish to draw;
- is suitable for use with photos or colour pictures as 'stick-ons';
- allows you to use the reveal technique by sticking pieces of paper over the parts that are not to be seen straight away and then peeling them off as required;
- can be prepared before the lesson so that you can take your time over neatness;
- can be semi-prepared so that you can complete it during the lesson. You can prepare using feint pencil (blue is best) and rule feint guidelines to help keep your writing level.

The disadvantages are that flipcharts are:

- bulky to transport (depending upon make);
- difficult to store;
- much smaller than a chalkboard which can be difficult to get used to.

It is a very flexible tool and especially useful if teaching away from your usual place.

With a prepared flip chart pad, you may find the writing on the next sheet showing through. If this is the case, have a blank sheet which you can place underneath the display sheet.

> *Possible Evidence to Show You have*
> *Achieved the Competence*
> *'Use Board Aids Appropriately'*

The type of evidence that you might collect to show that you have achieved the competence involves:

(a) State six types of board aids indicating, with reasons, which you have used and which you haven't used.

(b) State three advantages and three limitations of using THREE different types of board aids.

(c) With one of your classes, use TWO different types of board aid and, for each:

   (i) describe the layout that you have used;

   (ii) give reasons for your chosen design.

Possible Evidence

Progress Check

> *If you want to check your understanding*
> *of your role in using board aids*
> *appropriately, try the following progress check*

Progress Check 4.2

1. State six different types of board aids.

2. Give at least SIX important aspects that well designed learning aids should achieve in the teaching and learning environment.

3. State three advantages and three limitations of using THREE different types of board aids.

4. Why should charts be:

    (i)   displayed in teaching rooms; and

    (ii) changed frequently?

5. Handouts

Teachers vary in their views about handouts from 'essential' to 'the students file them and never read them'.

The copying of notes or diagrams from a chalkboard or OHP transparency is not usually effective use of class contact time. Class contact time is valuable and handouts are one means whereby this time can be saved. However, handouts take time to prepare and are relatively expensive. Consequently, once the decision has been taken to use handouts, you should ensure that they save class contact time.

Also, you should try to make them visually attractive and include some form of activity associated with them (for example incompleteness) so that your students have to use them. They should be 'user friendly' through the use of language and vocabulary that the students can understand. Sketches and drawings can replace a relatively large number of words. If you give instructions, ensure they are clear and correct - trial test them! If you have ring binder holes punched into the handouts, it will save a lot of noise and disruption as students try to borrow a hole punch in the lesson.

Handouts tend to be used a good deal. They can be used in a variety of ways:

- directly related to lesson content;
- supporting - to introduce the lesson;
- contain relevant (complex) formula;
- as a reading list;
- as a worksheet/jobsheet/operation sheet;
- information sheets - presenting rare or hard to find information.

There are different types of handout but all have one thing in common: they should help the student. *Information handouts* are used to provide students with data and facts. There are three main types:

Notes: these are directly related to the lesson content, for example the main points of a lesson;

Supporting: an introduction to a topic, definitions, complex formulae, graphs, tables and diagrams;

Reading lists: which can be related to the course as a whole or to an individual topic.

A *worksheet* is an incomplete handout which the student is expected to complete during or straight after the lesson. They can be used by individual students which economises the teacher's time allowing time for individual attention. They allow students to work at their own pace, in an independent manner.

Worksheets:

(i)   can save you repeating yourself especially if the students are working at different rates;

(ii) need to be foolproof or have been tried and tested.

There are several types of worksheet:

(i)   *Job Sheets*: which contain instructions or a specification so that a student can complete a piece of work. An example of a job sheet might be a specification for making a skirt or other article of clothing. Here the instructions are given so that students can complete the article on their own.

An alternative which can be completed by students is shown in the example in Figure 4.6. Completion can be achieved through inserting words in spaces left for the purpose for homework, through exposition as the lesson proceeds or by having an associated OHP transparency on which you can write in the appropriate words in the spaces as you go through each of the steps.

Plant Propagation
Hardwood Propagules

Significant points to be considered when preparing propagules.

1. Select only .... of the previous season's growth to form propagules.

2. Select wood where possible of about ...... thickness, preferably from the basal region.

3. Prepare the propagule by cutting it flat across the bottom ...., and at the top a slopping cut .... ensuring that any unripened wood is removed.

4. Each proagule should be about ...-... mm (. -8 inches) in length but try to make cuttings of equal size.

5. Dip the bottom end of the propagule in the ...., and tap gently to shake off any excess.

6. Make out a label in the prescribed way

| D A T E | Genus |
| | Specific Epithet |

7. Collect the propagules together and tie in bundles of .. .. .. together with the label

8. Insert the bundles of propagules in ... . where they can remain until the following spring when they can be lined out or inserted straight away.

200mm
8"
7"
6"
5"
100mm
4"
3"
2"
1"

Figure 4.6   Example Jobsheet - Incomplete Handout

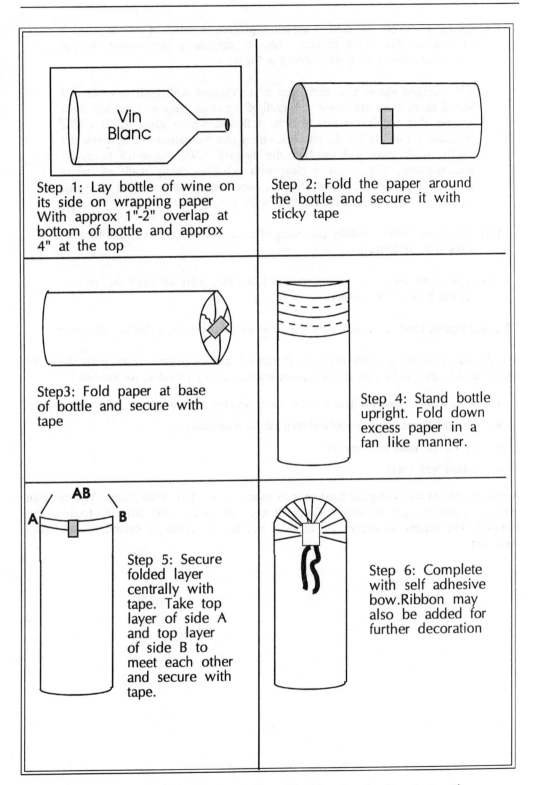

Step 1: Lay bottle of wine on its side on wrapping paper With approx 1"-2" overlap at bottom of bottle and approx 4" at the top

Step 2: Fold the paper around the bottle and secure it with sticky tape

Step3: Fold paper at base of bottle and secure with tape

Step 4: Stand bottle upright. Fold down excess paper in a fan like manner.

Step 5: Secure folded layer centrally with tape. Take top layer of side A and top layer of side B to meet each other and secure with tape.

Step 6: Complete with self adhesive bow.Ribbon may also be added for further decoration

Figure 4.7   Example Operation Sheet Showing Step-by-Step Instructions

(ii) *Operation Sheets*: are used to explain a process or series of operations such as how to take blood pressure, how to operate a photocopier, or the 'Decorative Bottle Wrapping' shown in Figure 4.7.

The example shows how each step is highlighted with both pictorial and verbal instructions associated with each of the steps. This seeming repetition ensures that the instructions can be followed where some students (the 'visualisers') will follow the pictures, others (the 'verbalisers') will follow the words, while most will use both the pictures AND the words to ensure understanding. The layout is clear with good use being made of 'white space'. Thus, after a demonstration (or even without one) students can work on their own to complete the Bottle Wrapping.

(iii) *Assignment Sheets*: usually consisting of a number of questions, problems or tasks to be performed;

(iv) *Experiment Sheets*: frequently used in laboratory work although the 'recipe' approach should be avoided.

Whatever type of handout is used, they should be well designed and checked for errors.

The danger of handouts is that they are distributed and the learner never reads them. To overcome this, the handout should have some learner activity included, for example:

- leave blanks - students have to listen for or find key facts/words etc.;
- give the learner time to read and then ask for a summary;
- or use questions and answers;
- follow with a test.

A valuable use of an incomplete handout is to issue it at the start of the lesson. You can then use it as a test of entry behaviour. Completion of the handout can form the focus of the learning. The student then uses the handout and has a permanent record of the issues discussed.

> *Possible Evidence to Show You have*
> *Achieved the Competence 'Use Handouts*
> *aids appropriately'*

The type of evidence that you might collect to show that you
have achieved the competence involves:

(a) Choose THREE different handouts that you have designed
and used with your students. For each of them:

   (i)   classify them into either worksheets or information
         handouts;

   (ii) describe how each of them was used in your lesson(s);
         and

   (iii) explain what students did with them.

(b) Explain the general design principles that you use when
making your handouts.

Possible Evidence

Progress Check

> *If you want to check your understanding of your role in using handouts appropriately, try the following progress check*

Progress Check 4.3

1. Define each of the following:

   (i) information handout;

   (ii) worksheet.

2. State at least FOUR different types of worksheet.

3. List at least three different types of student activity that might usefully be associated with their completion of a handout.

4. State at least THREE advantages of using handouts with students.

6. The Overhead Projector (OHP)

When to use an OHP

The OHP is in widespread use and has been so for many years. It can be used in a number of ways:

- as a record of discussion through the noting of key points as the lesson proceeds;

- as a summary at the end of a lesson especially when objectives have been noted in the introduction. At the end these can then become a basis of a question and answer to see how much has been learned;

- to reproduce a chart or map or some other type of prepared material;

- to build up materials using an overlay technique;

- to develop an argument which is similar to the complex drawing above except that it contains key words or phrases;

- can be linked with incomplete handout as suggested in Figure 4.6 to ensure that students read and use the handout when they are completing it;

Merits and Limitations

Its *merits* include;

- it is readily available;
- can be used in daylight conditions;
- it is reliable;
- user can see the learners - observe reaction and behaviour;
- easy to store transparencies;
- OHT's (OverHead Transparencies) last a long time;
- can make own to suit exact needs; can be colourful;
- can show movement;
- high quality especially when using a photocopier (enlarge/reduce), or a computer.

The *limitations* include:

- can be noisy due to the fan which operates all of the time to cool the bulb;
- can generate heat/draught from the fan;
- needing a screen or light coloured wall onto which to shine the image. This can be a disadvantage when sun shines onto the image surface. The screen should not be placed in the direct light but a silver screen can be used where the daylight is strong.

6.1 Care of an OHP

Care needs to be taken with OHPs:

- do not move them when hot. This can damage the bulb;

- do be careful of the cable so that you or your students do not;

- do not 'open' OHP to change the bulb unless the institution allows you (Health & Safety), and, if you do, ensure that it is switched off at the mains and the plug is removed;

- do not handle the bulb directly (use a soft cloth) as the grease from your fingers will cause a 'hot spot' on the glass from the intense heat that is produced;

The projector and screen should be positioned to avoid keystoning effect (where the image is wider at the top of the screen than it is at the bottom). This can be achieved by slanting the screen away from the wall at the top (see Figure 4.8). The keystone effect can be eliminated if the light beam projected by the OHP is at right angles to the screen.

Figure 4.8   Positioning of OHP to Avoid Keystoning

6.2 Using the OHP

When using the OHP:

- switch off when the image is not needed in order to reduce any possible distraction;

- keep out of the way of the image by standing to one side;

- use a pointer on the top of the OHP to indicate key points;

- give your students a chance to see the whole image before you start talking. This provides an 'advance organiser' for the students and can assist them in making their own notes;

- keep the caps on the OHP pens so that they do not dry up;

- don't mix up your transparencies - have a system. Pick up from left hand side - place on projector, remove and store on right hand side.

- try to involve the learners in your presentation of the transparencies. This might be achieved through question and answer, leaving spaces for either yourself or the students to complete, or just through expecting them to make their own notes;

- link with incomplete handouts as was suggested with Figure 4:6. This helps with the involvement of the students.

6.3 Transparency Design Principles

The following design principles for overhead projector transparencies are valuable:

- keep it simple, not too much detail;
- not too much information in words, nor too many drawings;
- one topic per transparency;
- design on plain paper before making the transparency;
- ensure there is a title on every transparency;
- put the main idea in the middle of the image;
- ensure an adequate space at each edge of the transparency;
- simple words - key words instead of sentences;
- not all upper-case - use both lower and upper case.

You should remember that the transparency should not transmit *all* of the information, but should "only" be a basis for reminding you of the important points of your exposition and an aid to students structuring their notes.

Skills in Making Transparencies

Making OHTs demands a whole new set of skills. If you are a good artist to begin with, then so much the better - you will already have a clear appreciation of design principles. But you do not need to be a good artist, there are many ways in which you can 'cheat' to produce a very professional effect.

Lettering may be achieved by:

- using computer or desk top publishing (make original on plain paper and use a photocopier with special OHT original). This produces a good quality but colour is not possible;

- dry letter e.g. *Letraset*. Good quality and available in colour. Letters and diagrams tend to age and crack;

- stencil - should be used with a drawing board. The quality is high but it can be time consuming;

- freehand using pens. Quality depends upon handprinting/handwriting but colour can easily be added;

- Remember that the size of lettering is important and the following can be used as a guide:

* 5 mm lettering seen from 10 metres max

* 10 mm lettering seen from 10-15 metres max

* 15 mm lettering seen from 15-20 metres max

Pens

Pens may be permanent (i.e. spirit based) or non-permanent (i.e. water based). These can be used as follows:

* Alterations may be made when you use spirit-based pens using an alcohol-based fluid or an OHP rubber/eraser;

* Water-based are easily changed. Unfortunately perspiration on hands removes the image. Ideal to have a permanent structure using spirit based pens and add temporary information using water based pens which may be removed before the OHP is used the next time.

Pens are available in various thicknesses:

* superfine - ideal for detail and lettering;
* fine;
* medium;
* broad - ideal for main headings;

You need to experiment with each and decide on the range which suits you. Special compasses are available if you wish to draw circles e.g. for pie charts. Templates are also available which help with drawing a wide variety of shapes. Highlighters are even available which have been especially designed for use on OHPs.

Colour often improves an OHT. It may be achieved using pens - (tends to be streaked) or with highlighters and colour film.

Colour Film

Colour film is material which can be cut to shape to colour areas on your transparency and is an alternative to colouring-in large areas with a pen. At first it appears to be expensive but it does seem to last a long time.

To colour an 'L' shape first draw the shape on an acetate sheet. Then roughly cut out a piece of colour film and stick it over the drawn 'L' shape. Finally, using a craft or stanley knife and a metal ruler, cut to the exact outline. The skill is using just the right pressure - to cut the colour film but not the transparency. Three colours on any transparency is sufficient.

Overlay Technique

Overlays help you to present complex issues. The base OHT is attached to a card frame and the overlaps can then be positioned. Masking tape gives a firm line whereas sellotape ages, bubbles and cracks. A maximum of 5 sheets is advised.

Overlay are ideal for: Bricklaying; Circuits (electrical/hydraulic); Maths solutions; Maps; Graphs; Chessboards, etc.

The example shown in Figure 4.9 indicates how you might design an overlay. You need to use a number of transparencies (two in the example). The first one (a) has the title and the first part to be shown (Part 1) while the second (b) has the addition of part 2. In designing the overlay it is an advantage if you draw the whole thing first on a piece of paper and then trace first part 1 (a) and then part 2 (b). The two (or as many as you have,) can then be hinged at the sides with masking tape to ensure that the parts fall over in place easily.

(a) **Showing Part 1**   (b) **Adding Part 2**

Figure 4.9 Transparency Overlay Technique

Reveal Technique

A reveal technique is where part of the transparency is initially shown, then a little more, and so on until all is revealed. A piece of tracing paper may be used to cover what you wish to reveal. Strips of card or paper may be used to mask lines or key sections or you may reveal area by area. As each section is revealed, it is explained, commented upon and applied to a specific situation The use of the reveal technique ensures that students concentrate on a particular aspect of the transparency at a particular time.

Transparency Storage

Storing OHTs need not be difficult. Card frames are very useful and special ring binders and boxes may be bought. You can write on the frames any notes you may wish to make.

A4 wallets/Sleeves are relatively cheap and have the advantage of having 'multiholes' so that they can be stored in a ring binder. Do remember to buy glass quality so that the image is projected through the wallet.

Silhouette Effect

The OHP can be used to produce shadows e.g. of a leaf, layout of a room cut in card, moving figures/mechanisms etc. This silhouette effect can be very impressive. Animation can be achieved e.g. clock with pointers. A most effective example is demonstrating magnetic fields using magnets and iron filings. Be certain to have a blank OHT on the projector first so that you can remove the iron filings.

As you make more use of the OHP and you develop expertise in making transparencies with both a pen and the computer, you learn some useful ideas. Some such ideas are:

(i)   You can highlight a word (or words) using a different coloured pen. However, if you put the colour on the reverse side it will stop the two colours interacting or 'bleeding'.

(ii)   Put the titles at the bottom of the page as opposed to the top.

(iii) Highlight titles, key words or phrases using boxes, or clouds, or thick borders, and so on.

(iv)   Bubble or graffite writing can be effective, particularly if the 'hollows' are filled with colour. The use of 'bubble' writing will highlight key words and headings.

(v)   When using colours it should be remembered that 'hot' colours advance, and 'cold' colours recede. This means words or phrases that you wish to stand out should use warm colours such as red, whereas background should be cold colours such as blue.

(vi) Landscape format allows 20% more writing, on average, than portrait format. However, you should consider the shape of the OHP lens when using landscape format for transparencies.

7. Other Techniques

7.1 Video

Videos are being used more and more in teaching. Unfortunately, this powerful medium is often used as a time-filler to keep the learners quiet for an hour. A video can be shown in daylight which means that students have the opportunity to take notes or complete handouts whilst watching.

Videos should be used with care and planning. You need to watch the video yourself prior to showing it to a class. From this initial showing you can highlight the main points. You might also design an associated (incomplete) handout to accompany it.

Interactive video is being used more and more but the high cost and solo use are drawbacks.

7.2 Audio materials

The radio can provide some excellent learning material, for example dealing with politics. The problems are fixed transmission time, no replay and fixed pace. These limitations may be overcome by taping the transmission and playing it back at a suitable time and stopping it where you want to.

7.3 Audio Cassettes

The use of audio cassettes, either made by you from a taped radio transmission, or bought specially for the purpose, allows you to: use material at any time; stop and start at own choice; replay; edit.

Audio cassettes are widely used for foreign language training and special language laboratories are used for the purpose, where students have their own headphones and can start and stop the tape themselves. This allows an activity to be built into the process where students can speak the foreign language and hear themselves using a playback facility. In these laboratories, the teacher can 'tune in' to any particular students and monitor their progress.

7.4 Tape Slide Programmes

The use of audio cassettes can be supplemented by 35mm slides so that the showing of the slides can have an accompanying commentary. The two can be synchronized so that a pulse on the tape will automatically change to the next slide.

Tape-Slide can be made by most people. It is relatively cheap.

The pictures may be taken by yourself or they may be bought.

This medium is ideal to recap on a visit to a factory, foreign location or field trip where you have taken slides which can be shown to the class to remind them of specific points.

7.5 Use of IT

Information Technology, particularly the use of computers has greatly enhanced the ability of the individual teacher to produce quality visual aids. Most teachers have access to a personal computer (PC) with a word processing package attached. This has resulted in much better production of handouts. The use of Desktop Publishing (DTP), is available in most organisations and an increasing number of teachers are familiar with its use.

> ### *Possible Evidence to Show You have*
> ### *Achieved the Competence*
> ### *'Use the Overhead Projector appropriately'*

The type of evidence that you might collect to show that you have achieved the competence involves:

(a) Choose THREE different overhead projector transparencies that you have used with your students. For each of them:

    (i)   state how you made them (e.g. drawn freehand, traced from books, what type of pens you used);

    (ii) describe how each of them was used in your lesson(s); and

    (iii) explain what students did with them.

(b) Explain the general design principles that you used when making your transparencies.

(c) Explain how you set up the room to use the overhead projector.

Possible Evidence

Progress Check

> *If you want to check your understanding of your role in using the overhead projector appropriately, try the following progress check*

Progress Check 4.4

1. List FOUR advantages and TWO limitations of the use of the overhead projector

2. List FOUR different ways in which the overhead projector might be used as a learning aid.

3. List at least FIVE principles of design of overhead projector transparencies.

4. Describe the difference between water and spirit-based overhead projector pens.

5. Explain at least TWO different techniques that you might use for the production of an overhead projector transparency.

6. Describe what is meant by 'reveal' and 'overlay' techniques.

8. Copyright

There is a tremendous amount of printed and recorded material available and some of it is ideal for teaching purposes. The use of photocopiers, video recorders have made it easy and cheap to make copies of these works. However, the need to protect copyright is important. Copyright law is a specialist area of law and, before making copies, you need to be clear about your right to do so. If you work for a college or training organisation you should be able to seek guidance from your management colleagues.

Briefly, copyright is a right given to or derived from work and not a right in the novelty of ideas. The types of materials included under copyright include:

- literary works, written and including written tables or compilations;
- music works;
- dramatic works;
- artistic works;
- sound recordings;
- films;
- broadcasts;
- published editions.

An exception to copyright is for 'fair dealing' which in this case means research or private study. You are allowed to make one copy of anything which is protected under copyright so long as it is only for your own research or your own private study. Also, you are allowed to copy part of a document, so long as it is *not a substantial part* of the work. This, however, is not very helpful to us as the definition of a 'substantial part' is open to interpretation. A substantial part could be 'the most vital part' of a book, the main thesis, even though in terms of volume, it is not a large proportion.

However, many colleges and institutions, through their Local Education Authorities, have a CLA (Copyright Licensing Agency) Licence which allows them to copy 'for immediate use in no more than one course of study in any academic year:

- up to one chapter or (if greater) 5% of a book
- up to the number of copies required for the personal use by each member of the class plus the teacher ...'

Clearly this scheme is of major benefit to us but, before using this process, you should ensure that your organisation is a member of the scheme and you should read the conditions very carefully.

9. Selection of Visual Aids

Having described some of the important design characteristics of a range of visual aids, it is necessary for you to select a particular type of aid for a specific purpose.

Unfortunately, like so many aspects of teaching, there are no definitive answers for the selection of a particular aid. The design of aids starts in your own mind. A good aid is one which does a particular job to assist in the learning of a particular topic for a particular group of learners. But all learners are different. So, what works for one group does not necessarily work with another. However, there are some general rules that you can use as a guide.

9.1 Factors Affecting Choice of Visual Aids

Some of the factors affecting the choice of visual aids are shown in Figure 4:10. First, the choice of a particular method will often dictate (or at least limit), the choice of aids. For example, if you decide to use a method involving group discussion and the sharing of experiences, then obviously the use of a one-direction medium such as a film would not be suitable as it limits the opportunity to exchange ideas. Secondly, the type of learning task facing the learner will eventually influence the choice of visual aid because it dictates the choice of teaching method. Thirdly, the special characteristics of some learners will also bear an influence on choice. For example it would be unrealistic to instruct a group of slow readers using handouts. Finally, the practical constraints, both administrative and economic, will limit the choice of methods and aids. It appears reasonable, therefore, to consider:

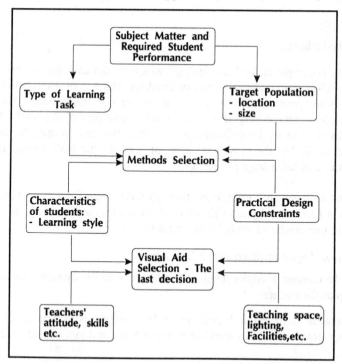

Figure 4.10   Factors Affecting the Choice of Visual Aids

- teaching methods;
- learners;
- type of learning;
- practical considerations; *and then*
- make decisions about visual aids.

Perhaps one further factor should be added to the list - and that is yourself. You may either love or hate using the overhead projector. If you hate it, you are unlikely to use it. Also you may have no training in its use and be afraid of it. Thus, you must have the skills to be able to use it properly.

Cost and Content Suitability

Figure 4.11 reviews the cost and content suitability for each of the main visual aids described in this chapter. These two selection tools can be used with some assurance that the 'right' visual aid is being selected if all factors are considered in making the decision.

Type of Aid	Production Costs	Duplication Costs	Type of Audience	Suitable Content		
				Cognitive	Affective	Motor
Handouts	Very low	Very low	Individual	Excellent	Fair	Good
Boards	Low	High	Group	Fair	Good	Poor
OHP	Mod Low	Low	Group	Fair	Fair	Fair
Film/ TV/video	High	High	Group or Individual	Good	Poor	Poor
Charts	Low	Low	Group	Fair	Poor	Poor
Work card	Low	Low	Individual	Fair	Poor	Good

Figure 4.11   Suitability Factors of Common Visual Aids

Possible Evidence

> *Evidence that you might collect to show that*
> *you have achieved the competence*
> *'Select, adapt or construct learning resources*
> *for a specific programme'*

(a) Identify and present a number (at least three) of lesson plans which use a range of learning resources.

Justify the choice of resources in relation to the objectives of the sessions.

(b) Identify the constraints and problems that might exist in the use of the chosen resources.

(c) State how you have shown an awareness of equal opportunities in the design or use of the resources (for example how you have considered all ranges of ability).

N.B. In collecting this evidence it is suggested that you use at least five different resources and that at least one of these should use information technology in its production.

If you want to check your understanding of your role in selecting, adapting or constructing learning resources for a specific programme try the following progress check

Progress Check 4.5

1. State how you would choose aids for a specific session.

2. For a chosen visual aid, indicate the process that you would go through to design it.

Progress Check

10. Evaluation of Aids

As with all of your teaching, it is important that you consider how to evaluate the aids that you use.

The checklist shown in Figure 4.12 on the next page will help you in considering the aspects that you might use to evaluate your design and use of aids. It should be completed through answering all of the 18 questions with either a 'YES', 'NO' or 'NOT APPROPRIATE'. If you have any answered with a NO, you should reconsider that aspect of the design, use, etc.

An alternative way to evaluate your aids is to ask students questions about their suitability, whether they assisted the learning, whether they appreciate them, and so on. Students are the ones for whom the aids are designed - they have to suit their needs.

Also you might ask colleagues what they think about your various aids. Indeed, it is useful in a department to have a pool of aids so that you can use each others' and file them in a central place. In this way the time taken in their design and production is shared.

Evaluation of Aids	YES	NO	N.A
Preview			
1. Have you checked in advance:			
(a) that you have not used too many aids?			
(b) that you have not used too few aids?			
(c) that your aids work?			
Presentation			
2. Can the aid be seen/heard?			
3. Is it used for too long/not long enough?			
4. Is it clear (does it aid learning)?			
Design			
5. Will it work (blackout, bulbs, leads)?			
6. Is there a logical sequence?			
7. Is the time for use about right?			
8 Can it be misinterpreted?			
9. Is there enough/too much variety?			
10. Is there enough/too much colour?			
11. Is it well made?			
Use			
12. Have you invited co-operation of the students?			
13. Does it attract attention?			
14. Have you decided how it will be introduced?			
15. Does it supplement verbal information?			
16. Does it hold attention?			
17. Is it challenging for the students?			
18. Does it consolidate learning?			

Figure 4.12 Checklist for the Evaluation of a Learning Aid

Possible Evidence

The type of evidence that you might collect to show that you have achieved the competence involves:

Design a visual aid for use in one of your classes and then make, use and evaluate it.

1. State the objectives that it will achieve, where it will be used and how it will assist in the learning process.

2. Use it with a class.

3. Evaluate its effectiveness through completion of the checklist in Figure 4.12.

4. Evaluate its effectiveness through its efficiency (for example time taken to prepare compared with increase in learning effectiveness), and suitability for the content and gather learner views.

5. State what amendments are necessary before it is used on another occasion.

> If you want to check your understanding of
> your role in evaluating your use of
> visual aids, try the
> following progress check

Progress Check 4.6

1. Explain at least FOUR factors that effect the choice of visual aids when used with students.

2. Which TWO aids have low production costs?

3. List an aid which is suitable for each of the following:

   (i)   group audience;

   (ii) individual student.

Progress Check

Further Reading and References

Further reading and references relating to this chapter can be found in the following:

Audio Visual Products Division (1987) — *How to Make Successful Overhead Projector Transparencies* 3M UK plc.

Brown, G. (1975) — *Micro-Teaching: A Programme of Teaching Skills*, Methuen.

Buzan, T. (1974) — *Use Your Head*, BBC.

Curzon, L. B. (1980) — *Teaching in FE*, Cassel.

Ellington, H. and Race, P. (1993) — *Producing Teaching Materials*, Kogan Page.

Folex Ltd. (1988) — *Successful Presentations*, Folex, Zurich.

Kemp, J. E. (1980) — *Planning and Producing Audiovisual Materials*, Harper and Row.

Lloyd-Jones, R. (1986) — *How to Produce Better Work Sheets*, Hutchinson.

Newble, D. (1987) — *A Handbook for Medical Teachers*, MTP Press.

Osborne, P. et al. (1987) — Graphics in Training, Vol 8, *Training Technology Programme*, Parthenon Publishing.

Perrott, E. (1982) — *Effective Teaching*, Longman.

Pringle, J. (1966) — *Chalk Illustration*, Pergamon.

Reece, I. and Walker, S. (1995) — *A Practical Guide to the Overhead Projector and Other Visual Aids*, Business Education Publishers.

Rominszowski, A. J. (1988) — *The Selection and Use of Instructional Media*, Kogan Page, (2nd Edition)

Thorpe, R. (1987) — Projected Still Images in Training, Vol 10, *Training Technology Programme*, Parthenon Publishing.

Walkin, L. (1990) — *Teaching and Learning in Further Education*, Stanley Thornes.

Waller, Chris (1983) — *Using your overhead projector and other visual aids,* Fordigraph.

Chapter 5

Planning and Design for Teaching and Learning

Overview of Chapter 5

Competences Related to this Chapter

The teacher competences and associated performance criteria related to this chapter are:

Overall Competence - *Design Learning Programmes and Schemes of Work*

Competence	Performance Criteria
1. Analyse a syllabus document for deficiencies.	(a) List possible deficiencies in a syllabus document. (b) Identify measures that may be used to overcome deficiencies.
2. Identify learning outcomes for specific programmes.	(a) Specify learning outcomes which include conditions and criteria for success. (b) Relate outcomes to identified needs.
3. Design learning programmes related to specific needs of learners.	(a) State learning needs, prior experience and capabilities of the learners. (b) Clearly state outcomes. (c) State relevant factors influencing the programme design (syllabus, etc.). (d) Seek active participation in the design of the programme. (e) Specify learning resources, time and other factors in the design of the programme. (f) Specify content, learning methods and student activity in the design of the programme. (g) State the means of assessment clearly in the programme design.

FENTO Standards

FENTO Standards Related to this Chapter

A.	**Assessing Learners' Needs**
a1	Identify and plan for the needs of potential Learners
B.	**Planning and Preparing Teaching and Learning Programmes for Groups and Individuals**
b1	Identify the required outcomes of the learning programme
b2	Identify appropriate teaching and learning techniques
C.	**Developing and Using a Range of Teaching and Learning Techniques**
c1	Promote and encourage individual learning
c2	Facilitate learning in groups
c3	Facilitate learning through experience
D.	**Managing the Learning Process**
d2	Plan and structure learning activities
E.	**Providing Learners with Support**
e2	Provide effective learning support
e4	Provide personal support to learners
F.	**Assessing the Outcomes of Learning and Learner'sAchievement**
f1	Use appropriate assessment methods to measure learning and achievement

Based on the FENTO Draft standards by kind permission

1. Curriculum Development

1.1 Introduction

Educational institutions are fundamentally about learning. It follows that one of your duties as a teacher and a classroom manager is to review your curriculum at regular intervals. This involves you in reviewing what you teach and what your students learn, how that learning is organised and with what success. Any resulting changes from these reviews can be called curriculum development.

Russell and Latcham (1979) have suggested that you will need to ask three increasingly interlocking questions.

(a) "What is it that I want my students to learn?

(b) How can I get them to learn it?

(c) How will I know when they have done so?"

Although you are generally presented with some form of syllabus upon which to base your teaching, the answer to these questions falls firmly upon your shoulders not upon those of the syllabus designer. In order to find answers to questions, you must look at the aims and objectives of what is intended to be learned, sequence the objectives into a learning sequence, and choose appropriate teaching, learning and assessment methods. This, then, is what curriculum development involves.

Your 'syllabus' document may be stated in terms of the aims of the subject, a list of objectives, a list of competences with associated assessment criteria, a list of topics, or a mixture of some or all of these. It may also indicate the common themes to be developed and assignments that are to be completed by the learners. This document is the official guide to the course of study which is prepared by administrators, supervisors, an examining or validating body or by yourself.

The following characteristics may be identified for a syllabus document:

(a) aims of the course of study;

(b) pre-requisites/entry behaviour expected of the learners;

(c) expected outcomes (objectives, competences, etc.);

(d) number and names of major topics;

(e) time allocated for the coverage of the course;

(f) suggested teaching/learning methods;

(g) recommended textbooks and references;

(h) assessment procedures to be used.

However, not all syllabuses have all of these features incorporated into them which means that the curriculum developer - you, the teacher - have to interpret them for your students.

1.2 Possible Measures to Minimise Weaknesses in a Syllabus

By analysing a syllabus document, you can identify its weaknesses. You might use the following suggestions to minimise the effects of these weaknesses:

No.	Syllabus Deficiency	Possible effect on Teaching/Learning Process	Measure to minimise the effect
1.	Absence of depth of treatment	Previous exam papers become the only guide The effect being that teaching becomes based on recall of factual information	Convey thoughts to syllabus designers andDecide, with colleagues and industry what depth is required
2.	Absence of indication of ability and skills expected of student	As (1) above	As (1) above
3.	No indication of teaching strategies to be used	Most teaching styles revert to what has been used before and to the needs of the examination/assessment	List all teaching methods and show how much time is to be associated with each during the completion of the syllabus
4.	No indication of 'best' resources to be used	As (3) above	List all necessary resources for 'best' coverage of the topics and ensure that they are available when needed
5.	Not enough information on testing procedures	The classroom testing may be done with little thought to remedial and enrichment teaching and to modification	Review with colleagues how best to test and how best to use the results of testing
6.	Absence of logical sequence of topics and content	This is likely to lead to a serious discontinuity in the learning process	Individual teachers to plan a logical sequence and make any additions/ changes necessary
7.	Absence of indication of useful links with subjects	Compartmentalisation of teaching canalso lead to repetition of topics	All teachers involved, to share their individual schemes of work
8.	Absence of indication of links with industry,	This is likely to lead to inadequate and inappropriate learning experiences	Review tasks required of course graduates in industry and build these into the course
9.	Absence of abilities skills and attitudes to be developed	This can lead to teachers developing different abilities, or ignoring some important ones	Write objectives for knowledge, skills and social abilities that are needed in industry
10.	Absence of lesson plans	As in (9) above,	Individuals to write lesson plans and to share them with colleagues teaching on the same course

> *Possible evidence to show that you*
> *have achieved the competence*
> *'Analyse a Syllabus Document*
> *for Deficiencies'*

The type of evidence that you might collect to show that you have achieved this competence involves:

For a syllabus that you use for one of the classes that you teach:

(i) state the characteristics found in the syllabus;

(ii) using the list of characteristics given in section 1.1 of this chapter, identify those that are missing

(iii) for the characteristics that are missing, explain how the deficiency might be overcome.

Possible Evidence

Progress Check

> *If you want to check your understanding*
> *of syllabus analysis try the following*
> *progress check*

Progress Check 5.1

Explain what measures you would take to minimise the effects of
the following:

1.   Abilities and skills to be developed in the learner which are
     not stated in the syllabus documents.

2.   Lack of information on class and practical tests.

3.   Lack of information on teaching methods to be used.

4.   Lack of information on time to be devoted to each of the
     topics.

2. The Process of Specifying Learning Outcomes

Before we consider the details of course planning and design, it can be helpful for you to consider the totality of the process and the components that are involved in the specification of learning outcomes. The diagram below (Figure 5.1) shows the various components of the curriculum development process: the manner in which a syllabus may be expanded for teaching purposes to show the learning process.

The diagram shows us two main things:

(a) that the development process is *sequential* in nature starting with the aims of a course and progressing, through increasing detail, to the more specific outcomes of the learning process; and

(b) that there are *alternative specifications* of learning behaviour that can be written as outcomes. These are:

   (i) product objectives which concentrate upon what the student will be able to do as a result of learning; .

   (ii) process objectives or statements which specify the use and application of knowledge and skills that are required for work;

   (iii) statements of competence which specify the knowledge and skills required in the workplace for a particular occupation and, in consequence, what is required by employers.

The diagram suggests that the outcome statements are offered as alternatives. This is sometimes true. It is, however, often the case that there is a need to be eclectic: that is borrowing from each of the sources as the need arises for a single syllabus.

The next sections of the chapter expand upon each of the aspects identified in the diagram and, indeed, show the importance of the increasing specificity: from aims to specific objectives, to common skills and to competences.

3. Course and Subject Aims

Courses often consist of a number of "subjects" or "units" (Business Studies may include accounts, law, word-processing etc.). The development of courses and subjects, as suggested by Russell and Latcham (1979), can be considered at course, subject and lesson levels.

Course Level - development at this level is concerned with the whole of what the student is intended to learn. It is sometimes, but not always, carried out by awarding bodies.

Subject Level - a subject is sometimes called a module or a Unit. Quite often a subject is apportioned to one member of staff and the development is the responsibility of that member of staff. The subject is broken down into lessons or other learning situations.

Most teachers are required to complete development work at subject and lesson levels. However, most of the external bodies like Edexcel, City and Guilds as well as GCSE Boards are changing and placing more and more responsibility for the development work in the hands of the teacher.

The starting point for this development work lies with the AIMS. Again, the aims are at the two levels indicated above. Course aims are fairly general and describe the overall purposes of the course. Davies (1971) describes these as 'ultimate goals' - goals that are to be reached by the learner at the end of the course in all of the subjects and all of the lessons. A Course aim is a general statement which gives both shape and direction to the more detailed intentions of the course. Aims are a starting point for curriculum development and are necessary in order to mould the more precise decisions that are to be taken about the curriculum.

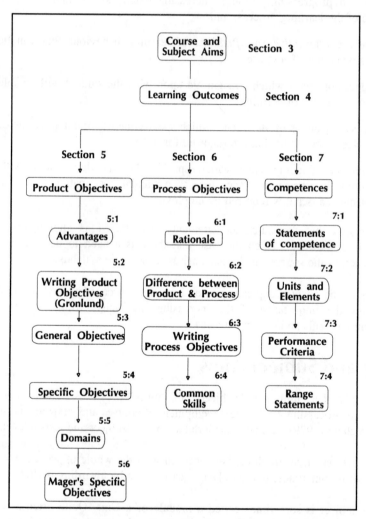

Figure 5.1   Specifying Learning Outcomes

The aims of a Civil Engineering technician course might be to:

- develop accuracy in measurement and methodical scheduling of quantities;
- assist in understanding the factors which affect the cost of buildings;
- develop knowledge of contractual procedures concerned with construction;
- develop the ability to work as an effective member of a team;
- develop the ability to prepare working drawings, sketches, specifications and planning data.

You will see that the aims are all related to the course of civil engineering and are obtained from the specific requirements of the industry. However, the course will consist of a number of subjects (i.e. surveying, maths, services, building science, drawing) and each of these subjects will require its own aims. The course aim 'to develop the ability to prepare working drawings and sketches' suggests a drawing subject. This will have its own aims and these might be:

- develop skill in the use of formal drawings as a means of communicating technical information;
- understand architectural and working drawings containing services in symbol form;
- show skill in the production of simple working drawings of plant rooms and their associated equipment;
- etc.

3.1 Aims: Some Characteristics and Some Examples

It is important that you are able to differentiate between aims and the more specific forms of learning outcome - objectives.

Product objectives and competence statements have "rules" or procedures which help to make them unambiguous. There are no rules to assist with writing aims but Figure 5.2 gives some characteristics of aims which may help you to formulate your own course or subject aims.

Aims:

- are broad ranging and often cover several subjects or topics. They are general statements;
- often cover more than one domain of learning, perhaps encompassing all three domains;
- are long term. The aims of a degree course may take three or more years to achieve;
- often contain more than one verb;
- are difficult to observe directly;
- give a sense of direction and "flavour" of the course.

Figure 5.2   Characteristics of Aims

The list of verbs shown in Figure 5.3 can be useful to you when you are writing your own aims or when ou classify them for curriculum development purposes.

Cognitive	Affective	Psychomotor
Identify Develop knowledge Give an understanding Apply Enable Provide a foundation Equip students with	Develop confidence in Give an appreciation of Assist flexibility with Promote a positive attitude in	Develop skill in Develop competence in

Figure 5.3   Useful Verbs for writing Course or Subject Aims

The following examples of aims, Figure 5.4, illustrate the broad nature of aims and how they relate to a range of subject areas. You may find some of the phrases useful when you write aims for your own courses. A tip which we find helpful is to think about your course-leaflet, or how you advertise your course. The course aims should "sell" your course to the students. They should give an idea of what the students should be able to do at the end of the course. They should be realistic and not misleading.

- Develop road sense, driving skills and a mature and safe attitude to driving.

- Develop the necessary knowledge and skills of a good bar manager and instil confidence in both colleagues and customers.

- Increase the knowledge and skills needed to decorate a home.

- Develop a creative and mature attitude to their work and customer relations.

- Develop practical skills and confidence in handling cash and credit card sales.

- To be able to apply a range of materials, colours and techniques in order to create a suitable decor in a variety of situations.

- To provide a foundation for practising as qualified accountants in both the private and public sector.

- Give an understanding of the world of work.

- To prepare students to be able to budget their grants/loans appropriately, and develop confidence in cooking meals which are quick, cheap and nourishing.

Figure 5.4   Examples of Course Aims

You can use the checklist shown in Figure 5.5 for either writing your own aims or, alternatively, for the analysis of aims that are presented to you as part of your syllabus.

	Yes	No	Not Required
1. Do the aims cover: (a) knowledge required? (b) skills required? (c) attitudes required? (d) personal development?			
2. Do the aims identify priorities or are they all inclusive?			
3. Do the aims identify competences to be developed as well as topics or subject areas?			
4. Are the aims of practical use to the teacher or just decorative?			
5. Can the aims be used to write objectives?			
6. Are the number of aims about right to be useful (not too many or too few)?			

Figure 5.5   Checklist for the Evaluation of Aims

Not all of the aspects identified in the checklist will be required in all specifications of aims. Consequently, when completing the checklist for a specific set of aims, you will tick one of the columns 'yes', 'no' or 'not required'. For a well written set of aims, none of your ticks should appear in the 'no' column. If they do, the aims should either be re-written or modified.

Possible Evidence

Possible evidence to show that you have achieved the part of the competence 'Identify Outcomes for Specific Programmes' related to Aims

---

The type of evidence that you might collect to show that you have achieved this part of the competence involves:

1. Identify and list the aims of a subject that you currently teach.

2. Critically analyse the aims using the checklist given in Figure 5. 5.

3. For any deficiencies that you find, rewrite the aims stating how such new aims will overcome the deficiency.

> *If you want to check your understanding of
> the writing of aims try the following
> progress check*

Progress Check 5.2

Consider the aims for the course given below:

Aims for a Vocational Preparation Course

1. To identify the vocational aspirations, potential abilities and aptitudes of trainees.

2. To provide the opportunity to develop basic skills in a number of areas and then develop particular knowledge and skills in a specific field.

3. To give the trainee an appreciation of opportunities in local industry.

4. To develop confidence, motivation and interview techniques to improve the prospect of gaining employment.

5. To develop personal qualities relevant to maintaining employment including safety consciousness, mature attitudes, response to discipline, time keeping and tidiness.

(a) What do you consider have been used as sources to arrive at these aims?

(b) Classify each of the aims into the domain into which each predominantly falls. i.e. cognitive, affective or psychomotor.

(c) Critically analyse the aims by the completion of the checklist given in Figure 5.5.

4. Learning Outcomes

4.1 Different Types of Learning Intentions

In the previous section we discussed the aims of a course. These aims, however, are insufficient to convey to the teacher (or the students) the intended learning. More specific intentions, in other words objectives, will be needed. As we can see from the examples shown in Figure 5.6, an objective is a mixture of a *student behaviour* together with an element of *subject content*. Consider the three different categories of objective shown in Figure 5.6.

Objective Type	Example
Product objective	Define raising agents in a recipe
Process objective	Prepare a window display
Competence	Demonstrate competence in laying a table for guests

Figure 5.6   Examples of Different Types of Objective Statements

It is important that you can not only recognise each type but you can also write them. Thus, the discussion of each type gives suggestions for writing and interpreting them. In doing this each type of objective will be considered in isolation but you should remember that, in a syllabus, or for a learning experience, a mix of types might be appropriate.

4.2 Learning Behaviour

As a teacher, your concern is that your students should learn aspects which are considered desirable or educationally important. When we use the words 'learn' or 'learning' they can often have many meanings. To be useful to us as teachers we have to agree upon an operational definition of the terms.

Suppose the students mentioned below were observed on two different occasions. Say that they were observed for the first time a year ago and then a year later. There will be a difference between the two observations such as:

- Alan can read music
- Susan can solve equations
- Kalo can turn a table leg on a lathe
- Ram can recite a poem
- Jane observes laboratory safety precautions
- Ali can ride a bicycle

Between the period of the two observations something must have occurred so that these students can now do what they did not, or could not, do earlier.

You will see that what the students have learned is very different - each of them involved different behaviours. In educational terminology *behaviour* is used to represent any act that is performed by a person - physical, mental or emotional. We must remember that this use of the term behaviour is different from the one used in everyday language when it is normally used to describe the *good* or *bad* behaviour of a person.

If we agree that the term behaviour is used to denote any activity, it can be said that students are displaying a behaviour *after* learning that they did not display *before* their learning. In other words, the process of learning has resulted in a *change of behaviour*.

Therefore, if we can observe a change in the behaviour of a person, we may conclude that learning has taken place. In education, learning could be defined as:

> a *relatively permanent change in behaviour as a result*
> *of experience, training or practice.*

Progress Check

> *If you want to check your understanding of the concept of behaviour, try the following progress check*

Progress Check 5.3

You have observed that students in the list below have learned certain things during a particular period. Against each statement write:

Y   If you think that this is a result of instruction from a teacher;

N   if you think it is not because of instruction from a teacher;

U   if you are unsure whether it is or it is not a result of instruction.

1.   John has learned to appreciate poetry.   _____

2.   Ram has learned to hate history.   _____

3.   Rahim has learned to swim.   _____

4.   Jane has learned the definition of force.   _____

5. Product Objectives: A Concept

5.1 The Advantages of Product Objectives

Product objectives were the first of the three types of learning behaviour shown in Figure 5.6. Earlier in the book we suggested that objectives were useful for:

1. Communicating intended learning outcomes

2. Teachers in teaching

3. Students in learning

4. Assessing the learning that has taken place

5. Improving teaching

We should also have noted that objectives should be written in terms of **intended learning outcomes** that are expected after instruction.

The second point to note here is that as objectives are used by so many people (such as students, teachers and examiners,), to be effective they must convey the same meaning to everyone who reads them. In other words, they must be unambiguous.

Consider the following statement written as a product objective:

> 'This lesson is intended to demonstrate the blood circulation system to the students'.

What is wrong with this? You will notice that it describes the method of instruction but it does **not** specify the intended learning outcome. What does the teacher expect the learners to learn? What changes in behaviour will the students display? If the teacher does not know this, how can the learning be verified?

Technically speaking the above objective will be achieved as soon as the teacher completes the demonstration, irrespective of whether the students have learned anything or not.

Now consider the following objective:

> "At the end of instruction the student will understand the working of a petrol engine."

Note that in this case the objective is stated in terms of *learning outcome*; in other words that at the end of learning, the student will *understand*.

But, does it convey the same meaning to everyone? What does the term 'understand' mean? What will the students have to do to demonstrate that they actually understand? Will they have to describe the petrol engine? Will they have to draw a sketch of the parts? Will they have to identify the working parts? Or will they have to complete all of these?

Although the understanding of the working of the petrol engine may be a desirable learning outcome, the use of the word 'understand' does not clearly communicate the intent of the objective and therefore it is not useful in guiding the teaching and testing. The term has to be further clarified.

There are many verbs similar to the verb 'understand' which are open to many interpretations: for example, such words as 'know', 'appreciate', 'enjoy', 'believe', 'think critically' and many others The main reasons for the different interpretations is that these verbs attempt to describe what goes on in the mind of the student. Since an observer cannot enter the mind of the student, a teacher does not know when students understand or when they appreciate.

What is required is a description of some observable behaviour which can be accepted as proof or indication of the student's understanding or appreciation. In other words, a product objective should specify what the student should be able to do which can be observed by an outsider. For instance, if it is agreed that a learner can DO the following, it should be accepted that they understand Newton's Laws:

1.   *States* the laws in own words.

2.   Gives *examples* where each law is applicable.

3.   *Distinguishes* between the situations where each law is applicable.

Note: Each of the words that are written in italics describe actions which could be observed and indicate specific behaviours which could be measured (tested) to find if the objective had been achieved.

When the objective is written using a verb which specifies an *observable behaviour* it is known as a *product objective* (or sometimes called a behavioural objective, or specific objective).

Verbs such as 'write', 'state', 'identify', 'classify' or 'draw' describe actions which can be observed and, therefore, **can** be used when writing product objectives. Verbs like 'know', 'understand', 'appreciate' or 'think' do not describe observable action hence they cannot be used in specific product objectives.

There has always been a tension in education regarding detailed specification of learning outcomes and more generalised statements. The debate will go on. You may have a choice or you may be constrained to follow a certain model. Which ever, you need to be aware of the benefits and limitations of product objectives. Interestingly, competence statements have very similar advantages and disadvantages. Figure 5.7 gives a summary of the main points.

Product Objectives	
Advantages	**Limitations**
• gives students a clear target	• limits student learning
• gives teachers a clear framework	• constrains teacher
• communicates to third parties e.g. employers	• can be too detailed
• informs assessment	• may be perceived as trivial
• informs selection of teaching strategies	• may not help achieve overall aims
• provides clear standards	• are time consuming to write
• encourages planning	• may be given undue status
• gives a reliable system	• may be perceived as too narrow
• are unambiguous	

Figure 5.7   **Product Objectives: Advantages and Limitations**

Progress Check

> *If you wish to check your understanding of the concept of behavioural objectives, try the following progress check*

Progress Check 5.4

1. Which of the following correctly describes a specific objective written using observable behavioural terms?

   A. Communicating the activities of the teacher in behavioural terms.

   B. Containing words to indicate what is expected from the student at the end of instruction.

   C. Containing words to indicate changes in student behaviour that can be measured.

   D. Communicating student behaviour in measurable terms prior to instruction.

2. Two objectives are stated below. Which of these objectives uses *observable behavioural terms* to describe the learning outcome?

   A. At the end of instruction the student should be able to appreciate the importance of heat treatment of steel.

   B. At the end of instruction, the student should be able to select an appropriate heat treatment process for steel.

3. A list of verbs usually used to indicate learning outcomes is given below. Indicate which of these verbs are open to many interpretations and which are open to few interpretations.

   (a) Know   (g) Think   (l) Enjoy

   (b) Understand   (h) Solve   (m) Believe

   (c) Write   (i) Distinguish   (n) Remember

   (d) Construct   (j) Compare   (o) Draw

   (e) Explain   (k) Differentiate   (p) Design

   (f) Really understand

5.2 Writing Product Objectives - Gronlund's Approach

In the previous section we defined Product Objectives as a statement which uses a verb specifying observable behaviour and we identified the difference between observable and unobservable behaviours.

There are situations where the teaching of specific observable behaviours is very useful; particularly for knowledge level objectives.

However, much education is directed to the more complex behaviours of understanding and applying knowledge. Employees need not only to know the principles of their vocation, but they need to understand them so that such principles can be applied to specific situations.

Earlier, we noted that verbs like 'understand' and 'apply' do not describe an observable behaviour. Hence they cannot be used for the writing of product objectives in behavioural terms. If we sought to specify all of the learning outcomes, the number of objectives required for a subject/topic would be too great. Too many product objectives may restrict the scope of teaching.

In an attempt to ensure that (a) the totality of the subject matter for teaching purposes is covered and (b) the specific behaviours are suitable for the formulation of assessment, Norman Gronlund (1970) suggests writing product objectives at two levels. These are:

1. *General objectives*, and

2. A sample of *specific objectives* corresponding to and representative of each general objective.

Gronlund further suggests that *teaching* should be directed towards the achievement of the general objectives whereas the specific objectives should form the basis of *assessment*.

An example of the Gronlund approach is shown in Figure 5.8

General Objective:	1. Understand Newton's Laws of Motion
Specific Objectives:	1:1 State Newton's Laws of Motion.
	1:2 Define force, momentum, action and reaction.
	1:3 Explain the units of force.
	1:4 Derive the relation $F = m.a$
	1:5 Etc.

Figure 5.8   Example of Gronlund Specific Objectives

Note that verbs like 'know', 'understand' 'apply' and 'appreciate', which we considered unsuitable for stating behavioural objectives, may now be used for stating general objectives. The general objective describes a general learning outcome which, by itself, is not observable. It is, however, further clarified through a representative sample of specific behaviours which use terms to describe observable behaviour.

Progress Check (vertical text in left margin)

If you wish to check your understanding of the difference between general and specific objectives try the following progress check.

Progress Check 5.5

A list of product objectives is given below. Indicate which of them are general objectives and which of them are specific objectives.

1. Understand the working of the heart.

2. Calculate the power required to lift water through a given height by a pump.

3. Apply Pythagoras' Theorem.

4. Appreciate the need for providing incentives to workers giving excess production.

5. Erect a tripod with the help of given tools and equipment, so that the apex is 3 metres above the ground.

6. Measure the length of a wall using a tape to an accuracy of 0.1mm.

7. Understand the method of setting-up a levelling instrument using a bubble tube.

8. Know the steps in boning a chicken.

5.3 General Objectives: Guidelines

Guideline 1.   Objectives should be stated in terms of student performance.

Consider the following two objectives:

1. To teach Faraday's Laws of electro-magnetic induction.

2. Understand Faraday's Laws of electro-magnetic induction.

The focus of the first of the objectives is on what the teacher does, whereas the attention of the second one is on what the student does; in this case what the student understands. Objectives should always be stated in terms of student behaviour rather than in terms of teacher behaviour.

Guideline 2.   Objectives should be stated in terms of the learning outcome and not in terms of the learning process.

Examine the following statement:

'The student gains knowledge of Bernoulli's theorem'.

The statement emphasizes the gaining of knowledge (the learning process) rather than the type of behaviour that provides evidence that learning has taken place.

Words like 'gains' 'acquires' and 'develops' generally indicate the learning process rather than the desired outcome of the learning experience.

Guideline 3.   Statements of objectives should be an amalgamation of subject matter and the desired behaviour.

Examine the following:

1. Armature reaction.

2. Understands armature reaction in a D.C. machine.

The first statement is merely subject matter and contains no verb or student behaviour. The second tells the general outcome of learning with the addition of the desired student behaviour; it is an amalgamation of the subject matter and the student behaviour.

Guideline 4.   Avoid the use of more than ONE type of learning outcome in each General Objective.

Read the following objectives:

1. Uses appropriate experimental procedures in solving problems.

2. Knows the scientific method and applies it effectively.

The second objective includes both 'knows' and 'applies' as possible learning outcomes. It is better to have a separate statement for each because some students may 'know' the scientific method (that is be able to state it) but may not be able to 'apply' it effectively.

The checklist shown in Figure 5.9 can be used for either writing your own general objectives or for assessing those written in your syllabus. It indicates the important aspects of the writing of these objectives.

	Yes	No
1. Does the general objective indicate an appropriate outcome for the instructional unit?		
2. Does the general objective include desired outcomes such as knowledge, skills, attitudes, etc?		
3. Is the general objective attainable taking into account the ability of the learners, facilities, time, constraints, etc?		
4. Is the general objective relevant to the course aims?		
5. Does the general objective begin with a verb?		
6. Is the general objective clear, concise and well defined?		

Figure 5.9   Checklist for Evaluating General Objectives

5.4 Specific Objectives: Guidelines

The following guidelines should assist you to write specific objectives which will expand upon the general objective and give a representative sample of behaviours showing how the general objective could be assessed.

1. State the general objective.

2. Begin each specific objective with an action verb which indicates what the students have to do.

3. Write the specific objectives which explain the general objective.

4. State the objective including conditions and criteria, where possible, in order to reduce ambiguity.

5. Do not omit complex objectives (e.g. appreciation) simply because they are difficult to state in behavioural terms. Reference materials may have to be consulted in such cases.

6.   Write a sufficient number of specific objectives for each general objective so as to adequately describe the student behaviours for achieving the general objective.

7.   Write a specific objective to communicate each learning outcome.

8.   Sequence the specific objectives in such a way that the learning outcome of one becomes the pre-requisite for achieving the learning outcome of the next.

A checklist is shown in Figure 5.10 which is similar to the one for General Objectives. It, again, provides the important facets for the writing or checking of this type of objective.

	Yes	No
1. Are the specific objectives relevant to the general objective?		
2. Does the specific objective contain a verb which is an observable behaviour?		
3. Is the specific objective stated in terms of student behaviour as opposed to teacher behaviour?		
4. Does the specific objective communicate only one learning outcome?		
5. Have the specific objectives been arranged in a logical sequence?		
6. When seen as a whole, does the list of specific objectives reflect what is intended by the corresponding general objective?		

Figure 5.10 Checklist for Evaluating Specific Objectives

Writing general and specific objectives must be within one of three domains and at a specific level within that domain. The process relies upon the specification of the *verb* which is specific to both domain and level. The lists shown in Figures 5.11 and 5.12 are adapted from Gronlund (1970) and give an indication of the verbs that might be considered for writing general and specific objectives. Notice that some of the verbs appear in more than one domain and more than one category in the cognitive domain. The reason for this is that the verbs are only *illustrative* of the domain and level and the specific level depends upon the context within which the verb appears. For instance the verb 'solve' (a specific objective cognitive verb) can be at three levels.

'Solve two times two' is recalled as 'four' and is *knowledge*. 'Solve a problem' by putting numbers into an equation is *comprehension*. 'Solve the height of a building' by devising an equation for the first time is *application*. Thus, the verbs given in the lists are to assist with writing objectives: there are many others and the ones given are only an indication of those that you might use.

Level	Illustrative General Objective	Illustrative Verbs for Specific Objectives
Knowledge	**Knows** common terms. **Knows** specific facts. **Knows** basic concepts. **Knows** principles. **Knows** basic procedures.	Defines, describes, identifies, labels, lists, names, outlines, reproduces, selects, states.
Comprehension	**Understands** facts. **Understands** how to interpret charts and graphs. **Understands** how to translate verbal material to maths formulae. **Understands** how to estimate future consequences from data.	Converts, classifies, compares, contrasts, defends, determines, distinguishes, estimates, explains, extends, generalises, gives new examples, infers, justifies, paraphrases, reviews, suggests, summarises.
Application	**Applies** concepts and principles to new situations. **Applies** laws/theories to practical situations. Constructs charts and graphs.	Changes, computes, demonstrates, discovers, manipulates, modifies, predicts, prepares, produces, relates, shows, solves, uses.
Higher than Application (Analysis, synthesis & evaluation)	**Recognises** unstated assumptions. **Integrates** learning from different areas into a plan for solving a problem. **Judges** the logical consistency of written materials.	Breaks down, discriminates, infers, outlines, relates, separates. Categorises, combines, devises, designs, modifies, plans, rewrites, summarises. Appraises, compares, concludes, justifies.

Figure 5.11   Illustrative Verbs for Specific Objectives in the Cognitive Domain

Domain	Illustrative General Objective	Illustrative Verbs for Specific Objectives
Affective	**Appreciates** the need to show sensitivity to human needs and social problems. **Appreciates** the need for class discussion. **Appreciates** safety rules. **Appreciates** a healthy diet.	Asks, chooses, selects, answers, assists, complies, practices, follows, forms, initiates, influences, shares, studies, works on own volition.
Psychomotor	**Shows skill in** writing. **Shows skill in** operating. **Shows skill in** typing. **Shows skill in** preparing food. **Shows skill in** cutting hair.	Assembles, builds, calibrates, changes, cleans, connects, composes, creates, designs, hammers, makes, manipulates, mends, paints, saws, sews, sketches, starts, stirs, weighs.

Figure 5.12   **Illustrative Verbs for Specific Objectives in the Affective and Psychomotor Domains**

Progress Check

> *If you wish to check your understanding of writing general and specific objectives try the following progress check.*

Progress Check 5.6

1. Write two general objectives for a unit or topic of the course subject you are presently teaching and, for each general objective, write at least three specific objectives which will show achievement of the general objective.

2. Use the checklists (Figures 5.9 and 5.10) to evaluate the objectives that you have written.

3. State whether the following general objective behaviours are likely to represent Cognitive, Affective or Psychomotor behaviours.

    (i)   understands

    (ii)   appreciates

    (iii) shows skill in

    (iv)   judges

    (v)   knows

4. State the level in the cognitive domain that the following specific objective behaviours are most likely to represent.

    (i)   list

    (ii)   explain

    (iii) predict

    (iv)   justify

    (v)   give new examples

    (vi)   name

5.5 Domains

Selecting the Domain

You should note that few objectives are purely cognitive, psychomotor or affective. The major criterion that we use in selecting the domain in which the objective belongs is the *primary behaviour* called for: if it relates primarily to 'knowing' about the subject, it is cognitive; if it relates primarily to physical 'skill behaviour', it is psychomotor; and if it relates primarily to 'feelings' or 'attitudes', it is affective.

The checklist shown in Figure 5.13 can be used for either writing your own product (general and specific) objectives, or for assessing those written in your syllabus.

	Yes	No
1. Does each objective use an observable verb?		
2. Does each objective contain only one behaviour?		
3. Does each objective in the cognitive domain deal with knowledge and intellectual skills?		
4. Does each of the objectives in the psychomotor domain deal with physical skills?		
5. Does each of the objectives in the affective domain deal with attitudes, feelings or emotions?		

Figure 5.13 Checklist for Evaluating Product Objectives

Progress Check

> *If you wish to check your understanding of domains of objectives try the following progress check*

Progress Check 5.7

The following is a list of product objectives. Read each and indicate the *domain into which each primarily falls* by placing the letter 'C' if it is cognitive, 'P' if it is psychomotor, or 'A' if it is affective.

1. __ Stitch given materials.
2. __ Identify the given samples of legume seeds by name.
3. __ In the clinical setting, demonstrate concern for apprehensive patients by answering the call lights promptly.
4. __ Define the editing symbols on a given list.
5. __ Select the appropriate forms for transferring doctor's orders.
6. __ Given ten lists of three digit numbers, calculate totals for the lists on any adding machines found in the simulated office practice laboratory.
7. __ Choose the most suitable option among several alternatives in business careers.
8. __ Specify any missing or incomplete information on the completed short- term loan contracts provided.
9. __ Compute the missing value on a given list of Ohm's Law problems.
10. __ Determine the kinds of nutrients to be applied to a given soil to grow a certain crop.
11. __ Select the proportions of concrete mix required for a given job.
12. __ When confronted with a hazard, demonstrate concern for safety practices by observing all safety precautions.
13. __ Given ten shafts with differing diameters, measure the diameter of each with a micrometer.
14. __ Outline the qualifications for a given job.
15. __ Change the ribbon of a typewriter.
16. __ Identify the sequence of operations for constructing a house.
17. __ Grease all points in a car, as outlined by the manufacturer for routine maintenance.
18. __ After reviewing a film presentation, criticise the presentation using the outline form provided.

Precision in Classification into Levels within a Domain

In many instances you can classify a given objective as belonging to one level from one point of view and to another level from a different point of view. In such cases, particularly for psychomotor and affective objectives, it may not be advisable for you to classify them as strictly belonging to one level or another: the dividing line between any two successive levels is not sharply defined and either level would be acceptable. For most occasions you will find it acceptable if the following simplification of the levels is used for operational purposes:

1. The levels in the cognitive domain are classified as:

   (a) Knowledge   (b) Comprehension

   (c) Application   (d) Higher than Application

You should note that level (d) includes the levels of Analysis, Synthesis and Evaluation. This level is sometimes called 'Invention' and this is descriptive in that it is a high level cognitive behaviour which involves the learner in doing something new. Very little of many syllabuses will contain a high percentage of this level and some, particularly in the initial years of a course, may not contain any at all.

2. No sub-division of the Psychomotor and Affective domains need be used.

Instructional Uses of Taxonomic Levels

You will notice that classifying product objectives into the different levels in domains will assist you in your teaching in the following ways:

1. To *sequence* objectives for teaching so that learning progresses from known to unknown and simple to complex.

2. To include objectives at all of the required levels within a domain. This ensures that you emphasise the different levels required by the overall aims of the course.

3. To construct appropriate test questions to measure desirable changes in behaviour at the required levels.

Taxonomic Levels in Teaching/Learning Programmes

You may not find it possible or desirable within the time available to develop all cognitive, psychomotor or affective abilities to the highest level in each domain. For example, some motor skills may be developed to a naturalization level (done automatically and with ease), but it would not be possible or even realistic to expect all skills to be developed to this level. Similarly, in the affective domain you will find it likely that most of the objectives may not go farther than the valuing level and it has already been indicated that the Higher than Application level in the cognitive domain is a high level skill with only small amounts in any one year of a course. The tasks which students have to perform determine, to a large extent, the taxonomic levels to which they have to be developed during the educational programme.

Progress Check

> *If you wish to check your understanding of*
> *taxonomic levels try the following*
> *progress check.*

Progress Check 5.8

Identify the levels of objectives in the list below as Knowledge (K), Comprehension (C), Application (A) or Higher than Application (HA) by placing the appropriate symbol in the blank space adjacent to the item.

(a)		Identify the given samples of legume seeds.
(b)		Define the editing symbols on a given list.
(c)		Select the appropriate forms for transferring doctor's orders.
(d)		Specify any missing or incomplete information on the loan contracts provided.
(e)		Determine the kinds of nutrients to be applied to a given soil to grow a certain crop.
(f)		Select from the tables the proportions of concrete mix required for specified jobs not previously tackled.
(g)		State the qualifications for a given job.
(h)		Design a method you would use to accomplish the given task.
(i)		Identify the objectives on a given list as primarily cognitive, psychomotor or affective.

5.6 Mager's Approach to Writing Product Objectives

In the previous sections we described Gronlund's approach to writing general and specific objectives and we identified the taxonomic levels of the three learning domains. Gronlund's approach to writing objectives has much to commend it. However, you will find that the specific objectives are often open to interpretation due to their lack of specificity. Robert Mager (1970) suggests a method of overcoming this problem.

Since the intention is to make specific objectives unambiguous so that everyone who reads them gets the same meaning, there are two ways in which we can achieve this:

1. Write all product objectives using terms which describe only the specific observable behaviours as intended learning outcomes; or

2. Use non-observable terms to describe the intended learning outcomes **BUT** further clarify such terms by indicating a sample of specific behaviours.

The first method of writing product objectives is the one favoured by Robert Mager while the second one is the one that we have already described as suggested by Norman Gronlund.As a teacher you will find both methods useful. You will find some situations in which the Mager type objective is useful and others where the Gronlund approach helps.Mager suggests that objectives should be written which specify what the learner should be able to perform (or do) to demonstrate mastery of the subject/topic. As many statements as necessary should be written, he suggests, to describe all of the learning outcomes.

He further recommends that to make the objective more specific, it should contain three elements. According to Mager it is, however, not always essential to include all three elements in every objective. If all of the three elements reduce ambiguity, then they should be included. The three elements are:

1. *Terminal Behaviour* (behaviour to be demonstrated by the student at the end of instruction).

2. Important *conditions* under which the terminal behaviour is expected to occur.

3. *Criteria* of acceptable performance.

Terminal Behaviour

The terminal behaviour describes what the student will do or perform after instruction. It is essential that it should specify observable behaviour like 'repair', 'state', 'write', 'select'. Verbs like 'know', 'understand' and 'appreciate' which are not observable behaviours do not qualify to describe terminal behaviour in Mager's approach.

Conditions

Conditions refer to what the learner will be given, for example, with the help of 'handbook', 'tools', 'references'. It can also specify what the learner will be denied, for example 'without the use of a calculator', 'from memory'.

Criteria

Criteria refer to the extent or standard of attainment. They may specify speed or efficiency, for example, 'within 40 minutes'. They may make reference to quality or quantity, for example 'to the second place of decimals', 'eight out of ten correct'.

The following example may assist to clarify for you the three elements:

> Given a 7.5 kW DC motor, that contains a single fault and given a standard kit and references, the student must be able to repair the motor within 45 minutes.

In the above objective:

1. *repair* communicates the desired terminal behaviour.

2. *given a 7.5 kW DC motor that contains a single fault and a standard set of tool and references* communicates the conditions under which the behaviour is expected to occur.

3. *within 45 minutes* tells us the criteria of acceptable performance.

A simplified approach to this is to ask yourself three questions:

> **What** do you want your students to be able to do?

> **How** do you want your students to demonstrate that they have learned?

> **How well** do your students have to perform?

An example of this approach is as follows:

What: Swim 50 metres,

How: in a swimming pool, wearing outdoor clothes,

How well: within ten minutes.

Figure 5.14 illustrates some examples which may help you. But please bear in mind that it is not always possible to stipulate the conditions and/or the criteria.

What (Behaviour Performance)	How (Conditions)	How Well (Criteria)
Lay a table for 20 places	given a menu and 30 minutes	correctly
List the sequence of steps needed to change a circuit in a P.C.	without reference to notes or manual	correct sequence without error
Identify O.S. signs	given an O.S. map	with 9 out of 10 correct
Change a car wheel	on a drive, observing safety precautions	within 10 minutes

Figure 5.14   Examples of Objectives with conditions and Criteria

5.7 Examples of Product Objectives

We have discussed several guidelines which are intended to help you to write objectives. You may feel overwhelmed! This section gives examples of general and specific objectives which cover a range of subjects. We hope these may give you some ideas and some encouragement. A range of styles is used and you are encouraged to adopt your own style.

Example 1 Resuscitation

1.0   **Know basic anatomy and physiology of the heart.**

1.1   State the main functions and components of the heart.

2.0   **Understand the need and procedure for basic life support.**

2.1   Describe the method for carrying out cardio-pulmonary resuscitation (CPR).

2.2   Explain the procedure of CPR using appropriate medical terminology.

2.3   List 3 causes of cardiac arrest.

2.4   State the signs and symptoms of cardiac arrest.

2.5   Explain the role of the nurse during and after a cardiac arrest.

3.0   **Show skill in carrying out basic life support.**

3.1   Perform basic life support unaided and with assistance.

3.1   Carry out immediate post resuscitation care.

Example 2 Music

1.0   **Know composers and compositions.**

1.1   List five composers.

1.2   State at least two works of the above composers.

2.0   **Understand concepts which influence musical sounds.**

2.1   State the effect of rhythm

2.2   State the different keys

2.3   Explain how minor keys influence the mood.

Example 3 Food Hygiene

1.0   Know the correct storage conditions for all raw materials.

1.1   State 3 storage conditions for raw meats given four examples.

2.0   Appreciate the importance of correct procedures.

2.1   Choose to follow correct procedures.

3.0   Show skill in raw food preparation.

3.1   Prepares two items of raw food to prescribed standards within specified time.

Example 4 Driving

1.0   Know the Highway Code.

1.1   State 90% of road signs correctly.

1.2   State correct braking distance on wet and dry roads.

2.0   Appreciate the importance of road sense.

2.1   Choose to drive with safe distances.

2.2   Choose to comply with speed limits.

3.0   Show skill with driving techniques.

3.1   Complete an emergency stop safely.

3.2   Use gears correctly.

Example 5 Bar Management

1.0   Know the law relating to bar management.

1.1   State opening hours.

1.2   State age limits.

2.0   Appreciate the need for good customer relations.

2.1   Choose to engage customer in conversation.

Example 6 Painting and Decorating

1.0   Understand the importance of thorough preparation of surfaces.

1.1   State how to prepare a surface.

1.2   Explain the implications of poor preparation.

2.0   Appreciate the importance of safety.

2.1   Choose to ensure adequate ventilation.

3.0   Show skill in painting.

3.1   Paint a door to a smooth surface with total coverage.

Example 7 Information Technology

General Objectives	Specific Objectives
Know the basic components of a computer	• Name the parts of a PC
Show skill in the use of the component parts of the computer	• Manipulate the appropriate keys of the keyboard
	• Manipulate the mouse correctly
	• Use diskettes correctly
	• Manipulate the floppy disk drive correctly
Appreciate the need for safety whilst using a computer	• Choose not to eat or drink whilst working on a computer
	• Choose to adopt a correct posture and position whilst working
	• Choose to take breaks away from the computer at 2 hour intervals
Understand the concepts of how to store and retrieve files	• State the correct commands for saving files
	• State the correct commands for loading files
	• Explain the rules governing the naming of files
Understand the concepts of disk drives and directories	• Explain the difference between the hard drive and the floppy drive
	• Explain the structure of file directories
Appreciate the need to organise files and disks	• Choose to organise his/her files correctly and logically
	• Choose to store diskettes safely
	• Choose to use appropriate file names
	• Choose to back up files regularly
Understand the basic WINDOWS concepts	• Name the various parts of the WINDOWS screen
	• Explain the principles of multiple windows
	• Define 'icons'

Progress Check

> *If you wish to check your understanding of Mager's approach try the following progress check*

Progress Check 5.9

Complete the table below to identify the three components of the objectives (a) to (e). If you do not find a particular element in the objective, leave the cell blank.

Objective No.	Terminal Behaviour	Conditions under which behaviour occurs	Criteria of acceptable performance
a.			
b.			
c.			
d.			
e.			

(a) Given ten rock specimens, identify all sandstones without the use of any equipment.

(b) The students shall be able to name the parts of an electric motor.

(c) Using the standard code of practice for Steel Design, the students shall design a suitable section for the column (pillar).

(d) Given samples of bricks from four brickmakers, the students shall select those that are first class.

(e) The students shall state the quantity of bricks required for wall construction to an accuracy of 10%.

6. Process Objectives

6.1 Rationale for Process Objectives

In the previous section, we concentrated upon writing product objectives and we suggested that general and specific objectives were a useful method to convey their meaning. We further suggested that this type was useful for the acquisition of knowledge and skills. However, apart from knowledge and skill, a workforce needs to be adaptable and flexible due to the rapid changes in technology. The knowledge and skills associated with product objectives do not necessarily give us this required flexibility - hence the need for process objectives which concentrate upon the use and application of knowledge and skills and attempt to provide us with the additional competences that are required for work.

Traditional examination assessment is characterised by:

- a dependence on memory and speed;
- a judgment made on a single occasion;
- a judgment made by someone remote from the learner;
- the need for contrived problems to suit designated examination times;
- a lack of acknowledgement of transferable skill development;
- a likelihood that they are norm referenced.

We can identify two major problems with product objectives:

(a) there is a likelihood for curriculum developers to (over) concentrate on the low level skills associated with knowledge because these are the easiest product objectives to write and assess;

(b) teachers tend only to teach to the behaviours stated in the specific objectives and ignore the more all-embracing general objective which precedes them.

Work-based assessment is characterised by:

- a need to investigate, inquire and be reliable;
- the fact that assessment is continuous;
- judgment being carried out by oneself and peers, providing feedback;
- real-life problems;
- skill development being continuously demonstrated as circumstances change;
- being criterion referenced because a certain level of competence is required.

If our courses are to reflect the needs of the workplace then the objectives should reflect processes or competences that are important at work.

The addition of process objectives to a course specification is an attempt to ensure that students not only acquire knowledge but, also, apply it. Such activities are more likely to lead to learning which is flexible and durable as it will allow our students to change to meet the needs of a changing technology. Additionally, the inclusion of such process objectives is likely to lead to increased student motivation when they realise that the competences are relevant to their work.

Justification for the process mode is given by Cole (1982) where he suggests that promotion of process education 'stems from the realities of a satisfying and productive life in the present world'. He suggests the following eight justifications:

1. The world is changing so fast .... that it is impossible to predict what knowledge individuals will need in the next few years.

2. The state of knowledge is so vast that only a small proportion can be taught to students.

3. The acquisition of processes ensures an individual who can solve problems.

4. Processes are more widely applicable than knowledge and information.

5. Processes are more permanent than other types of learning.

6. Information is easily obtained when needed but processes cannot be 'looked up'.

7. An emphasis on processes is needed to prevent academic isolation and social irrelevancy.

8. Processes are required for learning to occur through formal education.

6.2 Differences between Process and Product Objectives

The key features of the process model are:

(a) a focus on student activities, and

(b) the teaching and assessment of transferable skills which are common to a number of subject disciplines.

These key features mean that process-based curricula focus on a clear description and identification of the learning activities like the following :

- communication skills;

- problem solving skills;

- self appraisal and evaluation;

- working as an effective group member.

As you will see, these types of competences are common to all work personnel and are required as life skills. Of course, they need to be aligned to relevant subject content and it is suggested that this is completed in one of the two ways shown in the next section.

The Product and Process models may be better understood by comparing and contrasting key features as shown in Figure 5.15.

Product Model	Process Model
Concentrates on the output i.e. the end or terminal behaviour, the end product	Concentrates on the learning experiences and student activities
Students tend to learn very similar things	Students may learn very different things because the experiences are individually interpreted
The teaching and learning are seen as a means to an end	The teaching and learning activities are seen as inherently worthwhile
Learning is observable or measurable	Learning may not be observable or measurable
Outcomes are predictable	Outcomes may be unpredictable
Content important and dominant	Content not so important

Figure 5.15   Features of Product and Process Education

The examples given in 5.16 will serve to illustrate the main facets of the models. First, you should notice the difference between product and process types and see that product objectives concentrate upon student terminal behaviours whilst the process type concentrate upon student activities.

Product Objectives	Process Objectives
State the principle of movement	• Establish the effect of a force rotating about a point.
Draw a histogram from specific data.	• Collect, tabulate and summarise statistical data.
List at least 5 reasons for planning lessons.	• Participate in a discussion on lesson planning.

Figure 5.16   Examples of Product and Process Objectives

Progress Check

> *If you wish to check your understanding of the rationale for product objectives and, the differences between process and product objectives try the following progress check*

Progress Check 5.10

Give three reasons for the inclusion of process objectives within a course specification

Below are ten objectives. Choose those that are product objectives and those that are process type.

1. __ State the principal sources of hydrocarbons.

2. __ Work on tasks where measuring and estimating of materials and time are required.

3. __ Define the meaning of the term petty cash.

4. __ Choose from a given list, the tools required to carry out a major service on a motor car.

5. __ Prepare a window display.

6. __ Obtain, by a variety of means, information on the characteristics of the range of job opportunities available in the catering industry.

7. __ Investigate how a business is run by identifying the factors involved in selling, choosing location, borrowing, employing, etc.

8. __ Convert fractions to decimals and vice-versa.

9. __ Experience various roles in groups (e.g. leader, recorder, participant, chair).

10.__ State the ingredients required to make chilli.

6.3 Writing Process Objectives

You will remember from the previous section that process objectives concentrate upon student experiences. Using the following criteria when writing your own, you should:

1. Reflect the general learning that the subject/course aims to achieve.

2. Blur the boundaries between topics and often make reference to personal qualities, skills, attitudes and practical knowledge.

3. Rely more on the generalised process skills of analysis and problem solving, personal qualities such as resilience and responsibility, the ability to transfer knowledge and skills acquired in one context to other problems and situations.

4. State them in terms of the experiences that students will undergo.

BTEC (1988) suggest alternative methods of writing process objectives. Both of these employ what they call principal objectives, the bases of learning, and these are supported by either indicative objectives or indicative content. The methods are outlined below:

Figure 5.17 Methods of Writing Process Objectives suggested by BTEC

You can see from this that a system of principal objectives is the start of the curriculum specification and that these are like the general objectives discussed earlier. However, it is suggested that these contain a significant amount of process-based objectives. Associated with these principal objectives are either *indicative objectives* or *indicative content*. The word 'indicative' is obviously important in that the principal objectives may be achieved in a number of different ways. The subsequent content or objectives is just one of the ways in which this might take place. The main difference between the two methods of specification is that 'A' has less process-based objectives than 'B'. If indicative content is given as in 'B', then more of the principal objectives are required to be process-based.

To illustrate the use of principal objectives and indicative objectives and indicative content, the following examples are given.

Principal Objective

> '*Obtain information on basic financial accounting procedures used in a variety of offices.*'

Indicative Content

The principal objective might cover items such as:

- invoices, order forms, credit purchases and sales, delivery notes, statements of accounts.
- methods and procedures used to record transactions and verify payments.
- documenting, recording and valuing stock.
- payroll operating.
- computer-based and manual systems.

Here, you will see that the principal objective concentrates upon the process of obtaining information; students are required to find their own information on financial accounting procedures as opposed to it being given to them. The content is only indicative and covers a variety of aspects that might be obtained by the students.

An example of principal objective followed by indicative objectives is related to workshop safety and shown below.

Principal Objective

Simulates the appropriate procedures which should be adopted in the event of workshop accidents.

Indicative Objectives

The principal objective might cover items such as:

- giving mouth to mouth resuscitation using dummies,
- describing the effects of various types of fire e.g. oil, electrical, chemical.
- bandaging various types of physical injury.

Here the process involves the simulation of procedures in the event of workshop accidents. The indicative objectives are of the process type except for the describing of the effects of fire - this is a product type.

You can use the checklist shown in Figure 5.18 for writing process objectives or for evaluating those process objectives that are presented to you as part of a syllabus.

	Yes	No
1. Are the principal objectives written in terms of processes (e.g. as a statement of a competence)?		
2. Are the process objectives written to: (i) Reflect the general learning of the course? (ii) Blur boundaries between topics? (iii) Rely on process skills? (iv) State experiences that the learners will undergo?		
3. Do the indicative objectives include a significant element of process-based objectives?		
4. Are the student learning experiences explicitly defined?		

Figure 5.18 Checklist for Evaluating Process Objectives

6.4 Key (Common or Core) Skills

The term skill denotes cognitive (or thinking) skills as well as the more purely technical or manipulative (psychomotor) abilities. Thus, we see that there are two kinds of skill:

- *vocationally specific*, that is those applying to a particular vocational area;
- *common*, that is those general or transferable skills like the ability to acquire new knowledge or to cope with problems of an unpredictable character.

We previously suggested that the key features of the process model are the transferable, common, key or core skills and that these are based on competences that are common to a number of subject disciplines.

The term 'key skill' is to be used in this book but synonyms for it are often used such as 'transferable skills', 'general skills', 'core skills' or 'core competences'.

Definition of Key Skill

A key skill can be defined as:

> *The possession and development of sufficient knowledge, appropriate attitudes and experience for successful performance in life roles. This includes employment and other forms of work; it implies maturity and responsibility in a variety of roles; and it includes experience as an essential element of competence.*

BTEC defined seven major key skills areas although, they agree, these will be developed in different ways for different courses to take into account the needs of their vocational area.

The seven areas are detailed below with each area given examples of how they might be achieved.

self-development skills e.g.:

- manage own roles and responsibilities;
- manage own time in achieving objectives;
- undertake personal and career development;
- transfer skills gained to new and changing situations/contexts.

working with and relating to others e.g.:

- treat others' values, beliefs and opinions with respect;
- relate to and interact effectively with individuals and groups;
- work effectively as a member of a team.
- communication e.g.:
- receive and respond to a variety of information;
- present information in a variety of visual forms;
- communicate in writing;
- participate in oral and non-verbal communication.

managing tasks and solving problems e.g.:

- use information sources;
- deal with a combination of routine and non-routine tasks;
- identify and solve routine and non-routine problems.

applying numeracy e.g.:

- apply numerical skills and techniques.

applying technology e.g.:

- use a range of technological equipment and systems.

applying design and creativity e.g.:

- apply a range of skills and techniques to develop a variety of ideas in the creation of new/modified products, services or situations;
- use a range of thought processes.

Thus, when process objectives are written, you might well use a representative sample of the above seven areas of key skill *together with* process objectives from the other skill areas associated with your specific subject area.

In 1996 the term Core Skills was changed to 'Key' skills and given considerable prominence in the Dearing Report (HMSO 1996). One of the three main issues raised in the report involved:

"the need to make a determined national effort to raise the standards in communication and the application of number, and to build competence in the use of information technology" (Summary Report 1996)

This was probably the most demanding of the recommendations made by Dearing for both pre and post-16 education organisations to address. The three key skills of communication, the application of number and information technology permeated nearly every curriculum recommendation. These included:

- separate grading in GCSE maths for calculation, estimation and statistics;

- separate grading in GCSE English for spoken English;

- a review of all A level cores and syllabuses;

- a new AS level in key skills;

- review of GNVQ core skills alongside the new AS in key skills;

- development of tests to assess key skills;

- strong recommendation to incorporate key skills within NVQs;

- emphasis on key skills for Entry Level Qualifications;

- award of National Certificates and Diplomas dependent on achieving key skill awards;

- strong recommendation to HE to insist on key skills awards at admission.

The emphasis, then, is to be placed on the three key skills of Communication, Number and IT and this has clear implications for curriculum delivery and staff development. It is argued elsewhere in this book that IT is fast becoming a 'basic' skill that is required by all teachers and, if IT is to be taught integrated with other vocational areas, then teachers will also have to teach it to their students.

Possible Evidence

Possible evidence to show that you have achieved the competence 'Identify Learning Outcomes for Specific Programmes'

The type of evidence that you might collect to show that you have achieved the competence involves:

1. For a subject or topic that you teach, write learning outcomes in the form of:

    (i)   general and specific objectives;

    (ii) Mager type product objectives;

    (iii) process objectives which include both subject and key skills areas;

2. From the different types of learning outcomes that you have written state which are more likely to be appropriate to meet the needs of:

    (i)   your students;

    (ii) the vocational area that you serve; and

    (iii) your own teaching.

3. Write a critical analysis of each type of learning outcome in (1.) above.

> *If you wish to check your understanding of competence and writing process objectives, try the following progress checks.*

Progress Check 5.11

Define the term 'key' skill and give three examples from your own subject area.

State the three components of Mager's product objectives.

Describe the main differences between Gronlund's and Mager's product objectives.

The four criteria for the writing of process objectives are:

(a) Blur subject boundaries;

(b) Experiences of students explicitly stated;

(c) Reflect aims of the course to give general learning;

(d) Generalised process skills stated.

Choose which of the four criteria is predominant in each of the following statements.

1. Experience, either vicariously or directly, a variety of personal encounters and a range of responses in them.

2. Be able to read and understand written questions and requests (e.g. memos, questionnaires, worksheets).

3. Investigate the outlets for surplus fish and poultry.

4. Recognise the basic personal and technical skills necessary in electronic engineering with particular reference to hygiene, cleanliness and appearance.

5. Identify and assess the nature of specific environmental problems.

7. Competences

7.1 Components of Competence Statements

The National Council for Vocational Qualifications (NCVQ) was established following a review of vocational qualifications in 1986. Industry is seen as the 'owner' of National Vocational Qualifications (NVQs): the qualifications which receive the 'seal of approval' of NCVQ. All new courses and schemes which are to be accredited by examining and validating bodies (e.g. City and Guilds, NCFE, and so on) should be written as though they were to be approved by NCVQ. Many validating bodies have, therefore, adopted a competence based model for the specification of their accredited qualifications. The model is based on a statement of competence in a particular vocational area together with standards of performance for the achievement of the competence. The specified competences are those that are required in the work place and, in consequence, those that are required by employers. In future it is anticipated that all vocational qualifications will be competence based and validated by NCVQ through National Awarding Bodies.

The vocational qualification in these terms is a statement of competence relevant to employment. It is the basis from which assessment procedures, recording and certification are derived. This brings about changes in post-16 education and training which include:

(i)   identification of competences for the vocational areas;

(ii)   the specification of assessment criteria for each competence and each part of the competence;

(iii) liaison with industry for:

(a)   assessment of competence (e.g. in the work place);

(b)   provision of prior skills;

(iv) greater marketing procedures.

Units and Elements of Competence

A competence is defined by NCVQ as the 'ability to perform an activity within an occupation'. Competence is a wide concept which embodies the ability to transfer skills and knowledge to new situations (Bloom's application level in the cognitive domain and a high level ability) within the occupational areas and includes aspects of 'key' skills. In order to receive a qualification, candidates need to accumulate the *units* of the competence which make up that qualification. Each unit is usefully subdivided into appropriate *elements*. The relationship between the qualification and its units and elements are shown diagrammatically in Figure 5.19.

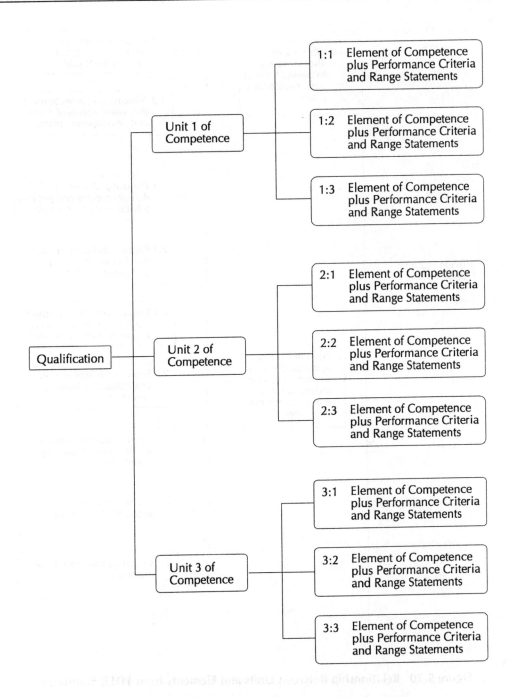

Figure 5.19 Relationship between Units and Elements

Figure 5.20 shows how the units and elements have been applied by the Training and Development Lead Body to one of their areas (Provide Learning Opportunities, Resources and Support) with its two elements and associated units.

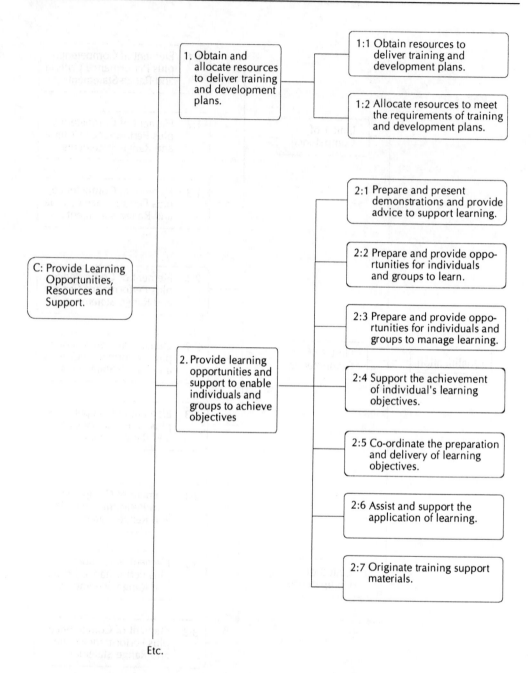

Figure 5.20   Relationship Between Units and Elements from TDLB Standards

Units of Competence

Thus, the qualification is made up of a number of Units and each Unit consists of a number of Elements of Competence (with associated Performance Criteria and Range Statements). Examples of Unit titles from different occupational areas are:

- Establish ornamental borders (*from Horticulture*)
- Design posters (*from Design*)
- Handle power - aerated doughs (*from Bakery*)
- Filing (from Business Administration)
- Devise a Scheme of Work (*from Teacher Training*)
- Manage Learning Activities (*from Teacher Training*)

Units of Competence should be written in terms of what an employee must be able to do to achieve the overall competence for the qualification. Units are a mechanism for sub-dividing the qualification into manageable parts for both learning and assessment.

The writing of a unit should conform to the general guidelines for all statements of competence. It should: refer to outcomes rather than activities, tasks or skills; follow the structure of action verb followed by object.

The following example from Business Administration illustrates the component parts of a Unit of Competence:

action verb:	process
object:	petty cash and invoices

The following checklist can be used for written units:

Checklist for Units of Competence

Is each Unit:

(a)   expressed in a language which is precise, and is an acceptable and distinct work role, within the industry or occupation?

(b)   composed of elements, performance criteria and range statements which have a coherent relationship with each other and which describe outcomes, achievements, or results of activity?

(c)   of sufficient size and scope to recognised as a creditable achievement in its own right?

Do the Units taken as a whole:

(a)   identify all the work roles within the occupational sector?

(b)   identify emerging as well as current work roles?

Elements of Competence

The purpose of Elements is to make units manageable for the purposes of assessment and learning design. The element title should be a precise description of what somebody should be able to do, but still phrased as an outcome rather than a specific task or activity. For example:

> Maintain reception area.
>
> as opposed to:
>
> Reception duties
> Display boards and publicity materials

An element is a precise description of what someone should be able to do as a necessary part of the unit. Elements are expressed in functional form; that is, they are expressed as outcomes rather than processes. This is shown in the examples below from horticulture:

Unit	• Establish ornamental borders
Elements	• Build the border with attractive shapes;
	• Create colour matching schemes
	• Choose plants which flower in succession; etc.

and from *Teacher Training*:

Unit	Assist and support the application of learning.
Elements	• Assist individuals to apply learning;
	• Provide advice to support the application of learning;
	• Monitor and assess the effectiveness of the learning process.

Alternatively an element may describe knowledge and understanding which is essential if the performance is to be sustained or extended to new situations. An example of this from *Information Processing* is:

Unit	Process records in a database
Elements	• Define styles and formats of organisations;
	• Describe security and back-up procedures;
	• State relevant aspects of Data Protection Act.

Performance Criteria

One or more performance criteria apply to each element. Each criterion defines a characteristic of competent performance of the element. All criteria attached to an element *have to be met* for the performance to be considered competent. Thus, the criteria discriminate between satisfactory and unsatisfactory performance: the assessment criteria give an answer to the question 'how should I know that a candidate is competent in ..?' Performance criteria are precise descriptions which are used as a specification to guide and structure assessments. As with elements, the results may be tangible products or nontangible results of processes. The example below gives an indication of the type of performance criteria expected:

Element:	Promote the sale of products to potential customers.
Performance Criteria	• Appropriate and accurate information about the product/service is offered;
	• Potential needs and status of customers are identified accurately and politely;
	• Options and alternatives are offered where products andservices do not directly meet potential customer needs;
	• Customers are offered the opportunity to make a purchase;
	• Potential customers are treated in a manner which promotes goodwill.

Thus, in the example, the main outcomes which are reflected in the criteria are the quality of the information given *plus* the treatment of the customer. They give a clear indication of what must be assessed and how it will be assessed.

An example from the Training and Development Lead Body (TDLB) is:

Element:	Provide advice to support the application of learning.
Performance Criteria	• Appropriate advice and support is given to those whosupport the application of learning;
	• Information about the learning needs of individuals andgroups is provided for those who support the application of learning;
	• Opportunities and facilities for giving and receiving feedback are given to those who support the application of learning;
	• Etc.

Checklist for Elements and Performance Criteria

Elements, performance criteria (plus range statements, see below) indicate the 'content' of units for those involved in the design of learning or in the writing of competences. The following checklist can be used for the writing of competences to ensure that they are acceptable, or for you as a teacher if you do not find given competences acceptable for your design of learning sessions, to adapt or modify them.

Checklist for Elements and Performance Criteria

1. Does each element:

   (a)   use precise language to indicate a distinct work role within the industry or occupation?

   (b)   describe outcomes, achievements or results of activity rather than activities or procedures themselves?

   (c)   describe outcomes that can be demonstrated and assessed?

   (d)   Possess appropriate associated assessment criteria?

2. Do the elements taken as a whole:

   (a)   identify, within appropriate limits, critical aspects of work?

3. Is each performance criterion:

   (a)   given as a clear evaluative statement?

   (b)   expressed in a manner which facilitates a mode of assessment?

4. Do the criteria, taken as a whole:

   (a)   describe only those outcomes which are essential for successful performance?

Range Statements

A range statement is a description of the range of application to which the element and performance criteria apply. They give suggestions of the range of situations where the competence must be assessed.

An example of the need for a range statement is for the competence to 'drive a motor vehicle'. Does it only apply to cars or will it include lorries? Is it only in UK or on mainland Europe as well? The range statements can help clarify these matters for the candidate and the assessor. Thus, the range in which the driving certificate applies might be:

- all vehicles up to 3 tonnes;
- all road conditions (light/dark, wet/dry);
- all roads including motorway;
- all European countries (on left or right).

An assessor would have to make the judgment as to whether a 30 minute driving test in one vehicle provided adequate evidence of competence. Generally this is supplemented with oral questions to give an assessment of other driving abilities as well as to assess the underlying knowledge and understanding.

An example of an assessment criteria with associated range statements from the TDLB Standards is:

Element:	Originate visual display and support materials	
Performance Criteria	(a)	Visual and written materials are developed which are relevant to the learning outcomes to be achieved;
	(b)	visual display materials are legible, accurate and conform to display conventions;
	(c)	equipment used to produce visual materials is operated according to manufacturer's instructions;
	(d)	written support material is in a language, style and format which is appropriate to the learning needs of the target audience;
	(e)	materials from external sources are appropriate to the content and are adapted and used within the constraints of copyright law.
Range Statements	1.	Display media: OHPs; flipcharts; whiteboards.
	2.	Written materials: tutor notes; participants' brief; summaries; handouts.
	3.	Equipment: computer based; OHP material; production equipment.

A range statement describes significant categories in order to expand upon the scope of the performance criteria. Such categories are shown in Figure 5.21. They are not assessment options. They are assessment sampling categories so that each should be sampled. The particular instances within the categories which should be sampled are identified when the assessment system is in place, not in the specification.

Category	Example	Sample Range
Tools, equipment, machinery, plant	Visual aids	flip charts, white boards, video recordings, OHP and slides.
Products and services	Lending services	mortgages, further advance, personal secured loans, unsecured loans, credit cards.
Methods, processes and procedures	Information	oral, computerised and paperback sources
Clients and customers	Customers	minors, teenagers, 16+, middle aged, pensioners, professional contacts, non residents.
Physical constraints	Health	normal, ill health, early and late retirements.
Environments	Where assessed	on-the-job, in a simulated situation.

Figure 5.21   Example Categories of Range Statements

The following checklist can be used to assess the effectiveness of written range statements.

Checklist for Range Statements

Does the range statement:

(a)   describe both existing and emerging practice?

(b)   specify classes and categories (not each individual instance) in sufficient detail to enable an assessment schedule to be developed at a later stage?

(c)   only include categories where a difference in application is significant?

(d)   set specific boundaries of application, each of which MUST be included in an assessment sample?

(e)   act as a reminder of specific instances which might be missed?

7.2 Designing Assessment Systems for Competence Schemes

7.2.1 Introduction

The basis of assessment is the generation of evidence by individuals to show that they can achieve the assessment criteria associated with units of competence. The evidence is judged and verified by assessors as to whether it is sufficient to merit accreditation. National awarding bodies' certificates are awarded to individuals on the basis of accredited achievement of the competences. This system is shown diagrammatically in Figure 5.22.

Figure 5.22   Assessment System

The requirements of the assessment system are, therefore:

(i)   The generation and collection of evidence by individual students which is relevant to the elements of competence, the performance criteria and the range statements. They also need to judge whether the evidence that they have collected is sufficient and relevant.

(ii)   The assessor then needs to judge whether the collected evidence is sufficient and relevant and, if so, to verify this fact.

(iii)   Finally, the Awarding/Validating Body provides a certificate to indicate achievement of all of the units and elements.

The different layers of the pyramid are discussed separately below. In reality, however, they all interact together. The overall objectives of the system are:

(i)   the units and elements, and their associated performance criteria must be assessed. The assessment must cover, but be limited to, the units which make up the certificate;

(ii) the evidence should relate clearly to the elements;

(iii) the evidence should cover the range of contexts for the element;

(iv) the assessment must be open to verification by an assessor.

7.2.2 Generation of Evidence

As shown in Figure 5.23, there are three basic sources of evidence that can be used to assess the ability of an individual.

Figure 5.23   Sources of Evidence of Competence

Evidence from prior achievements results from activities which have been undertaken in the past. The evidence may be clearly available, e.g. articles that have been made or designed or, even, qualifications previously gained. Alternatively, candidates may need to generate the evidence in terms of, say, written reports of work that has previously been completed but which has no tangible evidence e.g. from being a member of a working party or from working on a project.

Performance evidence can result from observations of individuals completing tasks as part of their normal work OR from specially set tasks and simulations. Again, the evidence may already be available e.g. from the individual's employer's normal work records, or it may be generated while the individual works. Both the process of work and its outcomes may be considered as evidence. The specially set tasks can be skills/proficiency/competency tests or projects or assignments. Traditionally this has been the most commonly used method of collecting evidence for accreditation.

Supplementary evidence relates to all forms of questioning (both oral and written). This is often required, as suggested in the range statement example of the driving test above, to assess the individual's underpinning knowledge and understanding of applications which might otherwise be difficult to assess.

The evidence can be built into a portfolio which might, for a teacher, include, for example:

direct evidence:
- artefacts: photographs, models
- video recordings
- audio tapes
- teaching materials
- plans: schemes of work, lesson plans
- visual aids: handouts, transparencies, slides, charts
- evaluation materials: tests, test results, questionnaires, interview data
- development work: papers from working parties, proposals for new programmes/courses
- reports: meetings, conferences, visits, discussions with colleagues
- summaries: books, articles, radio or TV programmes
- projects or assignments
- analysis of classroom and other activities

indirect evidence:
- references and testimonials
- reports on practice
- feedback from employers
- certificates and awards

reflections:
- on learning activities during a course
- on development of competence
- on someone observing teaching
- on a project or an assignment

7.2.3 Collection of Evidence

Assessment must cover every element. The amount of coverage depends upon both the element, the performance criteria and the range required. In some cases it is not possible to collect evidence for all of the activities: there is not time and it would be too expensive. The individual needs to make this judgment. However, this sufficiency of evidence is crucial. Imagine collecting evidence which suggests that a candidate has only a 50:50 chance of being judged proficient. More evidence can then be collected using the same assessment method, or a different one might be used to provide the additional evidence. For example a test can be supplemented by oral questioning.

In deciding the frequency and spacing of assessments there are three variables which you should take into account:

(i)   assessment should be more frequent the closer one gets to being judged competent;

(ii) if there is some doubt as to the competence, it may be necessary to continue assessment after the student is first judged to be competent;

(iii) if the assessment is particularly large, it is practicable to subdivide it into smaller component parts.

7.2.4 Portfolio Building

Why Portfolios?

With the advent of National Vocational Qualifications, there has been a need to produce evidence related to the competence. The assessment for an NVQ consists of three stages:

(i)   planning what to do to meet the standards;

(ii) collecting together the evidence;

(iii) judging of the evidence against the standards by an assessor.

The second of these stages, the collection of evidence, is at the heart of the NVQ process. Carrying out the job whilst being observed by a qualified assessor is the best source of evidence that can be used. However, where this is not possible, candidates may perform in a simulated environment, or present a product of their work, or carry out an assignment, or answer questions, or present a statement by a colleague detailing their performance.

Generally at levels 1 and 2, the presented evidence is typically as a result of assessor observations. At the higher levels of 3 and 4 candidates are operating in a more complex environment and direct observation is not always possible or appropriate. It may be suggested in the assessment requirements that the evidence could be based on observation by an assessor or other sources such as reports, designs and other forms or written work. This mixture of evidence from diverse sources is typically gathered in a **portfolio** of evidence.

A portfolio is an organised 'folder' of evidence compiled by a candidate in relation to an element of competence. It should contain evidence that the candidate has reliably demonstrated the skills, knowledge and understanding to be given recognition of competence.

NIACE (1991) suggests that a portfolio is not only useful for qualification purposes, but is also useful for gaining employment and for personal development. In terms of gaining employment the portfolio can provide a systematic overview of past learning and achievements through its lists of verified competences which can be used as evidence for interview purposes. In terms of personal development it can encourage self assessment as well as increasing self-confidence and self-esteem through it completion.

What might be in a Portfolio?

The key features of a portfolio are shown in Figure 5.24. City and Guilds (1994) suggest that a portfolio should contain the evidence that the candidate is competent in relation to the element of competence.

> A portfolio is a 'folder' which contains details of:
>
> - skills
> - knowledge
> - understanding
> - achievement
>
> which may arise from:
>
> - observation of employment tasks
> - products resulting from performance
> - documentary evidence of completed tasks
> - written accounts of activities

Figure 5.24   Key features of a Portfolio

The source of evidence should include:

(i)   notes from an assessor detailing what has been observed and how the performance criteria and ranges were covered;

(ii)   products of candidates performance at work such as letters, memos or reports produced as part of normal work. For teachers this may be lesson plans, schemes of work, assessment plans, test instruments, or audio visual aids;

(iii)   evidence from others about the individual candidate's work and abilities. These may be letters, reports or appraisals from managers, colleagues, clients or others involved in the work process. These types of document are sometimes referred to as 'witness testimonies';

(iv)   evidence produced from supplementary activities. To ensure coverage of the standards it may be necessary to write about activities that have been completed. This may be in the form of a project or assignment that has been suggested by the assessor.

Criteria for a Good Portfolio

The assessment process is much easier if the evidence is presented in an orderly manner. The main criterion is that the portfolio should be easy to follow with the different pieces of evidence easy to locate. It should have a clear structure which makes it easy to follow. This means that the candidate needs to be logical in the design of the portfolio and have an index and cross reference system which relates the evidence to the elements of competence and performance criteria of the NVQ.

The aspects that should be included within the portfolio are:

(i)   autobiographical account indicating name, address, date of birth, job description and any other relevant details;

(ii) a list of the competences, performance criteria and range to be covered (i.e. a copy of the standards which are subdivided in the format that is to be followed);

(iii) an index for the evidence (i.e. where the sections are located);

(iv) an indication of how the elements are covered (i.e. where each of the pieces of evidence is located);

(v)   evidence (probably best divided element by element); and

(vi) supplementary written evidence to show how range has been covered (again element by element).

These are indicated diagrammatically in Figure 5.25. The indexing system presupposes that each of the pages are numbered for ease of location and some sort of dividers are used to separate each of the elements. This will further facilitate understanding of the materials.

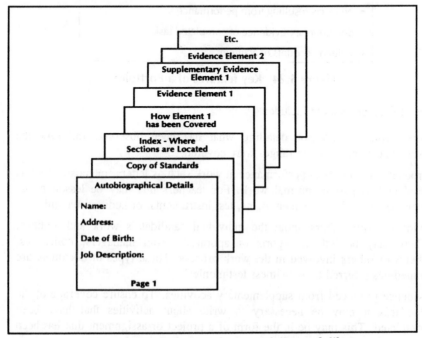

Figure 5.25   What Might a Portfolio Look like?

Portfolio Checklist

All portfolios must follow the four basic rules of evidence. These are:

(i) validity: that the evidence is directly related to the standards;

(ii) authenticity: that the evidence relates to the candidates own abilities;

(iii) currency: that evidence is up-to-date;

(iv) sufficiency: that there is enough evidence (and not **too** much) to demonstrate competence.

Figure 5.26 may provide further indications of what to do when completing portfolios. Each of the aspects should be ticked with 'Yes', any ticked with a 'No' need further consideration.

		Yes	No
1.	Does the evidence cover the performance criteria?		
2.	Does the evidence indicate how the range of situations is covered		
3.	Is the evidence relevant to the requirements of the element(s)?		
4.	Is the evidence clearly your own work?		
5.	Is there variety of types of evidence to show competence?		
6.	Have you shown reasoning why particular evidence has been chosen?		
7.	Is all of the evidence relevant?		
8.	Have the pages been numbered?		
9.	Is the indexing system and subdivisions logical?		
10.	Does the standard of presentation lead to easy location of evidence?		

Figure 5.26 Portfolio Checklist

7.2.5 Judgment of Evidence

The pyramid in Figure 5.22 suggests that judging the competence of the individual with respect to performance criteria is the responsibility of both the individual and the assessor. The assessor will likely be both internal and external. The internal assessor will be the line manager or the course tutor and will need to concentrate upon the validity and reliability of the assessment. Assessors need to guard against:

(i)   lack of direction. They need to know what is being looked for and base their judgment on this;

(ii)   halo effects where, because the individual has generally worked well, he is expected to continue to do so;

(iii) assessing progress and effort rather than achievement.

Verification

The awarding body will appoint an external examiner who will verify the judgments of the internal assessor. The primary purpose of this is quality assurance: ensuring that individuals from different centres are assessed in the same way with a common interpretation of the performance criteria.

External assessors must be:

(a)   available to carry out assessments. Meaning, that they must be in a position to observe performances or outputs;

(b)   able to interpret the performance criteria with specialist knowledge in order to recognise when it has been met;

(c)   able to manage the assessment process and be aware of the pitfalls and know how to avoid them;

(d)   willing to undertake the work involved.

In some instances it is only possible for the external assessor to sample some of the range of assessments that have been made. This, however, is not ideal and means should be found to make any sampling as effective as possible.

Certification

Individuals' achievements are recognised by the certificates of the Awarding Bodies. Once the external assessor is satisfied of the achievement of an individual or group of individuals, they will inform the Validating Body and certificates will be awarded accordingly.

The Validating Bodies have a central data bank which records credits over time. The issue of certificates depends upon the flow of accurate, timely information from the assessors. Each system will have its own appeals procedures. The first line of enquiry for this procedure is generally through the internal assessor. If this is not satisfactory then the second line is through the Validating Body who will, in turn, refer it to the external assessor.

Summary and Inter-relationships of Learning Outcomes

Once you have understood how to write various styles of learning outcomes, it is interesting to compare the methods and see how they inter-relate. Figure 5.27 gives such a guide.

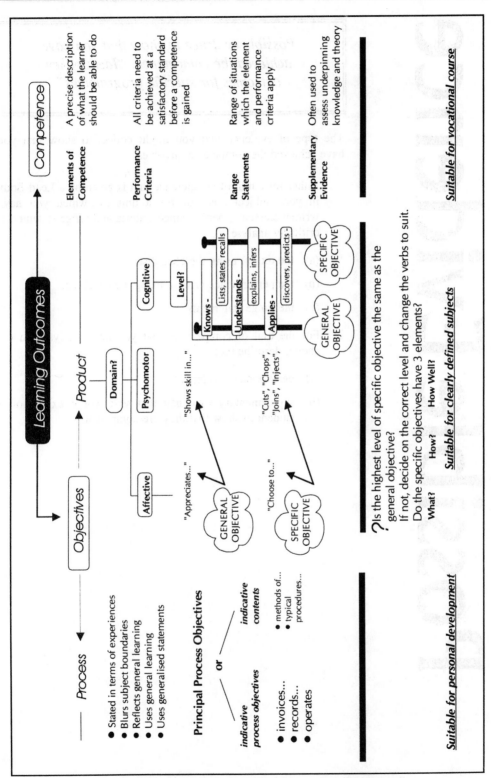

Figure 5.27   Inter-Relationship of Learning Outcomes

Possible Evidence

> *Possible evidence to show that you have achieved the competence. "Identify key outcomes for specific programmes"*

The type of evidence that you might collect to show that you have achieved the competence involves:

1. Either for a unit of competence that is given by a Lead Body in your subject area, or for a unit for which you have written elements, performance criteria and range statements, critically analyse:

    (a) the unit(s) using the checklist;

    (b) the performance criteria using the checklist;

    (c) the range statements.

2. For the unit of competence that you have analysed in (1) above, describe the:

    (a) performance evidence;

    (b) supplementary evidence that you would expect of a student to show that they are competent.

Progress Check 5.12

1. Write a definition of each of the following:

    (a) unit of competence;

    (b) performance criteria;

    (c) range statement;

    (d) performance evidence;

    (e) supplementary evidence;

    (f) evidence from prior achievements.

2. What process would you go through to judge a student competent in a unit of competence?

3. What three aspects do internal assessors need to guard against when assessing an individual's competence?

8. Scheme of Work (sequence of topics)

8.1 Definition of a Topic

At the start of a course, as the teacher, you are faced with the task of planning a series of topics and learning experiences for your students. This plan is sometimes known as a Scheme of Work. There are many ways of deciding upon the order of topics but, perhaps, difficulties occur in the identification of the word 'topic'. There is no fundamental definition of the term 'topic' (in the educational literature) as it is applied to a learning experience

For an Introduction to Teaching Course (such as C & G 730) the following may be identified as topics:

- Lesson Plans;
- Assessment;
- Memory;
- Motivation;
- Law and the Teacher;
- Profiling.

Topics like 'evaluation' 'psychology' and 'preparation for teaching' are all too large to be usefully considered as topics. So, a topic is part of a subject.

8.2 Sequence of Topics

The sequence of topics is often derived from a syllabus or list of issues to be taught. There are several ways in which you can establish your order of teaching. Some of these are:

1.	easiest topics first	in this way you can gain the confidence of students.
2.	a theme	two or more themes make-up the scheme of work. For example Parliament: theme, elections.
3.	logical sequence	in mathematics there is a need to learn addition and subtraction before multiplication and division.
4.	begin with the topics that you as the teacher are familiar with	you may be in the position of being familiar only with part of the syllabus, and teaching what you know allows you time to prepare the other topics.
5.	historical/chronological order	the causes of the First World War are taught before the battles. This is a logical and natural order. However, starting the teaching with a major battle, might create impact and the interest to see the causes.
6.	normal/abnormal	start with the normal situation and move toward the abnormal or unusual.
7.	seasonal	many topics are influenced by the seasons, e.g.

		cooking - availability of vegetables.
8.	anatomically	start at the feet and move up towards the head.
9.	fear/apprehension	with an antenatal class, first-time mums are concerned about labour pains - so deal with this first.
10.	sensitivity	if dealing with a healthy lifestyle, perhaps smoking should be one of the final issues - otherwise students may leave early in the course!
11.	most helpful	if your students' course is related to their work, then start with topics which are most relevant to them, hence creating maximum impact.
12.	controversial	starting with the least/most controversial topic.
13.	theory/practice	you may wish to integrate/mix theoretical issues with the practice or may wish to keep them discrete.
14.	geographical	this is a way to link social issues or natural resources.
15.	negotiation	set out the issues and agree a sequence with the student.
16.	availability	of resources, eg, video, workshop, laboratory, computers.
17.	group confidence development	in order to discuss sensitive issues e.g. child abuse or to use challenging teaching strategies e.g. role play.
18.	demands of other subjects	scientific or technological subjects may need to be preceded by certain mathematical topics.
19.	opportunistic	responding to the latest political news as part of the lesson on politics.
20.	must know, should know, could know	many syllabuses are overcrowded so the essential topics are addressed, then the next most important and so on. For example, with a driving and car ownership course.

Must know
know position of controls; switch on and start engine; change gear and brake; drive in a safe manner.

Should know
check oil and water levels; change wheel; tyre pressure.

Could know
change light bulbs; change windscreen wiper.

21.	order of the textbook	rarely written with sequence of teaching in mind.
22.	safety	Health and safety concerns may dictate certain issues are addressed at a very early stage in the course.
23.	evaluation	previous cohorts when evaluating the course may suggest a different sequence of topics.

A **Scheme of Work** may be defined as:

> *a series of planned learning experiences, sequenced to achieve the course aims in the most effective way.*

The scheme of work may include subject content, teaching strategies, student activities, assessment, evaluation and resources. The decision making process you go through in designing a Scheme of Work is complex and may be influenced by such aspects as:

- student entry behaviour
- course aims
- course content
- time available for learning
- teaching strategies to be used
- assessment techniques required
- resources available

The process is further complicated when 'your' subject is part of a course which must develop key (or core) skills and may have core themes like BTEC courses. Each subject planning is interdependent on the other subjects. A procedure that can be used is the Topic Precedent Diagram (TPD). This gives you a useful overview from which you can achieve an optimum learning sequence for your learners.

8.3 Topic Precedent Diagrams

You should try to make the planning process as rational as possible and Topic Precedent Diagrams will help. It is a means of achieving a logical sequence of topics so that both the learning and the teaching are readily understandable to the students. The following series of steps provide the essentials of the process:

Step 1	Identify the topics.
Step 2	Write each topic on an individual card. Place the cards in random order and then number them. This process is one way of changing the order of topics as provided by the syllabus.
Step 3	Now introduce the precedence of topics. Pickup any two cards. If the first two cards selected are 'A' and 'B', then the following questions give their relationship:

    (i)   must 'A' be taught before 'B'? Yes   (A) → (B)

    (ii)   must 'B' be taught before 'A'? Yes   (B) → (A)

    (iii) no relationship between 'A' and 'B'   (A)

    (B)

Thus, dependence upon the precedence decided by the criteria that you are using, such as historical, logical, simple to complex, decides how the cards are positioned to give the teaching and learning sequence, and the cards can be placed in

Step 4

Now pick a third topic card, 'C' and, using the criteria for precedence again, compare it with the topic in the earlier pair that has the greater precedence. For example in (i) above, compare 'C' with 'A' (the topic with the greater precedence). If

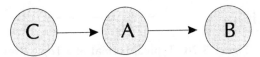

However, if 'C' does not have to precede 'A', compare it with 'B'.

You might find points of divergence when there is no direct relationship between 'A' and 'B' but 'C' must be taught before 'A' and 'B'.

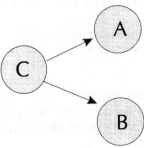

Alternatively you may find points of convergence when 'A' and 'B' have no direct relationship but must be taught before 'C'.

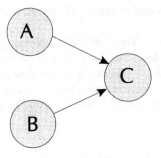

Step 5

Use a table or desk, and arrange the cards to form the TPD of the subject. This allows you to identify the TPD by movement of the cards. Once you have completed the procedure, the results are recorded in a diagram as shown below. Remember, the topics to the left must be taught before those to the right.

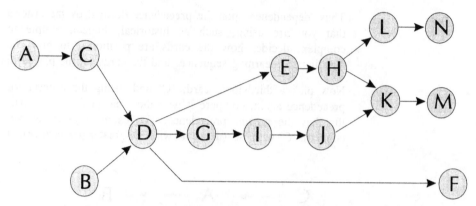

Figure 5.28   Typical Format of a Topic Precedent Diagram

Figure 5.28 shows a typical format when all of the cards have been sequenced. The diagram shows alternative starts (for example you may start with topics 'A' or 'B') and multiple finishes (you can have three optional finishing points, 'N', 'M' or 'F').

You should note that the points of convergence ('D' and 'K') indicate that the entry behaviour to that topic is complex and you may need careful revision before tackling them.

Note also that the points of divergence (that is 'H' and 'D') show the importance of these topics for subsequent learning. As such, you need to ensure that these topics are understood before you progress.

Once you have completed the diagram, the important topics that need assessing should be clear to you. These are the points of convergence and divergence. Also, you may need to revise certain topics before you can make progress. For instance, if the order is:

you may find it of value to revise 'H' before starting the teaching of 'K'.

Figure 5.29 shows a Topic Precedent Diagram for a course of applied mathematics of approximately 'A' level standard. It may be seen that the topics are linear and show their relative interdependence. Some topics are dependent upon others and themselves serve as an essential for others (for example topic 8 - basic differentiation). Other topics are relatively independent and you could consider them at almost any time (for example topic 23 - complex numbers).

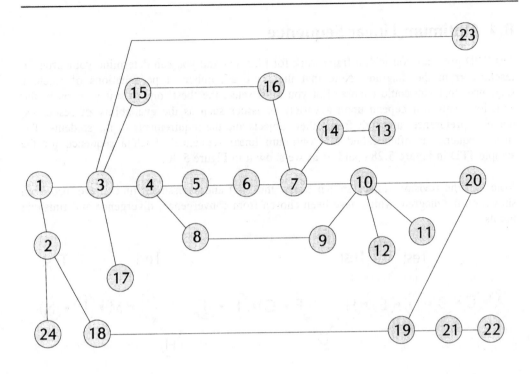

1.	Sets	13.	Taylor's Approximation
2.	Binary Ops	14.	Optimisation
3.	Mappings	15.	Functions
4.	Sequences	16.	Particle Differentiation
5.	Limits	17.	Morphisms
6.	Basic Differentiation	18.	Vector Spaces
7.	Differentiation Techniques	19.	Vector Space Trans
8.	Basic Integration	20.	Second Order Diff Eqn's
9.	Theorem of Calculus	21.	Matrices
10.	Integration Techniques	22.	Linear Equations
11.	First Order Diff. Eqn's	23.	Complex Numbers
12.	Application of Integration	24.	Relations

Figure 5.29 Example Topic Precedent Diagram - Mathematics

8.4 Optimum Linear Sequence

The TPD provides you with a framework for planning and you can determine your order of teaching from the diagram. Note that there are a number of permutations of teaching sequences that you could choose. But you must select the 'best' one to suit your particular situation. This will depend upon a variety of issues such as the availability of resources, personal preference, demands from other subjects and the requirements of the students. The 'best' sequence is often called the 'optimum linear sequence'. Such a sequence for the sample TPD in Figure 5.28 could be as we show it in Figure 5.30.

Note that the revision (topics shown below the line) and assessment times have also been shown on the diagram which have been chosen from convergence, divergence and finishing points.

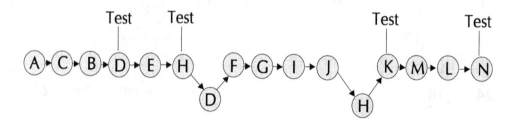

Figure 5.30   Optimum Linear Sequence of Topics from TPD, Figure 5.28

Figure 5.31 shows a TPD for Electrical Principles and it also indicates the designer's Optimum Linear Sequence (OLS). This is only one of many possible permutations. 'A' on the OLS denotes an assessment point and is usually placed after a topic which forms the basis for more advanced work. For example, many topics depend upon the learner understanding Topic 10.

You may also usefully indicate revision points on the OLS. For instance, you might find it beneficial to revise topics '2' and '9' after topic '28' before proceeding to topic '37'.

Mathematical, scientific and historical subjects lend themselves to this type of approach to planning a Scheme of Work. However, can the more creative subjects be considered in this structured manner? This really depends upon the subject matter and the will of the planner to reflect upon the planning process with care.

The world of Fashion is a creative area and Figure 5.32 shows an approach to planning this subject. There are fewer topics in the TPD but the use of the diagram helps stop a 'random' approach which sometimes is a feature of creative subjects. The need to be able to justify the sequence of study is an important part of the professional's task.

The use of the Word Processor is a rich area for training. One approach to planning is to divide the subject into practical and theoretical elements (see Figure 5.33). This may have benefits at the planning stage whilst in practice, learning theoretical and practical skills are well integrated.

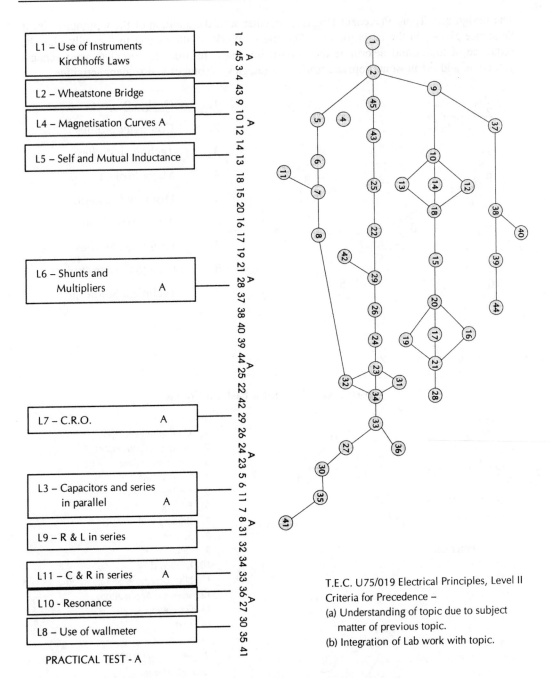

L1 – Use of Instruments
Kirchhoffs Laws

L2 – Wheatstone Bridge

L4 – Magnetisation Curves A

L5 – Self and Mutual Inductance

L6 – Shunts and
Multipliers A

L7 – C.R.O. A

L3 – Capacitors and series
in parallel A

L9 – R & L in series

L11 – C & R in series A

L10 - Resonance

L8 – Use of wallmeter

PRACTICAL TEST - A

T.E.C. U75/019 Electrical Principles, Level II
Criteria for Precedence –
(a) Understanding of topic due to subject
matter of previous topic.
(b) Integration of Lab work with topic.

Figure 5.31 TPD and Linear Sequence for Electrical Principles Subject

The teaching of various techniques in Graphics could take place in a number of different sequences. A justification of a well ordered approach is shown in Figure 5.34 which indicates a very structured sequence.

The design of a Topic Precedent Diagram together with the addition of the Optimum Linear Sequence gives you the basis for your Scheme of Work. It allows you to logically plan the sequence of topics and determine the assessment times. In order to complete your scheme you could add the most appropriate teaching strategies, resources and student activities.

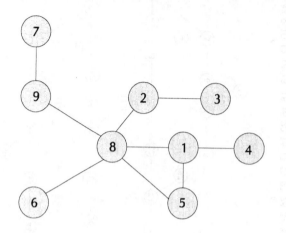

1.	Design Project
2.	Computer Studies
3.	Technical Studies I
4.	Major Project
5.	History of Fashion
6.	Art: Visual Studies
7.	Profession Studies
8.	Intro to Design Project
9.	Technical Studies II

Figure 5.32   TPD for a Fashion Course

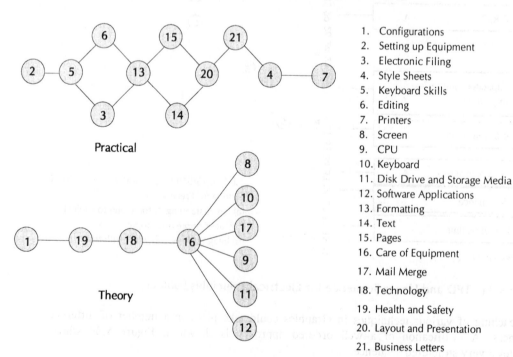

1. Configurations
2. Setting up Equipment
3. Electronic Filing
4. Style Sheets
5. Keyboard Skills
6. Editing
7. Printers
8. Screen
9. CPU
10. Keyboard
11. Disk Drive and Storage Media
12. Software Applications
13. Formatting
14. Text
15. Pages
16. Care of Equipment
17. Mail Merge
18. Technology
19. Health and Safety
20. Layout and Presentation
21. Business Letters

Figure 5.33   TPD for a Word Processing Course

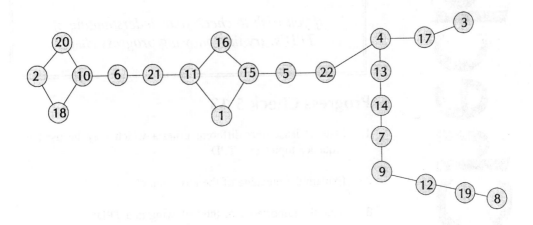

2 - 20 -18 - 10 - 6 - 21 - 11 - 16 - 1 - 15 - 5 - 22 - 4 -17 - 3 - 13 - 14 - 7 - 9 -12 - 19 - 8

1. Line – Pen + Ink
2. Correct Procedure – Drawing up art work
3. Positive + Negative – Gouache
4. Gouache Consistency – Flat colour
5. Halftone – Pen + Ink – Technical + felt
6. Image Grid – Enlarge/reduce
7. Cut paper – coloured
8. Applying Knowledge to Design Problems
9. Using Markers
10. Use + Care of Equipment: Brushes, Pens, Light, Light box etc.
11. Awareness of Techniques + Media
12. Experimental Approach
13 Gouache – Halftone
14. Coloured Pens – Halftone
15. Halftone – Monotone – Graphite
16. Basic use of Media Line Graphite
17. Flat Colour - Gouache
18. Correct use of Tracing Paper
19. Choice of Ground
20. Stretching Paper
21. Presentation of Finished Work
22. Understanding of Colour Theory

Figure 5.34 TPD for a Graphic Techniques Course

Progress Check

> *If you wish to check your understanding of TPD's, try the following progress check*

Progress Check 5.13

1. State at least four different criteria which may be used to sequence topics in a TPD.

2. Explain the meaning of the term 'topic'.

3. State the importance of the following in a TPD:

    -   point of divergence

    -   point of convergence

    -   finishing point

    -   optional starting points.

4. From a TPD, how could you decide:

    -   where best you might assess learning?

    -   where to revise a topic?

9. Topic Analysis

Having used the course aims, identified the main topics and organised the Optimum Linear Sequence for teaching, your next step in the planning process is to consider how you can present each of the topics to the students to make learning as simple and easy as possible. Some teachers go directly from the identification of the topic to the intended learning outcomes, for example by writing objectives or competences. If you wish to adopt a more rigorous approach, then you would include Topic Analysis which assists you in the identification of the main components of the topic (the sub-topics). Then proceed to order the sub-topics into a learning sequence which you will use in your lesson plan.

There are four main models of Topic Analysis which we will consider and these are ascribed to Davies (1971), Rowntree (1974), Gagne (1975) and Stenhouse (1975). Each model has its own advantages and limitations. Some subjects lend themselves to analysis by one (or more than one) of the models. Equally important is your preference for a model. If the model helps you to plan, then it serves a need. It is a valuable exercise to try each of the models in order to find which is the most helpful to you. You might find that you could use a combination of models for part of the subject (for example cognitive domain) and then use another for a different part (for instance affective domain).

9.1 Davies' Model of Topic Analysis

Davies suggests that you should ask five questions for each topic:

1. *What do you expect the students to demonstrate in order to show that they have learned the topic?*

This concentrates your mind on the objectives to be achieved through the learning of the topic.

2. *What questions do you expect the student to be able to answer?*

The questions that are to be answered by the students give an indication of the sub-topics that are required from the topic.

3. *What tasks, procedures and techniques should the student perform?*

Your response to this question forces you to concentrate upon the student activities required in the learning of the sub-topics.

4. *What discrimination must be made?*

Here a comparison is made between what has already been learned and what needs to be learned.

5. *What total change in behaviour do you expect and how will this be observed and measured?*

Your response comes back to the objectives and gets you to add criteria of acceptable performance.

Your responses to these five questions provide you with a framework for Topic Analysis and a series of prompts. It is a useful exercise in identifying sub-topics and objectives but is less helpful in the formulation of a learning sequence (that is the ordering of the sub-topics). Figure 5.35 shows how the five questions might be used to analyse the topic "painting a door".

Davies Question	Response
How will students demonstrate that they have learned the topic?	The students shall show skill in the application, of undercoat and gloss paint to a door, by brush.
What questions must the student answer?	The students must answer questions about: - need to protect surroundings from paint splash; - application of undercoat; - between coat procedures; - application of gloss paint; - the cleaning of tools, equipment and surroundings after each process.
What tasks, procedures and techniques must the student perform?	Skill of preparation. Skill of application of paint by brush. Working with others. Ability to work tidily.
What discriminations must be made?	Students should understand the difference between undercoat, gloss and emulsion paint. They should know how to avoid runs, misses, curtains, nibs, etc.
What total change in behaviour is expected?	The learner shall show skill in painting a door to a professional standard in a real or simulated environment.

Figure 5.35   Application of Davies Topic Analysis to Painting a Door

9.2 Rowntree Model of Topic Analysis

Rowntree's model uses a two dimensional perspective to Topic Analysis which allows you to use a chart or diagrammatic approach. The horizontal analysis shows you the 'component behaviours' while the vertical one shows you the 'contributory' or 'enabling behaviours'.

In the example given by Rowntree (Figure 5.36) the cognitive domain is on the left handside of the diagram with the right handside concerned with psychomotor abilities.

The horizontal aspects show the various components (that is the type of charts available). The vertical view shows what is needed to achieve the components (for example for a pie chart - draw a circle, divide the circle using a protractor, and so on). Thus, the horizontal analysis provides you with the sub-topics and the vertical provides you with the sequence with an indication, perhaps, of the required entry behaviour. This required entry behaviour is shown in italics at the bottom of each of the lines in the figure.

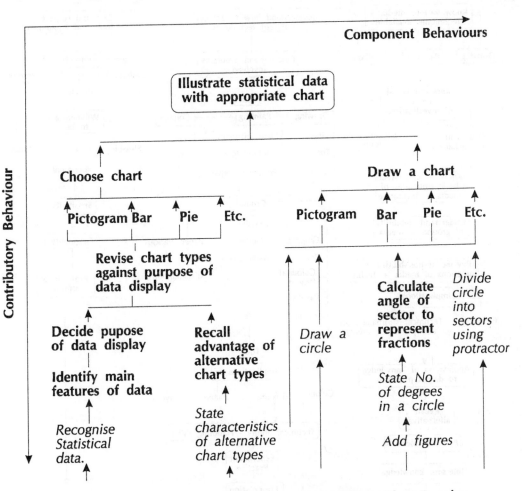

Figure 5.36 Application of Rowntree Topic Analysis to Chart Drawing

The Rowntree analysis can also be applied to 'Basic Graphics Techniques' and this is shown in Figure 5.37. Clearly this is a large topic but the analysis yields valuable insights which will enable you to identify the intended learning outcomes (that is the objectives and competences).

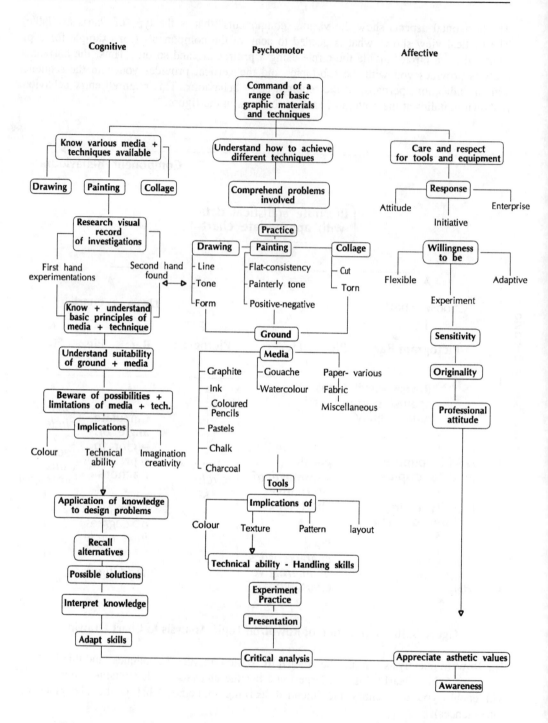

Figure 5.37 Application of Rowntree Topic Analysis to Basic Graphics

9.3 Gagné Model of Topic Analysis

The Gagné model is based on a hierarchy of learning; that is the student must learn simple things before learning complex ones. An example of the use of the model is shown (Figure 5.38) below with each of the Gagné stages identified for solving the problem 'How to Select an Appropriate Type of Holiday'.

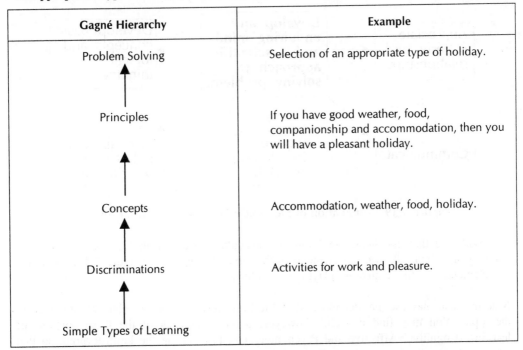

Gagné Hierarchy	Example
Problem Solving	Selection of an appropriate type of holiday.
Principles	If you have good weather, food, companionship and accommodation, then you will have a pleasant holiday.
Concepts	Accommodation, weather, food, holiday.
Discriminations	Activities for work and pleasure.
Simple Types of Learning	

Figure 5.38 Application of Gagné Topic Analysis to selecting a Holiday

In this way, learners start with simple types of learning (stimulus-response) leading to discriminations, through concepts and principles until, finally, they can use all of this learning in the solving of problems; the most difficult type of learning.

The advantage of the Gagné-type of Topic Analysis is that it allows you to sequence the work in terms of the order in which learning naturally takes place. The problem for you is that, in order to use the Gagné Model, you must be able to identify the types of learning with accuracy. Indeed, not all teachers subscribe to the Gagné learning types.

9.4 Stenhouse Model of Topic Analysis

The Stenhouse Model suggests that some course aims may be difficult to achieve merely by using the teaching topics. It suggests that you can use some aims directly to formulate the sub-topics and that you can use the model to achieve them. In the example given in Figure 5.39 'To Develop an Enquiring Mind and a Scientific Approach to Problems', learning may be achieved incidentally, but Stenhouse believes the analysis will help you structure teaching to ensure that activities take place which make the achievement of such aims more likely.

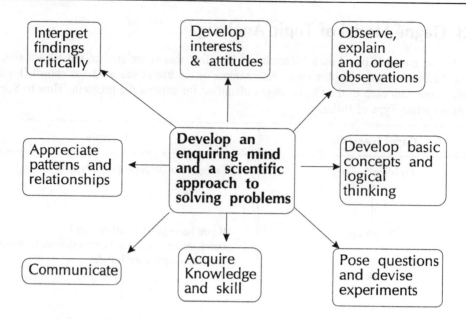

Figure 5.39   Application of Stenhouse Topic Analysis to Problems

You will find that the Stenhouse Model is particularly useful with 'creative' subjects. It allows you to 'map' the various elements of the topic. The example (Figure 5.40) shows the key elements in a first course in 'playing the violin'.

Note that you may use the Stenhouse Model to brainstorm the various elements involved in the topic. You may find it useful, however, to consider each of the three domains of learning (Cognitive, Affective and Psychomotor) in turn during the brainstorming so that you can be sure that you are being comprehensive in your coverage.

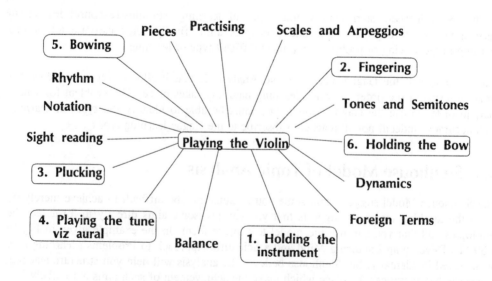

Figure 5.40   Application of Stenhouse Model to Violin Playing

> *If you wish to check your understanding
> of topic analysis try the
> following progress check*

Progress Check 5.14

1. What are the 5 questions that Davis suggests should be answered to analyse a topic?

2. What, according to Rowntree are meant by 'contributory' and 'component' behaviours.

3. Explain the Gagné hierarchy of learning which he uses as his basis for Topic Analysis.

4. What, in your opinion, is the most likely type of subject matter that can be applied to the Stenhouse method of Topic Analysis?

10. Scheme of Work (Planning Document)

We have already defined a scheme of work as 'consisting of a series of planned learning experiences sequenced to achieve the course aims in the most effective way'. Such a sequence is provided by the TPD technique outlined in section 8.3 above, giving the Optimum Linear Sequence as an example. However, to be of greater assistance, additional information can usefully be added to each of the topics to make the Scheme of Work into a really useful planning document. In order to design such a document, you need to arrive at answers to three major questions:

    (i)   for *whom* am I planning the scheme?

    (ii) what must I consider *before* planning?

    (iii) what must I consider *when* planning?

Answers to these questions might be:

    (i)   For whom am I planning the scheme?

This must be mainly for the students to increase the efficiency of their learning. In order to increase this efficiency students progress from ignorance to efficiency through three stages of:

(a)	wanting to learn	- consideration should be given to both long and short-term goals;
(b)	understanding	- you need to assess the students' initial level of understanding and assist them to find this level.
(c)	practice	- there is a need for students to be involved in the learning of their subjects and the amount of involvement will likely differ between vocational and nonvocational subjects.

    (ii) What must I consider before planning my course?

Prior to such planning you need to consider your own personal ability and the type of course which you are planning. Your own ability relates to:

    (a) your knowledge of the subject and your ability to keep up-to-date with the subject;

    (b) your own personal experience of the subject both as a student and a teacher; and

    (c) your ability to use the range of teaching strategies in terms of your knowledge of the range, and the facilities that you have available to use such a range.

    (iii) What must I consider when planning my course?

This, of course, is the main question that you must ask yourself. The answers might be:

(a) the *aims of the course* which give you an indication of the ultimate goals and the intended course participants. Well written aims should also indicate the relative amounts of time that might be allocated to the cognitive, psychomotor and affective domains and the different levels in the cognitive domain required (whether it is knowledge, comprehension or application). Such time will not be direct in terms of the respective numbers of hours but this might be gauged from the different numbers of aims that are indicated.

(b) the *content* of the course. This again leads to subquestions. In terms of the required content, what do the students already know about the subject, or what are they likely to know? This will depend upon what courses are required as entry requirements for the course and what vocational experiences the students are likely to have received from their employment.

Additionally, there will likely be a difference between the various topics of content. The topics might be subdivided into what students *must* know and what they *should* know. In other words there are some topics that are basic to the understanding of the course while others are more peripheral.

(c) the *duration* of the course. The length of the course has a direct influence on, as indicated above, the content that will be covered and the manner in which that content is presented to the students and the activities that you are able to plan; a teacher-centred approach will take less time than a student-centred one. Thus, the available time has a direct influence on the teaching and learning methods that you use. Also, the time has a bearing on both the type and number of assessments that you are able to plan.

(d) the *teaching strategies* to be used. As indicated above, in your scheme of work you need to consider whether (and where) to use teacher and student-centred approaches. The teacher-centred approaches are more applicable for the knowledge aspects, whereas the student-centred ones are more applicable for higher levels in the cognitive domain and the psychomotor and affective domain learning. Thus you need to consider the domains of learning that are involved and whether formal or informal approaches are to be used. It is also important to obtain variety of approach across the syllabus.

(e) the *methods of assessment* to be used. As a 'rule of thumb' you need to plan not more than 10% of the total time to be allocated to assessment and feedback to the students. You need to decide the place of formal and informal assessment procedures and the place of phase tests, question and answer, examinations, assignments, practical tests, observation and self-assessment.

When planning the Scheme of work, apart from the aspects outlined above, you particularly need to consider the needs of the students. These are the people for whom the Scheme is designed and, unless they have priority, you may be involved in much work that is not worthwhile. The following checklist gives the type of questions that you might ask yourself in order to ensure that you do place them high on your list of priorities when designing your Scheme.

Checklist of Student Characteristics

- What are the details of the group involved?
- How old are they?
- What is their educational background?
- Where do they live?
- What is the social bias of their various communities?
- What moral standards are they likely to have?
- What things stand high in their list of values?
- What are their interests?
- What is their employment category?
- What are the details of the type of job that they have?
- What experience of the subject are they likely to have?

It is, of course, unlikely that you are able to answer all of these questions for all of the students in your group. You are going to have to make general responses to many of the questions and you may not be able to obtain the information on others. However, the consideration of answers to the questions is a useful guide to the design of your Scheme of Work. Answers to them can assist you to answer other questions which you, as teacher, need to consider, as indicated in the teacher checklist below.

Teacher Checklist for the Scheme of Work

- How long is the course?
- Are there any basic and necessary subjects to be included in the Scheme?
- What is the likely reaction of the students to the course?
- What type of teaching method will be appropriate to their abilities?
- What tutorial arrangements will have to be made?
- What resources are at my disposal?
- What assistance will I have whilst working on the course?
- How can I best assess progress being made towards achieving the aims of the course?
- What, if any, summative assessment is in place?

An example part of a Scheme of Work is shown in Figure 5.41. The basis of the Scheme is the list of *topics*. The sequence in which the topics have been placed has been obtained from the Optimum Linear Sequence of the Topic Precedent Diagram. The *content*, obtained from a Topic Analysis, has been added for each topic and, for each of the topics the *teaching activity, student activity and resources* have been added. The completed Scheme thus provides the teacher (and the students if it is decided to present the Scheme to them) with a comprehensive overview of the programme and an excellent basis for the design of individual lesson plans. It allows the teacher to consider the course as a whole, which is often difficult when considering the design of the individual lessons.

Lesson No.	Topic	Content	Teaching Activity	Student Activity	Resources
1.	Personal Hygiene	Cleanliness - importance of good hygiene habits: social effects of good personal hygiene. Fashion sense: Making the most of yourself; Make-up and hair care.	Exposition, drawing together information from students' lists. Collect pictures or draw latest fashions (asked to bring them in next week). Discuss pros, cons, of fashion today. Plan fashion show (for a later date).	List all of the advantages of good personal habits. Discuss in groups. Discussion.	Film "Looking Good". Unilever Fashion magazine for discussion with student pictures.
2.	Personal Relationships	Peer group relationships: Relationships with opposite sex; Sex Education: Birth Control; Sexually transmitted diseases.	Exposition and Discussion. Opportunity for students to air views and problems.	Discussion after exposition of facts and distribution of leaflets and booklets for guidance.	Health Education leaflets and booklets.
3.	Smoking Alcohol and Drugs	Social and Personal effects; Cost: Emotional Problems.	Factual exposition followed by film, supported by discussion and guidelines for preparation of project.	Start a project working in groups of 4: (a) collecting information on effects of smoking (b) on drinking and (c) on effects of drug abuse.	Film: "Abuses" Health Education Council.
4.	Etc.				

Figure 5.41 Example Scheme of Work for a Subject 'Healthy Living'

It is from a document such as this that an overview of both teacher and student activities can be gauged. If, for instance, there is too much teacher-centred activity, then a topic can easily be seen where a more student-centred approach might be chosen. An omission in this type of approach, however, is that no outcomes are indicated. When using an approach such as this, the objectives or competences would have to be written on a separate sheet.

To overcome this problem an alternative approach might be used where each topic is written on a separate 'card' which we have termed a 'Topic Card'. An example card is shown in Figure 5.42 with the general information related to the topic on the front side of the card and the specific information relating to content and teaching and learning approaches detailed on the reverse side.

It will be seen that there is much more information when the Topic Card approach is adopted but it has the disadvantage that not all of the course is detailed on one sheet. Thus you are not able to see the whole of the course at a glance.

TOPIC CARD

Subject	Total No of Lessons	Total Duration _____ Hours
Topic	Lesson No.	Duration: _____ Hours

Entry Behaviour:

_____

Outcomes:	Domain		
1.	C	A	P
2.			
3.			

Reverse side of Card

Lesson Content

_____   _____   _____

_____   _____   _____

| **Teaching Method(s)** |
| **Student Activities** |
| **Assessment Method(s)** |
| **Aids/Resources** |
| **Evaluation of Lesson** |

Figure 5.42 Topic Card Approach to Scheme of Work Design

11. Lesson Planning

If you observe experienced teachers you may find a wide variation in practice with regard to their approach to lesson plans. Some teachers have very detailed plans while others 'appear' to have little at all in the way of a plan. What is important is that the lesson is always planned with care. What follows is a guide to some ways in which you may plan. You should experiment with planning until you find the method which works best for you. When you are planning a lesson you will find that a range of factors influence you. Figure 5.43 gives a brief overview of the process you could use. The student, of course, is at the centre of the process.

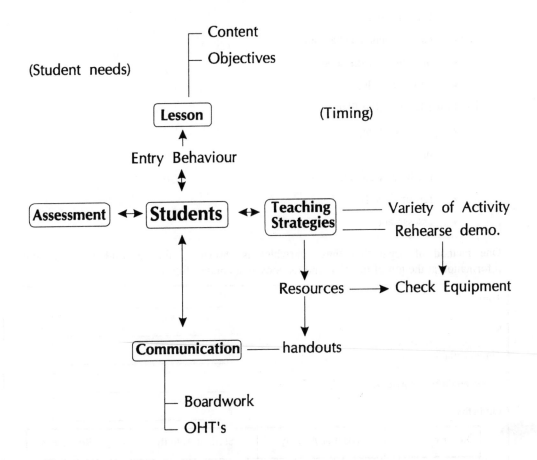

Figure 5.43 Factors which influence the Lesson Planning Process

You need to consider several strands. Begin with the intended learning outcomes (objectives/competences). In this case you need to identify the entry behaviour of the students - it could be that they know (a) too little and you have to start at an 'easier' level or (b) too much so that they do not need instruction. You should plan your communication with the students and aim to encourage communications between them. Use a variety of activities to maintain interest which will, in turn, influence your timing and your use of a range of teaching strategies and resources. When you use resources, check that the equipment does work and that you know (or remember) how to use it. For example, with demonstrations, check before you start that all of the equipment that you require is working. How long will it take to complete the demonstration?

At this stage you may wonder how you might plan all of this. The key features for a lesson plan include:

    (i)   Initial information:

- topic;
- class details;
- expected entry behaviour;
- objectives of the session;
- time available.

    (ii) In the Body of the Plan:

- student activity;
- timing;
- teaching strategies;
- resources/aids;
- assessment.

One method of organising these variables is shown in Figure 5.44 with the initial information at the top of the plan and its body in a column format.

| Topic _____ |
| Class _____ |
| Time available _____ |
| Expected Entry Behaviour: _____ |
| Objectives _____ |

Key/Time	Teacher Activity	Student Activity	Resources

Figure 5.44 Possible Layout for a lesson Plan

It is vital that you consider the lesson in three stages:

(i)   introduction;

(ii) development (the main body); and

(iii) conclusion (summary).

We have said of the lecture that the good lecturer 'tells students what is going to be told', 'tells them' and then 'tells them what they have been told'. This, in effect, corresponds to the three stages of a lesson.

In a student-centred lesson, your first phase may be to outline the activity to your students and check what they should know in order to complete it (the entry behaviour). Follow this by getting the students to attempt the activity. Finally, ensure that the learning has taken place through question and answer or a test or activity that makes the required check or, alternatively, review the main points of the session (the conclusion).

We have said previously in Chapter 1 that all lessons should have an introduction (beginning), development (middle) and conclusion (end). Consider the following scenario:

> *An inexperienced, young teacher, who works for St. John's Ambulance, has been asked to complete a 2 hour session on resuscitation to a group of twelve adults from an industrial background. He is nervous of the group because he has not met them before and realises that they have considerably more life experience than he has. He has planned a set of product objectives to cover basic anatomy and a set of procedures for carrying out resuscitation. He has put both of these (the objectives and the procedures) onto overhead transparencies. Additionally he has prepared transparencies for the main functions of the heart together with the causes of cardiac arrest and procedures for carrying out basic life support. He wants all of the group to practice the skills before the end of the two hours. He walks into the class with the twelve students there and they are all talking to each other. The introduction consists of showing the OHP of the objectives and briefly going through them. He then has a forty-five minute input about the heart, causes, signs and symptoms of cardiac arrest and the procedures for basic life support. The remainder of the session is spent with individuals practising life support on a dummy with others watching. Suddenly he realises that he has gone 5 minutes over the time and calls the end of the session.*

So, how can we critically analyse this lesson? There has been only a very brief introduction and no conclusion at all. The session has had a 'sudden' start with very little preparation of the students for the main part of the lesson. Also, he has no specific idea of what they already know about resuscitation and does not know specifically what their interests are or why they have attended. To make matters worse there is no conclusion which means that he has little idea of what has been learned and has not summarised the main points of the session for them. What might he have done during these two important phases, the introduction and the conclusion, of the lesson?

The **introduction**, as a general rule, should be about 10% of the overall time available - in the scenario above this means about 10 minutes. It should gain both the attention and interest of the students and begin to build rapport with them. At the end of this phase students should look forward to what comes next. It needs to be informative about the session itself so that students have some idea of what to expect both in terms of the subject matter and how it is planned to be dealt with. Aspects for this first phase of the lesson that he might have chosen from include:

- introducing himself;
- review the previous lesson by asking questions about it (from the previous lesson's objectives);
- assessing the entry behaviour by asking questions about the topic;
- describe the importance of the topic and how it might subsequently be used;
- show objectives;
- describe an overview of the session;
- inform students about the style of the lesson (make your own notes, there will be a test, there will be opportunity to practice for yourself);
- show end product (cake).

Choosing three or four of these should settle the class, get them thinking (about what has gone before and about what is to come) and set the scene.

The **conclusion** phase of a lesson is just as important. A lot has gone on during the session and much has been both said and done. It is important, for the sake of memory recall as much as anything, to highlight the main points from all that has gone on during the lesson: students need to be able to sort the important aspects from those that are less important. So, you need to condense the lesson into a few basic points that can be quickly presented to the students to make sure that they have understood the lesson and achieved its objectives. The summary should be brief but sufficient time should be allowed to answer any student questions which may arise. As with the introduction, about 10% of the overall time should be allocated to this part of the lesson so that in our scenario above, with 15 minutes to go, the teacher knows that he must finish the development phase and start the conclusion.

As a review, the conclusion is a way of reinforcing the lesson and drawing it together. At the same time you can obtain feedback from the students as to whether they understood the lesson. You should not think of the summary as an add-on to the end of the lesson which serves only to repeat the main points that you have covered. It should be more than a review, it should extend the lesson, rather then merely restate it. You can make suggestions to the ways that students might apply what they have learned to previous learning. It should further the students' understanding by allowing them to reflect upon what they have learned and look forward to what they will learn. Additionally, you should always include opportunities to obtain student feedback. This is needed for you to have some indication whether the students have understood the materials that you have presented in the lesson.

One method that is often used at the end of a lesson is to ask if students have any questions of their own about the topic. This is probably not the best time to ask such an open question. It is likely getting near a break time and students, even adults, do not want to hold back their colleagues to ask something that others may already know. It is probably better if you ask more specific questions that require students to answer with statements that summarise the main points covered in the lesson. You might do this by making reference to the objectives of the lesson. If you have put these onto an OHP transparency, you might show this again and pose specific questions related to each of the objectives. An informal quiz, based upon the objectives, is another good way to end a lesson. Students can exchange papers and mark each other's quizzes, or students can mark their own as the answers are discussed and explained.

If you get your students to take their own notes, you might want to ask them to refer to their notes and summarise the lesson themselves for the rest of the class. Two other ways of ending a lesson is to make a transparency of the major points and project it for the class, or to prepare a handout covering the main points and distribute it at the end.

These main ways of concluding a lesson are summarised as:

- revisit the objectives;
- assess the learning either by question and answer or by a quiz;
- review the main points either with a transparency, or the whiteboard;
- suggest how students might apply what they have learned;
- get students to review the main points from their notes;
- prepare for the next lesson by giving homework or reading.

The following lesson plans explain how you might complete these points in practice. The first example (Figure 5.45) is for a psychomotor skills lesson, the second (Figure 5.46) is to learn attitudes and the final one (Figure 5.47) is to achieve an objective with indicative content.

Topic:	Temperature Measurement
Class:	10 Student Nurses
Time Available:	60 Minutes
Expected Entry Behaviour:	State the components of a mercury-in-glass thermometer.
General Objective:	Show skill in the procedure for body temperature measurement.
Specific Objective:	Measure a person's temperature using a thermometer. Accurately record results.

Key/Time	Teacher Activity	Student Activity	Resources
Recap last lesson 5 min	Q. Normal readings of blood pressure?	Answering	OHP Transparency
Introduction 5 min	Need to take temperature. Thermometers. Use of records.	Listening	Thermometer
Development Temperature 30 min	Q. Why take temp? Q. How gain/lose heat? Use a thermometer. Body Temperatures	Answering Watching/Listening Practise on each other	OHP 1 Mediwipes List on Chalkboard
Conclusion 10 min 5 min	Recap main points Question Objective Test	Answer	Test No 6

Figure 5.45   Lesson Plan for a Psychomotor Skills Lesson

Topic:	Simulation of meeting.
Class:	15 communication students (Bus Stud).
Time Available:	70 Minutes
Expected Entry Behaviour:	State the procedures of formal meetings.
General Objective:	Appreciate the relative merits of meetings as part of the decision making process.
Specific Objective:	Listen to others. Contribute to decision making process. Support other members of the class.

Key/Time	Teacher Activity	Student Activity	Resources
Introduction 5 min 5 min	Purpose of simulation. Issue/allocate roles	Listening Reading	Suitable room. Role cards
Development 30 min 20 min	Agenda item 1 Agenda item 2 Agenda item 3 Debrief - questions	In role Feedback/discussion.	Agenda items.
Conclusion 10 min	Summary of key learning issues.	Note taking	OHP Transparency.

Figure 5.46 Plan for Lesson to Teach Attitudes

Topic:	Making a video 'Interviewing Consumers' Lesson 1.
Class:	10 Personnel Officers.
Time Available:	3 hours.
Expected Entry Behaviour:	Explain the components required in planning.
Objective:	Participate in the making of a video. Observe reactions of the interviewer and interviewee.
Indicative Content:	Use of camera. Team work. Planning work.

Key/Time	Activity
9.00	Meet class – discuss overall task. – distribute duties to students e.g. collect camera, etc.
9.45	Meet at 'scene'.
9.50	Confirm/discuss duties with individuals.
10.10	Coffee.
10.30	Questions.
10.35	Record interviews.
11.15	Adjourn to room to see tape.
12.00	Lunch (p.m. editing, etc.)

Figure 5.47   Example Lesson Plan Related to Indicative Content

> *If you wish to check your understanding
> of lesson planning try the following
> progress check*

Progress Check 5.15

1. List the six main aspects which could be included in the introductory information of a Lesson Plan

2. Give two useful activities which could be included in the introduction to a lesson.

3. Identify the headings that are useful for the body of a Lesson Plan.

4. What percentage of the total time for the lesson might be given to:

   (i) the introduction;

   (ii) the summary;

   of a lesson?

12. Negotiation

The needs of students clearly vary enormously and this is particularly true of adult learners. Using a standardised course you cannot hope to meet the range of abilities, expectations and temperaments of all of your students, but can only hope to meet some of their needs for some of the time.

If you negotiate an individual programme with a student, there is a greater likelihood that it will suit the needs of that individual. However, the system is not without its problems and in Figure 5.48 we outline some advantages and limitations.

Advantages of Negotiation	Limitations of Negotiation
- Increased motivation. - Course seen as 'right for me'. - Students active in the learning process. - Closer relationship with teacher. - Early identification of learning problems. - Increased opportunities for pastoral counselling. - Good for social skills. - Highlights (unknown) student skills	.- Can be difficult to manage. - Can be bureaucratic. - Students may not want to take on role. - Lack of rapport leading to lack of agreement. - Unrealistic goals may be set. - Practical considerations (e.g. laboratory availability) may cause difficulties.

Figure 5.48 Advantages and Disadvantages of Negotiation

12.1 The Process

The process of negotiation may be seen as a five stage model:

    (i)   preparing for negotiation

    (ii)   the first session(s)

    (iii) the contract

    (iv) monitoring the learning

    (v)   the review

(i) Preparing for Negotiation

Before entering into the negotiation process, you should have a very clear idea of what your student is to achieve. The limiting factors, or constraints, that you need to establish are, for example, whether the assessment is to be determined by a third party, if the institution has constraints such as 'supervision' at all times, what is the time scale (not only the end dates but, also, regular reviews). Unplanned difficulties arise and you need to build in some contingency for them. The student may be unfamiliar with negotiation and your planning needs to take this into account. Finally, decide the best place for the first and subsequent meetings.

(ii) The First Session(s)

Students often find negotiation difficult, if only because they may be adolescents dealing with an adult in a new situation. It is important, therefore, that you quickly establish a rapport. Perhaps a useful way to start is to find out more about the students as people by asking about their interests and ambitions. Establish the framework and limits or boundaries of the negotiation before the process begins properly. One approach that you could use is to start from details and proceed to agree detail by detail. This involves great expertise and time. You may find it more useful to secure a broad, wide ranging agreement and then explore area by area. Your role is to listen to the students, confirm beliefs and agreements by repeating them, and then to probe a range of issues. You will find that sticking points do occur. It is often useful not to spend too much time on these but to refer to them at a later stage.

(iii) The Contract

At some stage you will need to 'firm-up' or agree the proposals. You can do this in the form of a contract or agreement. This is best in writing and needs to be in a language that the students understand - in fact, get them to draft the contract. From the contract, your students should be clear about what is the intended learning, what is to be done, how it is to be done, what resources are available, what is the time-scale, how the outcomes are prescribed and, finally, what are the assessment criteria. Regular reviews need to be a feature of the contract.

(iv) Monitoring the Learning

It is important to have regular reviews to monitor progress. In this way you will set the student a series of deadlines in which to work thereby giving a structure to the process. You can identify progress, or lack of it, so that the final outcomes should be no surprise to you. The student should do most of the talking at the reviews. You can achieve this by posing questions such as 'How is the project going'? 'Have you any problems'? or 'What problems have you had'? 'What are you going to do next'? You might find it useful to note some of the outcomes in the contract itself.

(v) The Final Review

Your final stage is to review what has been done and learned. Your ultimate question is 'Has the student achieved the intended learning outcome'. This may include a discussion of a formal assessment. What is also important is 'What would you do differently?' and 'What have you learned in other (negotiated) learning?'

12.2 Summary

As you can see, the negotiated curriculum places very different demands upon both you and the student. The benefits for the student have been discussed. The benefits for you come when you can see your students working on their own initiative and discussing, in an adult or even enthusiastic manner, their work. You need to have, or develop, the skills of a negotiator, manage several different learning activities and, very importantly, manage your own time to ensure all students have sufficient support.

Possible Evidence

> *Possible evidence to show that you have*
> *achieved the competence*
> *Design Learning Programmes related*
> *to specific needs of students'*

The type of evidence that you might collect to show that you have achieved the competence includes:

1. Draw a Topic Precedence Diagram and Optimum Linear sequence for your own subject area. To complete this you will need to:

    (a) define the topics;

    (b) follow the suggested steps to produce the TPD;

    (c) design an OLS from the TPD and, on it, show revision and testing time.

2. Using the OLS as a basis, design a Scheme of Work where, for each topic, you indicate the learning time required, the teaching methods and resources to be used, and the assessment procedures that you will plan.

3. Select a topic from your TPD and apply the most appropriate methods of topic analysis to it. Give reasons for your choice of method.

4. Using the topic analysis that you have completed, plan a lesson using the criteria that have been suggested.

5. Critically analyse the written lesson plan either from the basis of having written it, or after you have used it with a class, from the basis of having used it.

6. Design a pro-forma which could be used as a basis for a contract for your students to negotiate effective learning. Critically analyse the design of the contract.

> *If you wish to check your understanding of negotiation try the following progress check*

Progress Check 5.16

1. List the 5 stages that might usefully be used in negotiating a learning programme with a student.

2. Identify at least three aspects that you should prepare before negotiating a learning programme with a student.

3. Define a learning contract.

4. Why are regular reviews important when questioning a negotiated learning contract with a student?

5. List the important questions that you should ask a student in the final review of a negotiated learning contract.

Progress Check

13. Classroom Management

What is classroom management? It seems to beg the question to define it as 'managing the classroom situation'. However, management is about control, about directing affairs, and about coping with uncertainties. Classroom management relates to the following:

- controlling the learning situation;

- directing the learning for the students; and

- coping with the individual student differences.

So classroom management can be defined as:

> *"managing the classroom situation to ensure that an **atmosphere** is generated where the most effective learning takes place for all of the students".*

You will know when the right atmosphere has been achieved in a classroom because the students will have drive (be keen to master the new knowledge), self-enhancement (strive to have esteem and satisfaction from a job well done), and affiliation (be eager to gain the approval of you as teacher and of other members of the class).

Much of the literature suggests that there are four main areas of importance in classroom management:

(i)	**arousal**	to ensure that students are motivated and ready to learn;
(ii)	**expectancy**	making sure that students know what is required of them and what they will be able to do after learning;
(iii)	**incentive**	ensuring students know how achievement will be rewarded; and
(iv)	**disciplinary**	ensuring that the work of a group is not disrupted.

We agree that these four are important for classroom management purposes, but we would add to this list a fifth area which is equally important. This is:

| (v) | **employment** | ensuring that students are gainfully employed in a variety of activities. |

It is thought that now, not only is this list comprehensive, but it is also in order of priority with 'arousal' probably the most important in terms of learning and, especially with adult learning, discipline being the least important.

The first of these factors, **AROUSAL**, relates to attention: to individuals paying attention to the learning and committing themselves to the task in hand. There are both external and internal factors that are associated with and influence arousal. The **external** factors are the ones that the teacher influences and the **internal** ones are the physical and mental dispositions of the individual.

External factors include:

(i)   the intensity of the stimulus that is being presented to the student can have an effect on attention. Loud noises, bright colours and strong odours are compelling stimuli. So, how can we use these in the classroom? You can ensure that your voice is heard and present whiteboard or OHP presentations in a colourful way.

(ii) **novel** stimuli attract attention. The reason for using *italics* in a textbook is to draw your eye to key concepts by printing the words in an irregular way. Similarly, using different teaching and learning methods which are novel to the student can assist arousal and commitment to the task.

(iii) a **variable or changing stimulus** can demand our attention. As a teacher you quickly discover how to use your voice by frequently changing the intonation. Wall charts and aids should be changed regularly, otherwise they no longer attract attention.

(iv) **spatial and temporal irregularity** affects attention adversely. Irregular presentation of stimuli improves attention. The spatial regularity of handouts can be improved by the use of sub headings and capitals to emphasise key points. Colour and underlining can also be used for this purpose. Variation in speed of speech is more likely to maintain attention than speech which has a temporal or tonal regularity.

Internal factors include:

(i)   **interest** is clearly a factor that can cause differential influence. Events that have relevance to the needs of an individual are more likely to attract attention. Attitudes and prejudice also affect the extent to which we are drawn to pay heed to events and ideas. Anyone who is prejudiced, for instance, against NVQ programmes, will pay attention when they listen to a point of view which is in agreement with this. You must, therefore, try to make topics and their application, relevant to the needs of the class.

(ii) **fatigue** has a detrimental effect on attentiveness. The implication here is to have frequent breaks, ensure that there are frequent changes of activity between ones requiring high concentration (like brainstorming) and those which do not.

(iii) **over arousal** can have an adverse effect on performance. Drive theory states that performance improves with increased arousal up to a point. Beyond this point, performance begins to deteriorate until, at high levels of arousal, performance is extremely poor. Attention is thought to operate in a similar way as the arousal level increases. The moral here is to ensure that individuals do not become overexcited, or discussion becomes overheated, in a classroom.

(iv) **personality characteristics** have a differential influence. Many behavioural distinctions exist between extroverts and introverts. Extroverts need more rest pauses while performing tasks requiring great attention. Consequently, their attention suffers in comparison with introverts. Extroverts do not like repetitive tasks and cannot concentrate consistently like introverts. So extroverts are more likely to wilt and become distracted during long periods of attentive activity.

The second factor, **EXPECTANCY**, relates to students knowing where they are going and also knowing, when they get there, that they are there. This can be used in the introductions to lessons by you telling your students what they are expected to learn. Telling them (in plain language) the objectives of the session. This, together with a brief overview of the main parts of the lesson, will provide them with an 'advance organiser' and set up an aspect of expectancy in their minds.

A second aspect of expectancy lies with having high expectations of individuals. An important experiment (Rosenthal and Jacobson 1968) involved **randomly** dividing students into three and telling one group that they were the worst, another group that they were the best, and telling the third group (the control group) nothing. They were then taught and tested. Who did best in the tests? The group who were told that they were the best. Who did the worst? The group who were told that they were the worst. A group of students will invariably live up to your expectations of them. So, always inform the class of your high expectations of them. Never tell your students that something is hard - always suggest that they are capable of doing well.

A final aspect of expectancy relates to the use of a behaviourist approach for consistency. Telling students of the objectives is the first part of behaviour modification and this should be continued in using other approaches especially with regard to **reinforcement**. Praise is usually preferable to punishment as the latter will often lead to avoidance and not the 'correct' behaviour. You should reinforce student achievement constantly and, especially with extroverts, publicly. You should avoid the use of sarcasm - it is the lowest form of wit. Also, always set a good example.

The third factor is **INCENTIVE**. No one becomes highly committed to a task when there is nothing in it for them (or for other people). Behaviourism is all about stimulus-response and advocates that responses that are rewarded (or reinforced) will be repeated. Thus, reinforcement (as indicated above) is important and students should know how achievement is to be rewarded. When an activity is set, or an assignment given, it is important that they also know how it will be assessed. Along with an assignment sheet, a **marking scheme** should also be given so that students know exactly how they are going to be assessed, what marks (or grades) are going to be used for which aspects of the work, and then they have an incentive and know where to place the effort for the work to be completed.

A second aspect of incentive relates to **relevance**. All the work that the students are asked to do should be relevant to their needs. If, for instance, the task is to learn theory for its own sake, then learning will not be as effective as it might be. It is important in the introduction to a session that you tell students **why** they are studying a topic, **how** it will help them, and **why** it is important to them.

The fourth factor, the **DISCIPLINARY** aspect of classroom management associated with adult learning, is less important than it is with children. Teachers of adults do not necessarily expect to have discipline problems like fighting or shouting at each other, or not doing as requested. The discipline problems associated with adult learning are of a more subtle nature. There can still be threats to your authority, there can still be disruption, there can still be poor time keeping, and so on. Such disruptions can lead to other members of the class being disrupted, with them finding it difficult to concentrate. An example of this is during group work when one member of the group wants to talk about something that has nothing to do with the topic. This makes it difficult for the other members to get on with their work.

The sensible teacher never allows a discipline problem to develop: it is much easier to deal with the initial stages of trouble than it is to deal with mass dissent. The problem comes with being able to recognise the signs and this is where personality can be a problem.

So, how should we deal with this type of discipline problem? You will find it useful to establish effective **rules for class conduct**: getting to class on time; telephoning about any absences; and those related to effective team work like ensuring that everyone has their say, offering only constructive criticism, and so on.

Dealing with adults is very different to dealing with children - even though, at times as adults, we all act like children. It is important that you **show concern** for individuals and treat them like colleagues.

It is very helpful to find out student interests (as well as their problems) as this can be effectively used during class contact time. Even if you do not like a student, try hard not to let it show. If you are rude to an adult it will be a long time, if ever, before it is forgotten. When discipline problems do occur it is beneficial for you to **address the management problem** rather than making an attack on an individual student.

The fifth and final factor related to good classroom management is **EMPLOYMENT**. It is important to adult learners that, at the end of a session, they feel a sense of achievement: that they have learned something. If adults do not feel a sense of achievement, then the atmosphere that you generate will not be one of effective learning. If they are not fully employed they will not look forward to coming to your classes. An important aspect of this lies with variety of activity. The more variety of different teaching and learning methods that you can employ, the more likely the concentration span of the students will be increased. Also, however, the **variety** must relate to effective activities. You should try to provide activities that are directly relevant to the achievement of the lesson objectives.

It has been suggested that good classroom management relates to five major areas of practice and, for each of them, suggestions have been made. The table at Figure 5.49 summarises the main points that have been made.

Areas of Classroom Management	Suggestions for Classroom Management
1. Arousal	• use novel strategies for a change and to break up any monotony
	• create interest through relevance
	• change the stimulus frequently between verbal, whiteboard, OHP and charts
	• have frequent breaks and change of activity to combat fatigue and to ensure that individuals do not become overexcited
	• get to know the personality characteristics of your students (extroverts and introverts) as soon as possible
2. Expectancy	• tell students the objectives of what is to be learned
	• have high expectations of your students
	• always praise student achievement
	• avoid the use of 'punishment'
3. Incentive	• ensure all students know how they are to be assessed
	• make work relevant to individual needs
	• tell students why they are studying a topic and how it will be of benefit to them
4. Disciplinary	• establish effective rules for class conduct
	• never use sarcasm or humiliate a student
	• address the management problem rather than attacking a student
	• show concern for individuals and get to know their interests
5. Employment	• ensure a sense of individual achievement
	• provide activities that are relevant to the achievement of the lessons' objectives

Figure 5.49 Suggestions for Classroom Management

> *Possible evidence to show that
> you have an understanding
> of Classroom Management*

The type of evidence that you might collect to show that you have an understanding of Classroom Management involves:

1. Write a definition of Classroom Management in your own words.

2. Give examples from your own teaching of:

   (a) arousal;

   (b) expectancy;

   (c) incentive;

   (d) disciplinary; and

   (e) employment.

   and indicate for each, with reasons, the amount of success that has been achieved in terms of increased learning for each of the examples that you have cited.

3. For adult learners, indicate and write about what aspects of classroom management are important for you.

Possible Evidence

Progress Check

If you wish to check your understanding of Classroom Management, try the following progress check

Progress Check 5.17

1.   Define classroom management in terms of efficiency of learning.

2.   Define each of the following as they relate to classroom management.

     (a)   arousal;

     (b)   expectancy;

     (c)   incentive;

     (d)   disciplinary; and

     (e)   employment.

3.   Identify six different ways that you mighty generate interest in a mixed class of adult students.

4.   Complete the grid below by putting the following in an order of priority from the most important for good classroom management to the least important and give reasons for your choice.

intensity of stimulus; novelty of stimulus; variability of stimulus; spatial irregularity.

Aspect	Reason for Choice
(i) most important	
(ii) second in importance	
(iii) third in importance	
(iv) least important	

Further Reading and References

Further reading and references relating to the topics in this chapter can be found in the following:

Brown, A. and
Haffenden, I. (1989)
Implications of Competence Based Curricula, HRW.

BTEC (1988)
Course and Unit Design, BTEC.

Bloom, B. S. (1964)
Taxonomy of Educational Objectives: Handbook 1:CognitiveDomain, Longmans.

City and Guilds (1994)
Producing a Portfolio of Evidence for an NVQ: Assessment Resource Book. City and Guilds of London Institute.

Cole, H. P. (1982)
Process Education, Education Technical Publications.

Davies, I. K. (1971)
The Management of Learning, McGraw Hill.

Fletcher, S. (1991)
Designing Competence-based Training, Kogan Page.

Fletcher, S. (1992)
Competence based Assessment Techniques, Kogan Page.

FEU (1988)
Learning by Doing, FEU.

Gagné, R. M. (1975)
Essentials of Learning for Instruction, Dryden Press.

Gronlund, N. E. (1970)
Stating Behavioural Objectives for Classroom Instruction, McMillan.

HMSO. (1996)
Dearing, R. *Review of Qualifications for 16-19 year olds.* DfEE.

Jessup, G. (1991)
Outcomes: NVQs and the Emerging Model of Education and Training, The Falmer Press.

Krathwohl, et al. (1964)
Taxonomy of Educational Objectives: Affective Domain, David Mckay.

Mager, R. F. (1970)
Preparing Instructional Objectives, Fearon Publishers.

National Extension College
(1970)
Developing Competence, National Extension College

Newble, D. and
Cannon, R. (1991)
A Handbook for Teachers in Universities and Colleges, Kogan Page.

Newby, T. (1992)
Validating your Training, Kogan Page.

NIACE (1991)
Assessment of Prior Learning and Achievement: A Study Guide and Resource Pack to Support Staff Development. National Institute of Adult Continuing Education – Replan.

Popham, W. J. (1978)   *Criterion Referenced Measurement*, Prentice Hall.

Reece, I. H. (ed) (1982)   *Aspects for Curriculum in Technical Education*, Colombo Plan Staff
                                College.

Romiszowski, A. J. (1976)   *The Selection and Use of Instructional Media*, Kogan Page.

Rosenthal, R. and   *Pygmalion in the Classroom*, Holt, Rinehart & Winston.
Jacobson, L. (1968)

Rowntree, D. (1984)   *Developing Courses for Students*, McGraw Hill.

Rowntree, D. (1974)   *Educational Technology in Curriculum Development*, Harper Row.

Russell, J. and   *Curriculum Development in FE* 3rd Edition. Further Education Staff
Latcham, J. (1979)   College

Simpson E. J. (1976)   *The Classification of Educational Objectives: Psychomotor Domain*,
                                University of Illinois.

Stenhouse, L. (1975)   *An Introduction to Curriculum Research and Development*,
                                Heinemann.

Vargas, J. S. (1972)   *Writing Worthwhile Behavioural Objectives*, Harper Row.

Chapter 6

Communication and the Teacher

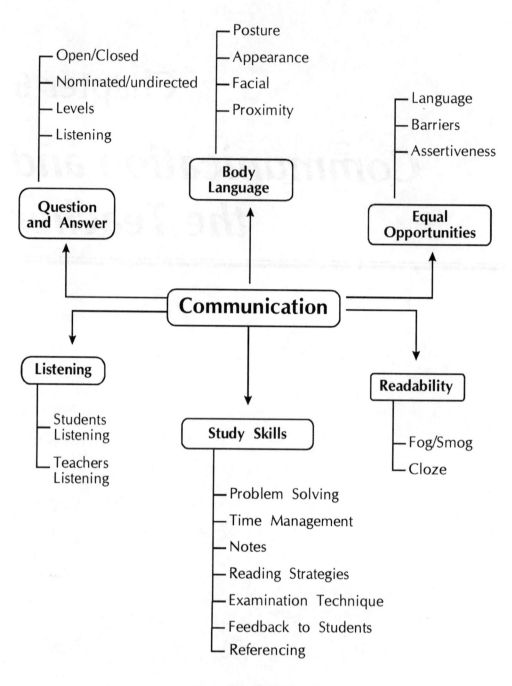

Overview of Chapter 6

Competences Related to this Chapter

The teacher competences and associated performance criteria related to this chapter are:

Overall Competence - *Employ effective Communication Techniques*.

Competence	Performance Criteria
1. Demonstrate effective communication skills	(a) Use language appropriate to the ability of the students
	(b) Use a variety of stimuli to enhance communication.
	(c) Select appropriate means of communication to suit the learners and the topic.
	(d) Use question and answer technique effectively.
2. Assist students to develop their communication skills.	(a) Identify the communication skills required by students.
	(b) Monitor progress in skill development.
	(c) Assist students to develop these skills.
	(d) Provide opportunities for students to practise these skills.

Competences

FENTO Standards

FENTO Standards Related to this Chapter

B. b2	**Planning and Preparing Teaching and Learning Programmes for Groups and Individuals** Identify appropriate teaching and learning techniques
C. c2 c3	**Developing and Using a Range of Teaching and Learning Techniques** Facilitate learning in groups Facilitate learning through experience
D. d1 d2 d3 d4	**Managing the Learning Process** Establish and maintain an effective learning environment Plan and structure learning activities Communicate effectively with learners Review the learning process with learners
F. f1	**Assessing the Outcomes of Learning and Learner'sAchievement** Use appropriate assessment methods to measure learning and achievement
H. h1 h2	**Meeting Professional Requirements** Work within a professional value base Conform to agreed codes of professional practice

Based on the FENTO Draft standards by kind permission

1. Model of Communication

Communication is essentially about one person who sends a message which is received by a second person. Some form of channel, or means of communication is needed. This channel could be sound, it could be movement, it could be smell. We have used models elsewhere in this book and Figure 6.1 shows us a basic model of communication

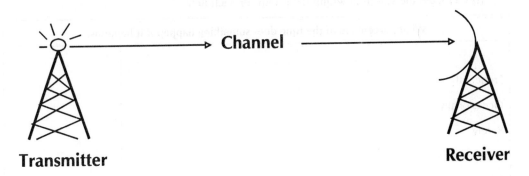

Channel

Transmitter

Receiver

Figure 6.1   Basic Communication Model

The model is satisfactory for most situations, for example, speech, non-verbal communication, reading; but in practice the situation is more complex.

In practice there are factors which distort the message or signal. This is called 'noise' and it is a barrier to good communication. If your classroom has a poor layout, the students may not be able to see or hear you. The lighting may be poor or there may be excessive sunlight. 'Noise' could be from traffic or people outside the room or it could be from the students themselves. Noise could be more difficult to identify, like pitching the level of the learning too high or too low for the learners. The vocabulary you use could be too difficult for the learner or use too much unfamiliar jargon. We have to do our best to minimise noise and make our message clear. Non verbal signals - or even verbal signals, from the students should give us valuable feedback on the quality of communications.

1.1 Are you sure your are communicating?

You are explaining to your students, they are responding and the body language is good. So everything is fine. But is it?

You can use the following game (see Figure 6.2) with your own students. Most teachers find a great variation in the answers given. Some students do not put 100% for "Always". This shows that even if the students think they understand the message - they may be understanding something which is not your message!

The game may be used as follows:

(i)   Give each student a copy of Figure 6.2 and ask them as individuals to allocate a percentage to each of the descriptors.

(ii)   Ask the group for their answers in order to find the lowest, and the highest percentage scores for each descriptor.

(iii)   For each descriptor, write the lowest percentage and the highest percentage.

(iv)   Discuss the variation within the group for each item.

What percentage of the time does something happen if it happens:	
	%
Frequently	
Occasionally	
Rarely	
Sometimes	
Usually	
Never	
Now and Again	
Always	

Figure 6.2   Percentages

We all have knowledge and skills and have formed attitudes, and many of us will even admit to some prejudice. All of these factors may have a significant impact on the effectiveness of the message. Figure 6.3 attempts to show some of the influences on communications and some of their complexities.

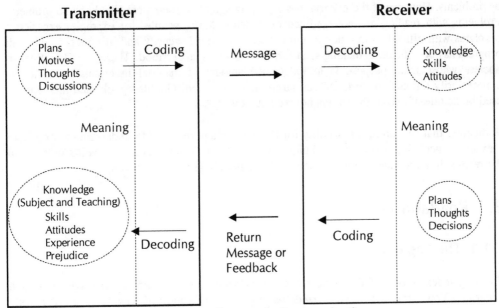

Figure 6.3   **Influences in Communications**

These complexities are involved with both the sending and the receiving of messages. Of particular importance are the affective domain aspects of the transmitter and receiver of a message. If we assume that you, the teacher, is the transmitter you have your own motives and thoughts associated with the message which influences the way that you encode (for example whether it is verbal, or done on whiteboard or a handout, or a mixture of these) the message. This is then passed on to the students who decode it in terms of, not only their knowledge and skills, but also in terms of their attitudes. Then there is the feedback element from the students back to you as the teacher. This is particularly important when you, as the teacher, decode the feedback message and your attitudes have a direct effect upon the process.

2. Reading Age and Readability

Almost all the students with whom we come into contact, will have attended school until they were at least 16 years old. We make assumptions about that experience and, in particular, we often assume that students have the ability to read the information we present to them. We give the students handouts, we write on the board and we recommend textbooks. But how often do we really consider the difficulty of the reading and the ability of the students to read well? Difficulties in learning may not be caused only by the way in which we teach, or the lack of intelligence of the student but may be the result of a reading problem. Consequently we should now look at how we can determine the reading age of a student and the readability of written materials.

Reading age is related to the reading age of the average child. So a reading age of 14 is the ability to read at the standard of the average 14 year old. *Readability* on the other hand considers the degree of difficulty with particular reading materials. Consider 14 year old pupils. If they are presented with material requiring a reading age of 16 then there could well be problems. However if the material has a reading age of 12 then there should be no problem. Problems with reading are not confined to students. Many people, for example, experience problems with official forms such as those relating to social security and income tax, although progress has been made in making such forms more easily understood. There is a Plain English Society whose main purpose is to reduce the amount of material in circulation which is unnecessarily difficult to read. Official jargon is often called 'Gobbledegook' and this word is used in the title of two of the techniques we will now look at.

Remember that calculating readability (or the reading age required to understand a text) is an inexact science. So, two of the techniques used, the FOG index and the SMOG index, and the results they produce, should be seen only as guidelines.

2.1 Readability

2.1.1 The Fog Index

The Fog index is one of the indices used to calculate the required reading age of written materials. You can use it on your handouts to give an indication of whether you are writing at an appropriate level for your students.

FOG is the *Frequency Of Gobbledegook* and may be calculated as follows:

1. Select a passage of 100 words

2. Count the number of complete sentences

3. Count the words in each of the complete sentences.

4. Find the average sentence length (L) by dividing the number of words in all of the complete sentences by the number of complete sentences (i.e. divide your answer to '3' by your answer to '2').

5. Count the number of words of three or more syllables (N) in the 100 word sample

6. Add L and N, multiply by 0.4 and then add 5 i.e. $0.4(L+N)+5$

7. This is the reading age

You may wish to select three or four passages of a textbook to find the average reading age.

The following text is designed for use with students who have a reading age of 14. The FOG index has been applied to determine its suitability for such students.

Note that in the following passage there are 100 words between the two stars.

Lamps and Lighting

(*)Filament lamps are available with a single coil of tungsten wire or with a double coil, or coiled coil, which gives more light. All common filament lamps have an average life span of one thousand hours. This light is best for normal domestic usage since it gives a good balance between the amount of life obtained and the cost of the electricity.

Filament lamps should be bought to suit the voltage of the mains supply. If, for example, your residence is supplied at 240 volts, buy lamps of the same voltage. The common size of domestic filament lamps range from about (*) 8 watts (for the dimmest of night lights) to 200 watts. Almost all household lighting needs are met by 40, 60, and 100 watt lamps but the greater the wattage, the greater the heat generated and the greater the cost.

Number of complete sentences	=	5
Average sentence length (L)	=	$\dfrac{\text{No of words in all sentences}}{\text{No of complete sentences}}$
	=	$\dfrac{90}{5}$
	=	18
Number of polysyllabic words (N)	=	11
Reading Age	=	$[(L + N) \times 0.4] + 5$
	=	$[(18 + 11) \times 0.4] + 5$
	=	$[29 \times 0.4] + 5$
	=	$11.6 + 5$
	=	16.6 Years

This means that the material would be unsuitable for students who have a reading age of 14 years. They would have too much difficulty with reading the text let alone with its content. You should recognise that the important aspect of Required Reading Age that makes the text difficult to read lies with the number of polysyllabic words and the length of the sentences. So to bring down the required reading age you must reduce the number of long words and the length of the sentences.

Consider the following text about the design of a teaching programme. It is intended to be used as a handout to students who have a reading age of 14 years. Will the students cope with the demands of the language?

(*) "*Basically* a teaching programme is a course prepared as a result of an *intensive analysis* of the learning task. It is *generally* presented to the students one stage at a time. Each stage presents *information* and demands a response from the students. They may be required to answer a question, make a *decision* or practise a *procedure*. The response that students make has two functions. First it ensures that they are *actively* involved in the learning process and practise the tasks that they are to master; *secondly* it provides a measure of their progress. This measure can be used by the (*) students as knowledge of results or by the course designer to identify and remedy weaknesses in the teaching."

Again use the FOG index to gauge the suitability of the text for these students. The two stars (*) represent the beginning and end of the 100 words. Within the extract there are:

(i)   six complete sentences within 94 words giving an average sentence length of 94/6 = 15.7 (L);

(ii) nine words have 3 or more syllables (N) - these are shown in italics.

Thus, for this extract the Required Reading Age is:

$$
\begin{aligned}
\text{Age} \quad &= \quad [(L + N) \times 0.4] + 5 \\
&= \quad [(15.7 + 9) \times 0.4] + 5 \\
&= \quad [24.7 \times 0.4] + 5 \\
&= \quad 10 + 5 \\
&= \quad \underline{15}
\end{aligned}
$$

The extract is too difficult for the students and should be simplified. To do this you need to either reduce the length of the sentences or the number of long words or both *without* losing the sense of the original text.

We have rewritten the extract to reduce the number of long words to six, the semicolon has been omitted and an extra sentence has been created. Thus, the extract becomes:

(*) "In essence a teaching programme is a course prepared as a result of a thorough breakdown of the learning task. It is *generally* presented to the students one stage at a time. Each stage presents *information* and demands a response from the students. They may be required to answer a question, make a *decision* or practise a *procedure*. The response that students make has two functions. Firstly it ensures that they are *actively* involved in the learning process and practise the tasks that they are to master. *Secondly* it provides a measure of their progress. This measure can be used (*) by the students as knowledge of results or by the course designer to identify and remedy weaknesses in the teaching."

Thus

L	=	95/7
	=	13.6
N	=	6
Age	=	[(L + N) x 0.4] + 5
	=	[(13.6 + 6) x 0.4] + 5
	=	[19.6 x 0.4] + 5
	=	8 + 5
	=	<u>13</u>

and the text will now be suitable for the students in terms of its Required Reading Age.

2.1.2 The SMOG Index

SMOG is the Simple Measure Of Gobbledegook and may be calculated as follows:

1. Take a sample of 30 sentences

2. Count the number of words with three or more syllables

3. Find the square root of this number

4. Add 8

This gives the reading age of the material. Again, three or four samples should be calculated to gain an average age of, say, a textbook. If your material contains fewer sentences you can try the following which should give very similar results.

1. Take a sample of 10 sentences

2. Count the number of words with three or more syllables

3. Multiply this answer by 3

4. Find the square root

5. Add 8

It has been said that calculations of Required Reading Age is an inexact science and, in fact, the SMOG index tends to indicate a required reading age about 2 years below that of the FOG calculation.

If the required reading age of the written materials appears to be too high then you can redesign the handout by reducing the number of words in each sentence and by reducing the number of words with three or more syllables. You cannot do this with books but you can consider recommending other books which your students may find easier to understand.

2.2 Reading Age

2.2.1 APU Vocabulary Tests

The Applied Psychology Unit (APU) at the University of Edinburgh have produced standardised tests which measure the reading age of learners. These are relatively quick and easy to administer and are considered to be reliable.

The test that they have produced consists of 75 multiple-choice questions asking students to identify the meaning of words. The initial questions start off very easily. For example, which of the following words means the same as the one printed in capital letters?

BEGIN   1. ask   2. start   3. plain   4. over   5. away

However, later in the test the words become much more difficult. For example, the final question is:

PUSILLANIMOUS   1. Loud   2. living   3. timid   4. averse

Thus, not only is the test assessing students' ability to understand words but it is also a time test. Once the test has been completed, it is marked and the raw score is placed on a graph to translate it into a reading age of the student.

2.2.2 CLOZE

Another technique that can be used to gauge whether students are able to cope with specific reading materials is the "cloze" technique. This, unlike the APU test, does not give us a specific reading age, but allows us to assess whether a student can cope with a particular part of a book, a specific handout or worksheet.

So far we have considered the required reading age of materials and the reading age of students. The cloze technique can be used with your own materials to find the required Reading Age. It is based on 'closure'; a concept used in Gestalt psychology.

For example when we look at the figure we see a circle because we close the gaps.

Similarly when we see gaps in prose we consider the meaning of the words before and after the gap and 'complete' the gap. The technique may be used on handouts, books, instructions etc. It matches an individual student with written materials and identifies if they have a concern.

The technique is relatively simple

1. Take a passage and omit every 'n'th word (say every 5th word)

2. The learners have to supply the correct word.

Interpretation of the scores is not exact and tends to vary with n, i.e. nth word which has been omitted. Figure 6.4 may act as a guide,

n = 5	n = 7	Comments
Score 50% +	Score 80% +	Learners should have no problems
Score 30%-50%	Score 65% - 80%	Some guidance needed
Score less than 30%	Score less than 65%	Materials too demanding

Figure 6.4   Interpretation of Cloze Technique to Determine Readability

Despite the problem of interpretation, the Cloze technique has several advantages.

1. It can be set for any student at any level because the learner relates to your material

2. Your own relevant text can be used

3. It is realistic to the student (own subject area)

4. It tests recognising words, semantics and skimming.

3. Listening Skills

"Some students just don't listen." The adage "in one ear and out the other" describes fairly accurately what happens in some lessons with some students. Students, and teachers, sometimes hear what they want to hear and this invariably results in a breakdown in communication.

Listening, like reading and writing and, indeed, all communication skills, needs practising and can be improved. The skill for the teacher involves motivating students to listen. It involves more than telling them to listen hard and trying to pick out all of the important points. While motivation is necessary and should be encouraged, it is not enough. Students need to know when to "tune in" and what to listen for.

To start with no one listens intently from one minute to the next. Students may look as if they are listening. But, while they may be hearing all of the time, only some of the time are they listening, that is, taking in information, storing, analysing or evaluating the content, and summing up what they hear.

The attentive periods when students listen vary depending upon their tiredness, anxiety, boredom or interest, the stimulation which you provide, and the extraneous noise that makes it difficult for them to concentrate. All people listen for periods ranging from twenty to forty seconds. This is followed by periods of processing of information. Listening involves this continual process of making sense of what is heard. If your talk has your student's attention, then the talk is making sense and students retain more information and are able to recall more details than if they are bored by what you are saying.

Both students and teachers listen: students listen to your explanations and you listen to your students' questions and explanations. Getting students to listen attentively involves using techniques of good talking. These are shown in Figure 6.5.

- Speak clearly and loudly so that all can easily hear;

- Do not read from notes; look at students when speaking and maintain eye contact;

- Be enthusiastic about the topic;

- Use gestures for emphasis and avoid distracting mannerisms;

- Use visual aids to assist the spoken word but be careful that they do not become the main form of communication;

- Encourage questions from the students.

Figure 6.5 Talking Techniques to Assist Student Listening

Each of these assist with student listening and, combined, should ensure that most concentrate. Each of the techniques will be more or less attractive to individual personalities and, as such, will assist the concentration.

Teacher listening skills involve skills that students should be encouraged to use. These are shown in Figure 6.6.

- Organise;

- Summarise;

- Beware of Distractions.

Figure 6.6   Listening Skills for the Teacher

The first of these skills involves *organisation* and can be achieved through asking questions in your mind whilst the student is talking. Such questions are:

(a)   What are the main points that the student is making?

(b)   What supporting facts or reasons are given?

(c) What advantages are being claimed?

(d) What disadvantages are mentioned?

The answers to these questions can usually be summarised from the key words that the student uses. Most student answers contain relevant and irrelevant information and you need to sort this out.

Secondly, it is useful, when a student has finished speaking, to *summarise* the main points that have been said. This ensures that the main points have been understood and greatly assists with two-way communication.

Most classrooms are noisy places. So, finally, any *distractions* can be a barrier to effective listening. If the noise is too great, quieten the class, move closer to the students and delay the communication until it can be heard. Sometimes the distraction is due to differences in accent or dialect or the disorganised way of speaking.

4. Questioning

4.1 Techniques of Asking Questions

Oral questioning is a very powerful way for you, the teacher, to interact with the students. It involves the student in the session through thinking and provides you with feedback on the level of learning.

Questioning is a skill which needs to be developed. 'Closed' questions usually only require the student to answer 'yes' or 'no' and as such are not particularly valuable. 'Open' questions cause the student to formulate a response. If you ask students to explain 'Why vaccines work', then they have to state in their own words their own understanding. This gives you feedback especially if you observe the students' body language - are they unsure?

Questions may be asked at various levels. For example in the cognitive domain you could ask: "What are the main parts of a flower?" (Knowledge). "What does this abrupt change in the graph mean?" (Comprehension). "Knowing the properties of Sulphuric Acid and the composition of water, predict what would happen if the two were mixed" (Application).

Questions may be built up from knowledge to comprehension to application and above. You may pose questions at comprehension level and find no response from the students. In that case you ask questions at knowledge level to ensure that the students have the basis upon which they can answer the question.

Communication is a two-way process, where you want to communicate to your students and you want your students to communicate with you. Question and answer is a good way to develop this interactional style of communication.

As a teacher you need a certain amount of confidence in order to develop questioning skills in yourself and in your students. When you pose a question, you have no ideas as to what the student is going to say, despite your hopes! So, it means that you have to have the courage and confidence to deal with any answer no matter how bizarre. When you develop the questioning skills of your students, you are going to experience a wide range of searching questions which places significant demands upon you. You have to be confident in your subject matter and be well prepared even though the best of teachers are sometimes posed questions which they cannot answer. If you do not already use question and answer in your teaching, plan a short questioning session in the near future. You can then gain experience and extend the duration and frequency of the question and answer sessions.

Pate and Bremer (1967) show that most teachers ask closed questions (that is questions that relate to specific facts and mainly to do with recall). What we should be trying to do is to get the students to think aloud. This gives a real insight into students' thought processes and assists both you and the peer group. You are also trying to get students to generate ideas and thoughts of their own and to explore the implications.

One of the first stages in questioning is getting the students to talk. This may seem strange when we are often trying to get them to be quiet. Students will engage in social talk very easily but your task is to get them talking about some aspect of your subject. It may be that the talking starts with an aspect not of immediate concern to the current topic.

For example you may be dealing with electrical circuit design and ask questions about the relative merits of using alternative sources of energy. Students talk to you but can also talk to their peers and it is at this stage that you ensure that you have control of the situation and do not allow a 'free for all'.

One thing about teachers is that we tend to talk far too much! What we need to do is to let others have a chance to speak. We need to plan our questioning. Before the lesson starts we need to think about the key questions which we should ask. The *order* in which we ask these questions is also important. Although we prepare these key questions before the lesson, we have to be prepared to change these questions, or use a series of unrehearsed questions, in order to respond to the answers that we receive. In other words we need to plan a questioning *strategy* but be prepared to develop *tactics* on the spot.

In Chapter 3, open and closed questions were discussed where closed questions require a one word answer or there is a single correct answer. Open questions, on the other hand, allow the students more scope to state their views, postulate what could happen or put forward an argument. Developing the technique to pose open questions is a skill that teachers should practise. These questions need not just be at the start of a lesson or during the development phase. It may be useful to pose open questions at the end of one lesson which stimulates curiosity about the next lesson.

Another facet of good questioning technique is to distribute questions around the whole class so that answering is not left to a few students. One technique to achieve this is:

1. Pose the question to the whole class.

2. Pause - allowing all students to think
    of the answer.

    P.P.P.
    --- Pose, Pause, Pounce

3. Nominate/name a student to answer.

4. Listen to the answer.

5. Reward correct answer with "yes, correct, that's right" etc.

6. Incorrect answer should not be.

7. Spread the questions around the class so that all can participate.

8. Encourage all to join in - in a regulated matter - for example by saying -
    "Jean, can you give an example of what David means?"

However, non-verbal cues can be given by establishing eye contact, raising eyebrows, and so on. If you work around the class in an obvious systematic order, those who have answered tend to relax a little. Use a technique which is not obvious. There is also a tendency for us to act like a torch beam as shown in Figure 6.7.

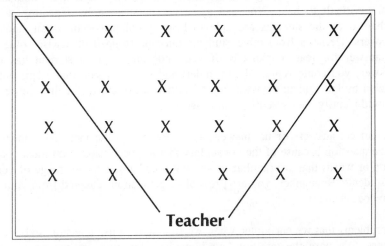

Figure 6.7   'Torch Beam' Arc of Questioning

If we are aware that most of us tend to concentrate our attention for questions on those students who sit in the beam, then we can deliberately pay attention to those we normally omit. There is also a tendency for students to sit in a classroom in such a way that it reflects their interest. Figure 6.8 shows the three zones into which students tend to sit according to their interest and you should try to relate it to one of your classes to see if it is true.

Figure 6.8   Areas of Maximum and Least Interest in a Class

The figure shows that 'A' is the area where students sit who have the most interest and 'C' is where they sit when they have the least interest. The least interested try to hide in the back corner of the room where they may not be seen and they may not have to answer questions.

Having posed our questions, dealing with the answers is another dimension. Student answers are sometimes difficult to hear. You can assist communication by repeating the correct answer so that all of the students are able to hear. Problems occur when students give incorrect answers. Derision from other students must be stopped otherwise some students will fail to answer for fear of ridicule. If you understand why a student has given an incorrect answer, you could reply, "I can understand why you said that Alan, but ...". If you are puzzled by the student's answer try "Could you explain that a little more, Peter?" This then should identify the cause of the misconception.

Sometimes incorrect answers or no answers at all are due to the fact that students do not understand the question because of the vocabulary that has been used. You must take care to explain jargon or words that are familiar to you but may be outside the range of vocabulary used by the students. Remember, you are probably a generation removed from your students and language does change!

One of the problems that we encounter when we first start to use question and answer may be nervousness. We pose the question, no immediate response, so we answer our own question. If we are asking an open question, the students need time to recall facts, think about the relationships and formulate a response. Give the students time and look at their faces for clues about puzzlement, deep thinking or even pain. Encourage the answer with nods and other non-verbal encouragement. Praise good answers without becoming sycophantic. In Chapter 3 we looked at the level or order of questions. It may be useful to 'warm-up' the students with questions of the lower order like recall, before going onto the higher order questions.

Teachers differ in whether it is a good idea to ask nominated questions (i.e. questions posed to a named student) or not. Jacobson (1984) discusses some interesting research. One of the aims of using question and answer is to increase student participation in the learning situation. However, a typical pattern is the teacher asking a question and then a student volunteering an answer. Those students who wish to be involved in the lesson participate and those not wanting to participate are unresponsive. This means that only a portion of the class are paying attention. (Some silent students may, of course, be paying full attention and learning.)

Research shows that teachers rarely direct questions at individual students (perhaps many teachers feel this is impolite). When teachers do ask nominated questions, these questions tend to be directed at the "good" students. Research by Kerman (1979) describes impressive results of tests which involved all students being asked an equal number of questions. Discipline and absenteeism decreased and student achievement increased.

4.2 Redirection

Redirection is a useful technique to use in question and answer sessions. This technique involves framing a single question for which there are many possible responses and allows responses from several students. The following example illustrates the technique:

T: "We have all read about British Prime Ministers. Who do you think was the greatest Prime Minister? Pat?"

S: "Margaret Thatcher."

T: "Chris?"

S: "Harold Wilson."

T: "Frances?"

S: "Churchill."

You may note that at this stage the teacher did not discuss the students' replies. The original question was redirected thereby increasing student participation.

In the next sequence, a similar technique is used.

T: "Why do you think these were great Prime Ministers? Yes, Jo."

S: "I think Thatcher was great because she was always right."

T: "David?"

S: "I think Wilson was good because he understood ordinary people and could communicate with them."

T: "Ruth, do you want to add anything?"

S: "They were all clever people and could speak well to large groups of people."

You can see the three students who answered may not have been thinking about the same person but responded to the single question.

It is important to see that the teacher's questions were divergent, that is a number of answers were possible. The questions were high level questions. For example, they required descriptions or comparisons.

4.3 Prompting

We have discussed what happens when students fail to reply and have stated that teachers often end up answering their own questions. Allowing a silence to develop can and does work. Another approach is to prompt the students. It may be that the students fail to answer because they do not understand part of the question.

Consider the following:

T: "Describe what is meant by equality of opportunity, John."

John appears to be puzzled. It may be that the concept of "equality" or the concept of "opportunity" may be the problem. If it is 'equality' then you could say "If I have 2lb of apples and 2lb of pears they are said to be ....?"

S: "Equal."

T: "Correct. Equal in what way?"

S: "Weight."

T: "Yes. If we put the apples on one pan of a scale pan and the pears on the other, what happens?"

S: "They balance."

T: "Right - so this is a form of equality" and so on.

It is not easy to prompt students. Many aspects of your teaching may be planned in advance but prompting forces you to "think on your feet". You have to listen to student answers, identify the problem and then formulate your prompt. It requires practice. However, once you acquire the skill, the rewards are great.

So far we have concentrated on our role as teachers and posing questions to students. But how about getting students to ask us questions? We could set up a situation where the students have to formulate questions to us for which we can reply either "Yes" or "No" and *only* "Yes" or "No". We will not give any other responses at all. This places real pressure on the questioner. An example could be: "My car will not start. Why?"

Student Question	Answer
Is there any petrol in the tank?	Yes
Is the petrol getting through to the carburettor?	Yes
Has the battery given trouble recently?	No

and so on.

The above technique helps the students to develop their communication skills and grow in confidence. However, there is a bonus. Such techniques give you interesting insights into how the students are thinking and, perhaps, show the concepts that they have attained and those that they have not.

Teachers at some stage in their careers, must be concerned about questions they cannot answer. The usual advice is to say that you do not know the answer but will find out for the next time. Perhaps someone else in the class may know. However, beware of the class who look for the most obscure question they can find for you each week! If you suspect this, give that question, or another, to the whole group as homework!

5. Transactional Analysis

5.1 The Theory

Transactional Analysis (TA) was originally developed by Eric Berne (1968) as a model of human personality. As with all models and theories, there are imperfections but may teachers find TA useful.

Berne postulated that there are three ego states viz Parent(P), Adult(A) and Child(C) shown diagrammatically in Figure 6.9.

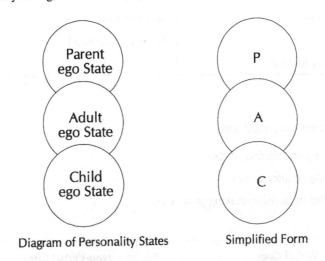

Diagram of Personality States   Simplified Form

Figure 6.9   The three ego states

Although people behave in many different ways, Berne argued that it is possible to classify their behaviour into the three ego states. All three states are usually present, but at any given time, one ego state tends to dominate. It is possible to move from one ego state to another very quickly although we are usually unaware which state we are in.

TA is based on two main assumptions: the first of these is memory. Memories from childhood are of particular importance as they contain many new feelings. Most of us have detailed memories of our parents or some guiding figures. The second main assumption is that we feel as a child feels. Perhaps this happens most when we are relaxing or when playing a sport.

As we move on to considering the three states it is important to say that TA does not imply that one of the ego states is superior to another. The TA suggests that the states are different from each other and that each person comprises three basic selves: parent; adult; child.

Parent

The Parent in us is often concerned with:

- prescribing the limits of behaviour;
- issuing moral edicts;
- teaching 'how to';
- protecting and nurturing.

Examples

Verbal Cues	Non-Verbal Cues
'If I were you ....'	Pursed lips
'There's no question......'	Wagging fingers
'That's ridiculous'	Horrified look
'Well done'	Pat on back or head
'This is the way to do it'	

Adult

The adult in us is often concerned with:

- the acquiring and sorting of data;
- the choosing of alternatives;
- the planning of decision-making processes.

Examples

Verbal Cues	Non-Verbal Cues
'My view is ....'	Open alertness
'In what way?'	Giving attention
'Can you say more?'	
'I think ....'	
'Why,, what,, where,' etc.	

Child

The child in us relates to frustration, anger, fear or conformity and is connected to curiosity, creative delight, desire to explore and trust. It may also include competitiveness and dependency.

Examples

Verbal Cues	Non-Verbal Cues
'I'd like ....'	Delight
'I don't care ....'	Rolling eyes
'I can't stand ....'	Shrugging shoulders
'Now!'	Laughter
'Oh no!'	Raising hand to speak

Before we consider how TA can help us with the teaching process, we need to develop the theory a little further. Two of the three ego states have subdivisions as shown in Figure 6.10.

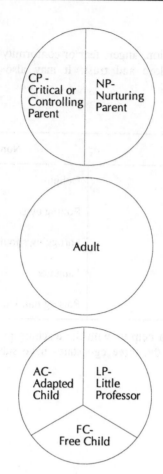

Figure 6.10   **Further Analysis of the three ego states**

The Parent

- Critical or Controlling Parent:

    - makes rules of behaviour;

    - strong, opinionated, prejudiced, critical;

    - authoritarian and judgmental.

- Nurturing Parent:

    - supports;

    - helps by reassuring;

    - protective, sympathetic, understanding.

The Adult

The Adult ego state is evaluating information from the other two states and this is "normal". However, if the adult cannot operate on its own, it is "contaminated" by the Parent or Child.

If contaminated by the <u>parent</u> this results in <u>prejudices.</u>

If contaminated by the <u>child</u> then this results in <u>phobias</u> and <u>delusions.</u>

The Child

- Free Child:

    - impulsive, natural, untrained, expressive;

    - self-centred, pleasure loving;

    - angry when needs are unmet.

- Adapted Child:

    - modifies behaviour with experience, particularly parental influences;

    - cooperative, obedient, sorry.

- Little Professor:

    - intuitive, hunches, creative, inventive.

Most of us have a favourite ego state but we can, with practise, change to another ego state at will.

5.2 Transactions

Transactions are:

- complementary when the ego state corresponds to that to which it is directed.

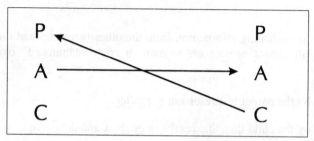

- crossed when the correspondence is not achieved.
- ulterior where one correspondence is intended but another conveyed.

5.3 Transactional Analysis and Teaching

Much teaching may be classified to be in the parent ego state. The danger of this is that transactions will be directed at the child ego state which produces a corresponding childlike response in our students which perpetuates the parent ego state. If the child ego state produces a passive, teacher-centred approach, we need to change.

Consider the following comment from a student to a teacher:

"I'm really fed up. You gave us a reading list and not one of the books is in the library".

This could be classified as C⟶ C or C⟶ P.

You could respond:

"You should have gone to the library straight after the lesson."

This may be P⟶ C

or you may respond:

"That's not my fault".

The transaction is C ⟶ C

However, if you say:

> "It is due to the usual underfunding of education. You could borrow my copy of Berne over the weekend and perhaps one of the group will help you with one of the other books."

This is then A ⟶ C

and should result in the student moving from the child ego state to adult and hence to a better communication situation.

5.4 Stroking

Strokes are acts of recognition one person gives another. With babies and very young children these strokes may actually be physical touching. In the adult world, these strokes tend to be symbolic. A positive stroke would be, "That's a really good essay". A negative stroke would be " You're hopeless".

We all need strokes (unless we are hermits!). Berne suggests that if we cannot receive positive strokes we will look for negative strokes. This is better than being totally ignored.

If you have disruptive students, they may have been conditioned to seeking negative strokes. However, if positive strokes are given but only for good performance, no matter how small or trivial, then the student will tend to look for strokes based on acceptable behaviour.

6. Body Language

A knowledge of body language is vital to every teacher. You need to be able to 'read' the students' body language and you need to be aware of your own. You cannot disguise your body language - but you may be aware of what sends negative feelings. You may not want to teach this particular group - and this may be communicated to the learners. You can minimise the negative signals and project more positive ones - which often means appearing to be more enthusiastic than you feel.

6.1 Posture

How you stand, sit and move indicate or communicate messages to others. Someone who stands and is constantly moving about is unsettled. Leaning forwards indicates interest, folded arms tends to indicate a defensive stance. A person who moves with confidence is very different from one who feels insecure.

6.2 Appearance

How you dress has an impact on those you meet. We dress more formally for an interview than we would for a social event with close friends. A dinner party with friends would indicate less formal dress than that worn for an official dinner. We all tend to wear uniforms. Teenage students tend to wear jeans and tee-shirt type clothes. Look at your fellow teachers - you can often see an indication of their subject specialism from their choice of clothes.

6.3 Dress

Style of dress can enhance or inhibit your relationship and hence your communication with the students. Some students expect their lecturer to maintain a certain standard of dress, for example business studies students may expect their teacher to wear "business wear". This may mean that if the teacher appears in old jeans and a tee shirt then that teacher may not be perceived as being credible and hence is not taken seriously. Conversely Arts or Sociology students may expect their teacher to wear jeans and tee shirt and if they appear in a "suit" then the teacher may not appear to be credible in the eyes of these students. Clearly, you need to develop a rapport or empathy with your students and the way in which you dress can be important.

6.4 Facial

The face is sometimes called the window on our feelings. When we are happy, we smile. It is difficult to stop doing so! Frowning can indicate difficulty with understanding or disagreement. There is a host of facial expressions and you need to look for the ones that signal the students are in trouble or following well. Asking if they understand almost always gets a "Yes" - not always a reliable indication. Eyes are a key to feelings. Strong eye contact is usually a good sign.

6.5 Proximity

We all have our own 'personal space'. If we are talking to a stranger and they come too close, we move to increase the space. However too much space can indicate a barrier. Walk around the classroom, move from the front and show the students that you are not frightened of them.

6.6 Touch

The usual advice is never to touch students in any circumstances! There are exceptions and the main one is when teaching students with severe special needs. When observing these classes, it is obvious that touching is an important form of communication and perhaps the most effective. Care needs to be taken that you follow the guidelines of the organisation.

There are other exceptions including teaching some psychomotor skills. You may need to stand very near to the students and guide their hands. If you feel you need to do this, you should ask their permission.

Finally, do take care because your norms of touching with friends and family could be very different from those of your students, especially those from different cultures.

7. Equal Opportunities

7.1 Language

Most of us become teachers because we enjoy helping others to learn. We agree that all students must have a fair and equal chance to learn. This essentially is embodied in equality of opportunity. We may be creating barriers to some students merely by the words we use. The following gives some examples.

Male - dominated language

Much of our language has expressions which contain 'man' e.g. mankind. We can, unconsciously, be creating barriers to some of our students. Further examples are listed below.

man in the street	average person
master copy	original copy
to man (the reception etc.)	to staff (the reception etc.)
to master	to learn
manpower	staff, workforce
manmade	synthetic, artificial
spokesman	official representative

Some examples of pronoun problems and how to overcome them are:

The student can complete his own enrolment form	Students can complete their own enrolment forms
A student with a physical disability should be able to gain entrance himself	A student with a physical disability should be able to enter without help
A student could get lost finding the college if he did not have a map.	One could get lost without a map.

There are many, many other examples and you can see that you really do need to take care.

7.2 Barriers

There are barriers to equality and you need to look carefully at your own practice and that of the organisation for which you work. Mistreatment of one group by another, more powerful, group is possible in three main ways,

1. individual   -   e.g. verbal or physical abuse

2. structural   -   e.g. employment, legal systems

3. Institutional-practice -   e.g. unequal provision of service

Values, attitudes and assumptions may be transmitted in three main ways,

1. expressed beliefs   -   e.g. they are all the same

2. cultural forms   -   e.g. books, jokes, literature

3. systems   -   e.g. the curriculum, learning resources

You must not allow any form of discrimination in your classroom or learning situation. Not only is it morally wrong, it is likely to be illegal.

7.3 Assertiveness

7.3.1 Definition

Assertiveness can help you to exercise your rights when you need to. The danger is that you meet some people with assertion training who appear to be demanding all of their rights all of the time. You need to appreciate the rights of others and use assertiveness in a mature and sensitive manner.

This section deals with some of the techniques which may help you to become more assertive. However, it is necessary that you practise these techniques. The likely situations in which you sometimes need to be assertive are in dealings with colleagues and some students. When we get into situations where there is a difference of opinion we can become aggressive; we can get angry and fight to win our 'rights'. We may get our own way on one occasion but it is likely to be a hollow victory because of the ill feeling it causes. On the other hand, we could act in a submissive way, agreeing with everyone and thinking it is not worth making a fuss or making enemies. We could lose the respect of others, certainly the students, and even lose self-respect. Between these two cases lies being passive and manipulative. We actually do as we are asked but let it be known, perhaps through non-verbal signs, that we are resentful. None of these three positions is really satisfactory.

Being assertive can help us to improve or retain our self respect and self esteem. This, in turn, should increase respect with the communities of colleagues and students. Assertion is all about being able to express our thoughts, opinions and feelings whilst at the same time allowing others to do the same. Expressing our own values without listening to others is not being assertive, it is being rude! We should not expect to get all our own way all of the time but should be prepared to negotiate to find a common workable understanding and agreement.

The situations in which assertiveness might be necessary include 'refusing', 'poor treatment', 'anger', 'criticism', and 'activity'. Each of these have possible techniques, argues Lindefield (1987), for dealing with them and are discussed separately below.

7.3.2 Refusing

Most of us when asked to do something we do not want to do either say "Yes" and resent or regret doing so, or say "No" and feel guilty. What we should do is think about the request and, if we do not want to do it, say "No". A technique to avoid feeling guilty is to rationalise it by refusing the request whilst showing that you are not refusing the person. Other helpful tactics are to ask for time to think about it. You might ask for more facts or information before making up your mind. If you decide to say "No", say "No" without thinking up excuses which could be attacked by the requester. Finally, you have said "No", so do not linger to reassure that person - move on.

7.3.3 Poor Assignments or Poor Treatment

Sometimes students present work to us which we feel is well below their best. When we try to redress the situation, we are presented with responses which are intended to side-track us. Consider the following situation:

Teacher:	Sam, I want you to resubmit this assignment. There are several spelling errors and your printer obviously needs a new ribbon. I can barely read the type.
Sam:	I was in a rush and have a lot to do today - other assignments. I am happy with it.
Teacher:	I appreciate your workload but I want the errors removed and a new printout.
Sam:	Could I pencil in the corrections? The content is O.K.
Teacher:	No, Sam. A new printout please. It is important that you present your work well at all times.
Sam:	But the printer was rubbish!
Teacher:	Some of the equipment should be serviced more effectively and I appreciate your frustration but please resubmit.
Sam:	O.K. I'll try my best.

This exchange showed the teacher using the 'broken record' technique, repeating the need to correct errors and for a new printout. The teacher was clear that the high quality of presentation was important and no amount of side-tracking had any effect. The teacher remained calm and did not criticise the student for sloppiness.

7.3.4 Anger

We are very fortunate if we never have to face a person who is angry with us. We tend to feel guilty and wonder why we have caused the situation. But, have we caused the anger? Perhaps it is up to that person to deal with situations without getting angry. Your task is to try to engage the person on a calm and rational basis. Dickson (1982) suggests a step-by-step approach similar to the following:

1. Gain the person's attention by repeating a suitable phrase such as, "Could I say something please?"

2. Establish and maintain eye contact.

3. As eye contact is established, try to make progress with something like, "I can see you are upset, could you explain to me why?"

4. Try to get a 'sitting down' situation as people tend to be less aggressive in this position.

5. Listen to the person and determine why the anger is there. Move closer if you are at some distance to the person to avoid the need for shouting.

6. Finally, if you reach this stage, you should now be able to move to try to solve the problem.

7.3.5 Criticism

We all like to be appreciated by others and be held in high esteem. However, we are all subject to criticism from time to time. We have to be honest with ourselves about whether the criticism is justified. A way of coping with criticism is to use a technique called "Fogging".

This involves the following options:

1. You can agree with those issues that are true and say things like "Yes, you are right about that. I will get in on time in the future".

2. You can agree with issues which might be true and say something like "Yes, you could be right about that. I'll check it".

3. You can see why certain perceptions are held and say "I can see why you think that".

Negative enquiry can be used with fogging or in place of it and involves asking for more information and/or asking for more criticism. For example, the following might be said:

"Why do my comments upset you so much?"

"I don't understand. What do you expect me to do?"

"Could you explain why I should give you special treatment at the expense of your peers?"

8. Classroom Control

Careful planning should ensure that students are challenged appropriately with relevant learning activities. This should ensure that motivation is high. However, some post-16 student groups are not mature enough to fully respond to this situation. When this happens you need to have a protocol; a code of practice.

The following guidelines have been found to be useful and are based on the Elton Report (1989).

- Set acceptable standards for work.
- Set high standards of behaviour and apply rules firmly and fairly.
- Give respect and accept respect.
- Treat everyone as an individual.
- Relationships are important so take the initiative and for everyone:
- greet and be greeted;
- speak and be spoken to;
- smile and relate;
- communicate.
- Students often try to see "how far they can go". Be prepared for this and be consistent and clear.
- All classes present problems; success is achieved by the way we deal with problems.

Remember it is helpful to:
- avoid confrontation;
- listen;
- establish facts;
- judge only when all facts are known;
- be careful with the use of punishments.

Within the college/organisation:
- start the dialogue;
- greet the students in corridors etc;
- do not ignore misbehaviour;
- set high standards of speech, manner and dress;

- enjoy relating to students.

In the classroom:

- arrive before the class and begin on time;
- be prepared for the lesson;
- keep everyone occupied and interested;
- extend and motivate all students;
- mark all work promptly and constructively;
- encourage student contributions;
- keep the room clean and tidy;
- maintain interesting wall displays.

Try to avoid:

- humiliation   students resent it;
- shouting   it diminishes you;
- overreacting   the problem will grow;
- blanket punishment   the innocent will resent it;
- over punishment   always have something in reserve;
- sarcasm   it damages you.

Try to:

- use humour   it builds bridges;
- listen   it earns respect;
- be positive and build relationships;
- know your students as individuals;
- be consistent.

Finally, if you have a problem, do not brood. Talk over the issues with a colleague. If you are a part-time teacher, talk to a full-time member of staff; they may have the same problem with those students!

9. Spider Diagrams

At the start of each chapter of this book there is a diagram which gives an overview of what is in each chapter. There are many names for this type of diagram such as 'spider diagram', 'concept map', 'framework' and 'mind map'. Using a diagram drawn by another person can be helpful because you can see the structure very quickly. However, drawing your own diagram really does help you to learn and understand. The diagrams are valuable for revision purposes.

A way to draw your own map or diagram is to place the main theme at the centre. Try to make this as visual and memorable as possible. Each strand may then be developed so that a branching network is developed. You may find it useful to start drawing diagrams from your existing topics but then, when you feel proficient, you could use the diagrams to plan the topic. You can even make an OHT so that the students can share the concept!

Figure 6.11 shows an example of a Spider Diagram for a lesson dealing with the 'Calculation of Area'. This subject was first dealt with in Chapter 1 where a lesson plan was presented for the topic. It is of interest to compare the lesson plan and the Spider Diagram.

At the end of a lesson, as a conclusion, it can be very useful to ask students to draw their own Spider Diagrams of their idea of what has taken place in the lesson. Such an activity not only provides a useful conclusion, but also provides you with an indication of what has been learned and the students' perceptions of the content of the lesson.

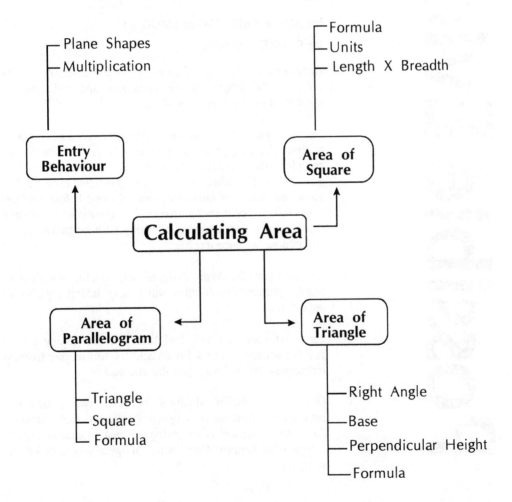

Figure 6.11 Example Spider Diagram for a Lesson 'Calculating Area'

Possible Evidence

The type of evidence that you might collect to show that you have achieved the competence involves:

1. Use some of the techniques to examine the suitability of the reading materials that you use for your students by using either:

    the APU test with FOG or SMOG; or

    the CLOZE technique.

2. Reduce the reading age of an inappropriate handout, say, by reducing the length of the sentences and reducing the number of polysyllabic words.

3. Design a question and answer session and ask a colleague to analyse what happened (if you cannot get a colleague to complete the analysis, try using a tape recorder). The analysis could include how many questions each student answered, levels of questions, time allowed before students answered correctly/incorrectly, questions needing rephrasing or restructuring, difficulty with language, verbal and non-verbal encouragement.

4. Examine your handouts, assignments, etc. for any signs of words, phrases or activities which may inhibit equality of opportunity.

5. The next time that you feel that you are getting into a conflict situation, take a breath and try to use assertiveness techniques. Record what you did and said.

6. Observe a conflict situation between two colleagues, between two students or between a colleague and a student. See what assertion could bring to that situation. Again, record what happened and what thoughts you have on the situation.

*If you want to check your understanding of
your role in Effective Communication Skills
try the following Progress Check*

Progress Check 6.1

1. Explain the basic model of communication.

2. State at least one way of ensuring that reading materials are suitable for your students.

3. Explain how you can reduce the reading age of written materials.

4. State at least three ways of helping students to listen.

5. Explain the difference between open and closed questions.

6. Explain the difference between nominated and un-nominated questions.

7. State at least two important categories of body language.

8. Give two examples of how to make language more gender neutral.

9. State two barriers to equality.

10. Draw a spider diagram for a topic that you are about to teach.

10. Study Skills

10.1 Introduction

Teachers teach and students learn! We have seen in Chapter 3 how people learn but we can aid the learning process by helping the student develop study skills. What are study skills? This is a difficult area but if we can help students take more responsibility for their own active learning processes then these can be included in study skills.

10.2 Problem Solving

Problem solving skills are important in everyday life such as, for instance, how to travel from A to B, or finding the best way to combine the demands of home life, working life and studying - and enjoy and benefit from each. With active learning we often ask the students to investigate a situation, explore a case study, and so on. We often leave the students to develop their own strategies for this and concentrate on our subject matter. Yet if we were to help with these problem solving strategies then the learning might be so much better. Three problem solving models are presented below and these are linked to Business, Science and Technology. You should use only one model depending upon the subject you teach. The models are only models and if experience shows that they could and should be improved to suit your students and their learning, then modify the models.

(i) Business Problem Solving

Problems in the Business Studies area often involve people and their behaviour. For example, why is absenteeism higher in one section than another? A structured approach which involves separating fact from opinion is achieved as shown in Figure 6.12.

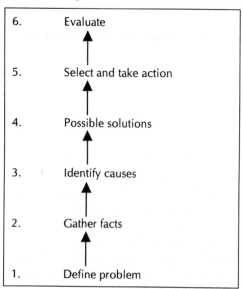

Figure 6.12 Model for Solving Business Problems

The first step is to state the problem. This seems to be rather obvious but if four people are working as a team to solve this problem then they may hold four very different perceptions, so it is useful to agree the problem (and any limitations). Secondly, facts need to be gathered and these need to be kept separate from opinions or conjecture. The third step involves exploring the cause or causes of the problem. There may be several interlinked causes. Some causes may be within your control but some may not. The fourth step is perhaps the most difficult. You need to get the students to generate at least three possible solutions. The danger, and it is a common trait in most of us, is that we identify a solution - the first idea - and use that. The difficulty is to structure the learning activity so that a number of solutions are generated. When using the problem solving model for the first few times, you may wish to set time limits for each stage and not allow progress until there are a number of possible solutions. The next step is to select the best solution and apply the solution to the cause(s) of the problem. Finally, students need to check that the problem has been solved by evaluating the solution.

(ii) The Technology Model

Technological Problem solving model is similar but often involves making something. The model is shown in Figure 6.13

Figure 6.13 Model for Solving Technology Problems

In this case the restrictions could include limitations on space available, costs, material etc. An example could be to make a building without internal supports, for example an aircraft hanger, so that supporting the roof becomes the major design problem.

(iii) The Science Model

Science Model is yet another variation as shown in Figure 6.14

Evaluate

↑

Select use best solution

↑

Inquiry - Action plan

⬆

Analysis of problem

⬆

Statement of problem

Figure 6.14   Model for Solving Science Problems

In this case the means of inquiry may be the most important stage. For example, how does temperature and humidity affect the strength of, say, nylon ropes? A structured approach to problem solving should give the students a framework for their learning activities. You may need to control the first uses of the models by setting time limits, checking progress, etc.

10.3 Making Notes

We often assume that because we can make notes, then our students can also make their own notes. Just check and see! We need to encourage the skill of note-taking and you can do this by starting with small topics and gradually building up to larger ones. Note making needs to be an active process and you may wish to start by helping with the first few sessions. The students need to know the three stages:

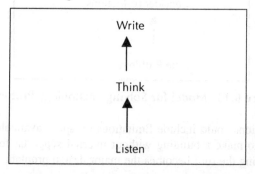

Write

⬆

Think

⬆

Listen

Thus the students listen to what has been said. They think - "What is the main issue here?" and write short/brief notes about the key points. You can help by giving clues, saying,

"There are four major points which influence ...". "The first is ..."At the first attempt at note taking you could promote examples of what the students' notes should contain.

10.4 Reading Strategies

We have already seen the importance of reading but know we need to help the students to develop good reading strategies. This may seem to be strange. If the students are good readers, what is the problem? The problem is that the students read everything in the book from start to finish when they need, and you want them, to be selective, that is read only three or four important pages. You may also want your learners to be able to skim read a chapter in order to identify and learn one or two key issues.

There are three approaches to reading a book, journal or part of them. These are:

(i) *Skimming* - is where the purpose is to get a general idea of what the writer is saying. The reader looks at the headings, general points, and so on, in order to get a quick overview of the text.

(ii) *Scanning* - is when we are trying to find specific information - for example finding out what brainstorming is and how to use it.

(iii) *Intensive reading* - is where the text is read very carefully and thoroughly. You should only use this technique when you find the specific information you are looking for or when an item of interest is found when skimming.

Can you help your students develop these skills? The answer is for you to design activities which are an integral part of your teaching, which allow the students to develop these skills. If you want to try a more structured approach you could use the SQ3R method. SQ3R stands for

Survey

Question

Read

Recall

Revise

You could set a research exercise, based on this technique, which could involve the use of the library.

Survey - is where you ask students to 'skim' the source of information in order to find specific information.

Questioning - includes asking, for example, is this the most appropriate source of information? Is it providing the answers I need? Is it too basic? Is it too advanced and detailed?

Read - is reading with a purpose e.g. scanning, and then intensive reading. Note making may be part of the process.

Recall - after reading provides a good check on understanding and helps memory.

Revise - does not mean intensive reading for examination but the periodic revision of the key points.

You may wish to structure an exercise in your own subject area based on this technique. We are being asked to 'teach' more material in a shorter time. This is one approach which may be helpful.

10.5 Examination Technique

There are still a great many courses which have formal written examinations. We often assume that our students know all about examinations and how to pass them. It may be worthwhile asking the students to form small groups and consider their worries about examinations, this may generate an agenda for discussion. The following five points may be in this agenda.

(i) *Research the Examination*

It is always valuable to see what the previous examinations were like. Again, the students should be guided to do this themselves. You could give them a framework as follows:

- Look at the syllabus
- Look at past papers - What questions are likely to be asked?
- Are the questions based on facts and/or application?
- Practise on previous questions.

(ii) *Practice Questions*

It is usually valuable to set the students some questions from previous papers - even under simulated examination conditions - and give the students feedback which could include the following. Have they:

- read the question carefully?
- answered the question that has been asked and not what they hoped it would be?
- answered all parts of the question and included all relevant facts?
- given superfluous information? - this is wasteful.

Essay type questions should have answers which have:

- paragraphs;
- an introduction;

- a middle which contains key facts and argues the case, gives examples and generally demonstrates understanding;

- a conclusion.

(iii) *Before the Examination*

The students need to be well prepared with all of the necessary equipment.. You could get the students to draw up a 'be prepared' checklist which may look like this.

Pens + spare (or refill, bottle of ink)	Instruments e.g. protractor, ruler, set square
Pencils (sharpened) plus sharpener	Eraser
Coloured Pencils	Reference books if allowed
Calculator	e.g. textbooks, dictionary
Watch/Clock	Sweets

(iv) *In the Examination*

Techniques which are common sense to you and I, often need to be explained to students.

(a) Read through the Paper:

- read instructions - any changes to previous papers;

- identify the questions you can - and want to answer.

(b) Plan the time:

- equal marks for each question then spend an equal amount of time on each;

- plan your answer (see mind maps);

- leave space at the end of each answer in case you want to add anything;

- allow pre-reading time;

- allow time at the end for checking through all answers;

- allow time for planning answers.

(c) *Answering the questions*:

- answer your best question first - but still to the time limit!;

- do not do less than the specified number of questions;

- write legibly;

- check spelling and grammar (when checking answers).

(v) *Multichoice Questions*

Multichoice questions are common because they give good coverage of the syllabus and are easy to mark. Marking can even be automated. Students need practise with this type of examination because the instructions need to be understood. Guidelines could include the following points:

- read the instruction carefully;
- do you have to answer all questions?
- is there only one answer?
- how much time is allowed?
- work straight through the paper and return to difficult questions later;
- do not spend too long on any one question.

10.6 Time Management

If you were to ask your students when they plan to go shopping for a new dress/shirt, to a disco, to buy the latest pop CD, and so on, they can probably give you a specific time because these are important events. If you were to ask which times in the week are set aside for study then you will probably find out that studying is fitted into 'spare' or unplanned time. It is important that time planning includes a positive approach to including studying.

(i) Planning the year

This indicates examinations and could include deadlines for various assignments and projects. Indication of review and revision times is important.

(ii) Planning the week

Some times cannot be changed e.g. coming to classes. It is important to stress that the students need to include time for sport, recreation, resting, meeting friends, and so on, but should also include study time. Does the planned study time reflect the importance of the learning programme?

(iii) Planning the studying

Research shows that an hour or so is the optimum time for studying a topic. For each hour the students should:

- set aside a few minutes to collect books and other requirements;
- set goals for the learning time;
- work for about 20 minutes;
- spend 3/4 minutes reviewing what has been learned;
- 5 minutes rest;
- 20 minutes working;
- 3/4 minutes reviewing;
- rest for 5 minutes or so;
- next topic or end there.

The above needs a disciplined approach but it is surprising how many students find it useful.

10.7 Feedback to Students

As we have said in Chapter 1, we tend to concentrate on the teaching of subject matter to the exclusion of core skills. But employers often tell us that they want their employees, our students, to be good communicators. The skills of communication pervade all subjects and all forms of education so each of us should help students to develop skills in oral and written communication. The use of question and answer will help students to receive oral information, process it and respond. Developing the students' own questioning skills is also a valuable asset. So, the frequent use of question and answer sessions in our teaching not only helps subject matter development, it aids the development of the students' oral skills. It is important that we encourage and support each student by giving feedback and encouragement. Written communication can be practised through assignments and homework tasks. You should mark this and return it to the students promptly. You should comment on the work rather than just give a mark of 6 out of 10. Comment about:

- how the work can be improved;
- what elements were missing;
- were some sections too verbose or unclear?

You should also correct any spelling and grammar errors. If you do not do it, no one else will and it is the only way that students will improve their written skills. With report writing, many students have problems writing in the third person, past tense. Re-write some sections for them correctly and get the students to practise this skill.

11. Key Skills

Key skills, common skills, transferable personal skills and core skills are all terms used for those skills and qualities people need in the world of work

The NCVQ (National Council for Vocational Qualifications) place great importance on these key skills and this follows the lead of many validating bodies such as City and Guilds, BTEC and the RSA.

Originally BTEC saw common skills as transferable skills which play an essential role in developing personal effectiveness in adult and working life. Workers with common skills are able to adapt and respond creatively to change.

Originally, the BTEC common skills were: managing and developing self; working with and relating to others; communicating; managing tasks and solving problems; applying numeracy; applying technology; applying design and creativity.

The implications for teachers are that the curriculum is student-centred and has assignments, projects, and so on. Common skills should help the students to apply knowledge and understanding to real situations, to cope with problems of an unpredictable character, and to acquire new knowledge.

GNVQs have three core skills which are *Communication, Applications of Numbers and Information Technology*. As students progress through the different levels of GNVQ, they are expected to develop their skills in those three areas. You may be concerned as to what these common skills contain and Figure 6.15, based upon Ashley et al (1993), may be helpful.

You may identify other key skills which you feel your students may need. The following could serve as a start for your own check-list.

Career and self development:

        - Study skills.

        - Managing time.

        - Managing self within an organisation.

        - Working with others.

        - Health and Safety.

        - Equal opportunities awareness.

        - Sending information.

        - Using information.

        - Problem solving.

        - Impact of science and technology.

        - Environmental issues.

        - "People" skills and relationships.

Communications:

        - Oral: speech; telephone; meetings.

        - Written: letters; memos; reports.

        - Reading skills.

        - Graphics: graphs; tables; charts.

Number:

        - Arithmetic; algebra, statistics.

Information Technology:

        - Word processing.

        - Spreadsheets.

        - Databases.

        - Graphics.

        - Desk Top Publishing.

Figure 6.15 Elements of Common Skills

Assessing Key Skills

Key skills develop during the learning programme so it appears to be appropriate to assess these skills in a formative manner. This provides regular feedback to students on their strengths and weaknesses as well as supplying you with information on the effectiveness of your strategies.

Assessment may take place via one or more of the following:

- Teacher observation of individuals working in groups or on their own; checklists of agreed criteria may be useful.

- Employers' assessment: using agreed procedures and criteria.

- Portfolios of work undertaken.

- Audio/video recordings.

- Students' diaries.

- Assignments.

- Peer assessment.

- Self assessment.

As with assessment of any learning, care needs to be taken with regard to validity and reliability and this is discussed in Chapter 7.

Possible Evidence

*Possible Evidence to Show that You have
Achieved the Competence "Assist Learners
to Develop their Communication Skills"*

The type of evidence that you might collect to show that you have achieved the competence involves:

1. Put the students into the role of questioner and pose them a problematic situation chosen from your subject area for them to solve. Tell them that you will only answer "Yes" or "No" to their questions to assist them to solve the problem.

    Record the situation and write a comment on how individual students respond.

2. Set tasks or homework in which students have to use a problem solving model. Comment on their use of the model. What aspects are well achieved and what aspects less well achieved?

3. Check student notes on a specific topic and compare with what you expected to see.

> *If you want to check your understanding of your role in Developing Student Communication skills try the following progress check*

Progress Check 6.2

1. Describe the problem solving model that is most applicable to your subject area.

2. Explain a technique that you might use to improve your students' reading skills.

3. Explain what you would include in a one hour session to teach study skills to your students.

4. Explain the aspects that you might teach students about examination technique in terms of:

    • practise questions;

    • before the examination;

    • in the examination.

5. How might you help students with their time management?

6. What aspects might your comments include when you mark your student's work?

12. References, Citation, Bibliographies and the Harvard System

12.1 Introduction

Written assignment often cause students to panic. Inexperienced students are usually confused by terms such as references, citation, bibliography, reading lists and so on. We need to help them to use the literature (and the Internet) in order to inform their learning. But we also need to help them to avoid infringing copyright.

Many Colleges and Universities standardise on a referencing system and you may need to adhere to that system. Given a choice, most students appear to find the Harvard system the most practical.

The advantages of the Harvard system include: easy to use; in widespread use; commonly used by the academic press; allows presentation to be made of all publications cited and other reading in one, alphabetical list.

Citation and **reference** are usually taken to mean specific reference to the work of other authors in the text of the students' own assignment. On the other hand, bibliography is generally understood to mean a complete list of all sources consulted whether or not they were specifically cited in the final work. The bibliography is usually presented at the end of the written work, before the appendices.

12.2 Be Systematic

Get into the habit of carrying around with you a number of index cards. Then when you see something of interest, note down all of the details of the publication - including any notes of your own. An example is given in Figure 6.16 below.

Reece, I. & Walker, S. (2000)
A Practical Guide to Teaching Training and Learning. 4th Edition
Sunderland: Business Education Publishers Ltd.
Own Notes:
A good overview of teaching
In College library at 374 but **must** buy my own copy

Figure 6.16 Example of an Index Card

12.3 Referencing in the Text

Single Authors

There are two main ways to refer to a publication using the authors name, the date of publication and page number.

e.g.

(i)   Smith (1996, 23) reports that less than half of the students used an accurate referencing system; or

(ii) less than half of the students used an accurate referencing system. (Smith 1996, 23)

Up to Three Authors

The same system can be used with up to three authors except all of the names are given.

e.g. Smith, Jones, and Thomas, (1996, 310) established a novel way to analyse student evaluations.

Multiple Authors

More then three authors can present problems but the Harvard system recommends the use of the first author followed by "et al", (meaning "and others").

e.g. Students did not appear to understand how to cite publications which emanated from multiple authors (Able et al,. 1996, 12)

Prolific Authors

Some authors are prolific, even to the extent of publishing more than once a year. Where do they get the time? In this case, you simply add a lower case letter after the year of publication.

e.g. Cookson (1996, a, 108) discovered an interesting phenomenon ...

In this case the bibliography would look something like this,

Cookson, K. (1996, a) Concepts in Evaluation. Durham: Hangman Publications

12.4 The Bibliography

Entries in the bibliography, at the end of the written work, are arranged alphabetically according to authors surnames. The bibliography entries usually include, authors' surname(s) and initials in capital letters, the year of publication (not of reprint!) the title surname(s) and initials in capital letters, the year of publication (not of reprint!) the title (which is underlined or bold or in italics), the edition, if it is not the first, the place of publication and the publishers name.

> e.g. Cookson, K. (1996, a) **Concepts in Evaluation**. Durham: Hangman Publications

> Reece, I. and Walker, S. (2000) **A Practical Guide to Teaching Training and Learning** 4th Edition. Sunderland: Business Education Publishers

> Smith, M. et al. (1996) **Serious Education**. London: Meldon Ltd.

We have given a brief guide to the Harvard system. If you need further, detailed help, ask your college librarian for publications or guides. They are only too willing to help you.

Further Reading and References

Reading and references relating to the topics in this chapter can be found in the following:

Ashley, R. et al (1993)   *Core Skills GNVQ,* Business Education Publishers.

Bond, T.(1986)   *Games for Social and Life Skills,* Hutchinson.

Brown, G. A. (1975)   *Microteaching: A programme of teaching skills,* Methuen.

Carey, G. (1992)   *Theory and Practice of Counselling and Psychotherapy,* Brooks/Cole.

Chishom, B. et al. (1986)   *Preventive Approaches to Disruption (PAD,)* Macmillan Education

Collins, N. (1986)   *New Teaching Skills,* Oxford University Press

Curzon, L. B. (1990)   *Teaching in Further Education: An Outline of Principles and Practice,* Cassell.

Davies, A. M. (1990)   *Equal Opportunities in the New Education Reform Act,* Tufnell Press.

Dickson, A. (1982)   *A Woman in your own right,* Quartet.

Dimbleby, R. and
Burton, G. (1992)   *More than Words: An Introduction to Communication,* Routledge.

Gray, J. and
Richer, J. (1988)   *Classroom Responses to Disruptive Behaviour,* Macmillan Education.

Hamblin, D. H. (1982)   *Teaching Study Skills,* Basil Blackwell.

Hargie, O. (1986)   *A Handbook of Communication Skills,* Routledge.

Harris, S. (1993)   *Human Communications,* NCC Blackwell

Jacobson, D. et al. (1984)   *Methods for Teaching,* Merril.

Jaques, D. (1991)   *Learning in Groups,* Kogan Page.

Kerman, S. (1979)   *Teacher expectations and Student Achievement,* Phi-Delta-Kappar 60, 716-8.

Kery, T. (1982)   *Effective Questioning,* Macmillan Education

Kyriacou, C. (1986)   *Effective Teaching in Schools,* Basil Blackwell.

Lindefield, G. (1987)   *Assert Yourself,* Self-Help Associates.

Myers, K. (1987)   *Genderwatch,* SCDC Publications Ltd

Nelson-Jones, R. (1986)   *Human Relationship Skills*, Cassell.

Northledge, A. (1990)   *The Good Study Guide*, Open University Press

Pate, R. and   Guiding Learning through Skillful Questioning, *The Elementary*
Bremner, N. (1967)   *School Journal*, 69(8).

Perrott, E. (1977)   *Microteaching in Higher Education*, SRHE.

Perrott, E. (1982)   *Effective Teaching*, Longman.

Rees, S. and   *Assertion Training*, Routledge.
Graham, R. S. (1991)

Turner, C. (1983)   *Developing Interpersonal Skills*, FE Staff College.

Robertson, J. (1981)   *Effective Classroom Control*, Hodder and Stoughton.

Severin, W. J. and Tankard, J.   *Communication Theories*, Longman.
(1992)

Wragg, E. C. (ed) (1984)   *Classroom Teaching Skills*, Croom Helm.

Chapter 7

Assessment of Student Learning

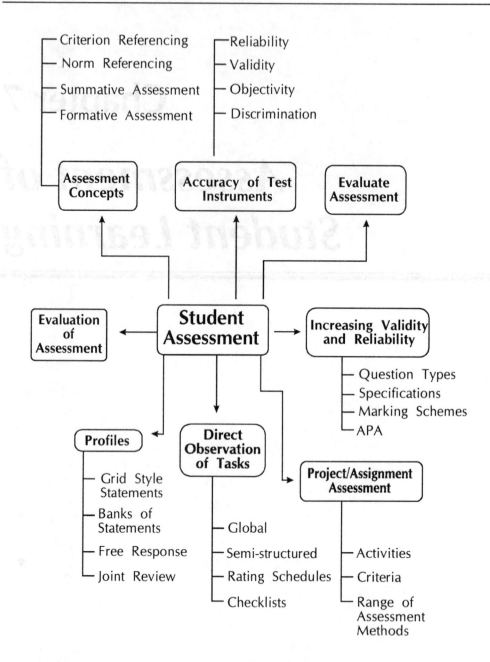

Overview of Chapter 7

NOTE: This chapter should be read in conjunction with, and after, the Assessment section in Chapter 1, Section 4, where the principles and techniques of supply and selection test questions are discussed.

Competences Related to this Chapter

The teacher competences and associated performance criteria related to this chapter are:

Overall Competence - *Employ a variety of effective methods of student assessment.*

Competence	Performance Criteria
1. Assess learners during a lesson or learning period	(a) Employ suitable short-term informal assessment methods (b) Rapid feedback is provided for the students. (c) Select assessment methods according to learning process and stated outcomes. (d) Motivate students through feedback. (e) Plan assessment into an overall lesson design.
2. Justify, use and record appropriate forms of measuring learner achievement.	(a) Provide a rationale for the methods and processes of assessment. (b) Clearly relate methods of assessment to appropriate objectives or competences. (c) Provide a rational explanation for any weighting, marking or grading employed. (d) Employ accreditation of prior achievement (APA) techniques as appropriate. (e) Record students' progress on suitable documentation. (f) Identify procedures for feedback to the students. (g) Review assessment procedure and provide evaluative comment as to its success, suitability and development (g) Draw clear distinctions between formative and summative methods employed
3. Employ appropriate assessment of student practical work.	(a) Use a range of test instruments for the assessment of practical tasks. (b) Use appropriate formats for the assessment of projects/assignments. (c) Employ effective student profiling formats. (d) Present feedback to students in a positive manner.

FENTO Standards

FENTO Standards Related to this Chapter

A.	Assessing Learners' Needs
a1	Identify and plan for the needs of potential Learners
a2	Make an initial assessment of learners' needs

B.	Planning and Preparing Teaching and Learning Programmes for Groups and Individuals
b1	Identify the required outcomes of the learning programme

D.	Managing the Learning Process
d7	Contribute to the organisation's quality assurance system

F.	Assessing the Outcomes of Learning and Learner'sAchievement
f1	Use appropriate assessment methods to measure learning and achievement
f2	Make use of assessment information

H.	Meeting Professional Requirements
h1	Work within a professional value base
h2	Conform to agreed codes of professional practice

Based on the FENTO Draft standards by kind permission

1. Introduction

We have already discussed some aspects of assessment in Chapter 1. Now we shall look at assessment in more detail. The first thing we should do is ask why do we assess? Figure 7.1 indicates some of the main reasons.

Diagnosis

- Establish entry behaviour
- diagnose learning needs/difficulties

Feedback

- feedback to students on their progress
- diagnose strengths and areas for development
- reinforce learning
- feedback to teachers
- motivate students

Standards

- maintain standards
- certificate achievement
- facilitate progression
- predict future performance/selection
- qualify as "safe-to-practice" e.g. driving, nursing
- data for Quality Assurance System

Figure 7.1   Reasons for Assessing Student Learning

It is important at the start of any study of assessment of student learning that you recognise the distinction between two types of assessment: formative and summative. The distinction between assessment to satisfy the needs of society ('summative' assessment) and assessment to help in both teaching and learning ('formative' assessment).

Summative assessment takes place at the end of a course or topic and is used for certification purposes. It is used to see if a student has learned the material and is capable of going on to further study. Formative assessment, on the other hand takes place during the course and is useful in telling the student how the learning is proceeding as well as telling the teacher about the success of the teaching. Figure 7.2 shows the different techniques that can be used for the two types of assessment.

Formative Techniques	Summative Techniques
Question and Answer Supply type questions Selection type questions Projects Assignments Essays Practical Tests	End examinations Supply type questions Selection type questions Projects Assignments Essays Practical tests

Figure 7.2   Formative and Summative Assessment Techniques

As you may see many of the techniques are the same but the purpose to which they are put is what distinguishes them. Figure 7.3 indicates the different uses to which the techniques can be put.

Uses of Formative Techniques	Uses of Summative Techniques
Teachers for ensuring that learning has taken place. Teachers for improving methods of instruction. Students to gain an idea of their success.	Employers for job selection. Curriculum developers for curriculum reviews. Examining/Validating bodies for award of grades and diplomas. Students for selecting courses of higher study.

Figure 7.3   Uses of Formative and Summative Assessment Techniques

2. Formative Assessment

The nature of formative assessment is essentially diagnostic. Black (1989) quotes research carried out by The Scottish Council for Research in Education, where teachers saw diagnostic assessment in terms of three basic modes as shown in Figure 7.4.

Mode	Focus of Assessment	Areas of Concern
I	The Class	The success of the class in learning what was intended.
II	The Individual Student	Which students have not attained the intended learning?
III	The Individual Student	What is/are the reason(s) for the learner not attaining the intended learning?

Figure 7.4   Assessment as a Contribution to Learning

The answers to the question in Mode III pose other questions such as:

(a) are the objectives suitable?

(b) is the teaching strategy suitable?

In this way, both you and your students see assessment as a positive contribution to learning.

So, how do you use formative techniques; what must you do in the classroom to ensure that these ideals are achieved? The following three principles can be employed.

(i) *Use short-term informal assessment.*
This first principle often means the use of question and answer but can also mean the use of test or homework questions which are given informally. The feedback concentrates upon the ways in which improvements might be made as opposed to giving a mark for the work, meaning more thorough marking which can be time consuming.

(ii) *Provide rapid feedback.*
If feedback is to be of most effect then it should be given immediately or as soon as possible. This is most effective through question and answer or through a tutorial situation. An effective technique is to get students to describe what they have done. In this way their understanding can be gauged and rapid feedback provided.

(iii) *Ensure feedback gives motivation to the student.*
The third principle relates to the manner in which the feedback is provided. It is often said that students are not really motivated to learn until they revise for an examination. Yet, here, we are making a case for you to use assessment methods which are part of the learning process; where feedback can be given without the formality of an examination or test situation and where the stress factors are removed as much as possible. In consequence, the motivation must come from the *manner* in which the feedback is given. The emphasis must, at least initially, be upon what has been done well. The aspects that are done less well must be highlighted as opposed to being condemned and suggestions must be given as to how they might be corrected.

These three principles for formative assessment are outlined in Figure 7.5 with suggestions of how they may be achieved.

To apply these principles means that the you should plan the use of the techniques as part of your overall lesson plan. It is probably sufficient to plan the assessment times in the overall plan and to ensure you give feedback. In both Chapters 1 and 5 suggestions were made as to the layout of a lesson plan with columns for teacher and student activities and it was proposed that the introduction could assess entry behaviour and the conclusion assess learning.

Principle	Methods of Achievement in the Classroom
Use short-term informal assessment	Concentrate upon way in which improvements can be made. Say why things are incorrect. Give comments as opposed to marks
Provide rapid feedback	Use question and answer as an assessment technique. Use tutorials to supplement assessment. Get students to describe their work.
Ensure that feedback gives motivation to the student	Comment upon the good aspects first. Ensure that praise is given where due. Do not condemn the incorrect responses.

Figure 7.5   Achievement of Principles of Formative Assessment

Formative Assessment Techniques

The types of technique that you can use for formative assessment have been outlined in Figure 7.2. You can, however, use each of the different types of question in a variety of situations. One of your roles as a teacher is to decide which type of test to use in a particular situation. The main type of questions that are used are the various kinds of objective questions and essay type questions.

Multiple-choice questions can be an effective test. They are suitable for:

- measuring a variety of complex learning outcomes such as vocabulary, explanations, calculations, facts and applications;

- providing diagnostic information to help with the identification of student learning problems;

- ensuring high test reliability.

Alternate-Choice (True/False) questions are **not** always particularly helpful as they are open to guessing and students have a 50% chance of getting them correct.

Matching Block questions are suitable for matching dates with events, causes with effects, principles with applications and symbols with meanings they represent. They are most suitable when:

- lower level (knowledge) outcomes are to be tested;

- associations between things are to be identified;

- all the responses are plausible alternatives to a premise.

Short answer questions can be useful for testing students' recall of names, dates, terms and generalisations. They are most suitable when:

- the learning outcome is recalling rather than recognising information;

- simple computational problems are used;
- a selection-type would be too obvious.

Essay questions usually allow greater freedom of response for students. They test the students' ability to structure a response. Both structured and extended essay type questions are most suitable when:

- the objectives specify writing or recall rather than recognition of information;
- the number of students is small.

Figure 7.6 gives a comparison of factors which are to be considered when selecting test questions. In general, multiple-choice questions give greater coverage of the syllabus and are easy to mark, but, on the other hand they are difficult to write. Essay questions are just the opposite to this, easy to write but difficult to mark and they do not give very great coverage of the syllabus.

Factors to Consider		Selection Type		Supply Type	
		Multiple Choice and Matching	True/False	Short Answer	Essay
Learning Outcomes	1. Number of specific learning outcomes which can be tested at a given time	Many	Many	Many	Few
	2. Coverage of the syllabus	Wide	Wide	Wide	Limited
	3. Abilities which can be tested	All	Knowledge Comprehension	Knowledge Comprehension	High Levels
Influences on Student Behaviour	1. Suitability for testing writing ability	Least	Least	Least	Most
	2. Suitability for testing reading ability	Most	Most	Medium	Least
Teacher Requirements	1. Ease of preparation	Hard	Hard	Medium	Easy
	2. Degree of skill required in preparation	High	High	Medium	Least
	3. Speed of marking	Quick	Quick	Medium	Slow
	4. Degree of skill required in marking	Low	Low	Medium	High
	5. Objectivity in scoring	High	High	Medium	Low

Figure 7.6   Comparison of Different Types of Test Items

> ## Possible Evidence to Show that you have achieved the objective
> ### 'Assess Learners during a Lesson or Learning Period'

The type of evidence that you might collect to show that you have achieved the competence involves:

Designing a lesson plan and highlighting the assessment points in the lesson and:

(a) select appropriate assessment techniques showing how these are related to the learning processes and learning intentions;

(b) describe how the feedback is to be (or has been) provided and show its rapidity and motivational intentions;

(c) after using the assessment methods, evaluate their effectiveness.

Possible Evidence

Progress Check

Progress Check 7.1

1. Write a definition of:

    (a) Formative assessment, and

    (b) Summative assessment

    which draws a comparison between the two types.

2. Give three uses to which formative assessment could be put.

3. What type of test would you construct for the following situations? You should list the types of question you would include and explain why you would use them.

    (a) A class of 20 students doing advanced chemistry need to be quickly tested across a range of topics. You do not have much time to prepare the test.

    (b) You have an average ability class in English. You want to test students' ability to present an argument.

    (c) You wish to test the students learning of a topic in mathematics at the end of term to see if you are able to go on to subsequent learning.

    (d) You are taking a cookery theory class for the first time and wish to assess their entry behaviour.

3. Norm and Criterion Referenced Assessment

End examinations are traditionally marked so that the normal curve of distribution (that is, a small percentage achieve distinctions and a small percentage fail, but the majority of the students obtain 'average' marks of between 40 and 60%) is achieved. This is termed norm-referenced assessment due to its relationship with the curve of normal distribution. This system is often employed in external examinations to ensure that standards are maintained. The argument is used that the level of the examination is difficult to maintain from year to year, whereas the level of students is more likely to be the same; the population remains more static than the level of the examination.

The forms of assessment related to norm-referenced assessment are the more traditional forms of end examinations and practical tests. These, of course, only assess a representative sample of the syllabus topics as time limits the amount that can be tested.

In terms of the marking of norm referenced tests, to ensure the normal curve of distribution, scripts are awarded a 'raw' score depending upon the correctness of the student response and they are then 'adjusted' to ensure that the range of scores fits the curve of normal distribution. This is usually only done by the larger examination/validating bodies.

More recently, it has been realised that the concept of *mastery* learning is important where all students need to master a subject prior to moving onto another subject. This has been facilitated by the introduction of specific criteria given in terms of objectives and competences which state in detailed terms what the student must achieve. This *criterion-referenced* assessment is becoming more widely accepted.

Criterion referenced assessment methods relate to the 'newer' types of assessment of assignments, projects; with profiles to record achievements as well as the more traditional forms of essays and the like. Also, criterion-referenced assessment is associated with continuous assessment so that many more of the objectives and competences are assessed.

The marking of criterion-referenced assessment relates to the the objectives/competences. In this case all of the students can achieve full marks if they attain the required standard suggested, or, alternatively, they can all fail, if they do not reach the standard.

You, as the teacher, need to decide whether ALL of your students need to master the objectives of a topic before moving onto the next topic, or whether only a certain percentage will achieve all of them. This latter approach leads to the identification of minimum essential objectives (or competences) and developmental objectives. All students will need to learn the minimum essentials with the better students achieving the developmental ones.

In Chapter 1 of this book we described assessment, we also described several types of assessment technique (supply, selection, practical and observation) and made some suggestions as to when the different techniques might be employed. We now need to look deeper into the assessment techniques, consider schemes of assessment and evaluate the use of the different methods.

4. Accuracy of Test Instruments

A test is a *measuring instrument*; it measures the achievements of the students. The desirable characteristics of a test are similar to those that would be looked for in any instrument. A set of scales is an instrument that is designed for weighing articles. The scales will have a tolerance of, say, plus or minus two grams, to which it will be accurate. Similarly, a test needs to be accurate, within limits, to what it is testing. As it consists of a series of items, questions or tasks, the quality of these is determined by their accuracy. Some of the desirable characteristics of the items, questions or tasks that effect their quality are:

- power of discrimination;
- objectivity of scoring;
- validity;
- reliability.

4.1 Power of Discrimination

A test that consists of easy items only cannot bring out the differences in achievement of students. All will score well and so it will not be effective in discriminating between good and poor achievers. A good test should have this power of discrimination.

You should, however, bear two points in mind about this:

(i)   it is not necessary on every occasion to discriminate between the students;

(ii) how easy or difficult the question is depends upon the group of students. A question, for example, may be difficult for first year students but easy for final year ones.

4.2 Objectivity of Scoring

Depending upon the type of questions included, a test will be either objective or subjective. If different people are asked to independently score an essay question they will probably award different marks. This is because they will place different emphases on various parts of the essay. In other words *subjective* judgment or personal preference will influence the score. Essay questions, therefore, cannot be scored with complete objectivity.

In an objective test the same scores will be awarded by different people. The multiple choice type of question has only one correct answer and can be marked by computer. A test made up of multiple-choice questions is *objective* in its marking.

4.3 Validity

Validity, in terms of assessment, is how well the test measures what it is supposed to measure. A paper and pencil test has low validity when assessing a student's ability to carry out a psychomotor skill but can have a high validity in assessing if a learner *knows* how to complete it. Thus a valid test is one which assesses a representative sample of the content.

It is evident that a valid assessment must also assess a sample of the abilities that are required in the curriculum. The questions must not only test the knowledge levels but also the comprehension, application and psychomotor skills; a cross section of all of the abilities that are required.

So, a test, having high **content validity** should:

(i)   be based on a sample of the objectives in a curriculum; and

(ii) have all of the questions relevant to the objectives which have been chosen from the sample.

What has been described above is 'content' validity. However, validity is also affected by the appropriateness of the method of testing. This latter type of validity is termed 'construct' validity. The **construct validity** of an assessment is the extent to which it is appropriate to the course, subject or vocational area concerned. Assessment of work done in the student's own time, group work, assignment work, oral work or assessment of skills at work might all be relevant to the course. If methods of assessment are chosen purely because they are easy to administer or because they are easy to mark, the construct validity of the assessment may be questioned.

Ensuring that a particular type of test is used for a particular application ensures construct validity. Figure 7.7 shows this in a different way to that shown in Chapter One.

Objectives	Possible Assessment Methods
Lower level cognitive	Multiple Choice questions Matching Block questions Short answer/completion questions
High level cognitive	Structured/Extended essay Assignment or Project
Psychomotor	Skill test observation Assessment of skills at work Self assessment related to a checklist Assignment or Project
Affective	Tutorial or discussion Peer assessment Observation
Personal effectiveness	Self assessment Discussion or tutorial Peer assessment

Figure 7.7   **Possible Assessment Methods to Improve Construct Validity**

There are no right or wrong answers for where you should use a particular test. There are too many variables to give more specific guidelines. What is right for one course might be different for other subjects or for different vocational areas.

4.4 Reliability

The reliability of a test refers to the extent to which it *consistently* measures what it is supposed to measure. If a test is reliable then the following things should happen:

(i)   different examiners assessing the same work should award the same scores;

(ii) examiners award the same score to the same script if they score it again on a subsequent occasion;

(iii) students get the same score on the test when it is administered at different times.

The reliability of a test is influenced by the objectivity of the scoring. If examiners are looking for the same aspects there is more likelihood of them awarding the same marks. Hence an effective marking scheme influences the reliability of a test. Also, the length of a test influences its reliability.

Figure 7.8 gives an indication of the possible merits of different forms of assessment.

Assessment Form	Power of Discrimination	Objectivity of Scoring	Validity	Reliability
Essay	Medium	Low	Low	Low
Supply-type	Low	Medium	Medium	Medium
Selection-type	Medium	Medium	High	High
Project	High	Low	High	Medium
Assignment	High	Low	High	Medium
Practical test	High	Medium	High	Medium

Figure 7.8   Possible Merits of Different Forms of Assessment

You will see from the chart that the essay type of assessment scores quite low in all of the aspects. The selection type, on the other hand, scores quite high on all aspects. So, why do you use essays at all and why do we not all only use selection type questions. The rationale is that some forms are more applicable to some types of learning than other forms. The multiple choice type of assessment is more applicable to knowledge and understanding whereas essays are applicable to the sorting and presentation of an argument. If the presentation of an argument requires assessment, you have to accept lower validity and reliability. However, there are techniques that can be used to increase validity and reliability.

If you are still uncertain about the two concepts, you may find the next two statements helpful.

Reliability is concerned with getting the **assessment right**.

Validity is concerned with getting the **right assessment**.

5. Increasing the Validity and Reliability

5.1 Increasing Validity by Designing an Assessment Specification

The success of your test instrument depends upon your ability to design a high level of content validity and a high level of reliability. You can increase content validity by using an *assessment specification*. This is a technique which attempts to ensure that you sample:

(a) the content of the course/topic; and

(b) the different abilities to be tested.

It is probably impossible that you will be able to cover *all* of the objectives or competences and all of the content in the time available for testing. You must ensure that this sampling is representative of both the content and the abilities. The *table of specifications* is used to show the relative importance of the various topics and abilities that are to be tested.

The following example specification (Figure 7.9) shows the percentage marks allocated to each topic distributed over the different abilities in the cognitive domain.

Topics	Knowledge	Comprehension	Application	Higher than Application	Total
A	6	6	2	3	17
B	8	6	2	2	18
C	4	6	2	4	16
D	6	4	4	3	17
E	6	8	10	8	32
Total	30	30	20	20	100%

Figure 7.9   Specification to Increase Content Validity

You can see from this table that, for instance, topic 'C' has been allocated 16% of the total marks and topic 'E', the major topic, has been allocated 32%. The first four topics have been allocated almost equal marks with the final topic allocated almost twice as much. On the other hand, the abilities of knowledge and comprehension are allocated the largest percentage of the marks (30% each). So, more marks are allocated within the assessment for the recall of information and its understanding.

You can design such a table by reflecting the objectives related to each of the topics and the abilities. This can be achieved either:

(a) by completing the totals columns first and then the cells;

or,

(b) by completing each of the cells from the objectives and then the totals to see if this reflects the time allocated to the learning of the topics.

Once the specification has been completed you need to design questions which match both the abilities and topics with marks being awarded on the basis of the numbers within the cells. If you are using multiple choice questions with one mark per question, you will need 17 questions at the different ability levels for topics 'A', 18 for topic 'B' and so on (or a percentage of these). If, on the other hand, you are using supply-type questions (say, structured essay-type) the number of marks need to be awarded as stated in the cells.

5.2 Increasing Reliability by the Design of a Marking Scheme

The value of *reliability* can be increased through using a *marking scheme*. A marking scheme is particularly important for those assessment forms which have low reliability like essays. An essay marking scheme, where the overall mark might be 40 marks, can be sub-divided as shown in Figure 7.10.

Aspect	Marks	Aspects
Style	15	Effectiveness of presentation in terms of sentence structure, and vocabulary range.
Accuracy	10	Spelling, grammar, sentence construction and use of tenses.
Content	15	How original and how relevant to the title.

Figure 7.10   Essay Marking Scheme to Increase Reliability

If you use a marking scheme such as this, whilst it does not ensure that all of the essays will be marked in exactly the same way, it goes some way towards ensuring that the basis of marking will be the same. You know that you are looking for the same things in each of the essays and, in consequence, you have increased the reliability of the marking.

A similar type of marking scheme can be used for a practical task where the abilities to be tested in each of the stages of the process are identified and marks awarded accordingly. An example for 'Flower Arranging' is shown in Figure 7.11 where the task is:

> "You are asked to decorate a table for a formal dinner party in June. All flowers and foliage must be available from the garden. Fruit and accessories may be included if desired.
> Table size 4ft 6in x 2ft 6in. Suitable covering to be used.
> Prepare a list of all plant materials used giving common and botanical names where possible.
> Describe briefly the china, glass, and cutlery that will be used."

This marking scheme could be applied to almost any task in flower arranging, particularly for the horizontal and vertical axes. Any differences could be catered for in the individual cells. A further advantage of keeping to the same marking scheme throughout the course, is that students get used to it and know the aspects upon which to concentrate.

Assessment Stages	A Technical Skills	B Method of Work	C Use of Resources	D Application of Knowledge	E Creative Ability	Marks Available
1. Choice of design (style)			Related to materials (5)	Suitable for occasion (5)	Concept (theme) (5)	15
2. Selection of plant material	Knowledge of plants (plant identify) (4)	Sorting and packing (3)	Est. of amount req'd (5)	Appropriate design qualities (4)	Unusual colour, texture, etc. (4)	20
3. Selection of other components		Faultless appearance (2)	Ingenuity (3)	Harmony and Compatible (3)	Harmony and Compatible (2)	10
4. Mechanics	Neat, firm and well hidden (3)			Suitable for type of plant material & style of design (2)		5
5. Execution of design	Manual dexterity (5)	Tidy and methodical work (4)	Materials used well (6)	Application of design principles (10)		25
6. Presentation	Condition of plant material (3)	Staging and display (6)	Value for money (6)	Degree of craft skill (overall standard attained) (6)	Originality & Distinction (4)	25
Marks % available awarded	15	15	25	30	15	100

Figure 7.11 Marking Scheme for a Practical Task

5.3 Weighting, Marking and Grading

Reliability can also be influenced through awarding more marks for the more difficult questions and less for the easier questions. The problem with the weighting of questions is how do you decide what is a difficult question and what is an easy one? There are two ways in which you can do this:

(i)   those questions that take longer to complete can be considered to be more difficult and be awarded more marks;

(ii)   those questions that require higher level abilities to be used (like application as opposed to knowledge) can be given higher marks. This is relatively easy with multiple choice questions as knowledge questions can be awarded 1 mark, comprehension level questions 2 marks and application level questions 3, and so on. With other types of question it is not so easy, as say, an essay question requiring a number of different abilities together.

Whatever weighting factors are used it is always advisable to tell students specifically what marks you intend to award for which questions or which parts of questions. When you do this, students know where to place their time and energies to obtain maximum marks.

Marks are notoriously unreliable as related to the assessment of student work. Even with a marking scheme it is very difficult to say with any conviction that a particular piece of work is worth, say, 56%. Depending upon the success of the marking scheme and the skill of the marker, there is probably a tolerance of plus or minus, at least, 5% on this mark. One way of overcoming this is to award grades instead of marks. On a graded mark scale the predetermined points are the pass and distinction or pass and merit points. For example a graded mark scale might have a pass mark of 40% and a distinction mark of 70%, or a pass mark of 50% and a merit mark of 65%. For example you might use:

Grade A - 75% and above
Grade B - 61% to 74%
Grade C - 45% to 60%
Grade D - 31% to 44%
Grade E - 30% and below

with D and E as fail, C as pass, B as merit and A as distinction. Also, for true criterion referenced assessment, this scale can be related to only Pass and Fail to indicate whether the objectives have been achieved or not.

5.4 Assessing Group Work

It has been suggested to you in various places in this book that group work has various advantages; indeed, certain objectives can only be achieved through the presentation of group tasks.

The size of the group depends upon the task and what is to be produced. However, you should remember that small groups are probably better than large ones due to the ability of the weaker members being able to 'hide' in larger groups. Some teachers do not like groups larger than three students and, even then, consider this quite large as one student will often do less than the other two.

This type of work can give rise to problems in assessment both between groups and within them. First, group work tends to be marked higher than individual work: groups can achieve more than individuals and individual weaknesses tend to be covered up by others' strengths.

Secondly, group marks tend to vary less than individual marks. If groups are randomly formed, the average ability will be similar and individual differences will be less. Problems within groups arise due to the differences in individual contributions.

To overcome some of these problems you can use mechanisms which will allocate different members of a group different marks which reflect their relative contributions to the work. Gibbs et al (1986) suggest that this can be achieved through (a) shared group grade, or (b) peer assessment.

The shared group mark means that students are invited to distribute a teacher's group mark amongst themselves. For instance if a group of four students were awarded 60% for a piece of work, they would be given 4 x 60 = 240 marks to distribute amongst themselves. Gibbs suggests that this distribution might be achieved by three different methods:

(i)   groups agree at the start of the work that all marks will be equally shared. This tends to motivate members into sharing the work equally.

(ii) groups can agree the basis upon which marks can be divided. This might include creativity, some value of workload, leadership, communication, and so on.

(iii) groups can decide at the outset of the work who will do which part of the work. This gives all members a specific task and, if this relates to the criteria for assessment can also lead to equitable distribution of the marks.

Another method is to allow, with the use of a rating sheet, each group member to rate every other member of the group in terms of several key aspects of their contribution to the group's work. An example is shown in Figure 7.12. These are only suggestions and might be very different depending upon the task. The average rating for each individual is then deducted from the group mark and allocated to that individual as their mark. Thus, a student who made a major contribution in every respect would have an average rating of zero and receive the group grade. Another student who contributed little in all aspects would receive the group grade minus 20 marks.

	Major	Some	Little
Leadership and direction	0	-1	-2
Organisation and management	0	-1	-2
Ideas and suggestions	0	-1	-2
Data collection	0	-2	-4
Data analysis	0	-2	-4
Report writing	0	-3	-6

Figure 7.12   Peer Assessment Sheet for Group Work Abilities

5.5 Selection Type Question Design

Selection type tests are so called because students **select** the correct answer to a question from a given list. Examples of selection type tests are multiple choice, multiple response, matching block and true/false.

The advantages of selection type questions may include:

- good coverage of syllabus
- ability to balance topics
- possibility of compulsory questions
- no need for students to write for long periods
- precise questions
- reliable marking
- consistent standard
- can be used each year (bank of questions)
- student marking possible
- discourages "question spotting"
- able to provide rapid feedback

Disadvantages include:

- the time and skill needed to produce really good questions
- students are able to guess answers
- no demand is placed on the students to express themselves in writing.

5.5.1 Multiple Choice Questions

At first encounter multiple choice questions appear to be easy to write and easy to answer. However, experience shows that multiple choice questions can be difficult to formulate - and can test student learning at a high level.

Why do we use multiple choice tests? The main advantages are:

- good coverage of the syllabus;
- tests at a variety of levels, e.g. knowledge, understanding and higher;
- questions can be used many times over the years;
- easy to mark (can be marked by a computer with an optical reader);
- cheap to mark (little or no use of expensive examiners' time);
- high reliability;
- short time to answer and mark - hence feedback can be given at the end of a lesson.

There are disadvantages:

- time-consuming to write;
- may lead to trivial questions or questions based simply on recall;
- students may guess.

An example of a multichoice question is given below and this shows the terminology used.

Q   If 6 is raised to the power of 2 then the answer is,   **stem**

a)   3   distractor

b)   12   distractor   **options**

c)   36   key

d)   64   distractor

You can see the terminology used in the above question. Some guidelines are given below.

- A well written question puts as much information as possible into the stem, the options are then brief and clear.
- There should be one correct answer (known as the key). The other answers, the distractors, should be plausible, i.e. common or likely errors, e.g.

    a) $6/2 = 3$
    b) $6 \times 2 = 12$
    d) $2 \times 2 \times 2 \times 2 \times 2 \times 2 = 64$

- Numeric answers should be in ascending or descending order.
- Take care with the "key". There is a tendency to make answer 'a' or answer 'c' correct. Look to see that you have a spread of correct answers e.g. some 'a's', some 'b's', some 'c's' and some 'd's'.
- The stem and options should be grammatically correct.
- The question must be based upon topics in the syllabus.
- The stem should be positive,
    e.g. Which one of the following substances occurs naturally?

    (a)   Nylon
    (b)   Plastic
    (c)   Formica
    (d)   Coal

- Avoid, where possible, double negative and "which of the following is not ..."
    e.g. Which of the following is not a measuring instrument?

     (a) thermometer

     (b) bandage

     (c) sphygmomanometer

     (d) ruler

If you must use a negative, emphasise it by either bold type or an underline.

- There should be only one correct answer.

- Diagrams may be used to reduce wording if appropriate.

- Try to avoid "none of these", or "any of these" as distractors.

If you are involved with the widespread use of multiple choice questions then it is worthwhile considering:

    (i)   the difficulty of each item (Facility Value);

    (ii) the discriminating power of each item (Discrimination Index);

    (iii) modifying the scores with a factor to account for guessing;

    (iv) ensuring each of the distractors are attractive to the uninformed.

    City and Guilds (1984) produce a comprehensive guide which will help with the above.

You may find the following examples of multiple choice questions useful as they have used the guidelines suggested.

    Q1. In which RAF Command did the Shackleton first see squadron service?

     (a) Bomber

     (b) Coastal

     (c) Fighter

     (d) Transport

    Q2. Which is the main ingredient in Stroganoff?

     (a) Chicken

     (b) Lamb

     (c) Beef

     (d) Pork

    Q3. The Norman Invasion of England occurred in the year:

     (a) 900 BC

     (b) 54 BC

     (c) 55 AD

     (d) 1066 AD

Q4. At what temperature °C would you cook scones?

1. 100
2. 150
3. 200
4. 250

Q5. In cookery terms "Au Gratin" means

(a) with grated potato
(b) with milk
(c) with cheese
(d) with mustard

Q6. A normal adult body temperature is:

1. 36.2°C
2. 37.1°C
3. 37.4°C
4. 39.0°C

Multiple Response Questions

Multiple response questions reduce the ability of the students to guess the answer correctly because there is a permutation of options. It is usual to award the mark only if the correct responses are made i.e. no half marks! It takes a little longer to mark the questions than with multiple choice. However, they do share many of the same advantages. Examples of multiple response questions are:

Q1. What ingredients would you require to cook cheese scones?

✓

(a) Sugar ☐

(b) Milk ☐

(c) Lard ☐

(d) Margarine ☐

(e) Cheese ☐

(f) Suet ☐

Q2. Which of the following are parts of the heart?

✓

(a) Atrium   ☐

(b) Cortex   ☐

(c) Ventricle   ☐

(d) Medulla   ☐

(e) Bundle of his   ☐

(f) Septum   ☐

Q3. Which of the following are ingredients of a Pina Colada cocktail?

✓

(a) Vodka   ☐

(b) Malibu   ☐

(c) Orange juice   ☐

(d) Bicardi   ☐

(e) Whisky   ☐

(f) Pineapple juice   ☐

Q4. Which of the following are towns in Germany?

✓

(a) Brussels   ☐

(b) Strasbourg   ☐

(c) Essen   ☐

(d) Insbruck   ☐

(e) Munich   ☐

(f) Cologne   ☐

Matching Block Questions

Matching questions require the students to match the correct answer to a series of questions. It is usual to have more answers than questions in order to reduce the guessing aspect.

Some guidelines for matching questions are:

- make the matches plausible;
- offer more responses than questions;
- use a logical order e.g. alphabetical or numerical.

Providing a response box eases the marking as the following examples show.

Q1. Match the RAF aircraft to the Command in which they principally served.

a. Bomber	1. Hurricane
b. Coastal	2. Lancaster
c. Fighter	3. York
d. Training	4. Zero
e. Transport	5. Shackleton
	6. Tiger moth

a	b	c	d	e

Q2. Match the make of cars in list 1 with the models in list 2.

List 1	List 2
a. Ford	1. Astra
b. Vauxhall	2. Civic
c. Fiat	3. Fiesta
d. Honda	4. Riva
e. Lada	5. Uno
	6. Micra

a	b	c	d	e

Q3. Match the stitch in list 2 with the correct type of needlework in list 1.

List 1	List 2
a. Tapestry	1. Double treble stitch
b. Knitting	2. Zig-zag stitch
c. Embroidery	3. Chain stitch
d. Crochet	4. Tent stitch

a	b	c	d

Q4. Match the sport to the trophy.

Sport	Trophy
a. Golf	1. America's Cup
b. Yatching	2. Davis Cup
c. Rugby	3. Calcutta Cup
d. Snooker	4. Benson and Hedges Cup
	5. Embassy Regal Cup
	6. Ryder Cup

a	b	c	d

Q5. Match the start of the letter with the ending

Start	Ending
a. Dear Sir of Madam	1. Lots of love, Bob xxx
b. Dear Ms McDonald	2. Love, Bob
c. Darling Rosie	3. Yours sincerely
d. Dear Philip	4. Yours faithfully
	5. Yours, Bob

a	b	c	d

Q6. Match the tools in List 2 with the operations for which they would be used in List 1.

Operation	Tool
a. Large surface	1. 2″ brush
b. Paper	2. Sponge
c. Artex	3. Roller
d. Window frames	4. Poster brush
	5. Blade

a	b	c	d

Q7. Match the human organ to the appropriate instrument.

Instrument	Organ
1. Sigmoidoscope	a. Lungs
2. Auroscope	b. Ears
3. Gastroscope	c. Rectal
4. Bronchoscope	d. Eyes
5. Opthalmascope	

a	b	c	d

True/False Questions

True/false questions are easy to design but the disadvantage is the very high guessing factor.

Well designed questions should:

- be plausible;
- avoid 'all', 'none', 'always', 'several';
- avoid negatives;
- test one idea at a time.

Examples include:

Q1. The Shackleton first saw RAF Squadron service with Transport Command.

    True   ❑

    False   ❑

Q2. Pearl Harbour was attacked on 7th December 1941.

    True   ❑

    False   ❑

Q3. The normal temperature of a healthy adult is 39°C

    True   ❑

    False   ❑

Supply Type Question Design

Supply type questions require the students to "supply" the correct answers to questions and the usual types include essays, short answer questions, and structured questions.

Essay or Free Response Questions

These are often referred to or regarded as "traditional" questions. Advantages include the student has to demonstrate:

- the ability to organise materials, develop a theory or argument, write fluently and to structure an answer;

- original thinking and approaches to problem solving may be measured.

Inevitably there are disadvantages, including;

- student may not know if they have really answered the question;

- poor coverage of the syllabus;

- variable examinations! If students have to answer six out of ten questions then there are 210 possible combinations of questions;

- marking may be subjective and is difficult;

- students may be penalised for poor grammar, spelling and style.

An example of an essay question is:

1. The introduction of National Vocational Qualifications was a major milestone. Discuss.

It is often better to use structured questions which will overcome some of the disadvantages (see below) such as - "how much do I write?"

Short Answer Questions

These questions are an efficient way of testing a wide coverage of the syllabus. They are particularly useful for recall type assessment. They are relatively easy to set and to mark. You could have questions where the student has to supply a missing word or where the student is required to answer with a single sentence.

Advantages of short answer questions include:

- the students know what is required;
- marking is reliable, and quick;
- no undue emphasis on writing ability.

However, the danger is that we assess rather trivial learning.

Examples of short answer questions are as follows.

1. Name ONE acid and ONE alkali.

2. Name SIX essential foods in a balanced diet.

3. State TWO advantages of the National Curriculum and TWO disadvantages

4. The most popular colour for private buyers of new cars is _____.

5. Give ONE reason why we should retain British Summer Time.

Structured Questions

Structured questions help the students to know what is required of them. They are more specifically defined than an essay question.

Other advantages include:

- marking can be more reliable;
- questions can be related to more of the syllabus;
- easier to test higher abilities.

The disadvantages include:

- difficult to set;
- time consuming to set and mark;
- subjectivity in marking;
- students may be penalised for poor writing, expression etc.

The essay question outlined above (e.g. The introduction of NVQs was a major milestone. Discuss) can be structured as follows.

Q1.

	Marks
(i) Explain why NVQs were introduced and the system they replaced	5
(ii) Discuss who were the main architects of NVQs	5
(iii) What were the initial reactions of	
(a) employers	2
(b) trades unions	2
(c) educationalists and trainers?	2
(iv) In practice, what have been the	
(a) benefits	2
(b) problems?	2

Total 20

As can be seen from the second version of the question, the student knows what the examiner is seeking rather than just guessing what the question is about. The marks allocated to each section helps the student gauge how much time to spend on each part of the question and the marking is more reliable.

The following examples may help you to make your questions more structured.

Q1. Describe the classes of bacteria likely to be found in cooked meats.

This may be improved as follows:

Q1. State THREE classes of bacteria likely to be found in cooked meats (with one mark for each class).

Q2. Discuss the materials used in the following situations

(a)   underground gas pipes

(b)   cavity wall insulation

(c)   ironing board covers

An improvement would be.

Q2. For each of the following state ONE suitable material and ONE reason for your choice.

(a)   underground gas pipe

(b)   cavity wall insulation

(c)   Ironing board cover

Q3. "Describe the construction of an electric bell".

This would be better as.

Q3.

	Marks
(a) sketch the circuit for an electric bell	6
(b) label four components	4
(c) describe how the system works	4
(d) state one likely fault	2

5.6 Summary of Methods

Figure 7.13 brings together various features of assessment instrument. As you may see if this is compared with Figure 7.8, there is no single ideal way to assess. If the test is easy to design, then it is likely to be difficult to mark accurately and reliably, and vice-versa.

	Validity	Reliability	Ease of Design	Ease of Marking
Multiple Choice	High	High	Low	High
Multiple selection	High	High	Low	Medium
Matching	High	High	Low	Medium
True/false	High	High	Low	High
Essay	Low	Low	High	Low
Short answer	Medium	Medium	Medium	Medium
Structured	Medium	Medium	Medium	Medium

Figure 7.13   **More characteristics of assessment Instruments**

6. The Accreditation of Prior Achievement

6.1 Assessment of Competences

With the introduction and proliferation of National Vocational Qualifications (NVQs) major changes are occurring in the assessment systems of education and training of adults. Fundamental to these changes is the competence-based approach and the ways in which we assess and accredit the levels of attainment achieved by adults.

The basis of Accreditation of Prior Achievement (APA) relates to the generation of evidence by students to show that they can achieve the competences. This evidence can be collected by:

- your students themselves;
- other course members or colleagues;
- the student's line manager at work;
- tutors;
- mentors at the place of work

Successful completion of a unit of competence will be on the basis of assessment. The requirements are illustrated in the pyramid below:

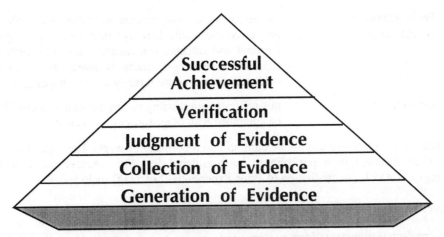

This shows that, at the base of the pyramid and the basis of achievement lies the generation of evidence. Students can generate evidence either on a course, or at work or through exercises which are linked to criteria of assessment associated with units of competence. Once the evidence has been generated it needs to be collected into an acceptable form so that it can be assessed. The collected evidence is then judged as 'reaching the necessary criteria' and then verified by an external assessor.

In order to be awarded an NVQ, students need to achieve a number of units of competence which make up the overall competence related to a vocational job. The following principles should be followed for the award:

(a) all of the competences must be achieved;

(b) the evidence should relate clearly to the competences;

(c) the evidence should cover the range of contexts for the competences;

(d) the evidence should allow distinction between those who meet the criteria and those who do not;

(e) the assessment must be open to verification by external examiners.

6.2 Generation of Evidence

There are four major sources of evidence that can be collected to show that students have achieved a competence. Sometimes a mixture of sources will be used. The four sources are:

(a)   Historical Evidence: this is evidence resulting from activities that have been undertaken in the past either at work or elsewhere. The evidence may already exist (e.g. curriculum materials) or it may need to be generated (e.g. written reports of projects in which you have been involved).

(b)   Performance at Work: this is evidence generated by the student at work. Again, the evidence may already exist or alternatively it may be generated as part of the assessment requirements.

(c)   Performance on Assignments: this relates to the assignments and projects completed as part of course work. This type of evidence gives greater freedom and students can demonstrate more fully their capabilities. However, there is more chance that the evidence will not relate directly to the competence.

(d)   Questioning: this relates to questioning during tutorial sessions. It may be combined with other sources of evidence.

The evidence collected can usually be built up into a portfolio of work. The type of evidence that can be included in a portfolio to be considered for APL (Accreditation of Prior Learning) and APEL (Accreditation of Prior Experiential Learning) includes:

direct evidence (students own work) such as:

projects/assignments from previous courses;
tutor assessments of projects/assignments;
artefacts - models, videos, photos, etc.;
documents used in professional practice;
evidence from written tests.

indirect evidence (information from others) such as:

reports of professional practice;
endorsed statements from an employer;
curriculum vitae;
certificates and awards;
references.

This book is partially based on a competence model where, at the start of each chapter you have been given a list of competences. Alongside each competence are a series of performance criteria to indicate how the competence can be achieved. Within each chapter are a series of suggestions as to what you might do to collect evidence to show that you can achieve the competence. This evidence, once generated and collected, can be placed into a portfolio and used for APA purposes. This will save you having to generate the evidence twice: once at work and secondly by sitting through a course and completing assignments.

> *Possible evidence to show that you have achieved the competence 'Provide a rationale for the methods and processes of assessment'*

The type of evidence that you might collect to show that you have achieved the competence include:

(a) For a particular test that you have used state how you have ensured that it is:

   (i) valid;

   (ii) reliable.

(b) State the reasons for the choice of the type of questions that have been used saying why they are appropriate for the objectives, students, topic, etc.

(c) For a particular course that you are teaching, write a competence statement and associated performance criteria that would show you that students have achieved the competence. Finally, decide and state the type of evidence that you would accept, that is related to the performance criteria, as proof of competence.

Possible Evidence

Progress Check

If you want to check your understanding of
validity and reliability, try the following
progress task

Progress Check 7.2

1. Which of the following correctly defines content validity of
    a test?

    The extent to which:

    A. The test measures the learning outcome related to
        instructional objectives.

    B. The process of sampling for test construction.

    C. Different examiners will award the same marks for a
        question.

    D. An item differentiates between good and poor students.

2. Categorise the following factors into those which
    predominantly influence validity and those which
    predominantly influence reliability.

    A. Sampling of objectives.

    B. Marking to a marking scheme.

    C. Relevance of test items to objectives.

3. Describe three different methods you might use in your
    classroom to assess group work.

4. List three types of

    (i)   direct evidence

    (ii) indirect evidence

    that your students might collect to demonstrate their
    competence.

7. Assessment of Student Practical Work

The usual technique for the assessment of practical work involves direct observation, where you watch the completion of the task and assess the process, (how the work is done), and the product, (what has been done).

7.1 Problems

Direct observation of practical work may be used to identify learning needs of students in relation to personality, attitudes, behaviours and skills. You can use direct observation in either a formative or a summative manner. Observation as a formal means of assessment over a long period, however, is subject to two problems. First, your students may feel threatened and second, your prejudices as the observer can affect the validity and reliability of the assessment. When identifying learning needs, therefore, it is best that you use short, focused periods of observation of a sample of tasks.

7.2 Direct Observation Assessment Instruments

There are four common methods of direct observation.

(a) *Global Impression*
which is essentially a technique where you 'look and describe what you see'. The method has no structure and, as such, lacks reliability. However, it is a useful first step in the development of the more sophisticated approaches.

(b) *Semi*-structured
which consists of a number of open questions which you determine in advance and are relevant to the task. You write answers to the questions for each student either during, or after, observation.

(c) *Rating Schedules*
where you rate a performance on a, say, five point scale as to your impression of each component of the task as carried out by the student.

(d) *Checklists*
where you mark whether the student did or did not carry out specific features of the task.

These four methods range from the global and impressionistic to the relatively specific and analytical. Each has its own strengths and weaknesses. Global methods allow you to take account of individual differences and spot unsuspected learning needs but they are also susceptible to personal idiosyncrasies. By contrast, semi structured observations do provide you with a framework which goes some way to checking your idiosyncrasies. Rating schedules concentrate your attention on the major aspects to be assessed but you may differ in your ability to interpret the 5-point scale compared with your colleagues. One assessor's 'very good' may be another assessor's 'mediocre'. Detailed checklists provide a very reliable method of diagnosing strengths and weaknesses but they may exclude some important unforeseen and rarely occurring characteristics. Of the four techniques, the checklist is probably the best for identifying student needs and provides you with some useful feedback for the improvement of your performance as a teacher. Once you have devised a checklist you can use it to develop rating schedules and to provide you with a framework for semi-structured observation.

Examples of the four approaches are shown below so that you can see the relative merits of each. An example of a global approach is shown below in Figure 7.14.

> Please write comments on the student's
>
> ability to decorate a table for a dinner party.
>
> Ring the grade you feel is appropriate: A B C D E

Figure 7.14 Global Observation

This approach is ambiguous as the instructions do not specify the items that are to be commented upon. Also, the notion of 'ability' is included so you are asked to predict as well as to comment upon present achievement. No criteria are given so it is difficult to compare a group of students. Finally, the meaning of A B C D E is not specified.

The semi structured approach (Figure 7.15) provides you with some guidelines in the form of questions. It can be used for observing the student but there is a temptation to answer the questions with a YES/NO. Additional instructions and questions would be required if you intend to estimate the student's achievement.

> 1. Did the student choose an appropriate style?
>
> 2. Were appropriate plant materials selected?
>
> 3. Were other components appropriately selected?
>
> 4. Were the mechanics of the design well applied?
>
> 5. Was the execution of the design completed well?
>
> 6. Was the presentation appropriate?

Figure 7.15 Semi-structured Observation Schedule

The rating schedule approach, shown in Figure 7.16, concentrates on the five broad dimensions of table decoration which are important. The rating scales are labelled but observers would have to be trained to ensure that they use the scales in the same way. It is, implicitly, a norm-referenced scale.

Please rate the student on the following:

1.	Choice of Style.	6 5 4 3 2 1
2.	Selection of appropriate plant materials.	6 5 4 3 2 1
3.	Selection of other components.	6 5 4 3 2 1
4.	Application of the mechanics of design	6 5 4 3 2 1
5.	Execution of design.	6 5 4 3 2 1

6 = very good, 5 = good, 4 = quite good, 3 = just satisfactory, 2 = unsatisfactory, 1 = very poor

Figure 7.16 Rating Schedule Observation Schedule

The checklist (Figure 7.17) approach sets out the criteria clearly. Even if you do not agree with the criteria, you do at least know what they are. The checklist, when given to learners, gives them a useful guide on how to cope with the decorating of a table for a dinner party. The terms "appropriate" and "correctly" clearly still require some personal judgment by you as assessor, but different assessors are more likely to agree when using such a checklist than they are when using a rating schedule. The checklist is, therefore, likely to yield reliable assessments and they may also be valid. It is essentially a criterion-referenced instrument.

CRITERIA	YES	NO	NOT OBSERVED
The student related to available materials.			
The design was appropriate for the occasion			
Choice of theme was appropriate.			
Plants were identified correctly			
Plants were sorted and packed correctly			
Correct estimate of quantities made.			
Appropriate design qualities used.			
Unusual combinations of colour and texture			

Figure 7.17 Checklist Observation Schedule

Thus, from the four types, the checklist is the most complex but is more likely to provide accurate results in terms of validity and reliability. It does, however, take more time and expertise to design and you need to observe a student closely in order to complete all of the aspects. In the class situation this latter point might cause difficulties. It is evident that the checklist is at one end of a spectrum with a high degree of structure with its closed, specific and systematic approach but there is less inference involved in interpretation of the instrument. The global approach is at the other end of the spectrum with low structure through its open, general and unsystematic approach, with the resultant high inference level required in order for you, as assessor, to interpret it, which results in different interpretations. The rating schedule and semi-structured approaches lie between these two ends of the spectrum as shown in Figure 7.18.

Figure 7.18   Relationship between Different Observation Techniques

7.3 Preparation of a Series of Practical Tests

You should follow logical steps in the preparation of a series of practical tests for your students. Such logical steps might be as shown in the following:

The *first* step is to prepare, from the syllabus, the objectives that require assessment by means of practical work. This will, in effect, be the minimum essential objectives from the syllabus.

The *second* step is to decide upon the number of tests that will assess the objectives and the type of test exercise that will be required for each of them. For this you will use:

(a)   the number of objectives noted in the list prepared from the syllabus;

(b)   the importance of each of these objectives;

(c)   the ways in which the objectives can be grouped together as relating to similar exercises;

(d)   the time which each of the tests can be expected to take, and the maximum time reasonably available from the course.

The *third* step is to prepare each test exercise. This is sub-divided into four parts:

(i)   Design a test exercise to ensure that students demonstrate attainment of the objectives which have been grouped together.

(ii) Decide how the test will be marked, by designing an assessment scheme which will comprise a list of criteria to show whether the student's performance is satisfactory. This might be a rating schedule, a checklist or a semi-structured format. Probably the most appropriate of these is a checklist which requires either a tick or a cross to show the student achievement or non-achievement of the criteria. The criteria should refer to both the final product *and* the method of work. It might also refer to the speed of work if this is important.

(iii) Decide how the result will be determined. Assessment criteria can be classified as either essential or desirable. Essential criteria are those which, when they are not met, can lead to the complete failure of the exercise, or, alternatively, lead to unsafe practices. The remaining criteria can be classified as desirable.

The requirement for a pass should include all essential criteria plus however many of the desirable criteria as is judged reasonable for a student to achieve.

(iv) Draft the test in three sections using clear, simple and unambiguous language. The three sections are:

(a)   Preparation which includes:

where the test will be held;
details of any necessary preparation;
a list of materials, tools and equipment required.

(b)   Student instructions which include:

what is to be done;
what materials, tools and equipment may be used;
a brief description of how the test will be assessed, including any time limits.

(c)   Design the marking scheme which comprises marking criteria listed in the order that will be most convenient to be checked

The example shown in Figure 7.19, for a task of wiring a three pin plug, demonstrates how such a test sheet might appear.

Preparation

The test should be held in normal working conditions. Students should be able to use tools and plugs normally available. They should be instructed to provide their 'usual' tools.

Student Instructions

This test is to assess whether you have reached a basic standard in wiring a 3-pin electrical plug. Using your own tools, a standard 3-pin plug and 13 amp wire, within ten minutes, wire the plug so that it is mechanically and electrically sound.

You should:

(a) collect the appropriate equipment

(b) strip the outer sheath and core insulation to the appropriate lengths

(c) secure the outer sheath correctly

(d) connect the cables to the correct terminals

(e) reassemble the plug correctly

(f) use the appropriate tools correctly

(g) check your work

Marking

Each point to be marked with a tick if satisfactory and a cross if it is not satisfactory. To obtain a pass, all the square boxes and 50% of the circles must be ticked.

Cable stripper used appropriately.   o

Cable cores bared to terminals but not away from them.   o

Connected cable to correct terminals.   ☐

Cables connected securely to terminals.   ☐

Outer sheath clamped securely   ☐

Fuse fitted correctly.   ☐

Body of plug reassembled securely.   ☐

Used correct screwdrivers for different screws.   o

Worked tidily and neatly.   o

Figure 7.19 Example Marking Scheme for a Practical Test

> *Possible evidence to show that you have*
> *achieved the competence*
> *'Use a range of instruments*
> *for the assessment of practical work'*

Design a test for the assessment of a practical skill for your students and describe:

1. How the objectives are meaningful.

2. How the test demonstrates achievement of the objectives.

3. How the preparation includes (a) where the test is to be held, (b) details of student preparation, and (c) a list of materials, equipment and tools required.

4. How the student instructions include (a) what is to be done, (b) what materials, tools and equipment may be used, and (c) how the test will be assessed.

5. How the marking scheme is valid and reliable including identification of essential criteria, time scale, listed order of tasks, pass requirements, safety requirements, and so on.

Possible Evidence

Progress Check

> *If you want to check your understanding*
> *of the assessment of practical tasks,*
> *try the following progress task*

Progress Check 7.3

1. Describe the differences between the following types of test instruments:

   (a) semi-structured;

   (b) rating schedule; and

   (c) checklist.

2. Identify the three important aspects that should be included in the *preparation* of a practical assessment.

3. Describe why it is important to:

   (a) design a marking scheme in the order of the completion of tasks;

   (b) give a copy of a marking scheme to students.

4. What are the aspects that define 'essential' criteria of a practical task?

8. Assessment of Assignments and Projects

You may encounter some confusion in the difference between projects and assignments. When used in the context of teaching methods the two are often ill defined despite being widely used and are sometimes inter-changed. The two are very similar and it is the time that is taken to complete them that often differentiates the two: an assignment generally taking a shorter time to complete than a project.

However, the major difference between the two lies in design. In a project the student decides the parameters of the work within overall guidelines whereas in an assignment the teacher decides on the parameters. Thus, a project is more open and is liable to more differences in the way in which it is tackled whereas the assignment has more structure which is likely to lead to similarities in the approaches taken by the students. In many ways a project may be considered as the extreme to which you may go in arranging student-centred learning approaches, whereas an assignment is more teacher-centred.

Both assignments and projects have the advantage that they provide the opportunity for the assessment of a great range of skills within all of the domains and at all levels within the domains. Also, BTEC have pioneered the use of what they term 'integrative' assignments where they also give the opportunity for assessment across the subject matter boundaries. They argue that this is the way that learning takes place at work; not within subjects but across them. The problem is the basis. This has given rise to 'work-based' assignments which also give the opportunity for the assessment of common (transferable) skills, which are problem based.

In this chapter we are going to concentrate only upon the methodology of assessing assignments. The reason for this is that (a) assignments are more commonly used than projects, but (b) the principles and techniques described are applicable to both strategies.

An example of a Work Based Assignment given by BTEC relating to National Awards in Leisure Studies is given below. The general guideline to the student is:

'You are to investigate security arrangements in a chosen leisure organisation'.

This, however, is only a general guideline that is given to the student. Remembering that an assignment has been defined as being:

(i)   structured by the teacher; and

(ii) giving opportunity for assessment across subject matter boundaries,

both student activities and the objectives from the different subjects need to be identified. These are shown diagrammatically in Figure 7.20 The student activities are shown as a step-by-step guide for the students to follow and it is from these that the objectives are identified from the different subject areas. The objectives become the basis for the assessment.

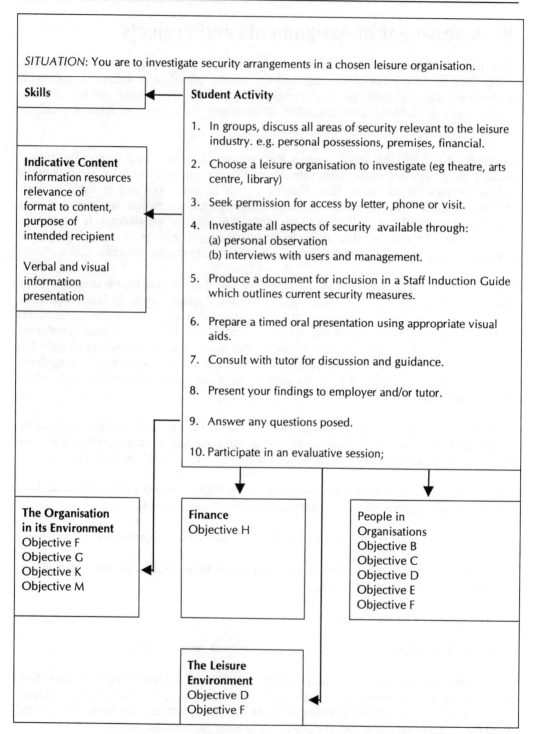

SITUATION: You are to investigate security arrangements in a chosen leisure organisation.

Skills

Indicative Content
information resources
relevance of
format to content,
purpose of
intended recipient

Verbal and visual
information
presentation

Student Activity

1. In groups, discuss all areas of security relevant to the leisure industry. e.g. personal possessions, premises, financial.

2. Choose a leisure organisation to investigate (eg theatre, arts centre, library)

3. Seek permission for access by letter, phone or visit.

4. Investigate all aspects of security available through:
    (a) personal observation
    (b) interviews with users and management.

5. Produce a document for inclusion in a Staff Induction Guide which outlines current security measures.

6. Prepare a timed oral presentation using appropriate visual aids.

7. Consult with tutor for discussion and guidance.

8. Present your findings to employer and/or tutor.

9. Answer any questions posed.

10. Participate in an evaluative session;

The Organisation in its Environment
Objective F
Objective G
Objective K
Objective M

Finance
Objective H

People in Organisations
Objective B
Objective C
Objective D
Objective E
Objective F

The Leisure Environment
Objective D
Objective F

Figure 7.20 Example Layout for an Integrated Assignment

The assessment of the assignment is based on amalgamation of the student activities and the objectives from the different styles. This means that you will need to identify assessment criteria for each of the student activities. There are also the common skills which must be included in the criteria. These can be achieved as shown in Figure 7.21.

Student Activity	Assessment Criteria
1. In groups discuss all areas of security relevant to the leisure industry.	Uses a variety of sources of information. At least three different areas of security should be discussed. Helps the group reach decisions. Participate in verbal and non-verbal communication effectively.
2. Etc.	

Figure 7.21 Assessment Criteria related to Student Activities

Thus, you need to design assessment criteria for each of the student activities and these can be given to the students along with the other information prior to the start of the assignment.

Instead of showing you all of the assessment criteria for each of the student activities in the above example, it is of more use to you to indicate a checklist as shown in Figure 7.22. This is subdivided into aspects to achieve validity (ensuring that it assesses what it is supposed to assess), reliability (ensuring that the assessment is the same for all the students who are observed) and utility (ensuring that it can be used effectively). In order to use the checklist for an acceptable assignment assessment all of the aspects should be checked as either 'YES' or 'NOT NEEDED'. Any aspects that are checked as 'NO' should be reconsidered in order to improve the assessment schedule.

	YES	NO	NOT NEEDED
1. Validity of Assignment Assessment			
1:1 Are the objectives of the assignment stated?	1	2	3
1:2 Do the objectives cover:			
(i) all the necessary domains?	1	2	3
(ii) all the necessary subjects?	1	2	3
(iii) all the necessary core skills?	1	2	3
1:3 Are the necessary student activities produced?	1	2	3
2. Reliability			
2:1 Do students receive:			
(i) written information of the assessment scheme?	1	2	3
(ii) details of how gradings are arrived at?	1	2	3
(iii) a timetable of key assessment events?	1	2	3
3. Utility			
3:1 Is there any duplication of sampling of student performance?	1	2	3
3:2 Is there an effective balance between process and product assessment?	1	2	3
3:3 Is informal observation of student performance possible to achieve?	1	2	3

Figure 7.22 Checklist for Assignment Assessment

You might use a wide range of assessment methods for assessing performance in assignments. The following examples illustrate some of the range that you might use:

- *teacher observation* of group activity, team tasks and, sometimes, individual activity;

- *student diaries* of work experience which include reflections on learning and students' strengths and weaknesses;

- *portfolios/work files* which may include students' working papers as well as completed assignment work and tutor comments;

- *self-assessment statements* on skills development at regular stages during the assignment

- *peer assessment* which may take the forms, for example:

- agreeing with a team member a statement of their contribution to the task;

- commenting in a group review on the work of different aspects;

- making a written comment, against set criteria, of the work of different teams.;

- *assignment products* which may be reports, designs, or artefacts;

- *process reviews* in which the students and tutor review the ways in which the assignment was approached.

Possible Evidence

For an assignment that you have designed for your students, explain the following for the criteria of assessment that you have included as part of the preparation:

(a) Why are you assessing the assignment?

(b) What are the subject objectives and core skills that are included?

(c) What is the rationale for the criteria?

(d) How does the assessment assist student self-assessment?

> *If you want to check your understanding of the assessment of projects/assignments, try the following progress check*

Progress Check 7.4

1. What three ways can you use to improve the validity of an assessment scheme for an assignment or project?

2. Explain how giving students:

    (i)   written information of an assessment scheme, and

    (ii) details of how gradings are arrived at might assist the reliability of an assessment scheme for a project or assignment.

3. Why is it important to include a mixture of process and product objectives in the design of a project assignment?

9. Student Profile Formats

You will realise from Chapter 1 that a profile is a way of reporting student achievements; it is not an assessment technique in itself. Profiles can be used for both formative and summative processes. Traditional methods of reporting student progress are through an examination and a brief comment about these results, the work completed in class and, perhaps, the attitude of the student. It can be argued that traditional methods :

- are very crude, global and mask individual differences;

- are subject-based reports which tend to hide the overall student abilities;

- offer little incentive to many students;

- offer little worthwhile information to students;

- give no real assistance to students with self-assessment;

- give teachers very little to go on when they are asked to give an account of their work;

- are very impersonal, giving students very little opportunity to discuss them.

Consider the aims of a typical vocational course given below in Figure 7.23.

Aims

To identify personal opportunities and prepare for progression.
Further explore selected occupational and non-occupational roles.
To become an effective member of a team.
Assist an ability for organisation and leadership.
Develop confidence in working independently.
Equip students to communicate effectively with a range of people in a variety of situations.

Objectives

Apply enterprise skills.
Recognise the need for a career plan.
Work co-operatively in a team.
Assist colleagues to plan tasks.
Assess results of own work without assistance.
Present a logical and effective argument and analyse others' arguments.

Figure 7.23 Typical Aims/Objectives of a Vocational Course

These mainly fall within the affective domain and, it is suggested, are not assessed and reported upon by traditional methods of assessment and reporting. Indeed, generally traditional methods of assessment neglect the affective domain to a large extent. Profiles attempt to pass information on to students, employers and other teachers on all aspects of learning.

Below, four different types of profile are described. When looking at each of them you should consider:

- the method that appears to be particularly helpful to you in your teaching situation;

- methods that might hinder you in your teaching situation;

- methods that might assist you to overcome problems that you might have presently in reporting on student learning.

The **first** example (Figure 7.24) is a *grid style hierarchical statement* which show the specific abilities that the students must exhibit and, alongside each, a three-point scale of individual progress in the abilities. A space is also provided for examples of how individual students have exhibited the abilities (what task they were involved in when they were observed, what they did, and so on). Additionally there is a space between each statement where either the teacher or the student can sign and indicate a date to confirm that, at that time, the student had achieved that level.

	Abilities	Examples of Abilities	Progress in Abilities		
C O M M U N I C A T I O N	*Talking/ Listening*		Can make sensible replies	Can follow and give explanations	Can present a logical argument
	Reading		Can read words and phrases	Can follow written instructions	Can judge materials to support an argument
	Writing		Can write words and phrases	Can write instructions	Can write a critical analysis
	Use of diagrams		Recognises everyday sign/symbols	Uses basic graphs/codes/ charts	Can make graphs to support conclusions

Figure 7.24 Grid-Style Hierarchical Profile

Only abilities in communication are shown in the example. However, practical, numerical, social and decision making skills can be added to cover all of the skills in a course of study.

It will be seen that the statements alongside each ability are graded starting from the simple and going to the complex. In the example given a three-point scale is used. This results in quite large jumps between each level. If a five-point scale were used the jumps between each would be smaller.

A completed example for a 'Practical' skill is given in Figure 7.25 to indicate how the spaces might be used. The ability has been assessed on two occasions with different tasks and shows the progression between the two dates.

Abilities	Examples of Abilities	Progress in Abilities		
Safety	1. Changed wheels & oil filter on a car	Can explain the need for rules	Can spot safety hazards	Can suggest safety improvement
		Sig. Date(1)	Sig. Date(2)	
	2. Changed points on a distributor			

Figure 7.25 Completed Grid Style Hierarchical Profile

The advantages of the grid style profile are:

- specific examples for the abilities can be identified;
- reliability is improved through the nominating of the three points on the scale;
- progress can easily be shown;
- can be completed by the teacher, the student, or through a mixture of both;
- can be used as either a formative or summative document;
- contains a lot of information for employers;
- has both tick box and statement information.

However, there are also the following limitations:

- can be restricting as there is no space for abilities other than those listed;
- can take employers a long time to read if they have a lot of them and if they are used as summative documents;
- teachers might think that all of the abilities need completing;
- can be time consuming to complete;
- there is no specific space for students to write their own comments.

The **second** example profile format consists of a *Bank of Statements* which the student should achieve. These, basically, are a set of objectives which are available for both the teacher and the student. The intention is that they are used as the basis for negotiation between teacher and student to decide how and when individual students will achieve the statements. The teacher will also use them as a basis for assessment and reporting.

Banks of Statements can be written for any area of the curriculum. However, they are mainly associated with affective domain areas covering the core skills such as 'personal development', 'career development', 'manual dexterity', 'evaluation of performance', and so on. Figure 7.26 shows an example bank of statements from the core area of 'personal and career development'. These are just a representative sample of the type of statement from this core area. Additionally, there would be objectives under other core areas of:

- Industrial, Social and Environmental Studies;
- Communication;
- Social Skills;
- Numeracy;
- Science and Technology;
- Information Technology;
- Creative Development;
- Problem Solving;

or whatever are the demands of the particular curriculum.

It will be seen that these are, as the name implies, just a bank of statements. The use of these in profiling is open to interpretation but, often, they are used as a checklist for teachers and individual students to check individual abilities.

FACTOR	Ref. No.	CORE COMPETENCE STATEMENT
Personal Development	01.1	Can identify own strengths and weaknesses.
	01.2	Can recognise opportunities to develop interests and abilities.
	01.3	Can make the most of opportunities to develop interests and abilities.
	01.4	Can show initiative in developing own interests and abilities.
Career Development	02.1	Can recognise the need for a personal career plan.
	02.2	Can identify factors influencing local job opportunities.
	02.3	Can make a realistic assessment of own career potential.
	02.4	Can produce a realistic career plan.

Figure 7.26 Bank of Statements related to Personal/Career Development

Again, this system has its advantages and limitations.

Advantages:
- gives a clear picture of what is intended in the curriculum;
- gives an excellent basis for negotiation with students;
- validity is assisted with the pre-specification of the statements;
- all students know what is required from the curriculum;
- can be used either formatively or summatively;
- contains a lot of information.

Limitations:
- there are a lot of statements;
- it can be difficult to keep track of all of the statements with what students do;
- students might not understand what is meant by the statements when tasks are negotiated;
- some form of overview sheet is needed for individual student records;
- it is likely to be time consuming to assess;
- can be constraining as only the nominated objectives are likely to be reported.
- there is no indication of need for open comments.

The **third** type of profile is one which allows for *free response*. This type of format is in the form of a booklet with headings under which both the teacher and the student make comments (see Figure 7.27). It can be completed at any time during the learning process and will form the basis of a summative report.

The advantages of this type of profile include:
- the compilation can be specifically geared to the needs of the individual students and the activities that they have completed;
- having a space for student completion ensures their involvement in the process;
- there are few restrictions for the teacher and the student;
- is used as a formative document but is a basis for a summative report.

On the other hand it also has limitations. These include:
- the openness might lead to bland comments being made about individual students;
- validity might be low due to the open nature of the profile;
- can be time-consuming to complete;
- relies on the writing ability of the tutor and the student;
- reliability might be low.

Page 1
Name of Institution
Student Name: ....
Date: ....
Course:
To teacher: ....
....
To Student:

Page 2	
Date	**Student Experience**
Please comment on the following: **Communication Skills**	
Practical & Numerical Skills	

Page 3
Attitude To Training
Planning & Problem Solving
Manual Dexterity
Computer Literacy
Areas of Aptitude/Improvement Give details of areas of aptitude and those needing improvement:

Page 4
General Comments
Tutor Signature: .... Student Signature: .... Date: ....

Figure 7.27 Example of Free Response Profile

The final type of profile is the Joint Review between the teacher and the student. This is basically a formative document (see Figure 7.28 for a typical example). It reviews what a student has completed over a period of time (say over a month) and sets targets for the following period.

Joint Review

1. What are the main tasks/work completed in the last 4 weeks?

> *These reviews are intended to be completed at least once per month.*
>
> *Review sessions must not be disciplinary sessions.*
>
> *What is written is intended to come out of a process of feedback to the student.*
>
> *The account is agreed between tutor and student.*
>
> *The original is on two A4 sheets giving more room than is shown here*

2. What has the student done particularly well?

3. After discussion, we have agreed that progress has been made in:

4. The next month will be spent on:

Student signature: Date:

Tutor signature :   Date

Figure 7.28   Example Joint Review Profile Format

The main difference between a Joint Review and the previous formats is the emphasis on the consultation between the tutor and the student. The principle here is that, if students see the need for change, then they are more likely to accommodate that change. Also, it places the emphasis upon self-evaluation by the student. This is a skill that must be learned and the format can be a useful teaching tool for that purpose.

The *Joint Review*, then, has the following advantages:

- the completion can be specifically geared to the needs of individual students and to the activities that they have completed;

- the involvement of the students assists the self-evaluation process and is more likely to be meaningful to them;

- setting targets can be useful for improvements;

- it is used as a formative document but also provides useful evidence for a summative report.

The format also has the following limitations:

- the openness might lead to bland comments being made about individual students;

- validity might be low due to its open nature;

- can be time consuming to complete, especially as it involves discussions with individual students;

- discussions must take place in private; a quiet room must be provided for this to take place;

- relies upon the writing ability of the tutor;

- may be used for disciplinary purposes;

- can be difficult to get the involvement of the more recalcitrant students.

We have already described profiling as a *process*; it takes place in a formative framework. In order for you to achieve this, the following principles should be followed:

1. Profiling requires one-to-one tutor-student reviews on a regular basis.

   The Joint Review format suggests completion at least once a month. This is time consuming but, it is suggested, is well worth the time that is devoted to it. A further problem is that this tutorial time must be completed in private and the remainder of the class might be unsupervised at this time.

2. Profiling involves *negotiation* with individual students.

   The negotiation with individual students, no matter which of the formats is used, is to ensure that students are involved in the process; involved in their own assessments, involved in making judgments about themselves and involved in their own target setting.

3. Profiling is a teaching strategy which allows student to:

   - reflect on success and failure;

   - take responsibility for their own learning and development.

   When considered as a teaching strategy, profiling is looked at in a different light. You should not consider it as an assessment strategy and your students should not look at it as a session for discipline. It is an opportunity to discuss both strengths and weaknesses.

4.   Profiles should record positive statements of achievement with respect to:

- abilities or skills/competences demonstrated;
- personal qualities exhibited;
- tasks or activities experienced.

You should note that the intention of a profile is that it reports what students can do as opposed to what they cannot do. You can see that, in all of the examples, the statements are written positively. In addition it should report the abilities, competences, personal qualities, tasks and activities in which the student has been successful.

Four different formats of profile have been identified and the advantages and limitations of each have been stated. The main points relating to these are contrasted in Figure 7.29.

Profile Format	Main Characteristics	Main Advantages	Main Limitations
Grid style Hierarchical Statements	Space for list of activities and nominated scale for indication of progress in abilities.	1. Has tick box and statement information. 2. Progress can be easily shown.	1. Might be restricting for some students. 2. No specific space for student comment.
Bank of Statements	List of objectives as basis of the curriculum.	1. Clear basis for negotiation. 2. Valid and reliable.	1. Lots of statements. 2. Can be confusing and limiting.
Free Response	A list of headings with spaces for mainly the tutor	1. Easy to link what student has achieved.	1. Relies on the tutor's writing ability
Joint Review	Similar to Free Response but more open in terms of headings.	1. Easy to link to what the student has achieved. 2. Space for setting of targets.	1. Is very open. 2. Might be hard to get the student involved.

Figure 7.29 Contrasting Different Formats of Profile

When you have designed your assessment it may be worthwhile using the following checklist based upon a CNAA/BTEC project report. Is your Assessment:

Reliable?   Reliable assessment will produce the same score from different assessors.

It is helpful to: - agree about what is being assessed;

                                 - agree standards;

                                 - have evidence and verdict open to scrutiny.

Valid?   Does your assessment measure what it is supposed to measure, i.e. the stated learning outcomes?

It is helpful to:	- match assessment to the standard/objectives/competences;
	- have clear performance criteria.
Credible?	Assessment is likely to be seen as credible if the assessors agree that it is effective.
It is helpful to:	- design simple methods of assessment as opposed to complex;
	- use tried and tested methods of assessment;
	- use a range of assessment instruments.
Authoritative?	If the assessors are experienced, knowledgeable, fair, and work to professional standards, then the assessment will be seen as authoritative.
It is helpful to:	- maintain standards;
	- have a sense of justice.
Feasible?	Assessment has to be manageable, i.e. it can only measure what it is cost effective to measure. Some skills and abilities are elusive and difficult to measure.
It is helpful to:	- have outcomes which are realistic and measurable;
	- have all resources available.
Enabling?	Assessment should influence and improve student performance.
It is helpful if:	- it encourages better practice;
	- it is motivating;
	- it encourages learning so that the student becomes competent.
Transparent?	Does everyone have a shared understanding?

To encourage openness and agreement it is helpful to agree:

- what is to be assessed;

- when assessment is to take place;

- what the consequences and outcomes will be.

Possible Evidence

> *'Possible evidence to show that you have
> achieved the competence
> 'Employ Appropriate Student Profiling Formats'*

1. For a profile format that you have used, give its advantages and limitations and state how it achieves appropriate objectives of your curriculum.

2. In using your chosen profile format, describe the process that you have used and identify the important principles that you followed.

> *If you want to check your understanding of profiling*
> *formats try the following progress check*

Progress Check 7.5

1. List FOUR advantages of profile formats that traditional methods of reporting student progress fail to achieve.

2. Define each of the following profile formats:

   (a) Grid-style hierarchical statements;

   (b) Bank of Statements;

   (c) Free Response;

   (d) Joint Review;

   and give two advantages and one limitation of each type.

3. Describe THREE principles of the profiling process that are important to make it successful with your students.

10. Motivate Students Through Feedback

You will know that the main aspect of formative assessment is the feedback that is given to students. If the assessment is to provide information that is going to lead to improvement in performance, then it must have a motivational effect. Feedback can be given as a mark or grade, or comments, or a mixture of the two. You will also know that if a mark is given then this is perhaps the first, and only thing, that is looked at. The comments take time to write, but should be of much greater benefit to the student in terms of future improvements. Comments can also be very discouraging to the student: often there seems little evidence that students have taken account of what has been said or even have understood it.

There is no doubt that immediate feedback is the most beneficial due to the work still being fresh in the mind of the student. This, however, is only possible with

(a) objective-type questions which can be marked immediately after completion;

(b) through direct observation when comments can be given either verbally or in writing and the student can question what is said.

There are ways of attempting to ensure that students pay more attention to your feedback. This can be done by relating the assessment and comments to the criteria of assessment which you have previously given to your students. Thus, if they have understood the criteria and put their effort into achieving each of the different aspects, they should more readily understand the feedback. This has the additional benefit, so long as you always formulate your feedback in this way, of ensuring that students pay attention to the criteria.

Alternatively you can ask students themselves what kind of feedback they want. If it is what they have asked for, they will be motivated to take it more seriously. They are in the best position to know what their difficulties are and to judge what kind of feedback is helpful.

Figure 7.30 (adapted from Gibbs, et al, 1986) gives a checklist for giving feedback to students.

1.	Keep the time short between the student writing and the feedback. Where possible make feedback instantaneous.
2.	Substantiate a grade/mark with comments both in the text for specific aspects and with a summary at the end.
3.	Balance negative comments with positive ones and ensure that negative ones are constructive.
4.	Follow-up written comments with oral feedback and aim for a dialogue.
5.	Make the criteria clear to students when setting the work and give them written criteria where possible.
6.	Make further suggestions (e.g. for further reading or for further developing ideas).
7.	Give periodic oral feedback on rough drafts.

Figure 7.30 Guidelines For Giving Feedback

11. Assessment in Overall Lesson Design

The timing of assessment throughout a course has already been discussed in Chapter 5 (section 8.4) when discussing the design of an Optimum Linear Sequence, where it was suggested that assessment points could usefully be included at the end of a teaching sequence of topics. It has also been discussed for an individual lesson, in Chapter 1 (section 1.3) when talking about the three phases of a lesson, suggesting that assessment could usefully be completed in the introduction to assess entry behaviour, and in the conclusion to assess terminal behaviour related to the objectives of the lesson. Both of these are important aspects, but assessment should be an on-going activity throughout both the lessons and the course. You will not only assess through written work but through question and answer of both individuals and the class. Different types of cognitive lessons are shown in Figure. 7.31 with different types of assessment taking place during the lesson. Three different sequences (A, B and C) are shown, but you must remember that these are only three from a whole number of different possibilities. The assessment can be by either a formal test or through informal question and answer. The test can be either supply or selection types and can be completed either individually or in groups. Whichever sequence is used, you must plan the assessment in your lesson planning so that it becomes a learning activity as well as an assessment opportunity.

	Introduction		Development				Conclusion	
A	State lesson aim	Entry level test	Concept No 1	Concept No 2	Review of Concepts	Test	Homework & next lesson topic	
B	Review test last lesson	State lesson aim	Introduce concepts by Q & A		Concepts 1 and 2	Application of concepts through Q and A	Test of concepts and next lesson topic	
C	Q & A last lesson	State lesson aim	Entry level test	Concepts1 and 2	Review of concepts through Q and A		Test	Next lesson topic

Figure 7.31   Assessment in a Cognitive Lesson

12. Revising Assessment Procedures

In section 5 of this chapter we have already discussed methods of increasing validity (through a table of specifications to ensure that a representative sample of topics and abilities are assessed) and reliability (through a marking scheme to ensure all scripts are marked in the same manner). The use of these techniques should not stop you from correcting anything that has been found wrong in the scheme. Indeed, you should still look for things that might be wrong. An appraisal of the table of specifications and the marking schemes can be useful in providing you with information on the aspects of the assessment which have worked the best. You can use statistical analyses to show you whether the questions are too hard or too easy for the students and whether they discriminate appropriately between the more and the less able students. If they are too difficult, is it the wording of the questions that is misleading or is it the subject matter that has not been learned or was your teaching poor? Do the better students get the questions right and the poorer ones get them wrong?

It is suggested that you periodically check all of these aspects. The checking may lead to recommendations for the change of syllabus content and course objectives as well as in the assessment itself. An evaluation might consider the following points which have been adapted from Ward, C. (1980):

(a) Does the assessment appear to be valid? Is it assessing all of the required topics and abilities in the right proportions?

(b) Does it appear to be meeting the needs of employers or prospective employers?

(c) Do the students see the assessment as valid and reliable? If not, why not?

(d) Is the standard of assessment appropriate to the aims of the course? i.e. does the table of specification relate to the course aims?

(e) Are most of the students succeeding in the assessment? If not does the fault lie in the selection of the students, in the teaching, in the students' motivation, or in some other factor?

(f) Are the results of most of the students consistent with your expectations? If not, why not?

(g) Were most students able to complete the work in the time available?

(h) Was the assessment of appropriate difficulty judged by the average mark obtained?

(i) Does the assessment differentiate between students of different levels of ability? This may be indicated by the numbers of students with high, low and middle range marks.

(j) Are all of the questions in the assessment appropriate, clear and technically correct?

The answers to all, or some, of these points can assist in giving you an overall view of how your assessment is working. The main point, however, is that you should periodically try to identify any problems that might occur in your assessment procedures.

> *Possible evidence to show that you have achieved the competence 'Justify appropriate forms of measuring learner achievement'*

1. Describe the process that you have gone through in designing a scheme of assessment at both course and lesson levels. You should draw the distinction between formative and summative procedures.

2. For particular assessment tests, describe how you have ensured:

    (a) Validity, and

    (b) Reliability

3. Evaluate an assessment test by answering some of the questions:

    *   Is the assessment appropriate to the aims of the course?

    *   Are most students successful? If not, why not?

    *   Were the average marks as expected? If not, why not?

    *   Was the range of marks as expected? If not, why not?

    *   Were the questions clear?

By answering the questions above, what changes would you make in the future if you were repeating the assessment to these students?

Possible Evidence

Progress Check

Progress Check

> *If you want to check your understanding*
> *of evaluation of forms of measuring*
> *learner achievement, try the*
> *following progress check*

Progress Check 7.6

1. Explain why it is important to give student feedback:

    (a) as quickly as possible, and

    (b) in a positive manner.

2. What ways can you ensure that criteria of assessment are understood by your students?

3. Suggest THREE techniques that could usefully be employed to evaluate your assessment techniques.

Further Reading and References

Further reading relating to the topics in this chapter can be found in the following:

Black, H. et al. (1989)   *The Quality of Assessment*, Scottish Council for Research in Education.

Black, H. et al. (1988)   *Assessing Modules*, Scottish Council for Research in Education.

Broadfoot, P. (1986)   *Profiles and Records of achievement*, HRW.

Castling, A. (1996)   *Competence – based Teaching and Training*, MacMillan

City and Guilds (1984)   *Setting Multiple-Choice tests*.

City and Guilds (1990)   *APL Handbook*, CGLI.

Fennell, E. (Ed) (1992)   *Competence and Assessment: Compendium Number* 2, Employment Department.

FEU (1987)   *Profiles in Context*, FEU.

Freeman, R. and   *Planning and Implementing Assessment*, Kogan Page.
Lewis, R. (1998)

Frith, D. S. and   *A Teacher's Guide to Assessment*, Stanley Thornes.
MacIntosh, H. G. (1984)

Gronlund, N. E. (1977)   *Constructing Achievement Tests*, Prentice Hall.

Gibbs, G. et al. (1986)   *53 Interesting Ways to Assess Your Students*, Technical & Educational Services Ltd.

Hitchcock, G. (1990)   *Profiles and Profiling: A Practical Introduction*, Longman.

Jessup, G. (1991)   *Outcomes: NVQs and the Emerging Model of Education and Training*, The Falmer Press.

Law, W. (1984)   *Uses and Abuses of Profiling*, Harper.

LLoyd-Jones,   *Assessment - From Principle to Action*, MacMillan Educational Ltd.
R. and Bray, E. (1986)

Rowntree, D. (1987)   *Assessing Students: How Shall we Know Them?* Harper Row.

Walkin, L. (1991)   *The Assessment of Performance and Competence*, Stanley Thornes.

Ward, C. (1980)   *Designing a Scheme of Assessment*, Stanley Thornes.

Chapter 8

Evaluation of Self and Teaching

Overview of Chapter 8

Competences Related to this Chapter

The competences and associated performance criteria related to this chapter are:

Overall Competence - *Employ effective evaluation techniques*

Competence	Performance Criteria
1. Engage in evaluation of own and other's teaching	(a) Identify central teaching tasks and other professional duties.
	(b) Devise strategies for monitoring and evaluating the effectiveness of teaching roles.
	(c) Develop appropriate feedback mechanisms.
	(d) Use feedback from students,, peers and colleagues to aid self-evaluation.
2. Engage in the evaluation of your courses	(a) Consider suitable methods of course evaluation.
	(b) Assess useful aspects to be evaluated.
	(c) Identify the components of an evaluation report.
	(d) Make suggestions for course improvements based on data from the evaluation.

FENTO Standards

FENTO Standards Related to this Chapter

C.	**Developing and Using a Range of Teaching and Learning Techniques**
c1	Promote and encourage individual learning
c2	Facilitate learning in groups
c3	Facilitate learning through experience
D.	**Managing the Learning Process**
d4	Review the leanrning process with learners
d5	Select and develop resources to support learning
d7	Contribute to the organisation's quality assurance system
E.	**Providing Learners with Support**
e1	Induct learners into the organisation
G.	**Reflecting upon and Evaluating One's Own Performance and Planning Future Practice**
g1	Evaluate one's own practice
g2	Plan for future practice
g3	Engage in continuing professional development
H.	**Meeting Professional Requirements**
h1	\work within a professional value base
h2	Conform to agreed codes of professional practice

Based on the FENTO Draft standards by kind permission

1. Introduction

Evaluation has already been described as the provision of the feedback loop of the Basic Teaching Model (Figure 8.1). Box D, assessment, consists of tests and observations that we use to determine how well the student has achieved the objectives. If this assessment tells us that the students, or even some of them, have fallen short of their learning, then one or more of the previous components of the model may need adjustment. This adjustment involves the evaluation of both ourselves and the courses that we operate.

Figure 8.1 Complete Basic Teaching Model

Thus evaluation, in its simplest form, is finding out as much as you can about the quality of teaching and learning and how to improve the various aspects which influence this quality.

2. Autonomy and Accountability

Evaluation, especially course evaluation, has emerged because of the increasing acceptance of two related concepts: professional autonomy and accountability.

The idea of autonomy is that professionals should be free to determine how they practice but, in return for this privilege, they should be rigorous in maintaining and developing their standards of practice. Accordingly, examining and validating bodies increasingly allow you, the teacher in post-16 education and training, to determine what you teach, to whom, and how you teach it. Your external syllabuses and externally set examinations are being replaced by college devised and assessed courses which are approved by central bodies and by lead bodies setting competences and associated performance criteria. However, in return, these central bodies are increasingly requiring you to monitor, review and evaluate your programmes and to report on them periodically. Such reports contain a critical analysis of the operation of the programmes together with proposals for improvements.

The public served by professionals, increasingly expect those professionals to be accountable to them or their representatives. In education, the move to accountability has been promoted by public concern over the relevance and standards of education in schools and colleges.

In consequence, apart from these external pressures, for your own peace of mind, you need to acquire knowledge and skills to evaluate your own performance and your courses. Some headings have already been suggested in Chapter 1 that might be used for a self-evaluation diary and that your own students might use to provide data on the effectiveness of your teaching.

3. Central Teaching and other Professional Tasks

In consequence of increasing autonomy and accountability, we need to consider the main tasks for which we, as teachers of post-16 education and training, are responsible. Once these have been identified, they can be the focus for a self-audit.

There has been a move recently to base many of the teaching tasks on a competence model. These moves have been spearheaded by two national bodies: the Training and Development Lead Body (TDLB) and the Management Charter Initiative (MCI). These, however, as yet, are far from being accepted generally by the teacher training profession. Not least of the problems is that there is no overt collaboration between the two. Yet teaching involves aspects of both; the teaching aspect as put forward by TDLB and the management (of the classroom) as put forward by MCI. Thus, in terms of competences that are required by the teacher, we need to consider (a) those aspects required to teach our subjects and (b) aspects of management of both the classroom and the curriculum. Thus, these tasks can be sub-divided into (i) teaching and (ii) other professional duties.

3.1 Teaching Tasks

Teaching tasks can be sub-divided into six main elements. These elements have been at the base of the thinking of TDLB and have various competences associated with them. The first of the elements relates to the preparation that you complete for your teaching. The associated competences are given in Chapter 1 and are:

(i) Preparation:

- identification of student needs;
- analysis of a subject/topic into a logical sequence;
- indication of expected student learning;
- selection of appropriate teaching/learning methods;
- writing systematic lesson plans;
- selecting and preparing learning resources.

The second element relates to the application of the preparation. Aspects relating to this element include:

(ii) Presentation:

- the implementation of selected teaching/learning methods;
- provision of appropriate:
  - introduction;
  - development; and
  - conclusion to a session;
- flexible response to classroom situations;
- using learning resources effectively.

The third element relates to the manner in which you as the teacher are able to relate to your students. This operates on the premise that the better the relationship between you and your students, the more likelihood there is of optimising learning. Aspects relating to this element include:

(iii) Trainee/Student Relationships:

- securing student participation in lessons;
- promotion of a classroom climate that facilitates learning.

An element that could be considered as going across all of the other elements is communication. However, it is considered so important that it is thought worthwhile to separate it and make it an element on its own. Aspects relating to communication include:

(iv) Communication:

- using appropriate language registers;
- employment of effective skills in verbal and non-verbal communication.

The next element is the final one in the basic teaching model, assessment of student learning. It is from here that you are able to identify any problems that might have occurred with the operation of the previous elements. Thus the aspect to be considered is:

(v) Assessment of Learning:

- making an assessment of the extent to which the students achieved the stated intentions.

The final element relates to your knowledge of the subject that you are teaching. It is thus:

(vi) Subject Matter:

- demonstration of mastery of the subject matter.

These aspects, then, provide you with the basis on which you can evaluate your own, or someone else's, teaching ability, or, on the other hand, the basis on which someone else might evaluate your teaching ability. They can be used in total to give an overall impression or they might be used one at a time to provide feedback on specific elements.

If you are inviting someone else to evaluate your teaching performance you might use a pro-forma like the one indicated in Figure 8.2.

PRACTICAL TEACHING OBSERVATION PRO-FORMA

Date: Class:

Time: Subject/Topic:

Place:

Competences to be displayed and assessed with associated comments:

Competences *(completed by you)*	Comments *(completed by observer)*

Additional comments by the observer:

(i) Preparation:

(ii) Presentation:

(iii) Trainee/Student Relationships:

(iv) Communication:

(v) Assessment of Learning:

(vi) Subject Matter:

Figure 8.2   Sample Pro-Forma to Assist Feedback from Observation

From the lesson plan it will be possible for you to identify the range of competences that will be used and upon which feedback can be given. If you identify these prior to the

observation and write them onto the pro-forma, you will obtain the spec
you desire. These might be, for instance:

    (a) use teaching strategies that are appropriate to the group;

    (b) organisation of the environment in a way that assists learning;

    (c) use appropriate language;

    (d) analyse strengths and weaknesses of the students.

It may be that you want to practise and gain feedback on a specific skill, such as your ability to use the question and answer technique effectively. In this case you might design and use a schedule related only to this specific aspect (see Figure 8.3).

An advantage of such a schedule is that you think about the main aspects of the competence related to question and answer both in the planning and the presentation stages. That is, you plan your question and answer technique to try to ensure that you cover the aspects that you have highlighted.

Question and Answer Technique		
	Circle as appropriate	
1. Questions were clearly understood by students.	YES	NO
2. Pauses were used after asking most of the questions.	YES	NO
3. Some of the questions were asked of specific students.	YES	NO
4. The questions were distributed amongst the whole group.	YES	NO
5. Prompting techniques were effectively used to assist students in answering.	YES	NO
6. Some of the questions were at the higher levels of thinking.	YES	NO
Comments:		

Figure 8.3   Example Schedule about a Specific Aspect of Teaching

This can, then, be used either by yourself or by an observer. If it is to be used by yourself, it can be useful to (a) write your impressions of what happened immediately after the teaching episode and (b) to arrange to either audio or video tape and, at your leisure, watch/listen to the tape and remark your schedule in the light of what you hear/see.

This type of self-evaluation allows you to compare your initial reactions with those that are evoked.

Tasks

...t you do in the classroom or in preparation for it, it also ... to make up the 'extended professional'. Tansley (1989) ... when discussing the role of the course team:

...tive	timetabling/accommodation, resource allocation
...s	arranging work experience, liaison with schools and employers
• Liaison w... ...sation	reporting to line management, liaison with other departments
• Student responsibilities	student guidance and tutoring/assessment/ discipline
• Course responsibilities	curriculum development, course evaluation and profiling
• Examination administration	clerical administration, examination administration, liaison with exam bodies.

This list gives some idea of the complexity of other tasks that the teacher is expected to complete. Although they are directly related to a course leader, many people tend to delegate these duties to different members of the course team. Indeed, there are distinct advantages in this delegation taking place so that it gives all of the course team members an overview of the whole of the course, its changes and developments. The line management and the course team are the best places for you to gain feedback about how you are doing with such tasks. Alternatively, you can make your own checklist of tasks and rate yourself on each of them.

3.3 Sources of Feedback on Teaching

There are several sources for obtaining feedback on your teaching performance which can give assistance with your evaluation. These include your students, peers, and your line manager or tutor. However, all of these people should give you feedback in such a manner as to assist with your own self evaluation. They can provide information (data and impressions) which it is difficult for you to gather when you are involved in the teaching yourself. The only true evaluation, however, is self-evaluation. You can find a multitude of excuses why someone else's evaluation is incorrect but, when you find a fault for yourself, there is less scope for such excuses. In consequence, the principles of providing feedback should be:

(a) to apply and have assessed competences identified by you;

(b) for the observer to provide constructive feedback about the identified competences and about aspects of practice;

(c) for the observer to collect data about practice for detailed subsequent analysis;

(d) for you to try out new methods and approaches to the development of student learning and obtain feedback on them as opposed to obtaining feedback on aspects in which you know that you are proficient;

(e) to assist you to evaluate your own teaching.

If these are the principles, it is important to look at the pros and cons of the different sources of feedback so that you can try to accentuate the positive aspects and minimise the negative ones.

Students are the people who have to suffer our teaching quirks and styles. They are omnipresent and, in consequence, you are not able to 'put on a show' for them. If you do something that is not usually done, they will be aware of it and are able to comment upon it from the standpoint of comparison with what they are used to. Thus, they have distinct advantages over the casual observer.

On the other hand students, especially adolescent ones, might not have the skill to be able to express themselves and tell you their feelings. Also, as you have the upper hand, especially as you assess their work and say whether they are to pass or fail their course, they are likely to give you answers that they think you expect. They might well be fearful of being honest, especially if this involves critical comment, thinking that it might have a bearing on their chances of success. Even if they complete a questionnaire anonymously you are going to know their handwriting so you are likely to be able to trace who has said what.

When you ask *colleagues* and *peers* to give you feedback, they are likely to be busy people and will have to find the time to complete the observation. Thus, any instrument that is given to them will have to be easy to complete and will have to be completed during the period of observation. Also they may make unfair comparisons between your practice and their own.

The main advantage of *tutors* is that they will have gained skill in observation and can provide effective feedback to you. However, they only see you on a limited number of occasions and might have some difficulty in 'tuning-in' to both your needs and requirements.

3.4 Checklist for your Teaching

As a final check on the aspects that you might consider in your teaching the following checklist can be useful. You need to consider each of the points and decide if specific points are applicable to your teaching and, if they are, whether you have taken them into consideration with a specific group of students. The completed checklist should be used with a specific group of students. It will be seen that the same headings have been used as those indicated in the 'Observation Pro-Forma' Figure 8.2.

	Yes	No	Not needed
Preparation Have you: a clear statement of aims/objectives/competences? explicitly identified the needs of the students? clear **plan** for the lesson with: • times indicated? • a choice of appropriate resources? • a choice of teaching strategies and learning styles? • an identified introduction, development and conclusion? • planned assessment of student learning? Is the amount of material about right for the time available? Have you anticipated problems and made the necessary contingency plans?			
Presentation Have you: identified the learning needs of the specific group? determined the entry behaviour of the students? considered the backgound, age, gender, racial and cultural issues? identified possible barriers to learning? managed the time effectively? In the **introduction** have you: • given an overview of the session? • shared with the group the required outcomes (aims/ objectives competences)? • made links with other sessions? • created interest?			

	Yes	No	Not needed
• negotiated with the students within the constraints that are set?			
In the **development** have you:			
• used a logical sequence for the sub-topics?			
• modified the plan to suit responses?			
Have you used a range of teaching/learning aids including:			
• OHP?			
• chalkboard?			
• handouts?			
• white board?			
• flip chart?			
• audio?			
• computers?			
• video?			
• programmed learning?			
• resource-based learning?			
Have you:			
- used a range of teaching strategies effectively?			
- paced the presentation to suit the students and the demands of the syllabus?			
In the **conclusion** have you:			
- given a summary of the lesson?			
- reviewed the key issues?			
- made links to the next lesson?			
Communications and Relationships			
Have you:			
- communicated effectively with the students?			
- spoken clearly?			
- introduced and explained jargon?			
- managed question and answer sessions effectively?			
- answered student questions clearly?			
- used clear diagrams via OHP, chalkboard, flip chart?			

	Yes	No	Not needed
- written clearly on the OHP, chalkboard, flip chart?			
- obtained student feedback?			
- provided positive reinforcement?			
- managed group work effectively?			
- used tutorial time effectively?			
- developed student communication skills (e.g. writing, talking, questioning)?			
- communicated enthusiasm for the subject?			
- motivated the students?			
- encouraged student contributions?			
- observed the non-verbal reactions of the students?			
- kept discipline and order?			
- managed disruptive student(s)?			
- been approachable?			
Assessment Have you: - identified prior knowledge and skills (entry behaviour)?			
- identified and used assessment criteria?			
- selected and used a range of assessment instruments?			
- designed a range of assessment instruments e.g.			
• essays?			
• practical tests?			
• observation?			
• objective tests?			
- ensured validity and reliability?			
- used assessment to facilitate learning?			
- selected and collected evidence of learning for profiles?			
- encouraged self-assessment?			
- encouraged peer group assessment?			
- kept accurate, up-to-date records in an appropriate, confidential system?			

	Yes	No	Not needed
Evaluation Have you: - used a range of evaluation techniques for: • lessons? • modules? • courses? • programmes? - reviewed teaching strategies? - taken appropriate action in response to evaluation?			
Subject Matter and Others Have you: - given due regard to the safety of the students? - given regard to equality of opportunity for all? - developed student study skills? - given appropriate guidance/referral for all aspects of guidance/counselling/development? - updated your own subject knowledge? - updated your own teaching expertise? - considered your own staff development?			

Possible Evidence

*Possible Evidence to Show You have
Achieved the Competence
'Engage in Evaluation of Own
and Other's Teaching'*

The type of evidence that you might collect to show that you have achieved the competence involves:

1. Devising a pro-forma (or using the ones given in this chapter) to evaluate your teaching in general or a specific aspect of it.

2. Completing the teaching to collect data about the episode and summarising the data.

3. Using the data summary to evaluate your teaching or have your teaching evaluated.

Progress Check

> *If you want to check your understanding of*
> *your ability to evaluate your teaching,*
> *try the following progress check*

Progress Check 8.1

1. Identify at least two aspects of teaching under each of the six main elements of (i) preparation, (ii) presentation, (iii) student relationships, (iv) communication, (v) assessment of learning, and (vi) subject matter.

2. State at least three different strategies for monitoring and evaluating the effectiveness of teaching roles.

3. State an effective way of developing appropriate feedback mechanisms.

4. Explain the main differences between obtaining feedback from:

   - students;

   - peers;

   - colleagues; and

   - tutors/line managers

   to give feedback on your teaching performance.

4. Course Evaluation

4.1 Aims of Course Evaluation

In order to take part in course evaluation in any realistic and motivated manner, you have to recognise the benefits that will accrue to you personally and to your teaching, your course and your students. This leads to your consideration of your aims of course evaluation; what is likely to accrue from them. Once the aims have been formulated, and only then, are you able to formulate an effective scheme to evaluate your course.

One of the problems of formulating a course evaluation scheme is the number of aims that might be achieved. Some of the aims are:

*   to find the appropriateness and achievement of the aims and objectives of your course/subject;

*   to consider the structure of your course, its progression, balance and coherence;

*   to identify the relevance and currency of the course syllabus;

*   to understand the quality and effectiveness of your teaching approach used on the course;

*   to find the abilities and skills of the graduates;

*   to assist with the student input profile and its match to the initial stages of the course/subject;

*   to improve and develop skill in your assessment methods and techniques in relation to the objectives and their effectiveness in revealing student achievement;

*   to give an appreciation of the staff who teach on the course, their development and cohesion;

*   to promote a positive attitude in the provision and deployment of resources.

As you can see, the aims are very comprehensive and to achieve them all would involve a very stringent evaluation. You need to be selective in deciding what you want to achieve in order to make a manageable task for your evaluation. You might achieve only one or two of the above aims in any one evaluation; you might make a three year development plan in order to achieve them all but only tackle some of them each academic year. You might decide, initially, on more general headings like:

*   finding information to improve educational processes and programmes;

*   identifying problem areas;

*   evolving new approaches; and/or

*   improving your ability to plan and effect the necessary changes.

Thus, you as an individual teacher, or with colleagues, might want to find the relevance of your course or subject to industry and students, find out if your teaching approaches are acceptable or if others would be better for your students, and so on. Once you have identified your aims, you might want to plan and effect the necessary changes. However, all of these should be reflected in your aims of the evaluation.

Figure 8.4 gives a typical list of aims for the evaluation of a subject.

Aims of the Evaluation of a subject
1. To consider whether the objectives are consistent with the needs of industry and other subjects in the course.
2. To examine the entry behaviour of the students and to link this with subject objectives.
3. To investigate the appropriateness of the teaching and learning approaches to (a) the curriculum documents and (b) the students' needs.
4. To find the trends in percentage of passes and 'drop-outs' over the past five years.

Figure 8.4   Typical Aims of Evaluation

Aims 1 and 2 are linked to the appropriateness of the objectives of the subject which will be found in the curriculum documents. However, their appropriateness to: (i) the industry that the course serves; and (ii) to the students, indicate that either questionnaires will have to be designed or interviews carried out. Similar methods may be used with respect to aim 3 where it is necessary to find out how appropriate the teaching approaches are to the students. The trends in pass rates and drop-outs will be obtained from course records.

A checklist for writing the aims of course evaluation is given in Figure 8.5.

Are the aims that you have written for the evaluation of your course or subject:	YES	NO
1. of practical use?		
2. able to be used in the design of evaluative instruments?		
3. able to be achieved through the process of evaluation?		
4. within your scope to achieve?		
5. sufficiently comprehensive to cover all of the aspects that you want to achieve?		

Figure 8.5   Checklist for Writing Aims of Course Evaluation

One of the problems that you will find in deciding the aims of evaluation lies in their scope. The aims have to be wide enough to cover all of the aspects that you want to achieve, but, on the other hand, they need to be manageable. In other words, you need not too many aims and not too few. They need to be written to be helpful in terms of the things that need to be identified and also to assist in the choice of evaluative instruments that you might design.

4.2 Model of Course Evaluation

In order to achieve comprehensiveness in terms of the design of the aims, you need to consider the types of question that you might ask. Several models of evaluation have been suggested but probably the most useful in terms of post-16 education and training is the one suggested by Stufflebeam (1971). He suggests that we should think of evaluation in terms of four main headings:

Context	This is the setting of the course or subject and relates to the aims of the curriculum;
Input	The input elements relate to the students, the staff and the resources that are used;
Process	This relates to the appropriateness of what happens on the course - how the input elements are used to achieve the aims and objectives;
Product	This relates to the outcomes - the students who have gone through the course and what they have learned.

Stufflebeam calls this the CIPP (the first letter of each of the elements) model and suggests that a comprehensive evaluation should answer questions relating to each of the elements. However, this might comprise quite an onerous task, especially for an individual teacher, and even for a course team. You might want to consider a long term evaluation and write aims only for one of the elements for one set of students. Thus, the complete evaluation might take two or more years to complete.

The type of questions that you might want to find answers to under each of Stufflebeam's elements could be:

Context

1. Are the aims of the curriculum consistent with the needs of industry/society/the individual student?

2. Does the curriculum foster purposeful co-operation and interaction with the world of work?

3. Are the aims broad enough to ensure further education and mobility of the students?

4. Are the aims up-dated regularly?

Input

1. Do the students possess the entry behaviour assumed when designing the curriculum?

2. Do the teachers have the competences required for implementation of the curriculum?

3. Are the resources for teaching and learning, explicit or implicit in the curriculum documents, available to the teacher and to the students?

Process

1. Do the teachers make use of the curriculum documents and, if so, for what purposes?

2. Do the teachers understand the curriculum documents?

3. Is there a system of feedback from students and teachers on the problems faced in the achievement of the aims and objectives?

4. Are the teaching strategies (classroom, laboratory and workshop) in line with those proposed in the curriculum?

5. What is the extent of the use of instructional resource material?

6. Is the student assessment system valid, reliable and practicable?

Product

1. What are the trends in percentage of passes and drop outs?

2. Do the students get absorbed into industry? Is there a time lag? Do they get appropriate employment?

3. What are the opinions of students and ex-students regarding the relevance of the course/subject/topics?

4. What are the staff development needs that have arisen and to what extent have they been met?

5. What are the views of employers on the curriculum?

This is not an exhaustive list of questions, but it gives an indication of the areas that a curriculum evaluation might want to address.

Each of the aims of evaluation, then, can have questions associated with them. Figure 8.6 shows how questions might be associated with the aims of the evaluation suggested in Figure 8.4.

Aim	Possible Questions
1. To consider if the objectives are consistent with the needs of employers?	Do the objectives cover cognitive, psychomotor and affective domains? Are any additions or deletions necessary? Do the objectives reflect industrial needs? How many employers take graduate students? What questions can be asked of employers to determine if the objectives are relevant?
2. To examine the entry behaviour of students.	Is an entry behaviour test available - if not, can one be designed? What is the best time to give an entry behaviour test? Does the entry behaviour for one subject need to reflect other subjects?
3. To investigate the teaching and learning methods.	What teaching strategies are suggested or implied in the curriculum documents? What teaching strategies are used and what strategies *could* be used? What questions should be asked of students and should these be through interview and/or questionnaire?
4. To find the trends in passes and drop-outs.	Who keeps records over the past five years? How can reasons for drop-outs be found - how can student addresses be found?

Figure 8.6   Questions Related to Aims of Evaluation

These, of course, are only a sample of the questions that might be asked. Each of the aims has a whole host of questions that might usefully be associated with them to find specific aspects of the operation of a course or subject. The skill in evaluation is to ensure that the questions are relevant to the information required and useful to the improvement of a course or subject.

4.3 Instruments for Obtaining Information

If the evaluation is to serve the aims that you have listed, it must be a continuous process rather than an intermittent or once only event. It must consist of constant observation, measurement and reporting of how the course/subject is being implemented so that appropriate corrective measures at the most convenient stage of curriculum development might be taken.

The methods of obtaining information can be:

- questionnaires;
- checklists;
- student performance; and/or
- structured interview schedule.

These might be used on the following sources of information:

- teachers;
- students: present, drop-outs, graduates employed;
- industry;
- support staff;
- organisational set-up;
- text and reference books;
- teaching/learning resources: availability, use.

4.3.1 Checklists

A checklist can be a useful *aide memoire* to ensure that you have covered all of the necessary aspects in an evaluation. It can also be used as a basis for the design of a questionnaire.

The example shown below (Figure 8.7) is a checklist of tasks that a course leader might wish to complete in order to consider the staff development of the course team.

	YES	NO
1. All of the staff teaching on the course understand their roles and responsibilities.		
2. Course team members have received specific training in working as a team.		
3. Structured curriculum-led staff development has been offered to all of the course team.		
4. The expertise of staff in helping other course team members to develop has been used.		
5. The following course tasks have been delegated as far as possible: • administration; • assessment design; • use of new teaching strategies.		
6. Part-time and support staff have been included in all staff development programmes for course teams.		

Figure 8.7   Example Checklist for Course Team Staff Development

Checklists must contain terms which the respondent understands and which more briefly and succinctly express views than would be the case with answers from open-ended questions. They are inevitably crude devices, but careful pilot work and design can make them less so. They are at their best when they are designed and used to be related to specific aims.

4.3.2 Questionnaires

An example questionnaire to be given to students about text and reference books is given in Figure 8.8 The aim of this evaluation is:

'To examine how students use the suggested reading list of books for the course.'

The questions associated with this are:

1.   How useful to students is the list of references given for the course?

2.   Why have students found additional reading useful?

3.   What use has been made of additional reading?

4.   How easy is it for students to locate the required reading?

Student Questionnaire - Use Of Reading List

1. How useful have you found the reading list given at the start of the course? Circle the number that best represents your feelings.

Of little use 1 2 3 4 5 6 Very Useful

2. What have you used the readings for? Tick the appropriate boxes.

Doing homework	
Completing assignments	
As a backup to lectures	
Preparation for examinations	
For topics missed when absent	
Others (please state)	

3. Which of the texts have you found MOST useful:

(a)

(b)

4. Why have you found them useful?

5. Which of the texts have you found LEAST useful?

(a)

(b)

6. Why have you found them least useful?

7. Where have you obtained the required books? Tick as appropriate.

	YES
Institution Library	
Home Library	
Bought	
Borrowed from friend	
Other (please state)	

Figure 8.8   Example Questionnaire for Students

You will see from the example that there is a mixture of open questions (those that require a written response) and closed questions (those that only require a tick). The closed questions are both easier to answer and easier to analyse. It is also simpler to collect data from them. Thus, a mixture of both qualitative and quantitative data will be collected.

Whatever the design, the questionnaire should be easy to answer and not take too long. A lengthy questionnaire will not get the necessary attention paid to it and will be difficult to analyse. As a general guide, the questionnaire should not take longer than 5 minutes to answer. The questions need to be directly related to the aims of what you want to find out and its design should be easy to follow and appealing to the eye. Plenty of white space is useful and each question should be clearly separated from the others. It could be helpful, for example, for questions 3 and 5 to indicate the titles of the specific texts that have been given as, say, required reading so that you are not relying upon the student memory to answer the questions. If this was the case you could combine these two questions with tick boxes for the most and least useful.

4.3.3 Structured Interview Schedules

An Interview Schedule is structured and prepared as a basis of a one-to-one interview with your target audience.

In a structured interview schedule you are unlikely to be able to cover as many aspects as you can in a questionnaire but it has the advantage that you can cover the items in greater depth: subsequent questions being dependent upon the response to the previous one. Also, you have much greater control over the responses in that you can ask the questions to ensure that they are understood and ensure that *all* of your questions are answered.

Although you are going to have a face-to-face discussion it is still important that you prepare a schedule upon which to base your questions. In such a schedule you should structure your questions from the general to the specific. You can ask questions about:

(a) knowledge and skills;

(b) common and study skills;

(c) work related skills.

Usually, you will want to find out opinions of individuals about various aspects of the course. The schedule shown in Figure 8.9 is for employers, to find out their opinion of a course of study upon which they send students.

It will be realised from the example schedule that the actual aims and objectives of the course, the knowledge and skills that are applicable, can be inserted into the design itself.

In completion of the schedule, spaces are left for you to insert notes on the responses that the employer makes. You make these notes as the discussion proceeds.

Your design should ensure the following:

- the questions must be directly related to the aims of what you want to find;
- there are a limited number of questions;
- adequately prepare both the schedule and any other information that is required.
- structure the schedule from the general to the specific.

Name: Position:

Company

No of Employees: Course Title:

Q1. Outline of course aims and objectives. Is this how you perceive the course?

Q2. If this is not what you thought, what differences would you wish to see?

Q3. Do you agree with the course content?

Q4. The course provides training in the following skills and knowledge.
     Does this reflect your requirements?

Q5. Stress will be laid on the following skills. Do you agree with this?

Q6. Where should the greater emphasis be laid?

Q7. How satisfied have you been with the student(s) who have attended the course?

Q8. How do you see your future needs?

Q9. What should be added or subtracted from the course?

Figure 8.9   Example Structured Interview Schedule for Employers

4.3.4 Student Assessment

Information about how well the course is going, can be obtained from the results of student assessments. If, for instance, a large proportion of the students fail the end examination, then this is important information and questions will need to be asked as to why this has happened.

This does not only have to be at the end of the course. If students do badly (or well) on your formative tests, then this is also useful information about the success of that part of the course which is being assessed.

4.4 Data Collection from Questionnaires

Data collection can either be qualitative, that is when it is related to opinion, or quantitative when it is related to a numerical scale. For comparative purposes it is easier to deal with and draw conclusions from quantitative data than qualitative. It is necessary, therefore, for us to look at transferring qualitative into quantitative data.

Figure 8.10 shows a small part of a questionnaire given to students to evaluate their opinion of the effectiveness of a short, in-service course for teachers. The part shown refers to the overall organisation of the course.

In your opinion was the overall organisation of the course:					
	QUALITY				
	Poor	Fair	Good	Very Good	Excellent
1. Well prepared?					
2. Properly sequenced?					
3. Intelligently time-tabled (e.g. to give variety)?					
4. Etc.					

Figure 8.10   Part of Student Questionnaire

It may be assumed that the questionnaire is given to a class of 25 students. In order to collate the data, each of the responses from the individual students can be transferred to a blank questionnaire. When this is done the completed blank questionnaire might look as shown in Figure 8.11. In each of the appropriate spaces a slash (/) mark indicates where a particular student has responded. The slash marks are then summated within each of the cells.

In your opinion was the overall organisation of the course:					
	QUALITY				
	Poor	Fair	Good	Very Good	Excellent
1. Well prepared?			///// //// (9)	///// ///// (10)	///// / (6)
2. Properly sequenced?		/// (3)	///// (5)	///// ///// //(12)	///// (5)
3. Intelligently time-tabled (e.g. to give variety)?	//// (4)	///// / (6)	///// ///// (10)	///// (5)	
4. Etc.					

Figure 8.11 Data Collection on a Blank Questionnaire

The next task involves changing the qualitative scale into a quantitative one (that is assigning numbers to each of the points on the scale). This can be done as follows:

Poor   = 1

Fair   = 2

Good   = 3

Very Good   = 4

Excellent   = 5

Another part of the questionnaire asked questions about the 'group tasks' involved in the course and students were requested to indicate their opinion of the tasks by either agreeing or disagreeing with a number of statements. A five-point scale of SD = Strongly Disagree, D = Disagree,; N = Neutral; A = Agree, and SA = Strongly Agree was used. This type of scale, known as a Likert Scale, is shown in Figure 8.12.

Similarly, the qualitative responses can be given a numerical value by assigning numbers to each of the five values of opinion.

	Opinion				
	SD	D	N	A	SA
1. The group work was useful in gaining insights into problems.					
2. The variety of group work helped to maintain interest.					
3. The group work needed more resource materials					
4. Etc.					

Figure 8.12   Example Questionnaire using a Likert Scale

Once the scale has been decided for each of the questions, the responses to them can be converted to the numerical scale and then correlated. So, for question 1 in Figure 8.11, the number of responses in each cell has to be multiplied with the number assigned to that point on the scale. As nine (9) students considered the preparation to be 'good' and 'good' = 3, a total for this cell would be 3 x 9 = 27. This can be completed for all of the cells as shown in Figure 8.13.

In your opinion was the overall organisation of the course:					
	QUALITY				
	Poor 1	Fair 2	Good 3	Very Good 4	Excellent 5	Mean
1. Well prepared?			9 x 3 = 27	10 x 4 = 40	6 x 5 = 30	97/25 = 3.9
2. Properly sequenced?		3 x 2 = 6	5 x 3 = 15	12 x 4 = 48	5 x 5 = 25	94/25 = 3.7
3. Intelligently time-tabled (e.g. to give variety)?	4 x 1 = 4	6 x 2 = 12	10 x 3 = 30	5 x 4 = 20		66/25 = 2.6
4. Etc.						

Figure 8.13   Calculation of a Mean (Average) Response

For comparative purposes the mean (average) response can be calculated for each of the questions. This can be achieved by adding the totals for each of the cells and dividing this by the number of students responding (25 in this case). So, for Question 1 the mean response is (27 + 40 + 30) = 97 / 25 = 3.9.

In consequence, the mean response for each of the questions will allow specific comparisons between the questions to be made. It can be seen that there is 1.1 difference between questions 2 and 3, but only 0.2 difference between questions 1 and 2, and that question 1 receives the 'best' result and question 3 the worst.

4.5 Writing a Course Evaluation Report

A necessary part of any evaluation that you have completed is the preparation of a report to convey the results and conclusions to interested parties. There are many different ways in which your report may be written but generally there are commonalities in the different formats. Reports usually contain four main divisions: an introduction, the methodology used, presentation and analysis of data, and conclusions and recommendations. This format reflects the stages of the evaluation process. The headings shown in Figure 8.14 expand upon each of the main divisions and may help you to write your report. This list of items is fairly comprehensive but is not meant to be a rigid guideline of every step you must take

1. Introduction

    (a)   Reasons for the evaluation

    (b)   Aims to be achieved

    (c)   Key questions to be answered

    (d)   Any limitations

2. Methodology

    (a)   Sources of data

    (b)   Data gathering instruments

    (c)   Procedures employed

3. Presentation and Analysis of Data

    (a)   Presentation of findings

    (b)   Tables and Figures (usually incorporated into the findings)

4. Conclusions and Recommendations

    (a)   Summary

    (b)   Recommendations

Figure 8.14 Format of a Report

Before deciding upon the final format it is necessary to ask yourself what is essential in order to provide an easily understood report, and how do you provide evidence that the recommendations are solidly based? An outline is effective if it helps to identify and order the sub-divisions of the report's major sections. Obviously the outline must precede the actual writing of the report since it is expected to serve as a guide for the writing that lies ahead. An effective outline is a check for coverage and an assurance for sequence and logical presentation of ideas and items.

4.5.1 Conclusions and Recommendations

These two aspects of the report are very important: they are why all of the work has been completed. Often, the two are confused but, in fact they are very different. The conclusion represents your judgment based on the evaluation data. There are two types of conclusion: (i) pre-determined decision situations and (ii) exploratory conclusions. In pre-determined decision situations a conclusion would be based on a synthesis of information about the particular decision. You have to draw your conclusion in the light of, say, political and social forces both inside and outside the education or training establishment. It is no good drawing conclusions that you know could not work due, for instance, to the need for resources. The second type of conclusion is more exploratory in nature. Exploratory evaluation is initiated to explore general concerns or feelings about the adequacy of a course. That is, if a course leader believes that a course has its shortcomings, but has not collected data on which to base the opinion, an evaluation study may be carried out to identify areas or components of the course which need changes.

Recommendations must be based on the conclusions. It can be useful to organise the recommendations around areas upon which you have placed special importance. For example the recommendations may be organised under content area, instructional methods, personnel, course management, or support services. Good organisation will assist the reader to have a clearer appreciation of the importance of your recommendations.

Conciseness in the recommendations section is a desirable characteristic. A lengthy section may produce boredom and lead to the rejection of even the good recommendations that are presented.

You should remember that the recommendations are a basis for action, and will be translated into policy by the decision makers. Therefore, you need to consider that decision makers have their own barriers to overcome. The recommendations, to assist this, may be presented in rank order. Recommendations that are socially, economically or politically unacceptable need to be adapted accordingly.

> ### Possible Evidence to Show You have
> ### Achieved the Competence
> ### 'Engage in Evaluation of Your Courses'.

The type of evidence that you might collect to show that you have achieved the competence involves:

1. Devising a set of aims for a course evaluation and, for each of the aims, writing a set of questions to show how the aims might be achieved.

2. Devising an instrument to collect data in order to answer the questions in (1) above.

3. Using the instrument and analysing the data that is collected.

4. Writing a short report on the basis of the data analysis.

Possible Evidence

*If you want to check your understanding of
your ability to evaluate your courses, try
the following progress check.*

Progress Check 8.2

1. List at least two aspects of your course that might be
    evaluated under each of the headings of:

    (a) Context;

    (b) Input;

    (c) Process;

    (d) Product.

2. Describe the advantages and limitations of the following
    instruments:

    questionnaire;

    checklist;

    student performance.

3. List at least five different sources of information that might
    be used to evaluate one of your courses.

4. Describe how to change qualitative to quantitative data.

5. List, in order, the aspects of a course evaluation report.

Further Reading and References

Further reading and references relating to the topics in this chapter can be found in the following:

Altrichter, H. et al. (1993)   *Teachers Investigate Their Work. Routledge: An Introduction to the Methods of Action Research*. Routledge.

Bell, J. et al. (1984)   *Conducting Small Scale Investigations in Educational Management.* Harper.

Bell, J. (1987)   *Doing Your Research Project*. Open University Press.

Cohen, L. and Manion, L. (1980)   *Research Methods in Education*. Croom Helm.

Dey, I. (1993)   *Qualitative Data Analysis: A User Friendly Guide for Social Scientists*. Routledge.

DES (1987)   *Managing Colleges Efficiently*. Department of Education and Science.

Drever, E. (1995)   *Using Semi-StructuredInterviews in Small Scale Research:A Teachers Guide*. The Scottish Council for Research in Education.

Eichler, M. (1990)   *Non-Sexist Research Methods*. Allen and Unwin.

FESC (1988)   *Responsive College Project*. Further Education Staff College.

FEU (1985)   *A Fragmented View? Professional Accountability and Maintenance of Standards in Vocational Curricula*. Further Education Unit.

FEU (1989)   *Supporting Quality in Y.T.S.* Further Education Unit.

Githin, A. (1989)   *Teacher Evaluation: Educative Alternatives*, Falmer Press.

Gibbs, G. and Haigh, M. (1983)   *Alternative Models of Course Evaluation*. SCEDSIP Occasional paper 13.

Hopkins, D. (1993)   *A Teacher's Guide to Classroom Research*. Open University Press.

Munn, P. and Drover, E. (1995)   *Using Questionnaires in Small Scale Research*. The Scottish Council for Research in Education.

NIACE, (1989)   *Replan. Further Education and Employment Training: A Quality Response*. Replan.

Simpson, M. and Tuson, J. (1995)   *Using Observations in Small Scale Research*. The Scottish Council for Research in Education.

Stufflebeam, D. (1971)   *Educational Evaluation and Decision Making*, Peacock Publishers Inc.

Tansley, D. (1989)   *Course teams: The Way Forward in FE*. NFER Nelson.

Chapter 9

Evidence of Competence in Teaching

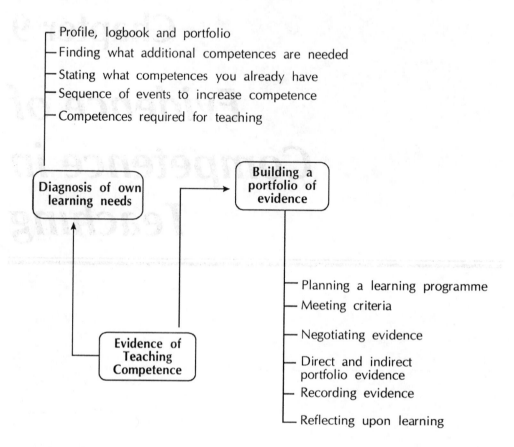

Overview of Chapter 9

Competences Related to this Chapter

The competences and associated performance criteria related to this chapter are:

Overall Competence - *Establish an effective system of gathering evidence of teaching competence*

Competence	Performance Criteria
1. Diagnose own learning needs to improve your teaching competence.	(a) Identify present competences
	(b) Collect evidence of present competences.
	(c) Identify competences that require improving.
	(d) Design a plan to achieve the competences that require improvement.
2. Build a portfolio of evidence of competence in teaching.	(e) Negotiate appropriate evidence of achievement.
	(f) Collect direct and indirect evidence in building a portfolio.
	(g) Have evidence validated if necessary.

Competences

FENTO Standards

FENTO Standards Related to this Chapter

C.	Developing and Using a Range of Teaching and Learning Techniques
c1	Promote and encourage individual learning
D.	**Managing the Learning Process**
d4	Review the learning process with learners
G.	**Reflecting upon and Evaluating One's Own Performance and Planning Future Practice**
g1	Evaluate one's own practice
g2	Plan for future practice
g3	Engage in continual professional development
H.	**Meeting Professional Requirements**
h2	Conform to agreed codes of professional practice

Based on the FENTO Draft standards by kind permission

1. Introduction

Many 'modern' syllabuses are being written in terms of the competences that are to be achieved and the assessment associated with them relates to assessment in the workplace. That is, the assessment is directly related to an individual's ability to perform specific competences at work. This places completely different demands upon the assessment process. The emphasis upon end examinations is becoming less and less and even the ability of an individual in projects and assignments is decreasing.

So, not only are the demands of the curriculum designers changing, but also the demands of the curriculum developer (which, we have already emphasised earlier in this book, is you, the classroom teacher) are changing. The emphasis of the teaching is on the ability of students to perform work-related tasks and for the student to have the necessary knowledge and understanding of these competences. Indeed, each of the Chapters in this book has emphasised the competences that are likely to be related to the knowledge and understanding of the concepts contained within the text. Also, the activities contained in each of the Chapters have tried to indicate how you might obtain evidence to show that you are competent in particular teaching skills. Thus, the skills of assessment in modern syllabuses mean that you have to be able to assess competence in the workplace or similar simulated environments.

This assessment of your teaching used to be referred to as 'Practical Teaching Assessment', carried out by tutors in Colleges of Education in conventional teacher training courses. This, along with many other courses, is in the process of change so that your practical teaching observation might be 'assessed' by someone in your own institution who will 'accredit your competence'.

As we described in Chapter 7 when discussing the assessment of competences, this requires a sequence of events from the generation of evidence, through collection of that evidence, to a judgment of whether it suggests competent performance or not, to, finally, its verification and successful achievement of competence. What we must do in this chapter is to look at how that applies to ourselves and to the teaching process so that we might successfully prove that we are competent teachers.

2. Competences Related to Teaching and Learning

At the beginning of each chapter in this book there has been an indication of the competences that relate to that chapter, along with an indication of the standards outlined by FENTO. These, we consider, are not the only competences and standards that you will be expected to perform, but are the *key* competences that are required for you to perform effectively in your first years of teaching. Many teacher training courses (for example, the City and Guilds 7307, and some Certificate in Education courses) and Industry Lead Bodies (for example the Training and Development Lead Body and Management Charter Initiative) identify slightly different competences although they have a similar base.

The competences identified as key to the role of the teacher of post-16 education and training are indicated in Figure 9.1.

	Chapter	Competences
1	**Basic teaching.**	1. Adopt a teaching role. 2. Plan and organise learning. 3. Manage learning. 4. Assess learning and evaluate teaching.
2	**Student learning.**	1. Identify the characteristics of the three learning taxonomies. 2. Demonstrate effective design of learning sessions through the identification of variables which effect learning. 3. Use the components of a range of theories of learning. 4. Identify variables which influence student motivation.
3	**Techniques of teaching.**	1. Deliver a programme of learning sessions. 2. Manage learning activities.
4	**Learning aids.**	1. Establish a basis for choosing learning aids. 2. Use board aids appropriately. 3. Use handouts appropriately. 4. Use the overhead projector appropriately. 5. Select, adapt or construct learning resources for a specific programme. 6. Evaluate the use of learning resources.
5	**Planning and design for teaching and learning.**	1. Identify learning outcomes for specific programmes. 2. Design learning programmes related to the specific needs of learners. 3. Develop procedures to assess learning and evaluate teaching.
6	**Communication and the teacher.**	1. Demonstrate effective teacher communication skills. 2. Assist students to develop their communication skills.
7	**Assessment of student learning.**	1. Assess students during a lesson or learning period. 2. Justify use and record appropriate forms of measuring student achievement. 3. Employ appropriate assessment of student practical work.
8	**Evaluation of self and teaching.**	1. Engage in evaluation of own and other's teaching. 2. Engage in evaluation of your courses.

Figure 9.1   Key Competences of the Role of the Teacher

Each of the competences listed has its own assessment criteria associated with it. In order to become competent you should ensure that you can achieve *all* of the assessment criteria. There can be no averaging, saying that you are excellent with one of the criteria so you will not bother with another of them. All criteria are equally important to the achievement of the competence.

3. Learning Competences

All teachers learn to be increasingly competent throughout their teaching careers. The teacher in training, however, needs to be more systematic about this process than does the more experienced teacher. The process described below has the following sequence associated with it:

(i) diagnose your learning needs;

(ii) plan a learning programme;

(iii) negotiate the further learning needed to provide evidence to show competence;

(iv) build a portfolio of evidence of competence;

(v) record evidence in a logbook or diary;

(vi) reflect on the learning activities.

There are many variations to this sequence but it seems to us that this is logical and covers the important aspects of the process. Such a process revolves around the *generation of evidence* to show competence in a particular aspect of the teaching role.

To assist with the learning process and to show that you have achieved evidence to prove that you are competent, it is suggested that you might use a Profile and a Logbook to record the above activities. The *profile* provides an accredited record of your learning activities. It can consist of:

(i) a record of the evidence that you negotiate with your accreditor;

(ii) your record of learning activities; and

(iii) reflections on those learning activities.

The *logbook* is a document for recording progress as you attempt the different aspects of competence. It is similar to a diary, and, indeed may be replaced by a diary consisting of A4 pages, and it runs parallel with the development of the profile of evidence. It assists you in reflecting on the learning process underlying that development.

It is becoming increasingly important when attending courses and going for job interviews that, as you learn, apart from the profile and logbook, you also keep a *portfolio* of work that you have completed as part of the learning process. This, like an artist's portfolio, gives examples of the different parts of work that you have completed whilst you are learning.

So, there are three important documents that are associated with the development of competence and each of them are interlinked. All of them are your responsibility to keep up to date and ensure that they are well written. You can, if you wish, ask your line manager, tutor, or a colleague to assess what you have done, comment upon it and sign that they have seen it.

The starting point, then, for the achievement of competence lies with the generation of evidence to show that you are competent and this evidence must be related to the assessment criteria.

4. Generation of Evidence

It is suggested below that the generation of evidence requires a sequential structure to ensure that it will be useful, show that you are competent and that you will not repeat what you have already done. In effect, you will need to plan and organise your learning programme. Each of the stages in the process is described below with suggested proformas which may be useful for the process.

4.1 Diagnosis of learning needs

You need to start with a diagnosis of your learning needs. For example, for each of the competences you should find answers to:

- What competence, if any, do I start with?
- What evidence do I have of existing practice?
- What competence do I need or want to achieve?
- What action do I need to take?
- How will I know when competence has been achieved?

Thus, suppose that you want to achieve competence in 'employ appropriate assessment of student practical work'. In order to diagnose your learning needs it will be necessary for you to think about your requirements for assessment of practical work. If you are attending a course you will be given assistance through the assessment criteria for that area of work. Thus, it might be as shown in Figure 9.2.

Competence	Assessment Criteria
Employ appropriate assessment of student practical work.	(a) Use a range of test instruments for the assessment of practical tasks. (b) Use appropriate formats for the assessment of projects/assignments. (c) Employ effective student profiling formats. (d) Present feedback to students in a positive manner.

Figure 9.2   Assistance with Diagnosis of Learning Needs

You can now link the five questions above with the content areas contained within the assessment criteria. So you ask yourself:

What competence have I with:

- a range of test instruments?

- using appropriate formats?

- employing profiling techniques?

- presenting feed back in a positive manner?

What evidence do I have with:

- a range of test instruments?

- using appropriate formats?

- employing profiling techniques?

- presenting feed back in a positive manner?

What competence do I need to achieve with:

- etc.

Figure 9.3 gives an example of what your diagnosis of needs might look like in response to the questions above.

Diagnosis of Need

I already use what I consider to be valid and reliable test instruments for workshop practical tasks. The evidence that I have for this includes test schedules and associated marking schemes for 1st year work.

I need to consider which type of marking scheme is best for the subject, for me and my students. I need to increase my competence in the assessment of project work for the end of year project for lst year students I need at least one and possibly three project briefs with associated marking schemes covering both content and common skills.

I have no experience with profiles but can see that they could be useful when associated with the practical work and projects.

Figure 9.3   Example of a Completed Diagnosis of Needs

Such a diagnosis needs to be carried out for each of the competences that you want to achieve. In this manner you start to identify:

(i)   the competences that you already have together with the evidence that you can assemble to prove that you have the competence; and

(ii)   those competences that you need to achieve to make you better at your job.

Possible Evidence

The type of evidence that you might collect to show that you have achieved the competence involves:

1. Make a list of the competences required by a teacher in your subject area. For each of these competences indicate those that you already have and those in which you need to become more proficient.

    For the competences that you already have indicate the evidence that you can produce to prove your competence.

2. For the competences in which you need to become more proficient, design a plan to show how they will be achieved.

> *If you want to check your understanding of your role in diagnosing own learning needs try the following progress check.*

Progress Check 9.1

1. For each of the following areas of teaching, identify at least two roles in which you should be competent:

    (a) Student Learning

    (b) Techniques of teaching

    (c) Learning aids

    (d) Planning for teaching

    (e) Communication

    (f) Assessment of student learning

    (g) Self evaluation

    (h) Evaluation of teaching.

2. Place the following into a logical sequence of activities which could be used to increase your competence in teaching.

    (i) Record evidence in a logbook or diary

    (ii) Plan a learning programme

    (iii) Diagnose your learning needs

    (iv) Negotiate the further learning needed to provide evidence to show competence

    (v) Reflect on learning activities

    (vi) Build a portfolio of evidence of competence.

3. Differentiate between the following:

    *   profile
    *   logbook
    *   portfolio.

4.2 Plan a Learning Programme

The next stage in the process involves the planning of a learning programme for yourself to rehearse the competence. From the diagnosis of need you have to sequence your activities to cover all of the aspects that you have identified. Look at each aspect and decide which to cover first, next, and so on. Your aim should be to finish with a full and balanced set of evidence which fully represents your professional ability.

Figure 9.4 gives an indication of what a completed Plan might look like for the diagnosis completed in Figure 9.3.

Plan of Learning Programme

1. Investigate different formats for the assessment of practical work and identify one that will be most appropriate for 1st year students. This to include:

    • whether to give marks, grades or pass/fail;

    • whether the marking will be on-going or terminal;

    • what will be given to the students (brief, assessment scheme, task sheets, and so on)

2. By looking through the syllabus and scheme of work, identify optional (possibly 5) practical tests.

3. Use one of these practical areas, to identify the skills (both subject and common) that students will need to complete the test. These skills to be limited to those that can be assessed.

4. Prepare a possible scheme of work that students can follow in the completion of a project area.

5. For each of the tasks identify the assessment criteria that will form the basis of the assessment scheme for marking the project.

6. Investigate profile formats to include:

    • where these are best used;

    • teacher and student tasks associated with their completion;

    • aspects to be included in their design;

    • what is available and what I need to design.

Figure 9.4   Completed Example - Plan of Learning Programme

The completed plan indicates not only what is required to be learned, but gives an indication of the order in which this might be completed. The criteria for making these decisions is likely to revolve around what you are doing at work and the type of possibilities that you see in the achievement of the competence with your students.

The argument here is that, when you plan your own programme, it is more likely to be relevant to your needs and be able to be applied, and be related to, your teaching. This, then, is more likely to give you motivation for your learning.

4.3 Understand, Agree and Meet the Criteria

After planning the learning programme, you need to concentrate upon how the assessment criteria will be met when you negotiate, collect and present evidence of your competence.

In meeting these criteria, it means that your work:

1. *'Establishes and maintains quality'*

    In all your work you need to ensure that its quality is the best.
    This is of prime importance in meeting the criteria.

2. *'Diagnoses students' learning needs and problems'*

    Your work needs to be based on the needs of your students.

3. *'Is based on an understanding of the learning process'*

    Not only do you need to gain the various competences based on doing your job better in the classroom, but the competences need to take account of a clear understanding of the learning processes.
    This might well mean wide reading of educational psychology which can often underpin classroom practices.

4. *'Demonstrates an awareness of the alternatives that can be used in achieving the criteria'*

    Often, in solving a problem, we use the first solution that comes to us.
    It is important that you consider the alternatives that are available to you and choose the most appropriate of these.
    The appropriateness might be in terms of what is available, what will best suit your students, what will best suit your situation, and so on.

5. *'Explores the use of IT'*

    The use of IT is a common skill upon which you must concentrate.

6. *'Contains its own evaluation'*

    In meeting criteria you must ensure that you can evaluate what you are proposing and doing. This self evaluation must become a way of life.

7. *'Demonstrates your research skills'*

    The achievement of all of the above indicates that you must be able to research what you are doing.
    Such research might involve reading, asking tutors and colleagues, asking students, trying things out and evaluating them, and so on.

All of these will not be achieved with every piece of work, every piece of evidence that you produce and for every competence. However, you should aim to achieve all of them by the end of a period of study. They are all equally important to the practising teacher. How you are to meet the criteria can usefully be recorded in a Logbook or Diary.

4.4 Negotiation of Evidence

The negotiation of appropriate evidence is a key stage in the overall process. Having decided on the competences to be achieved and having undertaken an initial diagnosis, the question is - what further learning and development is needed? What form will it take? What evidence will emerge that learning has occurred and that competence has been gained?

You may decide that no further work is needed to meet a given assessment criteria - you may feel competent enough and you can assemble evidence to prove it from work that you have already completed. If you do feel competent, gather your existing evidence in a document such as a portfolio of your work. You do, however, need to be fully prepared to justify your decision and to show that you have checked out all of the possibilities.

Sharing ideas and practices with colleagues and other teachers on a teacher training course can sometimes enable you to discover applications and practices that you have never thought about yourself. It is sometimes hard to identify the gaps in your knowledge until you know what is available. It is therefore important that you are 'open' about what you have done and be willing to show it to others and discuss its advantages and limitations. This sharing is an important learning tool.

An example profile form that you might use to negotiate your evidence to prove that you are competent is shown in Figure 9.5. Such a pro-forma, when associated with a teacher training course, would need to be completed either in association with the course tutor, or, when not on such a course, with your line manager. Whichever situation, when it is completed, it provides the basis for a discussion of what you are attempting to achieve.

Competence Area:	**Negotiation of Evidence of Competence**		
Competence:	*Establishment:* _____		
Aspects of Competence	*Proposed Evidence*	*Location of Evidence*	*Date*
1.			
2.			
3.			
4.			

Figure 9.5   **Possible Pro-forma for the Negotiation of Evidence of Competence**

The completion of the pro-forma becomes a simple matter when you have competently and accurately completed a diagnosis of need as suggested in Figure 9.3. Such a diagnosis might clearly indicate the type of evidence that is proposed (for example the project briefs and assessment criteria). However, you might have indicated that you can already meet some of the criteria and the type of evidence that you have to show this can be indicated on the pro forma.

We have provided a completed pro-forma in Figure 9.6 for the assessment of practical work competence which we suggested previously (assessment of student practical work).

Competence Area: Assessment	**Negotiation of Evidence of Competence**		
Competence:	*Establishment*: XYZ Adult Training Centre		
Aspects of Competence	*Proposed Evidence*	Location of Evidence	Date
1. Employ appropriate assessment of student practical work.	5 practical tests.	Year 1	October
	Marking Schemes		
2. Use a range of test instruments for practical assessment	Year 1 projects.		
	Marking Schemes		
3. Employ student profiling formats	Essay on formats	ABC college	December
	Report on discussion		
4. Present feedback to students in a positive manner	Results of questionnaire to student's practical assessment	Year 1 work.	July

Figure 9.6   Example Completed Pro-forma for the Negotiation of Evidence

The negotiation process can suggest alternative types of evidence that you might collect as well as assisting you with the things that are available. It is important that you have the evidence agreed before you start work. The evidence builds into a Portfolio which you should maintain and develop as you are achieving competences.

4.5 Building a Portfolio of Evidence

Probably the most important aspect of this new type of learning involves the building of a portfolio of evidence to demonstrate that you have learned a particular competence. Such a portfolio consists of all types of work that you have been involved with and shows the depth of skill that you have applied to the competence. Such a portfolio does not only show your assessor the work with which you have been involved, but is also available for future reference to be used as accreditation of prior learning for your future learning. It will ensure that you do not have to go through learning the same competence again.

So, what do you include as evidence in your portfolio? There is both direct evidence, that is the results of work that you yourself have completed; and indirect evidence completed by others as a result of your work, such as testimonials and certificates.

You can include many kinds of *direct* evidence in your portfolio like:

- teaching plans: schemes of work, lesson plans;

- visual aids: handouts, transparencies, slides, charts;

- evaluation materials: tests, projects, assignments, questionnaires, interview schedules, and the data from these;

- course work: papers from working parties, proposals for new courses, reports of meetings, conferences and visits;

- summaries: of books, articles, radio and TV programmes;

- analysis of classroom, workshop and other activities;

- artefacts: photographs, models, video recordings, audio tapes.

The types of *indirect* evidence that you might include are:

- reports on your practice (such as practical teaching reports);

- certificates and awards;

- references and evidence of work done on short courses;

Following the Kolb model discussed in Chapter 1 where we emphasised the importance of reflecting on learning, in addition to all of this material, the portfolio can also be a useful place to file *your thoughts* (or reflections) on:

- learning activities that you have undertaken;

- your development of competence;

- practical teaching visits;

- projects and assignments that you have completed.

Whichever of the above types of evidence that you keep in your portfolio, when it is part of a course, it should be in line with the evidence agreed in advance and must meet the criteria for that particular competence. The portfolio will also help you to decide whether, in your opinion, you are competent or not and, again if it is part of a course, whether you are ready to claim competence. In other words, it will be the means to support a claim for competence to yourself or to others.

The Process of Recording Evidence

A 'Logbook' or 'Diary' can be used to record progress as you tackle the different competences. You can keep a Logbook in parallel with the development of your Portfolio and it enables you to *reflect* on the learning process underlying that development. The process might follow the sequence of:

(i) start with your diagnosis of learning needs and continue with what has been agreed (Figure 9.3) and then record what is agreed in your learning plan (Figure 9.4); that is, the proposed evidence and the criteria by which it is to be judged that has been negotiated with a tutor (Figure 9.5);

(ii) make a note in your logbook/diary when you are actually engaged in the learning process. For example, record when you try a new method of teaching, use a particular visual aid, plan a lesson in a different way, try out a particular method of assessment, go to a meeting and try a new skill. A completed example is shown in Figure 9.7

Date	Competence: Assessment of Student Practical Work
Oct 6th	*Practical Test 1* *Designed a marking scheme by completing a breakdown of the complete job and for each sub-task, allocated marks (as appropriate) to (i) technical skills, (ii) method of work, (iii) use of tools, (iv) application of knowledge, and (v) creativity.*
Oct 10th	*Used marking scheme with Year 1. It was perhaps too thorough in that it took a long time to complete. I only completed three students.*
Oct 21st	*Practical Test 2* *Designed a marking scheme using a rating schedule.* *The scale designed using sub-tasks like Test 1.*
	Designed questionnaire to give to students to see which type of marking scheme they (a) find most helpful and (b) prefer.
Oct 31st	*Used Marking scheme and distributed questionnaire. The analysis of the results showed ...etc.*

Figure 9.7   Completed Logbook Entry to Show Record of Evidence

This shows the date on which aspects were completed for student practical work and it follows on from the entry in the Negotiated Evidence by expanding on the entry 'Design Five Practical Tests with Associated Marking Schemes'. The intention being to try different types of marking scheme and to try to find out which is preferable.

(iii) the next stage is to record how things went - to *reflect*. This can indicate what success you had, how you as the teacher felt about it (was it worth the amount of time and effort that was invested in it?), what results or feedback you obtained, what you need to do next, and so on. It is a record of your thoughts and actions. It does not, of course, have only to be your thoughts, for the reflection can often be most useful when you talk to someone else (a colleague, your students, and so on) about it and share and talk through the problems and difficulties. A completed example of such a reflection is shown in Figure 9.8.

Reflection of Learning Activity

Assessment of Practical Work

Test 1:   *The marking scheme took a long time to prepare (about 4 hours). It was decided to give a copy of the marking scheme to the students (which I had not done before) and they did not really know what to do with it. Perhaps I should get them to mark their own tasks which might make them concentrate more on each of the aspects.*
It was difficult to use the marking scheme for method of work as it was difficult to watch the 15 students at the same time and I felt that I missed some aspects. This was similar for Use of Tools. Students only tended to look at their overall mark when I gave them their results and not the marks for the individual sub-tasks. The reliability of the results was judged to be higher than my previous assessments as it is more closely related to the course aims.
The next scheme (rating scale) I will not add the marks for individual students.

Figure 9.8   Completed Example - Reflection of Learning Activity

This shows what was done, what success was thought to be achieved, and what would be done next in the light of the experience of the activity.

5. Competence Learning

An expansion of the Experience, Reflection, Learning Model described in Chapter 1, has been expanded by Kolb (1984) as shown in figure 9.9.

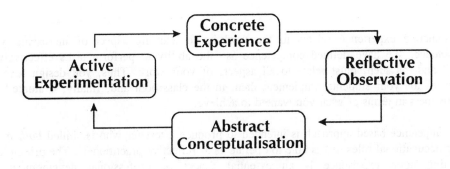

Figure 9.9 Kolb's Four Stage Model of Learning

It is suggested that the importance of this model of learning included:

(i)   being able to start the cycle at any stage;

(ii)   the importance of reflection as well as experience to optimise the learning;

(iii)   once the cycle is started, the sequence should be followed.

This cycle is equally appropriate for your own learning associated with your development of teaching competences. Each of the stages are, in effect, what has been described above in this Chapter. It involves the applications indicated in Figure 9.10.

Active Experimentation	Completing a needs analysis to decide what competences you already have and what are needed
Concrete Experience	Including work-based learning where you design, implement and evaluate aspects of your work in order to gain competence. This includes the gaining and recording of evidence for your portfolio.
Reflective Observation	The final part of your profile design involves reflecting upon what has been completed.
Abstract Conceptualisation	Placing what has been learned with all your previous learning and perhaps relating it to educational theory.

Figure 9.10   Relating the Kolb Model to Gaining Competence

Although Kolb suggests that the cycle can be started at any stage, we have suggested a specific sequence in this Chapter and Figure 9.9 has followed that sequence from needs analysis, through the learning by experience, to reflection and, finally relating the practice to theory. However, several aspects arise from this. For instance, you may wish to read about the educational theory first. This would be the traditional way of learning: to start with the theory and follow it with the practice. Whether this is more efficient is a matter of conjecture. Also, the learning of the theory may be part of the concrete experience, especially if it is associated with a course that you are completing and is a result of what your peers tell you and describe to you.

The concrete experience relates to the work-based learning aspect of increasing your competence. We have defined competence as "the ability to perform tasks effectively at work" and, as such, must relate to all aspects of your work. Thus, you design learning resources for your students, implement them in the classroom and, finally, evaluate their effectiveness in terms of what you wanted to achieve.

The competence-based approach is intended to produce a teacher who is skilled *both* in the major occupational roles *and* is able to operate as a 'reflective practitioner'. The principle of reflecting upon experience is an essential aspect of professional development. In consequence, it has been suggested that reflection is an important aspect of a profiling system. You need to reflect upon all aspects of your work; not just in terms of whether it has achieved its aims, but also in terms of how it was learned, whether the best learning techniques were used, whether you might have used different techniques, and so on.

Finally, you need to place what has been learned into your own personal 'concept map'; to align the new learning with what has already been learned. You need to be able to continually enlarge your concept of teaching and learning. Once you think that you know all there is to know, it may be time to give up teaching. We can all continue to learn different aspects all of our lives and, in consequence, continually improve our competence.

> *Possible Evidence to Show that you have achieved the Competence 'Build a Portfolio of Evidence of Competence in Teaching'.*

The type of evidence that you might collect to show that you have achieved the competence involves:

1. Choose a piece of work that you have recently completed for one of your classes (e.g. a lesson plan, a test, a visual aid) and show how that piece of work achieves AT LEAST FOUR of the following:

   - establishes and maintains quality;
   - diagnoses student learning needs and problems;
   - is based on an understanding of the learning processes;
   - demonstrates an awareness of the alternatives that might have been used;
   - explores the use of IT;
   - contains its own evaluation;
   - demonstrates your research skills.

2. For the piece of work identified in 1. above, indicate whether the evidence is direct or indirect.

3. For a competence that you consider needs improving, decide upon a plan of action to improve it and keep a logbook of all of the aspects that indicate that you are learning to improve the competence. The log should indicate the date and the activities that you have completed.

Possible Evidence

Progress Check *(vertical text in left margin)*

> *If you want to check your understanding of your role in building a portfolio of evidence of competence in teaching try the following progress check.*

Progress Check 9.2

1. Assume that you are attending a teacher training course and state at least three types of people with whom you might negotiate appropriate evidence of achievement of competence.

2. Explain the difference between 'direct' and 'indirect' evidence of competence.

3. List at least ten aspects of your work that might be included in a portfolio of evidence of competence in teaching.

Explain what is meant by 'validation' of evidence and state at least three people who might carry out this process.

Further Reading and References

Further reading relating to the topics in this Chapter can be found in the following:

Garry, A. et al (1986)   *Learning from Experience*. FEU/PICKUP.

Gibbs, G. (1988)   *Learning by Doing: A guide to teaching and learning methods*. FEU.

Hall, J. (1992)   *Crediting Competence - a Portfolio Development Technique for Managers, in Training and Development*. Vol 10 No 6, June.

Kolb, D. A. (1984)   *Experiential Learning - Experience as the Source of Learning and Development*. Prentice Hall.

Rae, L. (1991)   *How to Measure Training Effectiveness*. Gower Publishing Company, 2nd Edition.

Appendix

Appendix

Appendix

There can be little doubt that the Further Education National Training Organisation (FENTO) Standards will have a major impact on the whole of Furhter Education. They are likely to be the catalyst for compulsory training in futher education. At the time of writing, the standards are at the consultation stage but it is clear tha the majority of the profession welcome them. The standards shown in this appendix are for FE lecturers and will have an impact on teacher training courses such as City and Guilds 730 and the Certificate in Education/PGCE. Other standards for management, professional development, etc., are likely to be published in the future.

As the figure below shows the standards relate to seven Key Areas which provide the basis of what the proficient FE lecturer should demonstrate. This fourth edition covers the majority of the standards with the remainder being achieved in the workplace. Do remember that these are threshold standards and you are expected to develop beyond them as your career progresses.

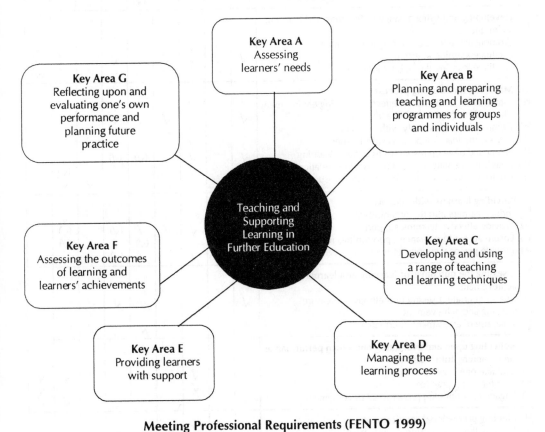

Meeting Professional Requirements (FENTO 1999)

FENTO Standard \ Chapter of the Book	Ch 1 An Introduction to Teaching	Ch 2 Student Learning	Ch 3 Teaching Strategies and Learning Styles	Ch 4 Learning Aids	Ch 5 Planning and Design for Teaching/Learning	Ch 6 Communication and the Teacher	Ch 7 Assessment of Student Learning	Ch 8 Evaluation of Self and Teaching	Ch 9 Evidence of Competence in Teaching
A. Assessing Learners' Needs									
a1 Identify and plan for the needs of potential learners	✓				✓		✓		
a2 Make an initial assessment of the learners' needs	✓						✓		
B. Planning and preparing teaching and learning programmes for groups and individuals									
b1 Identify the required outcomes of the learning programme	✓				✓		✓		
b2 Identify appropriate teaching and learning techniques	✓		✓	✓	✓	✓			
b3 Enhance access and provision in learning programme			✓	✓	(✓)				
C. Developing and using a range of teaching and learning techniques									
c1 Promote and encourage individual learning		✓	✓	✓	✓			✓	✓
c2 Facilitate learning in groups	✓	✓	✓	✓	✓	✓		✓	(✓)
c3 Facilitate learning through experience		✓	✓	✓		✓		✓	(✓)
D. Managing the learning process									
d1 Establish and maintain an effective learning environment			✓			✓			
d2 Plan and structure learning activities	✓		✓	✓	✓	✓			
d3 Communicate effectively with learners			✓	✓		✓			
d4 Review the learning process with learners			✓			✓			
d5 Select and develop resources to support learning	✓		✓	✓	(✓)	(✓)		✓	✓
d6 Establish and maintain effective working relationships			✓					(✓)	
d7 Contribute to the organisation's quality assurance system			✓				✓	✓	
E. Providing learners with support									
e1 Induct learners into the organisation								✓	
e2 Provide effective learning support			✓	✓	✓	(✓)		(✓)	
e3 Ensure access to guidance opportunities for learners					(✓)	(✓)		(✓)	
e4 Provide personal support to learners			✓		✓	(✓)			
F. Assessing the outcomes of learning and learners' achievement									
f1 Use appropriate assessment methods to measure learning and achievement	✓				✓	✓	✓		
f2 Make use of assessment information					✓		✓	(✓)	
G. Reflecting upon and evaluating one's own performance and planning future action									
g1 Evaluate one's own practice		✓			(✓)			✓	✓
g2 Plan for future practice		✓						✓	✓
g3 Engage in continuing professional development								✓	✓
H. Meeting professional requirements									
h1 Work within a professional value base		✓	✓			✓	✓	✓	
h2 Conform to agreed codes of professional practice			✓			✓	✓	✓	✓

FENTO Standards found in the various chapters of the book

Glossary of Terms

Affective Domain	Involves feelings, emotions, attitudes and values.
Andragogy	The science of adult learning (usually related to a student-centred approach).
Assessment	Measurement of how effectively the students have learned; usually measured against stated learning outcomes.
Assignment	Students are presented with a topic/subject or problem for an in-depth analysis.
Behaviourism	The prediction of human behaviour or learning through actions or tasks and based on responses to stimuli.
Brainstorming	Teaching strategy where students generate a large number of ideas in a short time.
Case Study	The examination of a real or simulated situation or problem.
Chalkboard	Either roller or fixed boards with a surface which will take chalk.
Checklist	A list of aspects (for example to assess) which can be 'checked-off' when they are completed.
Cognitive Domain	Involves mental processes.
Cognitivists	School of human learning with the focus on students and how they gain and organise their knowledge.
Common Skill	General or transferable skills (sometimes called core skills).
Competence	The ability to perform actions/procedures effectively in the workplace.
Concept	Mental pictures of relationships and qualities of objects or ideas.
Constructivism	School of human learning which believes in the need to identify current learning prior to constructing new meaning.
Contiguity	The almost simultaneous occurrence of stimulus and response in psychomotor skill learning.
Convergent	Search for a single correct answer or solution.
Copyright	The legal exclusive right that authors have to print, publish and sell their own work.
Criterion	Set standard, usually to be attained during assessment.
Curriculum	Programmes for learning and those factors which influence the quality of learning.

Debate	Teaching strategy where students put points for and against an argument or motion.
Deductive	Moving from generalisations to the particular.
Demonstration	Teaching strategy usually associated with showing students a practical skill which they will then practise.
Discussion	Teaching strategy where it is planned that students will talk to each other about a topic and report back on their findings.
Divergent	Process or search for a solution to a problem which has more than one answer.
Domain	A category of learning.
Entry Behaviour	What the student knows about the topic at the start of instruction.
Essay	Student response to a question where they have structured their response themselves.
Evaluation	Means of measuring the effectiveness of a learning situation (which *may* include student assessment).
Extrinsic	Coming from outside oneself. For example, extrinsic motivation is that provided by the teacher.
Feedback	The passing of information to the student of their ability to perform a task.
Feltboard	Board covered in felt which can be used to stick pictures, shapes or words.
Flipchart	Large pieces of paper fixed to a stand to be used in the same way as a chalkboard.
Formative	Type of assessment to help with teaching and learning. On-going assessment throughout the learning process.
Gestaltists	Study of human learning where understanding is based upon insight.
Humanist	Person who believes that learning should be based upon worth, self esteem and dignity of the individual.
Handout	Pieces of paper containing information to be given to students.
Inductive	Going from particular examples to a generalisation.
Intrinsic	Coming from within oneself.
Jobsheet	Handout containing instructions or a specification so that students can complete a piece of work.
Keller Plan	A personalised system of instruction which is individually paced and based on mastery learning principles.

Kinaesethetic	The perception of muscular effort.
Lecture	Teaching strategy where the passage of information is from the teacher to the student.
Lesson Plan	A guide to what the teacher plans for the students to do in order to achieve the intended learning outcomes.
Magneticboard	Board with a steel backing upon which magnets or magnetic-backed pictures can be placed and moved around.
Mastery Learning	Where a student must learn one topic (objective) before proceeding to another.
Matching Block	Type of question where students have to match aspects in one column with those given in another.
Memory	The ability to recall information.
Model	Theoretical relationships between aspects.
Module	Discrete units of identified learning materials.
Motivation	An inclination to become involved in the learning process.
Multiple-choice	Type of question where a student chooses from a number of options.
Norm	Related to the normal distribution of the population.
Norm Referenced Assessment	Relating performance with that of a typical student population.
Objective	May be behavioural (product) or expressive (process) but is concerned with what students must be able to do.
Open Learning	Sometimes called distance learning where the teacher and the student meet infrequently. The learning material is usually written.
Overhead Projector	Machine used to project images (words and diagrams) to students.
Pedagogy	The science of teaching (usually related to a teacher dominated approach).
Peer	Of equal rank or status (e.g. a colleague or fellow student).
Principle	A statement of the relationship between two or more concepts.
Problem Solving	A high level cognitive activity using two or more principles.
Profile	A means of recording achievement.
Project	A method of problem solving which involves the student in research, finding a solution and reporting either in writing or verbally.
Psychomotor	Involves physical movement and co-ordination.

Question and Answer	Teaching strategy where the teacher asks a question and a student responds.
Rating Schedule	Rating students according to a fixed scale.
Reliability	The ability of a test to consistently measure what it is supposed to measure.
Role Play	Teaching strategy where students act out a part or role.
Scheme of Work	The sequence in which topics are to be taught.
Seminar	Teaching strategy where a student researches a topic, presents the findings to other students and leads an ensuing discussion.
Simulation	An event or situation that is set up to be as similar to the real thing as possible.
Summative	Type of assessment used at the end of a period of instruction and used for certification purposes.
Transparency	Acetate sheet upon which words or diagrams are drawn to project to students.
Tutorial	One to one learning situation where teacher can give individual and in-depth help to a student.
Understanding	Doing something with recalled information (e.g. interpreting, translating or summarising).
Whiteboard	Similar to chalkboard but using dry-marker pens on a white plastic surface.
Worksheet	Incomplete handout given to students for their completion.
Workshop	Teaching strategy where students are given the opportunity to practise and develop practical skills in a real or simulated environment.
Validity	How well a test measures what it is supposed to measure.

Bibliography

Audio Visual Products Division (1987)	*How to Make Successful Overhead Projector Transparencies*, 3M UK plc.
Ashley, R., et al. (1993)	Core Skills GNVQ, Business Education Publishers.
Armitage, A. et al. (1999)	*Teaching and Training in Post-Compulsory Education* Open University Press.
Ausubel, D. P. (1968)	*Educational Psychology: a cognitive view*. Holt, Rinehast and Winston.
Bell, J. et al. (1984)	Conducting Small Scale Investigations in Educational Management, Harper.
Black, H. et al. (1989)	The Quality of Assessment, Scottish Council for Research in Education.
Bligh, D. (1971)	What's the Use of Lectures?, Penguin.
Bloom, B. S. (1964)	*Taxonomy of Educational Objectives: Handbook 1:Cognitive Domain*, Longmans.
Brookfield, S. D. and Preskill, S. (1999)	*Discussion as a Way of Teaching*. Open University Press.
Brown, G.(1975)	*Micro-Teaching: A Programme of Teaching Skills*, Methuen.
Brown, G. (1987)	*Lecturing Styles* in Engineering Design Education, Spring
Brown, G. and Atkins, M. (1988)	*Effective Teaching in Higher Education*. Methuen.
Brown, A. and Haffenden, I. (1989)	*Implications of Competence Based Curricula*, HRW.
BTEC (1988)	*Course and Unit Design*, BTEC.
Castling, A. (1996)	*Competence – based Teaching and Training*, MacMillan
Chishom, B. et al.(1986)	Preventive Approaches to Disruption (PAD), Macmillan Education.
City & Guilds (1979)	*Constructing Practical Tests*, City & Guilds.

Cole, H. P.(1972)   *Process Education*, Education Technical Publications.

Collins, J. (1998)   *Perfect Presentations*. Marshall Publishing.

Collins, N. (1986)   *New Teaching Skills*, Oxford University Press.

Cox, B. and   *Practical Points for Quality Assessment*. Kogan Page.
Ingleby, A. (1997)

Curzon, L. B. (1990)   *Teaching in Further Education: An Outline of Principles and
                              Practice*, Cassell.

Davies, I. K. (1971)   *The Management of Learning*, McGraw Hill.

De Cecco, J. P. (1968)   *The Psychology of Learning and Instruction: Education
                              Psychology*. Prentice Hall.

DES (1987)   *Managing Colleges Efficiently*, Department of Education and
                              Science.

Dewey, J. (1933)   *How we think: A restatement of the relation of reflective
                              thinking and the education process*, D.C. Heath, New York.

Dickson, A. (1982)   *A Woman in your own right*, Quartet.

Eggen,P. D.   *Strategies for Teachers*, Prentice Hall.
and Kanchak, D. P. (1988)

Eggen, P. D.   *Strategies for Teachers* 2nd Edition. Prentice Hall.
and Kauckak, D. P. (1998)

Ellington, H.   *Producing Teaching Materials*, Kogan Page.
and Race, P. (1993)

Employment   *Guide to the National Vocational Qualifications*, Employment
Department (1991)   Department.

FESC (1988)   *Responsive College Project*, Further Education Staff College.

FEU (1985)   *A Fragmented View? Professional Accountability and
                              Maintenance of Standards in Vocational Curricula*, Further
                              Education Unit.

FEU (1981)   *Experience, Reflection Learning*, FEU.

FEU (1988)   *Learning by Doing*, FEU.

FEU (1989)   *Supporting Quality in Y.T.S.*, Further Education Unit.

FEU (1992)

A Basis for Credit? Developing a post-16 credit accumulation and transfer framework. FEU.

Fletcher, S. (1991)

Designing Competence-based Training, Kogan Page.

Fletcher, S. (1992)

Competence based Assessment Techniques, Kogan Page.

Folex Ltd. (1988)

Successful Presentations, Folex, Zurich.

Freeman, R. andLewis, R. (1998)

Planning and Implementing Assessment, Kogan Page.

Fry, H. Ketteridge, S. & Marshall, S. (1999)

Teaching and Learning in Higher Education. Kogan Page.

Gage, N. L. and Berliner, D. C. (1975)

Educational Psychology, Rand McNally.

Gagné, R. M. (1975)

Essentials of Learning for Instruction, Dryden Press.

Garry, A. et al. (1986)

Learning from Experience, FEU/PICKUP.

Gordon, W. J. J. (1961)

Synetics. Harper & Row.

Gibbs, G. and Haigh, M. (1983)

Alternative Models of Course Evaluation, SCEDSIP Occasional paper 13.

Gibbs, G. Habeshaw, S. and Habeshaw, T. (1984)

53 Interesting Things to do in your Lectures, Technical and Educational Services.

Gibbs, G. et al (1986)

53 Interesting Ways to Assess Your Students, Technical & Educational Services Ltd.

Gibbs, G. (1988)

Learning by Doing: A guide to teaching and learning methods, FEU.

Gibbs, G. and Habeshaw, T. (1988)

253 Ideas for Teaching, Technical and Educational Services.

Gibbs G. (1992)

Improving the Quality of Student Learning, Technical and Educational Services.

Gibbs, G. and Jenkins, A. (1992)

Teaching Large Classes in Higher Education. Kogan Page.

Gray, J. & Richer, J. (1988)

Classroom Responses to Disruptive Behaviour, Macmillan Education.

Gronlund, N. L. (1970)   *Stating Behavioural Objectives for Classroom Instruction*, Macmillan.

HMI (1987)   *Tertiary Colleges.*

Habeshaw,S, Habeshaw, T, and Gibbs, G. (1984)   *53 Interesting Things to do in your Seminars and Tutorials*, Technical and Educational Services.

Habeshaw, S. Gibbs, G. and Habeshaw, T. (1992)   *53 Problems with Large Classes*. Technical and Educational Services Ltd.

Hall, J. (1992)   *Crediting Competence - a Portfolio Development Technique for Managers*, in Training and Development, Vol 10 No 6, June.

Hall, V. (1990)   *Maintained Further Education in the United Kingdom*, Staff College.

Heathcote, G. et al. (1981)   Curriculum Styles and Strategies, FEU.

Huddleston, P. & Unwin, L. (1997)   *Teaching and Learning in Further Education*. Routledge.

Jacobsen, D. Eggen, P. et al. (1981)   *Methods for Teaching: A skills approach*, Charles ER Merrill Publishing Co.

Jacobson, D. et al. (1984)   *Methods for Teaching*, Merril.

Jenkins, A. (1992)   *Break up your Lectures*. Teaching and Learning Vol 8.

Jessup, G. (1991)   *Outcomes: NVQs and the Emerging Model of Education and Training*, The Falmer Press.

Joyce, B. and Weil, M. (1986)   *Models of Teaching*, Prentice Hall.

Joyce, B. and Weil, M. (1992)   *Models of Teaching* 4th Edition. Allyn and Bacon.

Joyce, B. Calhoun, E. and Hopkins, D. (1997)   *Models of Learning – tools for teaching*. Open University Press.

Keller, F.S. and Sherman, J. G. (1974)   *The Keller Plan Handbook: Essays on a personalised system of instruction.*

Kemp, J.E. (1980)   *Planning and Producing Audio-visual Materials*, Harper and Row.

Kerman, S. (1979) *Teacher expectations and Student Achievement*, Phi-Delta-Kappar 60, 716-8.

Kerry, T. (1982) *Effective Questioning*, Macmillan Education.

Knowles, M. (1978) *The Adult Learners. A Neglected Species*. Gulf Publishing.

Kolb, D. A. (1984) *Experiential Learning - Experience as a Source of Learning and Development*, Prentice Hall.

Krathwoal, et al. (1964) *Taxonomy of Educational Objectives:Affective Domain*, David Mckay.

Kyriacou, C. (1986) *Effective Teaching in Schools*, Basil Blackwell.

Law, D. (1984) *Uses and Abuses of Profiling*, Harper.

Lloyd-Jones, R. (1986) *How to Produce Better Work Sheets*, Hutchinson.

LLoyd-Jones, R. and Bray, E. (1986) *Assessment - From Principle to Action*, MacMillan Educational Ltd.

Lindefield, G. (1987) *Assert Yourself,* Self-Help Associates.

Lovell, R. B. (1980) *Adult Learning*, Croom Helm.

Mager, R. F. (1962) *Preparing Instructional Objectives*, Fearon Publishers.

Maier, P. and Barnet,. L. (1998) *Using technology in Teaching and Learning*. Kogan Page.

Minton, D. (1991) *Teaching Skills in Further and Adult Education*, Macmillan.

National Extension College (1990) *Developing Competence*, National Extension College.

Neill, A. S. (1960) *Summerhill: a radical approach to child rearing*, Hart Publishing.

Newble, D. (1987) *A Handbook for Medical Teachers*, 2nd Edition, MTP Press.

Newble, D. and Cannon, R. (1991) *A Handbook for Teachers in Universities and Colleges*, Kogan Page.

Newby, T. (1992) *Validating your Training*, Kogan Page.

NIACE, (1989) *Replan. Further Education and Employment Training: A Quality Response*, Replan.

Nierenderg, G. (1982)   *The Complete Negotiator*, Souvenir Press, (London).

Oliver, D. and   *Teaching Public Issues in the High School.* American
Shares, J. P. (1966)   Educational Publishers.

Open University (1989)   *Delivering NVQs: a guide for staff development*, Open
    University.

Osborne, P. et al. (1987)   Graphics in Training, Vol 8, *Training Technology* Programme,
    Parthenon Publishing.

PCFC, (1992)   *Teaching More Students.* PCFC.

Parry, H. (1991)   *Successful Business Presentations.* Croner.

Pate, R. and   Guiding Learning through Skilful Questioning, *The Elementary
Bremer, N. (1967)   School Journal*, 69(8).

Perrott, E. (1977)   *Microteaching in Higher Education*, SRHE.

Perrott E (1982)   *Effective Teaching.* Longman.

Perrott, E. (1982)   *Effective Teaching: A practical guide to improving your
    teaching*, Longman.

Popham, W. J. (1978)   *Criterion Referenced Measurement*, Prentice Hall.

Pringle, J. (1966)   *Chalk Illustration*, Pergamon.

Rae, L. (1991)   *How to Measure Training Effectiveness*, Gower Publishing
    Company, 2nd Edition.

Ramsden, P. (1992)   *Learning to Teach in Higher Education.* Routledge.

Rawlins, K. (1993)   *Presentation and Communication Skills.* Macmillan
    Magazines.

Reece, I. H. (ed) (1982)   *Aspects for Curriculum in Technical Education*, Colombo Plan
    Staff College.

Reece, I. and   *A Practical Guide to the Overhead Projector and Other Visual
Walker, S. (1995)   Aids*, Business Education Publishers.

Rees, S. and   *Assertion Training*, Routledge.
Graham, R. S. (1991)

Robertson, J. (1981)   *Effective Classroom Control*, Hodder and Stoughton.

Robinson, A. (1987) *Study Skills*, FEU.

Rominszowski, *The Selection and Use of Instructional Media*, Kogan Page,
A. J. (1988) (2nd Edition).

Rogers, J.(ed) (1978) *Adults in Education*, BBC.

Rose, P. (1992) *53 Interesting ways to Write Open Learning Material*,
Technical and Educational Services.

Rosenshine, B. and *The use of direct observation to study teaching in Travers Rm.*
Furst, A. F. (1973) *Second Handbook of Research on Teaching.* Rand Mc Nally.

Rowntree, D. (1974) *Educational Technology in Curriculum Development*, Harper
Row.

Rowntree, D. (1974) *Assessing Students: How Shall We Know Them?*, Harper and
Row.

Rowntree, D. (1984) *Developing Courses for Students*, McGraw Hill.

Russell, J. and *Curriculum Development in FE* 3rd Edition. Further Education
Latcham, J. (1979) Staff College

Ryan, D. (1960) *Characteristics of Teachers.* American Council on Education.

Simpson, E. J.(1976) *The Classifcation of Educational Objectives: Psychomotor
Domain*, University of Illinois.

Stenhouse, L. (1975) *An Introduction to Curriculum Research and Development*,
Heinemann.

Stones, E. (1979) *Psychology of Education: a pedagogical approach.* Methuen

Stufflebeam, D. (1971) *Educational Evaluation and Decision Making*, Peacock
Publishers Inc.

Tansley, D. (1989) *Course teams: The Way Forward in FE*, NFER Nelson.

Tennant, M. (1988) *Psychology and Adult Learning*, Routledge.

Thorpe, R. (1987) Projected Still Images in Training, Vol 10, *Training
Technology Programme*, Parthenon Publishing.

Turner, C. (1983) *Developing Interpersonal Skills*, FE Staff College.

Vargas, J. S. (1972) *Writing Worthwhile Behavioural Objectives*, Harper Row.

Walkin, L. (1990)   *Teaching and Learning in Further Education*, Stanley Thornes.

Waller, Chris (1983)   *Using your overhead projector and other visual aids*,
                             Fordigraph.

Ward, C. (1980)   *Designing a Scheme of Assessment*, S Thornes.

Wragg, E. C. (ed) (1984)   *Classroom Teaching Skills*, Croom Helm.

Index

A

Accreditation of prior achievement, 438
Activists, 140
Adult. *See*
    Adult expectations, 9
Advanced organiser, 123
Affective, 23, 69, 136
Affective domain, 71, 96
Aims, 243, 245
Andragogical, 75
Andragogy, 11, 75, 117
Anger, 382
APA, 439
Appearance, 378
APU, 362
Arousal, 342
Asking questions, 365
Assertiveness, 380
Assessment, 49, 50, 490, 504
Assignment, 139, 420
Assignment sheets, 212
Assignments, 140, 451
Attitudes, 96
Audio cassettes, 221
Audio materials, 221
Ausubel, 123
Autonomous phase, 91
Autonomy and accountability, 481

B

Barriers, 380
Basic teaching model, 8
Behavioural family, 123
Behaviourism, 118
Behaviourists, 105
Berne, 371
Bibliographies, 400
Bibliography, 401
Boards, 203
Boardwork, 42
Body language, 377
Brainstorming, 136, 139, 144, 166

Business problem solving, 388
Buzz groups, 136, 139, 140, 144, 167

C

Case study, 136, 139, 140, 144, 172
Chaining, 108
Chalkboard, 204
Characteristics of aims, 245
Charts, 205
Checklists, 56, 443, 488, 498
Citation, 400
Classroom control, 383
Classroom management, 342
Closed questions, 366
CLOZE, 362
Cognitive, 22, 69, 136
Cognitive domain, 70, 76
Cognitive lesson, 28
Cognitive phase, 91
Cognitivism, 119
Cognitivists, 110
Common skills, 395
Communication, 355, 489
Competences, 250, 286, 517
Concept learning, 108
Concepts, 78
Conditions, 270
Confrontation, 383
Constructivist, 115
Content validity, 421
Context, 496
Contiguity, 109
Copyright, 225
Course evaluation, 494
Criteria, 270
Criterion-referenced, 417
Criticism, 382
Curriculum development, 239

D

Davies' model, 317
De Cecco, 78
Debate, 136, 139, 144, 155

Deductive, 114, 123
Deep and surface learning, 122
Deep learning, 122
Demonstration, 136, 139, 144, 148, 152, 184
Design principles, 217
Diagnosis, 520
Direct observation, 443
Disciplinary, 342
Discrimination, 418
Discussion, 136, 139, 140, 144, 153, 183
Domains, 265
Dress, 378

E

Ego states, 371
Elements, 286
Elements of competence, 290
Equal opportunities, 379
Essay, 420, 438
Evaluation, 49, 57, 181, 491
Evaluation of aids, 230
Evaluation report, 507
Evidence, 440, 520
Examination, 392
Examination technique, 392
Expectancy, 342
Experiment sheets, 212
Extrinsic motivation, 101

F

Facial, 378
Feedback, 395, 470
Feedback on teaching, 486
Feltboard, 205
Field trip, 136, 139, 140, 144, 168
First letter, 77
Fixative phase, 91, 92
Flipcharts, 206
Fog index, 358
Formative assessment, 410, 412
Free response, 435

G

Gagné Model, 321
Games, 140
Gaming/quiz, 136, 139, 144, 166

General objectives, 259
Gestaltists, 109
Global impression, 56, 443
Good teachers, 15
Gordon's synetics model, 124
Grading, 423
Gronlund, 257
Group size, 144
Group work, 140, 424

H

Handouts, 43, 152, 209
Harvard system, 400
Humanistic, 118
Humanists, 111
Humiliation, 384
Humour, 384

I

Ice breaker, 136, 139, 144, 170
Illustrative verbs, 262
Incentive, 342
Individual differences, 178
Individual work, 172
Individuals, 135
Inductive, 114
Information handouts, 209
Information Processing, 123
Input, 497
Integrated assignment, 452
Interview schedules, 502

J

Job Sheets, 210
Jurisprudential, 124

K

Key skills, 281, 395
Kolb, 532

L

Laboratory/workshop, 136, 139, 144
Language, 379
Large groups, 135, 144
Learning aids, 195
Learning outcomes, 22, 243, 250

Learning styles, 139
Learning taxonomies, 70
Lecture, 136, 139, 140, 144, 146, 185
Lesson planning, 27, 329
Likert scale, 506
Listening skills, 363
Logbook, 519

M

Mager's Approach, 269
Magnetic board, 205
Making notes, 390
Management of learning, 40
Marking scheme, 422
Maslow's, 100
Matching, 438
Matching block, 431
Matching block questions, 51
Memory, 76
Message, 357
Models, 75
Motivate, 470
Motivation, 100, 141
Multiple choice, 426, 438
Multiple discriminations, 108
Multiple response, 429
Multiple selection, 438
Multiple-choice questions, 51

N

National Vocational Qualifications, 438
Negotiation, 338
Neo-behaviourists, 107
Non-verbal cues, 373
Norm-referenced, 417

O

Observation techniques, 56
OHP, 44
       transparencies, 44
One to One, 136, 139
One-to-One (Coaching), 177
Open learning/distance learning, 177
Open questions, 366
Open/distance learning, 136, 139, 144
Operation sheets, 212
Optimum linear sequence, 312

Overhead projector, 215
Overlay technique, 219

P

Part test, 77
Pedagogical, 75
Performance criteria, 291
Personal family, 123
Plans, 27
Portfolio, 299, 519, 528
Portfolio building, 298
Pose, pause, pounce, 367
Posture, 377
Practical test, 52, 420, 446
Practical work, 443
Pragmatists, 140
Preparation, 488
Preparation of learning aids, 197
Presentation, 488
Principal objective, 280
Principles, 85
Problem solving, 86, 108, 388
Process, 497
Process objectives, 250, 275
Product, 497
Product objectives, 250, 253, 271
Professional tasks, 486
Profile, 54, 458
Project, 139, 420, 451
Project/assignment, 136, 144, 173
Prompting, 370
Proximity, 378
Psychomotor, 22, 69, 91, 136
Psychomotor domain, 72
Psychomotor skills lesson, 30

Q

Question and answer, 136, 139, 144,
       156
Questioning, 365
Questionnaires, 498, 504

R

Range statements, 292
Rating schedules, 56, 443
Readability, 357, 358
Reading age, 357, 362

Reading strategies, 391
Receiver, 357
Redirection, 369
References, 400
Reflect, 519
Reflection, 7
Reflectors, 140
Refusing, 381
Relationships, 489
Reliability, 420
Repetition, 77
Resources, 41, 195
Reveal technique, 220
Rhyme rule, 77
Role of the teacher, 5
Role play, 136, 139, 144, 169
Room layout, 45
Room requirements, 198
Rowntree Model, 318
Rule learning, 108

S

Sarcasm, 384
Scheme of work, 306, 324
Science Model, 390
Selection of visual aids, 225
Selection type, 420, 426
Selection type questions, 50
Self assessment, 54
Self directed (including open learning),
      140
Self evaluation, 17
Self test, 77
Seminar, 136, 139, 144, 163
Semi-structured, 56, 443
Short answer, 436, 438
Signal learning, 108
Simulation, 136, 139, 140, 144, 171
Skills lesson plan, 33
Small groups, 135, 161
SMOG, 361
Social interaction, 123
Specific objectives, 260
Spelling association, 77
Spider diagrams, 384
Stenhouse Model, 321
Stimulus-response, 108
Stroking, 377
Structured, 438

Structured questions, 436
Student learning, 45, 65
Study skills, 46, 388
Subject matter, 491
Suchman Inquiry Method, 123
Supply type, 420, 435
Supply type questions, 51
Surface learning, 122
Syllabus, 240
Synetics, 124

T

Tape slide programmes, 221
Taxonomic levels, 267
Teaching, 136
Teaching observation, 484
Teaching strategies, 144
Teaching tasks, 482
Team teaching, 136, 139, 144, 152
Technology model, 389
Terminal behaviour, 269
Theorists, 140
Three domains, 69
Time management, 394
Topic, 306
Topic analysis, 317
Topic precedent diagrams, 308
Touch, 378
TPD, 308
Transactional analysis, 371
Transmitter, 357
True/false, 434, 438
Tutorial, 136, 139, 144, 174

U

Units, 286
Units of competence, 289
Use of IT, 222
Useful verbs, 246

V

Validity, 418, 420
Values, 96
Verbal association, 77, 108
Verbal cues, 373
Verification, 302
Video, 136, 139, 144, 160, 221

Visual association, 77

W

Whiteboard, 204

Worksheets, 209, 210
Workshop, 165
Writing process objectuives, 279

